Transcendence and Non-Naturalism in Early Chinese Thought

Also available from Bloomsbury

The Bloomsbury Research Handbook of Early Chinese Ethics and Political Philosophy, edited by Alexus McLeod
Chinese and Buddhist Philosophy in Early Twentieth-Century German Thought, by Eric S. Nelson
Comparative Philosophy without Borders, edited by Arindam Chakrabarti and Ralph Weber
Confucian Ethics in Western Discourse, by Wai-ying Wong
Cultivating a Good Life in Early Chinese and Ancient Greek Philosophy, edited by Karyn Lai, Rick Benitez, and Hyun Jin Kim
Nonexistent Objects in Buddhist Philosophy, by Zhihua Yao

Transcendence and Non-Naturalism in Early Chinese Thought

Joshua R. Brown and Alexus McLeod

BLOOMSBURY ACADEMIC
LONDON • NEW YORK • OXFORD • NEW DELHI • SYDNEY

BLOOMSBURY ACADEMIC
Bloomsbury Publishing Plc
50 Bedford Square, London, WC1B 3DP, UK
1385 Broadway, New York, NY 10018, USA
29 Earlsfort Terrace, Dublin 2, Ireland

BLOOMSBURY, BLOOMSBURY ACADEMIC and the Diana logo are trademarks of
Bloomsbury Publishing Plc

First published in Great Britain 2021
This paperback edition published in 2022

A catalogue record for this book is available from the British Library.

Library of Congress Cataloging-in-Publication Data
Names: Brown, Joshua R., author. | McLeod, Alexus, author.
Title: Transcendence and non-naturalism in early Chinese thought /
Joshua R. Brown and Alexus McLeod.
Description: London ; New York : Bloomsbury Academic, 2020. | Includes bibliographical
references and index. | Summary: "Transcendence and Substance in Early Chinese Thought
offers a new account of the history of early Chinese philosophy, as well as a reconsideration of
current understandings of early Chinese thought, by focussing on transcendence and substance.
These two concepts are sometimes seen as being at odds with naturalist approaches to
philosophy. By offering a robust account of early Chinese thought, Alexus McLeod and
Joshua R. Brown argue that in fact non-naturalist positions can be found in early Chinese texts,
in topics including transcendence, substance, soul-body dualism, and divinity. Moreover, by
closely examining a range of early Chinese texts, and providing comparative readings of a
number of Western texts and thinkers, this book offers a way of reading early Chinese Philosophy
as consistent with the religious philosophy of the East and West, including the Abrahamic and
the Brahmanistic religions. Co-written by a philosopher and theologian, this book draws out
unique insights into early Chinese thought, highlighting in particular new ways to consider a
range of Chinese concepts, including tian, dao, qi, xing, and win"–Provided by publisher.
Identifiers: LCCN 2020019597 (print) | LCCN 2020019598 (ebook) |
ISBN 9781350082533 (hb) | ISBN 9781350082557 (ebook) | ISBN 9781350082540 (ePDF)
Subjects: LCSH: Philosophy, Chinese. | Transcendence (Philosophy) |
Naturalism. Classification: LCC B126 .B76 2020 (print) |
LCC B126 (ebook) | DDC 181/.11–dc23
LC record available at https://lccn.loc.gov/2020019597
LC ebook record available at https://lccn.loc.gov/2020019598

ISBN: HB: 978-1-3500-8253-3
PB: 978-1-3502-0403-4
ePDF: 978-1-3500-8254-0
eBook: 978-1-3500-8255-7

Typeset by Newgen KnowledgeWorks Pvt. Ltd., Chennai, India

To find out more about our authors and books visit www.bloomsbury.com
and sign up for our newsletters.

Contents

Introduction

The main goal of this book is to make an intervention into philosophical readings of early Chinese thought. Specifically, we seek to address a popular, yet in our view deeply flawed, presupposition about early Chinese thinkers that they universally possessed a "naturalistic worldview" devoid of any conception of non-natural entities or concepts such as transcendence. In many ways it is surprising that this view of early Chinese thought persists, given that scholars from other disciplines who study the same text (such as historians and religious studies scholars) or philosophical scholars from non-Western contexts (in this case, China is the best example) have freely associated Chinese thought with conceptions of transcendence and other non-naturalistic characteristics. But persist the presupposition does.

We find this presupposition problematic for several reasons. For one, we are not convinced the claim that Chinese thought is "naturalistic" is justifiable given the specific, Enlightenment-era career of naturalism and, paradoxically, the profound ambiguity of what philosophers mean by "naturalism." In this book, one of our tasks is to flesh out what is meant by claiming Chinese philosophy is naturalistic. Our conclusion, in this regard, is that naturalism is used as a label to make Chinese thought amenable to the fundamental projects of secular philosophy in the contemporary analytical framework.

This in turn raises two serious problems. First, there is a standard critique of Christianity-inclined interpretations of Chinese thought that such interpretations fail to understand Chinese philosophers on their own terms and in their own contexts. Harold D. Roth, for example, once called the presupposition by many Western thinkers that East Asian traditions were theistic a kind of "cognitive imperialism."[1] While we agree that a priori theological judgments should not be used to assess the nature of Chinese philosophy, we ask, is it only theists who stand at risk of cognitive imperialism? It seems to us that the sublimation of Chinese thinkers to the modern and Western project of naturalism (broadly construed) can be justifiably characterized as precisely this sort of dynamic.

We do not deny, of course, that a modern Western naturalist may utilize or leverage Chinese thought into a naturalist project, as a creative constructive proposal. Nor do we argue against the utility of naturalism to identify and understand some early Chinese thinkers and/or concepts. What we resist is that naturalism should be taken as the primary and universal lens through which Chinese thought should be interpreted.

Put differently, we do not think the fact that Chinese thought can be used within a naturalistic framework should not be taken to entail the claim that Chinese thought is itself naturalistic, though certainly it must have certain affinities or analogues with the naturalistic framework in order to be of use in these ways.

And so, it is this presupposition that Chinese thinkers were invested in or practiced the same kind of project as modern Western naturalism that we hold under suspicion in this book. Instead, we propose a different, non-naturalist framework for understanding early Chinese thought. To be clear, we do *not* mean to defend the opposite of the naturalist thesis and do not argue in this volume that non-naturalism is the primary lens through which Chinese thought ought to be interpreted. Rather, our aim is to demonstrate that Chinese thought can be convincingly interpreted in a non-naturalist way, and that there is a case to be made for a robust presence of concepts such as transcendence in the literature of early China. Our argument, then, is against the *dismissal* of non-naturalism and transcendence as adequate and helpful ways of understanding early Chinese philosophy, and our main task in the book is to demonstrate why such a dismissal is unwarranted.

Before turning to the main task of this volume, then, some words of explanation and contextualization are in order. First, one may justly ask, to what extent is naturalism really presupposed as a framework for understanding early Chinese thought such that non-naturalism is dismissed as a helpful interpretive approach? In other words, is this book really necessary? Although we deal with this problem at great length in Chapter 1, a separate introductory treatment is helpful here to give the reader insight into the project. Additionally, our task in this introduction is to clarify our methodology (primarily regarding Part 2 of the book) and offer a brief description of the content of the book's chapters.

The Naturalistic Presupposition: A Sketch of the Issue

It is quite common among scholars of early China to interpret early Chinese texts as "naturalist" and as lacking a concept of transcendence. There are, we argue, two main reasons for this. One group of scholars argues that there are intrinsic and fundamental differences between early Chinese and Western thought. Scholars who advocate such a position generally reject the existence of non-naturalism and transcendence as concerns in early Chinese thought on the basis of such a contrastive view, with the key contrast between early China and the premodern West. A different group of scholars argue for the fundamental similarity of early Chinese and *modern* Western thought. Like contemporary Western philosophers, these scholars argue, early Chinese thinkers were thoroughly naturalist, and thus either did not have or rejected non-naturalist concepts such as transcendence. From two very different positions, we get to the same place—early Chinese thinkers were naturalists and lacked a concept of transcendence. While we discuss in Part 1 of the book just how this situation came about, below we offer an overview of these positions and the core of our argument against them, which we develop throughout the rest of the book.

The Contrastive View

A number of scholars over the past fifty years or so have argued for a conception of early China as fundamentally different from the West in key ways. These contrastive views of Chinese thought generally center on a number of important concepts, such as truth, transcendence, substance, mind (as distinct from body), theoretical language, and "non-naturalism." The positions involve claims that early Chinese thinkers lacked some combination of the above concepts (or all of them). We seek in this book to address two of these in particular: non-naturalism and transcendence. We most commonly find rejections of the entire group of concepts, which are linked together in important ways as we demonstrate below. Our focus in this book surrounds non-naturalism and transcendence because we believe that these are two of the concepts closest to the core of the larger debate between "contrastive" scholars of early Chinese thought and those more like ourselves who find more diversity within the early Chinese tradition and continuity with other traditions. It is an old debate, and one we certainly will not settle here. We can, however, demonstrate that non-naturalist views and transcendence can be found in a number of senses (including ones vehemently rejected by "contrastive" scholars) in early Chinese philosophy.

A key move of many scholars who support a contrastive view of early China is that the nature of the Classical Chinese language precluded the development of certain philosophical concerns in early China. This position usually presents the Classical Chinese language as primarily pragmatic, active, and unable to formulate abstraction. Marcel Granet wrote of the Chinese language that it was concerned with "the effect of action" rather than "analysis of ideas."[2] Chad Hansen develops this idea further, arguing that features of the Chinese language led early Chinese thinkers to have a pragmatic rather than a semantic focus. Hansen claims he does not want to make the strong claim that such purported features of the language *required* a pragmatic philosophical focus and precluded semantic focus, but rather argues that that these features make a pragmatic focus more natural and likely.[3] Despite this claim, in many places Hansen does seem to make a strong linguistic determinative claim for Chinese thought, which he uses as the centerpiece of his argument.[4] Indeed, in the introduction to his *Daoist Theory of Chinese Thought*, Hansen writes,

> The key to my view of Chinese thought is this. I attribute a theory of language and mind to Chinese thinkers that differs fundamentally from the popular Western view. This theory of language makes sense of the philosophical disputes between the ancient philosophers.[5]

Another contrastive approach to early Chinese thought is that of David Hall and Roger Ames. The Hall and Ames contrastive approach is even more radical than that of Hansen, making Western and Chinese thought almost polar opposites. Like Hansen, Hall and Ames locate the purported absence of the important concepts listed above, including non-naturalism and transcendence, to features of Chinese language. They write in an extended passage very useful for our purpose here:

Differences between the Chinese and Indo-European senses of the verb "to be" will make for significant differences between the two traditions. It is clear that Parmenides, among other Greek thinkers (Aristotle is the great exception), conflated existential and copulative senses of "being." Whether this is to be counted as a confusion, as is often said, is a matter of dispute. At the very least this conflation contributed to the tendency to think of Chaos (as "nonbeing") in a negative manner, investigating it with suggestions of the Nihil, the Void, the Naught. By contrast, the absence of this kind of cosmogonic tradition in China may be considered both cause and consequence of the fact that the verb, *you*, "being," overlaps with the sense of "having" rather than "existing." If *wu*, "not to be," means only "not to be present," there is certainly less *mysterium* and *tremendum* attaching to the notion of Not-being.[6]

We see here that the claim Hall and Ames go on later to draw out in more detail, that there is no conception of transcendence in early China, is grounded in a particular view of Chinese language. Our view is that both the contrastive view of Chinese language and the rejection of transcendence are deeply problematic. One of the things we go on to show in this book is that there is indeed a cosmogonic tradition in China, one that involves transcendence in numerous senses. We also argue that the Classical Chinese language does not in fact have the limitations Hall and Ames, like Hansen, attribute to it, and that it would be a conceptually impoverished language if it did. Indeed, if it were ever the case that Chinese language lacked terms with the sense of "existence" as well as "having," someone would have had soon invented a term or a use of the old term with the necessary sense. It is doubtful that any human being can long have a concept of "having" without the thought occurring to them at some point that some things are had by nothing and are had nowhere. To not have something that is had or haveable is very different than not to have something that is not-had or not-haveable. I might recognize that I fail to have the original copy of the US Constitution, yet know that *someone* has it. It would not take a thinker with a concept of "having" very long to recognize the difference between this situation and that of not having the sword Excalibur, knowing that *no one* has it, and that it cannot be had. The latter is surely an understanding that Excalibur *does not exist*. How could features of a language bar a person from having such thoughts? As soon as a person thinks in this way with the concept of "having," the person thereby develops a concept of "existence" or "being."

According to Hall and Ames, early Chinese thought is thoroughly concerned with immanence, and there is no conception of transcendence in play. This absence of transcendence entails, they argue, the lack of a host further ideas, particularly a number of "dualistic" distinctions, "God and the world, being and not being, subject and object, mind and body, reality and appearance, good and evil, knowledge and ignorance, and so forth."[7] They go on to attribute a concept of transcendence to these distinctions, writing,

> The mutual immanence of the primary elements of the Confucian cosmos—heaven, earth and man—precludes the use of the language of transcendence and therefore renders any sort of dualistic contrast pernicious.[8]

We are highly suspicious of claims that early Chinese thought or language lacked key features found in Western thought or language. What would stop early Chinese thinkers from developing the same concepts as thinkers in the West, especially ones as seemingly basic to philosophical discourse as the distinction between being and nonbeing or reality and appearance? And note that this language is hardly ever deployed in the opposite direction. We seldom hear that some concept or view was not held in the West because Western thought or language lacked some key feature of Chinese. Why think that Classical Chinese was conceptually impoverished in a way that languages like Greek or Latin were not? It is uncontroversial that in the ancient Greek and Roman world, we find both naturalist and non-naturalist views, both acceptance and rejection of transcendence.[9] Indeed, this is classical contrast artistically depicted in Raphael's "School of Athens" painting—the non-naturalist mystic Plato pointing upward to the heavens, and the naturalist Aristotle with his hand downward toward the earth. Why would this variety of thought fail to exist in early China? Because Greek is a more expressive and permissive language, which allows for pragmatic as well as semantic consideration, for a focus on the theoretical and abstract as well as the concrete and active?

This is a highly implausible view, particularly when we compare languages. There is nothing you can do in Attic Greek that is impossible to do in Classical Chinese, and vice versa. And if there *were* some linguistic bar to thinking in a particular way in either of these languages, what would have stopped people from *creating* a way to express these thoughts in that language? One of the nice features of language is that it is not static. We're not simply provided a set language at birth that we are then confined within—as our thinking changes, our language changes, and as we gain new concerns and considerations, we create new ways to talk about these things in our languages. This is why linguistic innovation is always possible. The English of Shakespeare was not the English of Beowulf, and our English is neither, even though it is influenced by both. Indeed, the way we *learn* language is dynamic. We do not simply internalize rigid rules, but we adapt, create, and modify things as we learn to communicate through language.

The Similarity View

As mentioned above, another source of claims that non-naturalism and transcendence are not found in early China is the work of scholars who argue that early Chinese thought represents a worldview in key ways similar to that of modernity. A key feature of this worldview is the commitment to naturalism.[10] A number of scholars offer interpretations of key early Chinese texts as offering naturalistic systems, including ones that seem like the best case for non-naturalism in early China, such as the *Mozi*. Chris Fraser offers a view of the *Mozi* as presenting a thoroughly naturalistic system, writing,

> The *Mozi* presents the earliest explicit version of what I will call Chinese metaphysical and metaethical "naturalism" … reality just is the world of nature and observable natural phenomena, and accordingly whatever exists is to be explained as part of nature. Ultimate reality is not an abstract realm of ideal forms,

nor one of a supernatural, transcendent deity or spirits. Instead, it is simply "the stuff of people's ears and eyes," as the *Mozi* phrases it.[11]

This seems to us a surprising claim, given that the *Mozi*, more than any other pre-Han text, seems on the face to offer an agentive and theistic conception of *tian*. Fraser tries to explain this away, by claiming that *tian* (heaven) is a "quasi-personal nature-deity ... for the Mohists *tian* just is a semi-personified conception of nature—in effect, 'Nature' with a capital 'N.'"[12] As we discuss further in Chapter 4, the only reasons to read Mohist claims about *tian* as less than fully theistic or transcendent in nature are either the assumption that there is no transcendence in play or the assumption that a naturalist, non-transcendent *tian* "makes more sense" than alternatives. Fraser seems to take the second tactic in his *Philosophy of the Mozi*. He claims that his aim is "the philosophical 'rehabilitation' of Mohism," associated with demonstrating that "numerous features of Mohist thought are interesting, instructive, and worthy of attention."[13] But worthy of *whose* attention? And why? If Mozi is a non-naturalist, a theist who accepts a transcendent conception of *tian*, then he may not be of interest to naturalistic contemporary analytic philosophers. But he would certainly be of interest to theologians!

Jeeloo Liu offers a similar explanation for her rejection of non-naturalism and transcendence in early Chinese texts, writing that she "aims to demystify the notion of *qi* so as to render Chinese cosmology a respectable metaphysical position."[14]

While we certainly do not object to the project of interpreting early Chinese texts using contemporary concerns as a framework (which may then illuminate aspects of the texts of interest to certain audiences), we do object to readings of early texts that require these texts to fit a desired worldview that one finds plausible. Early Chinese texts should be allowed to speak on their own terms as much as possible, and if it turns out they adopt views that are not "respectable" by the lights of contemporary analytic philosophy, then so be it. Indeed, it strikes us as somewhat arrogant and intellectually rigid to begin with the assumption that naturalist positions are the only ones worthy of countenancing, when one has not done the work of considering arguments for alternative positions, and without being willing to interpret possible alternatives as alternatives, lest they "not make sense."

In terms of their central motivations, the contrastive view and the similarity view are actually closely linked. Indeed, we find proponents of each often making very similar claims to the other. What seems to be at the heart of both is an association of Chinese thought with many of the features of Western modernity, including the rejection of key features of premodern Western thought. Indeed, Hansen shows his hand early in his *Daoist Theory of Chinese Thought*. What he calls the "standard theory," which attributes a much more familiar view of language to early Chinese thinkers, renders Daoist thought more akin to the non-naturalist thought of the premodern West. According to Hansen, this requires us to interpret the Daoists as holding "an incoherent, mystical, irrational set of beliefs."[15] Offering an interpretation of early Chinese thought as a whole that renders the views of the Daoists more plausible to modern Western philosophical audiences who largely reject the non-naturalism of the premodern West is, then, to "make sense of Daoism."

One question of ours, which recurs through much of this book, is the following: Why think that making sense of early Chinese thought requires making sense of it in terms of modern Western thought? Isn't it a far safer assumption that early Chinese thought is closer to premodern Western thought, with its abundant non-naturalism and lack of revulsion at ideas like mysticism? What happens when we use a premodern Western frame to try to make sense of what is going on in early China? Better yet, why not try to the extent possible to simply listen to early Chinese thinkers without the assumption of any preestablished framework, and simply use our background knowledge of ideas like naturalism, non-naturalism, transcendence, immanence, and so forth as available tools to use for understanding what is going on in these texts? We don't owe early Chinese thinkers an account that will make most sense to *us* (as philosophers, theologians, or whatever else), but rather an account that would make most sense to *them*. Mysticism, transcendence, and non-naturalism may be anathema to contemporary analytic philosophers, but why think they would have been such to early Chinese thinkers? We contend that to think that the only ways we can learn from early Chinese texts is to render them either identical to "us" or the polar opposite of "us" represents failure of imagination, failure to listen with an open mind to what early Chinese thinkers were trying to say, and failure of willingness to critically evaluate one's own worldview in light of alternatives. These are unbecoming of members of a profession supposedly committed to the "examined life" and who regularly tout that one of the central benefits of training in their discipline is to enable the capacity to critically examine one's own assumptions and viewpoints.

A Methodological Clarification

In the main part of this book (Part 2), we undertake a close examination of a number of early Chinese texts, but we do not provide the kind of digital humanities textual analysis that scholars such as Ted Slingerland offer (in works like his recent *Mind and Body in Early China*), which we think can be a valuable tool. Additionally, we make substantial use of comparative methods in various degrees: some chapters see very little influence from non-Chinese sources; others are built upon such encounters. Readers may also note many of our comparative sources from the Christian theological tradition, Thomas Aquinas and Pseudo-Dionysius the Areopagite being the clearest examples. This might lead to two objections to our project. First, that we have "cherry picked" our material, focusing on passages and texts that lend support to our position, while ignoring passages and texts that problematize it, and that the passages and texts we discuss are not representative of the Chinese tradition as a whole. Second, that our comparative approach is underdeveloped, and too heavily influenced by Christian sources, thus revealing that our project is really crypto-theology in philosophical garb. In this section, we seek to head off both of these objections.

First, regarding the possible "cherry picking" objection, it is important to recall from above that we are not making blanket claims about the nature of the Chinese tradition as a whole, and believe that such claims are most often either wrong or highly problematic. The Chinese tradition, like that of the West or any other region of the world, is diverse and multifaceted. There are few, if any, ideas that *everyone* holds (at least in the same way), or views that *everyone* accepts. We know this is the case in the West—why should it be any different in China? Our argument in this book that robust conceptions of non-naturalism and transcendence are present in early China is not meant to show that naturalism or rejection of transcendence cannot be found in early Chinese thought (certainly they can). Rather, our argument is against those views that *dismiss* non-naturalism and transcendence as genuine concerns in early China. All our argument requires, then, is that we demonstrate that these ideas are held and discussed in depth at least *somewhere* in the early Chinese tradition. We think we do better than this in the book by showing that these ideas are not only present but also prevalent in early Chinese thought. The textual evidence we marshal here has been carefully chosen to show the importance (if not universality) of non-naturalist and transcendence concepts in early China. Thus, the "cherry picking" objection has little force here.

More generally, the "cherry picking" objection only has force, it seems to us, against those attempting to make blanket claims about early China, who argue for the *absence* or the *dominance* of some concept in early Chinese thought. In order to show that early Chinese thinkers did not have a certain concept, or that features of the Classical Chinese language would not allow the development of such a concept, one has to demonstrate that the concept in question comes up *nowhere* in the early Chinese discourse. On the other hand, those who argue, as we do in this book, that a particular concept can be found and was even quite widespread in early Chinese thought have nowhere near as enormous a burden. Truly, we cannot "cherry pick" in a negative sense, because any textual evidence we find, cherry-picked or otherwise, itself constitutes evidence of the existence of a discourse concerning the concept in early China.

Again, our intention here is not to show that every thinker in early China was concerned with non-naturalist concepts and transcendence (nor could we plausibly show that). Rather, it is to (1) show that there are non-naturalist ideas and that there is a concept of transcendence discussed in early Chinese texts and (2) detail the variety of ways early Chinese texts offer conceptions of transcendence, with the aid of premodern texts in other traditions sharing key features with the ones in question. Indeed, it turns out that there are a number of different senses of transcendence to be found in early Chinese thought. This, we contend, should not surprise us. Intellectual traditions, after all, are not monoliths. If everyone in them shared the same concepts and views, interpreted terms in the same way, and had the same understanding of language, then presumably a philosophical tradition could never have got off the ground in the first place, because there would have been no ground for disagreement.

Regarding the concerns about our comparative method and reliance upon Christian theological sources, this is a more difficult clarification to make, if only because it is more complicated. We agree that the very best comparative work makes use of concrete interlocutors whose approaches and frameworks can be developed in depth. This approach was not only utilized but also admirably articulated in the two standard comparative works on China and the West thus far, those by Lee H. Yearley and Aaron Stalnaker.[16] We have not indulged that preferential method here due to our purpose. Although we do not seek to make a universal positive claim about early Chinese thought, we do seek to unseat such a claim. Hence, this requires that our rebuttal of the naturalistic presupposition gesture toward this universality. Consequently, we see little rhetorical benefit in arguing our case based on a deep comparative engagement with a prominent Chinese thinker and, consequently, little benefit in a deep engagement with a single non-Chinese thinker as a comparative interlocutor.

So why, then, do we turn to a comparative approach at all in our argument? One of the main problems we face in this book is that the claim that early Chinese thought is naturalistic is itself somewhat amorphous (as we demonstrate in Chapter 1). All that advocates of this view seem to agree on is that early Chinese thought is naturalistic inasmuch as it rejects transcendence. However, scholars often fail to define what they mean by "transcendence" at all. Instead, there is an assumption about transcendence, that is, the authors presuppose that early Chinese thinkers dismiss transcendence in the way that modern Western naturalists understand the term.

But this raises an important question: how do modern Western naturalists understand transcendence, and is this historically the dominant meaning of transcendence? As we cite often in this book, one of the few definition of transcendence in the literature is the following offered by David L. Hall and Roger T. Ames: "A is transcendent with respect to B if the existence, meaning, or import of B cannot be fully accounted for without recourse to A, but the reverse is not true."[17] While there is some value in this definition, it is also woefully incomplete as a description of how transcendence actually functions in non-naturalistic traditions. In fact, Hall and Ames's definition is a clear example of what we present in Chapter 2 as a "contrastive" view of transcendence (borrowing from the work of Kathryn Tanner). And this in turn is significant because, as we also contend in Chapter 2, this contrastive conception of transcendence is decidedly not the dominant or primary way that the Christian tradition, at least, has historically understood transcendence.

Therefore, we cannot simply argue for the presence of transcendence in this work. We must also strategically recover a conception of what transcendence is and how it works in non-naturalist traditions. Since Christianity is at least the implicit (and often explicit) foil that naturalist readings of China use to make their case, it is apt to draw upon Christian thinkers to show that, in fact, there is much in common between classical non-naturalist Christian thought and early Chinese philosophy. Consequently, Christian non-naturalism makes for a fitting framework for unseating the naturalistic presupposition of early Chinese thought, but we do not mean to imply that early Chinese thought imitates transcendence or non-naturalism in the Christian tradition.

Before describing the chapters of the book, we should note a few other concerns that have shaped this book. We recognize that any interpretation or translation will require a particular framework. But, even the finest scholars often do not recognize the ways in which our interpretive frameworks guide our understanding of target traditions and texts, necessitate or privilege certain readings, and lead us to overlook or render invisible other possible readings. Thus, while naturalist frameworks might help us understand certain aspects of early Chinese thought, they blind us to other aspects. The danger is that only through employing only such interpretive frameworks, we come to a one-sided view of the Chinese tradition, one that neglects the existence of robust parts of the tradition. Part of our task in this book is to demonstrate which aspects of the tradition emerge when we apply non-naturalist interpretive frameworks.

A second problem arising from assuming Chinese philosophy is naturalistic is that it obscures those features of early Chinese thought that do not fit this paradigm, and does this in two ways. On the one hand, it means that texts or positions that do not fit neatly into the naturalistic framework can be ignored or classified out of the corpus of texts representing the Chinese worldview. An historical example—though not primarily due to reasons of transcendence—is the bifurcation of "philosophical" and "religious" Daoism (*Daojia* 道家 and *Daojiao* 道教, respectively). Even though this species of distinction between "religion" and "philosophy" did not exist until modern times even in the West, the distinction has served to peripheralize certain texts and/or historical perspectives on texts as being "not philosophical." The naturalistic presupposition also obscures features of standard texts, and leaves dissatisfying accounts of important features of early Chinese thought. An example is Mengzi, whose views of tian 天—the chief deity of the Zhou dynasty—have been remarkably underexamined in modern Western scholarship.

Finally, as comparative scholars, we are especially cognizant of a third problematic consequence of assuming Chinese thought is naturalistic. Such a presupposition unfortunately serves to isolate Chinese thought from non-naturalistic traditions, and thereby undermines comparative analysis of these traditions. This is important because, on the one hand, it means that Chinese philosophies are neglected as helpful resources for analyzing problems or themes other traditions may have in common with Chinese thought. For example, if Chinese thought is genuinely naturalistic, then it seems of little use to robustly theistic traditions such as Hinduism or Christianity on questions such as the problem of evil, except as an atheistic foil. More importantly, however, the naturalistic presupposition means that scholars are potentially blinded from recognizing the presence of genuine and robust analogues for non-naturalistic themes and problems in early Chinese texts. Put simply, the presupposition of naturalism would rule out a priori the possibility of something like the divine or revelation in early China.

Thus, to summarize, in this book, we demonstrate that non-naturalist ideas can be found in the early Chinese intellectual tradition. We focus in this volume on the concept of transcendence specifically, as a non-naturalist concept that numerous scholars deny played a role in early China.[18] We argue that not only do we find transcendence in early Chinese thought, but we also find it in a number of different forms across texts, schools, and periods. Our focus on transcendence in this volume demonstrates one way that a non-naturalist framework can be used to better understand certain aspects of early Chinese thought that are commonly neglected in contemporary philosophical scholarship on early China.

Transcendence, we argue, comes in many different forms. In addition to certain theistic forms of transcendence common to the Abrahamic traditions, we find a host of others throughout global thought, from the formalism of Plato and Plotinus to the soul/mind transcendence of classical Indian schools such as Vedanta. Part of our task in this book is to show that transcendence appears in early China in a number of different ways, across different texts, movements, periods, and schools. There is no "one size fits all" when it comes to transcendence, nor is there a single unified view on transcendence in early China. Though we do not claim to uncover all of the ways transcendence emerges in early Chinese philosophical work in this book, we show a number of the ways it does. We also suggest interpretive possibilities that become available once we recognize the role of transcendence and other non-naturalist concepts in early Chinese philosophy.

Outline of Chapters

The book is organized in two parts, with the second part itself comprised of two halves. In Part 1, we offer a genealogy of the idea of naturalism and its use in contemporary philosophy and in scholarship on early China in the Western academy. We focus in on the concept of transcendence and its relationship to naturalism, arguing that the rejection of transcendence in naturalist philosophical theories and interpretations of early Chinese philosophy are based on an association of a particular kind of contrastive transcendence with theistic commitments naturalists try to avoid. We argue that there are a number of different ways of thinking about transcendence, that these distinctions are often ignored by naturalist opponents of transcendence, and that because of this, interpreters often miss signs of transcendence in early Chinese texts. In the final chapter of Part 1, we argue that much of the evidence that naturalistic interpretations of early Chinese relies upon originates not in the pre-imperial period, to which these interpretations are most often applied, but in the early Han Dynasty, or "Western Han" (202 BCE–9 CE). We see what we call a "naturalistic shift" in the late Warring States and early Han period, in which certain terms previously associated with non-naturalist concepts take on a more naturalistic (if not physicalistic) meanings. While certain concepts are naturalized in the late Warring States and early Han, we do not see the kind of global naturalist revision of the tradition that we see in European modernity. That is, a host of non-naturalist concepts and views can still be found in the Han post "naturalistic shift." In addition, new kinds of non-naturalist concepts are developed. We find in the early Han the extension of old forms of transcendence and the construction of new ones. At least, part of what is behind the rejection of transcendence and other non-naturalist concepts by contemporary scholars of early China is neglect of Han Dynasty texts and consideration of the ways numerous concepts undergo critical changes in the period between the late Warring States and the end of the Western Han.

Part 2 of the book comprises of concrete examinations and demonstrations of the presence of transcendence and non-naturalism in early Chinese texts. Chapters 4–6 concern various ways that *tian* 天 plays a part of non-naturalist themes in early Chinese thought. Chapters 8–10 focus on *dao* 道 as the central concept, and Chapter 7 concerns both. By and large, each chapter is focused on analyzing a specific (and usually different) concrete text, and non-natural themes within it. We freely admit throughout these chapters that transcendence and non-naturalism are not perfect categories for describing the diverse aspects of early Chinese texts. Many times, we'll note there are either naturalistic components in these texts or ambiguities vis-à-vis transcendence that show certain texts are not concerned to emphasize or overly define the functions of transcendence. However, we also resist the tendency of modern philosophers to read these as failing a standard of transcendence that is the theological norm in the Judeo-Christian tradition. Rather, we accept that early Chinese thinkers did not have a tremendous concern to fully and clearly distinguish the naturalistic and non-naturalistic aspects of concepts like *tian* and *dao*. This does not mean, however, that the transcendence and non-naturalistic aspects are any less real or present, as our analyses show.

In Chapter 4, we examine the multivalent concept of *tian* in the Han-era Confucian text *Chunqiu Fanlu*, assessing how transcendence both is and is not part of the way this text understands *tian*. Chapter Five analyzes a significant point of debate in early China: in what sense *tian* does and does not will. Primarily drawing upon the *Mozi*, we seek to map out the ways in which the affirmation that *tian* has a will involves also affirming transcendence in some degree. Chapter Six turns to examine the relationship between *tian* and humanity, focusing on the discussion of this theme found in the *Xunzi*. Although the *Xunzi* has been claimed by recent scholars to be a prototypical naturalistic text in early China, we argue that it is at least plausible to interpret Xunzi as possessing a transcendent conception of *tian*, wherein he emphasizes the differentiation between *tian* and humanity. In Chapter 7, our attention falls on the concept of the "patterns of *tian*" (*tian li* 天理) in texts such as the *Zhuangzi* and *Huainanzi* in order to examine the ways in which early Chinese thinkers use something like transcendence to understand how the world is ordered or "patterned."

Chapter 8 examines the transcendental aspects of the *dao*, drawing upon the *Daodejing*, *Huainanzi*, and *Liezi*, by analyzing how the *dao* fits within the structure of change and causation in these texts. Our contention is that while these texts do not offer an account of *dao*-immutability that mimics the clear transcendence framework of divine immutability in the Christian tradition, there are senses in which the *dao* transcends other things as a changing cause that cannot itself be changed by anything else. Finally, Chapters 9 and 10 take up two sides of a common question: whether there is a transcendent source of the cosmos. In Chapter 9, we approach this issue by placing the *Daodejing* into conversation with the works of the medieval Christian writings of the Dionysian corpus (ascribed to Pseudo-Dionysius the Areopagite). Touching on themes of apophaticism and transcendental perfections, we show the *Daodejing* does indeed describe the *dao* as generative cause in ways that we can fittingly call transcendent. In Chapter 10, we examine the presence of transcendence in *dao*-discourse by focusing more intensely on the themes of affirmation and negation (cataphaticism and apophaticism) in relation to generative agency. Our goal here is to show that early Daoist texts do not endorse a view of divine creation (i.e., generation through creative agency); they still affirm the *dao* as a different kind of transcendent generative cause of the world.

Part One

1

"Naturalism" in Western Philosophy and its Use in Scholarship on Chinese Thought

Naturalism is a difficult idea in contemporary philosophy. It's a worldview almost everyone accepts, but almost no one understands.[1] Naturalism has increasingly become the flag under which philosophers rally in the contemporary academy (at least within certain widespread traditions), and scholars of Chinese philosophy are no different in this regard. Indeed, there is a history of looking to the philosophical and religious systems of China as alternatives to theistic or otherwise "non-naturalist" systems of thought once dominant in the West. Philosophers through much of the Western history of engagement with Chinese thought, such as Christian Wolff[2] and John Dewey, as well as more contemporary philosophers such as Herbert Fingarette[3] and Roger Ames (among others), have looked to early China as the source of a nontheistic spirituality and ethics they deem to be associated with naturalism, in the sense of acceptance of a monistic, single-world system that rejects "supernatural" or transcendent entities.

The idea that there is something beyond what we can access through the senses is not in itself particularly problematic to many today. Much of what is established by the sciences, for example, does not refer in any way to the senses, but explains the way things are experienced in a way that posits necessary additional entities, forces, or activities.[4] Such facts can make it unclear just what the naturalist is rejecting. Even the mystic recognizes that it is in what we cannot sense or perhaps even comprehend that the sensible world of experience is maintained. The mystic provides an explanation of our experience, just as does the naturalist. And it is unclear that the mystic's explanation rests on any shakier a foundation than that of the naturalist, one who takes scientific method (in its current or future forms) as the basis for truth.

If we are to take such a clear stand on the issue of naturalism versus non-naturalism, then we ought to at least have a reasonably secure sense of what the distinction amounts to. However, in most cases our commitment seems to greatly outpace our understanding. Within philosophical circles, it is often the case that one is far more firm in one's commitment to naturalism than one is confident in one's knowledge of what naturalism is.

The moniker "naturalist," we contend, works much more like an *affiliation claim* than it does like a marker of a substantive philosophical position. The naturalist/non-naturalist distinction is much more similar to the political Democrat/Republican distinction in US politics than it is to a distinction based on clear philosophical differences—such as moral realism/anti-realism (although the boundaries here can often be blurred as well). The key difference between these two distinctions, however, is that the latter generally tracks an underlying philosophical orientation whereas the former, we argue, does not. And if this is right, it makes sense of why we see a variety of different and incompatible versions of "naturalism." Part of the reason it is so difficult to get a handle on naturalism is that so many different and incompatible things fly the banner of naturalism, of such disparate kinds, that to make sense of them all as the same kind of view, one would have to define naturalism so broadly as to be almost completely free of content. These difficulties are resolved if we understand naturalism as an affiliation claim.

The naturalism numerous scholars see in early Chinese philosophy is taken as the counterpoint to ancient and medieval Western philosophy.[5] At the same time, it is taken to fit well with contemporary Western sensibilities.[6] It disavows non-natural entities, supernaturalism, transcendence, and all kinds of dualism (mind–body, multiple world, etc.), according to these scholars, and thus presents us with something we can accept, unlike the mysterianism of the ancient and medieval Western philosophers, with their metaphysical systems requiring transcendent entities such as God, souls, substances, and other "naturalistically" objectionable concepts. Such non-naturalism of course is not limited to the European tradition. Islamic philosophy, Indian philosophy, and Mesoamerican philosophy, for example, are similar to ancient and medieval European philosophy in these ways.[7]

The origin of naturalism in contemporary philosophy traces back to debates that arose toward the end of the modern period, with the beginnings of modern science. Akeel Bilgrami traces this back to debates in the Royal Society in England concerning the clash between the mechanistic system of Isaac Newton and classical Christian theology.[8] We see the slow removal of God from nature to a distant and initiative role, first with the influence of deism, in which God's direct activity in nature is rejected in exchange for a God more akin to Aristotle's "unmoved mover" or first cause. Bilgrami argues that contemporary naturalism can only be understood in terms of its historical origins and the debates in which it was situated. We agree with this position, and this historical bounding of the idea of naturalism is something that philosophers and other scholars, including scholars of early Chinese thought, often overlook. Bilgrami writes,

> Some of the philosophical debates of our time are secular echoes, indeed secular descendants, of disputation some centuries ago that was no less intense and of measurably greater and more immediate public significance. If some of this sort of significance persists in our current debates, it is seldom on the surface. This is because of our tendency in analytic philosophy to view our metaphysical and epistemological concerns in relatively autonomous terms, unburdened by any political and cultural implication or fallout. Hence, such wider significance as still might exist can only be unearthed by paying some *genealogical* attention to the antecedent disputes in which the issues at stake loomed larger and more visibly in public and political life.[9]

This disenchantment of nature that entered into the scientific mindset and tradition in the seventeenth and eighteenth centuries precluded the possibility of a God acting in or through nature, or anything not captured by the principles of the new science in its generally material nature. Though many scientists were still happy to accept the existence of a God, this God was placed well outside of nature, and thus outside of the realm of what could be known through science, and outside of the possibility of human knowledge altogether. Nature came to be understood as inert. God was thus *silenced*, and as this worldview developed, the idea of God began to be discarded altogether. Once we have made the move to isolate something from any explanatory or explicit place in our philosophical system, it is a natural next step to simply eliminate it. If an entity plays no explanatory role in a complete account of the world, has no causal connection to anything in that system, and is for this reason unknowable, it becomes natural to eliminate the entity as an extraneous element of the system. What was held onto by an earlier generation because of the seeming necessity of such an idea that was so prominent in their time is easily jettisoned by later generations, who have always known the concept as an inert and mysterious addition.

Naturalism in the modern Western tradition developed in the historical context of the distinction between the natural sciences as inert and shorn of normativity and the Abrahamic conception of God as operating in the world. The primary aim of the naturalist was (and is, we argue) to reject such entities as God, soul, or nonphysical Platonic realms. The hallmark of the "non-natural" or supernatural, given this historical background, is a concept arising from the non-naturalist affiliation group, explanations that go beyond what is provided by the natural sciences. Systems other than those of Western theism, of course, will be rejected by those with such a naturalist worldview. The concept of "vitality" we find in many philosophical traditions, such as the Chinese, Mesoamerican, and African traditions, will generally be rejected, mainly because of their resemblance to the objectionable ideas of the Western tradition around which this scientific naturalism defines itself. We thus stretch the meaning and significance of naturalism when we apply it to traditions like that of early China, but it can still be done and the framing of early Chinese thought in terms of naturalism or non-naturalism can still be useful.

Naturalism, of one form or another, has become the nearly unanimously accepted philosophical worldview in most corners of academia and contemporary scholarship. The best way to make sense of this naturalism in contemporary scholarship is as an affiliation claim connected to a commitment to science and its general methods, and to ontology consistent with and limited by this science and scientific method. The idea seems to be that all that can be known is known by the methods of natural science, and that all that exists is what is posited by the natural sciences. A naturalist commitment must consist in more than simply a commitment to *consistency* with science and scientific method, as it turns out that anything, including explicit rejections of science, might be made consistent with science and scientific methods. Consistency with science is a necessary but not sufficient condition of naturalist worldviews. Even something seemingly as extreme as Berkeleyan idealism (or other forms), which many would contrast sharply with naturalism, can be easily made consistent with all of science. If the world is idea, these ideas still follow the observed laws of nature. The very motivation for Berkeley's idealism was to eliminate what he thought of as empirically undemonstrated—the view that there is some thing in itself independent of our ideas that causes these ideas to be as they are. If we have access only to experience, we need no more than this to make sense of the world. Material things are not strictly necessary to explain our perception of the world, which could be just as we experience it even if nothing but ideas exist. All we ever perceive, according to Berkeley, are ideas, and objects of perception are themselves ideas.[10] Nonetheless, idealism is often taken as contrary to naturalism, presumably because of its rejection of *materialism*. Philosopher and theologian Edgar Brightman wrote in 1933,

> The only genuine opposition must be that between naturalism and idealism, and the realist, as one who believes in the real existence of a world of external objects which do not depend for their being, on being perceived, may, indeed, as he turns to metaphysics, embrace either naturalism or idealism.[11]

We argue that part of the reason we find drastically different accounts of naturalism is that on some accounts of naturalism, only consistency with science and scientific method is taken as necessary to make a system naturalist. Scientistic affiliation carries with it a certain perceived legitimacy and prestige, and even those who want to accept or endorse views that otherwise might seem non-naturalist still want the legitimacy scientistic affiliation accords. If one's views don't really mesh with scientific naturalism, one can simply make them fit by relaxing their conception of naturalism.

To see the pride of place enjoyed by the sciences and scientific methods, one needs look no further than contemporary academic institutions and their hierarchies. We can also see the place of the sciences in the influence and position of physical scientists among scholars in our culture, especially in comparison with scholars of the arts, humanities, or even social sciences. Even in these latter fields, adoption of or attempts to imitate the methods of the sciences are given the highest priority.[12]

Part of the difficulty here, even with the affiliation claim, is that naturalists take their commitment as a kind of promissory note, one that engenders a kind of faith in the ultimate development of the natural sciences that goes beyond what we can take them to have shown today. Naturalists will often point out[13] that their commitment is not to the view that only the entities (and methods) of *current* natural science can be accepted, but that only the entities and methods of a complete future natural science can be accepted. There are, of course, a number of problems with this formulation of the naturalist commitment. Probably the most difficult of them is the epistemological problem—that is, how do we know what a complete future natural science will posit? We of course cannot know what will fill the current "gaps" in our knowledge, and thus cannot know whether such possible information is naturalistically respectable or not. We also cannot know whether the entities (and methods) posited by our current natural science will still be accepted in an ideal future completed science. After all, we have come to understand that many ideas consistent with past scientific knowledge turned out to be false. At one point, Newtonian mechanics was accepted as natural law, until the theories of relativity showed it false. At one time, the phenomenon of burning was understood as a release of the element of *phlogiston*.[14] As scientists came to better understand combustion, they came to see that phlogiston does not exist, and revised their theories accordingly. Examples such as this show us that the fact that an entity is posited by the natural sciences today does not entail that it will be posited by the natural sciences in an ideal and complete science of the future. Thus, if naturalistic respectability is based on this future science, we cannot know whether any single entity accepted by the natural sciences today is in fact naturalistically respectable.

A better way to understand naturalism and to make sense of these naturalistic commitments is to think of naturalism as affiliation with the natural sciences such that one is committed to using only those entities and methods that the natural sciences accept, *as they are constituted at any given present moment.* This allows one who accepts naturalism today to accept all and only the entities and methods prescribed by the natural sciences, while leaving open the possibility that these might change as the sciences themselves change. In essence, this conception of naturalism amounts to "whatever the sciences say, and nothing else." While what this gives us would have been very different in 1850, today, and in the ideal complete future science (assuming such a thing is possible),[15] what counts as naturalist can change with changing science. This also makes sense of a number of attempts to "liberalize" naturalism, to make it consistent with a number of entities and methods not necessarily part of the natural sciences, but not clearly contradictory to them or incompatible with them. And such a project turns out to play an important role in many naturalistic interpretations of early Chinese thought.

Some advocates of "naturalism" seem to conflate two understandings of the term "nature," or at least associate a more general understanding of nature with the specifics of contemporary empirical science. A general conception of nature need not, and indeed cannot, eliminate transcendent entities or others not posited by the sciences. For to discuss nature in this sense is to simply discuss *all there is*. The ninth-century Irish philosopher and theologian John Scotus Eriugena offered a conception of nature (*natura*) along these lines. In his *Periphyseon*,[16] he expresses this point, in a dialogue between a master and student:

Master: Nature, then, is the general name, as we said, for all things, for those things that are and those that are not.
Student: It is. For nothing at all can come into our thought that would not fall under this term.[17]

This shows us a conception of nature that many contemporary philosophers adopt implicitly, but associate with the material posited by the empirical sciences. This conflation of a general conception of nature and one linked to the sciences is part of the reason that the whole notion of naturalism often seems trivial and uninformative in contemporary philosophy. But there is a great deal of hidden content in the positions of most contemporary "naturalists," and claims to naturalism generally have to do with commitment to scientistic affiliation.

The following chapters in this book, though focused mainly on interpretation of early Chinese sources, also include a heavy comparative element, particularly with the Western philosophical tradition. The reason for this is that it turns out, we argue, that clearly non-naturalist views, particularly concerning transcendence (as perhaps the central and most contentious non-naturalist view), found in various places in the Western tradition have clear analogues in the early Chinese tradition. Thus, if it is acceptable to call these Western positions non-naturalist (and indeed these positions are *definitive* of non-naturalism for Western scholars), then we should also see their early Chinese parallels as non-naturalist. As one example, the early medieval philosopher, theologian, and bishop Augustine of Hippo (354–430 CE) adopted the view that God endowed the world with "seminal reasons" in his creation, corresponding to principles by which things develop as they do.[18] This explains the development and change of things in a way that does not require the continual operation on those things by God. Rather, the entirety of the history of the cosmos is built into the principle through which things continually unfold, and this unfolding itself can be understood as the manifestation of this inherent principle. This position is very close to one we find in early Daoist texts (later adopted and developed somewhat differently by neo-Confucians) that attributes the change and development of things in the world, particularly the arising of things from an initial undifferentiated *dao*, to what they call the "patterns of *tian*" (*tian li* 天理).

Mario De Caro offers a bare-bones definition of naturalism that serves as a good beginning point for understanding how many contemporary philosophers and scholars of Chinese philosophy use the term. He offers as a definition of a broad kind of philosophical naturalism "the conception that stresses the indispensability of the scientific worldview and rejects any appeal to the supernatural."[19] This, of course, leaves open as many questions as it answers. Part of the definition includes rejection of the "supernatural," but presumably "supernatural" should be understood as "that which is not natural." So this part of the definition seems to collapse into the triviality that the supernatural "rejects that which is not naturalist," which is to say that naturalism is that which is not non-naturalism. We don't find much more helpful than this in other formulations of the definition. The rejection of "supernatural" elements seems to be a common feature of definitions of naturalism, but what lies under the surface here, when those accepting naturalism offer broader explanation of their view, is a certain kind of commitment to science in terms of affiliation. If this is the case, then the key to determining what naturalism is, or what its various proponents see it as being, is to determine the conditions of affiliation necessary for a position to count as naturalist. Affiliation, unlike doctrinal orthodoxy, can take a number of different forms, and of greater and lesser strength. To be affiliated with a group can consist in anything from sharing their goals to agreeing with them about method or sharing a general attitude. This, we take it, is the reason there is such wide divergence in positions among those who affiliate with a particular political party or even religion, as well as why political and religious views can change so readily. If the condition of being a Republican is not a matter of holding a particular position, but of affiliation with a particular group of other people or institution, then views might radically change while one's identity as a Republican remains the same. Notice that this cannot happen with substantive positions. The condition for being a moral realist, for example, is that one holds that morality is a genuine mind-independent and sui generis feature of the world, rather than reducible to nonmoral components or otherwise reduced or eliminated. If one moves to a view that morality is invented by humans in order to facilitate the development of orderly society, then one is no longer a moral realist, regardless of whether they maintain affiliation and commitments with people and institutions that accept moral realism. Note that the same is not the case for the Republican. If the Republican gives up the view that cutting taxes is the best way to create economic growth, he or she does not thereby abdicate Republicanism. As long as the person still affiliates with the Republican Party, they are a Republican. Indeed, we have seen throughout American history numerous realignments of political party platforms. Changing one's political views does not necessarily change one's party, because party affiliation is primarily based on *who* and *what* one wants to affiliate with. In this way, party association is closer to family or national affiliation than to doctrinal acceptance.

Much the same is the case with religion in practice, despite what on the surface appears to be clear doctrinal identification. Although religious traditions are often highly structured with normative sets of rules and doctrines (e.g., orthodoxy), religions change their doctrines, sometimes radically, over time, while maintaining their identities. This is also why we tend to find a wide variety of individual and offshoot beliefs within religious groups, even ones with highly structured and normative sets of rules and doctrines, such as each of the Abrahamic religions. If naturalism is primarily an affiliation claim, we should expect to see various forms of naturalism based on diverging positions within the naturalist camp, and this turns out to be exactly what we find.

The commitment to science of the contemporary naturalist is so basic that it is not always clear just what *about* the sciences proponents of naturalism are committed to. In some formulations of naturalism, the key claim is one of ontology—only entities posited by the natural sciences are real and can be posited as part of any philosophical theory. In other formulations, methodology is the focus—the claim that all that can be known is known through the methods of science. This second form of naturalism seems somewhat trickier. As a philosophical position, it has the potential to be self-undermining. It is far from clear that the methods of a priori philosophy are scientific in any serious sense of the term, especially as understood in terms of the natural sciences. This also goes for the methods of any other nonscientific pursuit, such as art, law, or philosophy. And certainly, a claim that only through the methods of natural sciences is knowledge possible cannot itself be a claim demonstrated via the methods of the natural sciences. Ontological naturalism may have a slightly easier path to take, but it too seems to rely heavily on intuitions about the supremacy of science as a complete and summative explanation of the universe. Some accounts of naturalism attempt to combine these two features. Boyd, Casper, and Trout offer such a combinative definition,[20] writing that naturalist views hold "that all phenomena are subject to natural laws, and/or that the methods of the natural sciences are applicable in every area of inquiry."

Hilary Putnam criticized this definition for what he saw as its vagueness,[21] but *every* definition of naturalism that we have seen is vague in similar ways. Recall the above definition offered by Mario de Caro involving the rejection of supernatural entities. This move is made by a number of other scholars in discussions of naturalism in Chinese philosophy, including Jeeloo Liu,[22] Janghee Lee,[23] and Chris Fraser,[24] among others. One helpful aspect of the definition offered by Boyd, Casper, and Trout is its explicit reference to the methods of the natural sciences as playing a central role in the definition of naturalism. If we take the affiliation approach rather than the doctrinal approach, we can see naturalism as a commitment to standing with the sciences, to adopting views and constructing systems that are respectable from the point of view of the physical sciences and their practitioners, or at least do not directly oppose them.

The affiliation claim implicit in naturalism seems to go beyond the positive claim of affiliation with the natural sciences, however. It also includes the *negative* claim of the rejection of "supernaturalist" or "non-natural" views. As we pointed out above, if we take these claims on their face, they are simply trivial—naturalism is not non-naturalism. But if we see the core of naturalism as an affiliation claim, we can make sense of this. It includes the claim that the naturalist is *not* affiliated with other groups they refer to as accepting non-naturalism. We contend, given the genealogy of the concept of naturalism, that this primarily refers to *religion*. Not all non-naturalist positions rejected by naturalists will fall under the heading of religion. However, most of these claims do. And it is critical to any study of naturalism (including our own) that we get clear on just what it means for something to be *supernatural*. This is something that proponents of naturalism often overlook, but it is far from clear what they mean by supernatural, and if naturalist commitment is going to be defined at least partly based on what the naturalist rejects, we must have a good idea of what that rejected category is, other than simply "what's not naturalism."

We can look to a very telling quote from Jeeloo Liu, who offers a naturalist interpretation of early Chinese metaphysics that she refers to as "*qi* naturalism":

> This cosmology has a naturalistic spirit in that it does not posit any supernatural, transcendent realm prior to the original cosmic state, and yet it has not been accepted into the naturalistic camp for the lack of any working reduction between *qi*-terminology and contemporary physical terms.[25]

Liu associates transcendence here with existence *prior* to the cosmos (it is unclear whether she associates the supernatural with this as well). There are a couple of different ways we might understand the claim of priority here—metaphysical or temporal priority, for example. It is unclear whether early Chinese systems posit anything like the temporal priority of any "realm" or entity to the cosmos—though it is less than clear in Western traditions that there exists such temporal priority either. For the Abrahamic traditions, it is not quite right to say that God existed *before* time and the cosmos, but rather God exists *outside* of time and the cosmos. Thus, the priority of God to the cosmos cannot be understood in these traditions as temporal priority. If we understand priority in the sense of conceptual dependence, however, then there is a good deal of evidence that a number of schools and texts in the early Chinese tradition do hold that there are entities, realms, or principles prior to the "original cosmic state." This is a claim we spend much of this book defending.

"Liberal Naturalism" and Other
Naturalism-Adjacent Views

If a kind of full naturalism is an affiliation with the natural sciences alone, we can understand it as something approaching *scientism*. On such a view, only what the natural sciences posit exists, and every entity must be reduced to those posited by the natural sciences.[26] This scientistic position can be understood as the default with concern to naturalism, even though there are hardly any naturalists in contemporary philosophy who accept such an extreme scientistic view. The various forms of naturalism we see today tend to relax the scientistic requirements built into this fundamentalist naturalism. They do this in different ways, and to the extent necessary to incorporate whichever entities or methods the philosopher in question is committed to. Generally, we see the proliferation of a variety of naturalism because while almost everyone wishes to retain the affiliation with the sciences that the naturalist badge comes with, they also want to accept entities and/or methods that scientism would reject. In this sense, many philosophers want to have their cake and eat it too. We wish to remain scientistically oriented, even when we want to accept scientistically illegitimate entities or methods.

Naturalism as an affiliation and commitment to the natural sciences might be seen as at least compatible with the view that every entity one accepts that is not itself an entity posited by the natural sciences is at least *reducible* to entities posited by the natural sciences. There is thus a strong presumption for physical reductionism as associated with naturalism. In recent years in contemporary philosophy, however, there has been increasing pushback on the idea that physical reductionism, or what we might simply call "physicalism," is the only kind of naturalism. Clearly if one is a physicalist then one is a naturalist, but many would today claim that the entailment does not hold in the other direction—it is not the case that if one is a naturalist then one is a physicalist.

The most well-known contemporary objections to physicalism by those who take themselves to be naturalist come from the philosophy of mind.[27] Resistance to physicalism also comes from those who think that the social sciences, arts, or humanities have distinctive subject matters and methods that cannot be reduced to those of the natural sciences. How, they sometimes say, can we make sense of artistic creativity or evaluate the aesthetic value of a novel, for example, based on the methods of the natural sciences? Many of these objections to physical reductionism rely on the view that the natural sciences have no way to deal with the *normative*, and that normativity on this kind of reductionist view must be reduced somehow to the merely descriptive. This, we argue further below, is one of the most glaring blind spots of the scientific tradition. In banishing normativity from the realm of science, the contemporary tradition cast it into an abyss from which it seems almost impossible to retrieve it, other than via insisting on normativity as basic alongside the elements of descriptive natural science. Something has gone wrong here. We see that in a number of other traditions, including in that of early China; there is not the kind of cleft between the normative and descriptive, between value and fact, that we see in the contemporary scientific and Western traditions.

Due to this recognition of the inability of the scientific worldview to account for normativity, a number of philosophers who otherwise accept a naturalist worldview try to make room in this worldview for irreducible normativity and other such "liberal" entities. The argument most adherents of this kind of view make is that while the entities or explanations they accept are not reducible to physical states, they are nonetheless consistent with an overall naturalistic viewpoint, because the nonreducible entities are not "supernatural" in nature. Tyler Burge, in explaining a liberal naturalist view in the philosophy of mind (concerning the irreducibility of psychology), writes,

> The notion of representation—of reference or attribution that can be correct or incorrect and that helps type-individuate kinds of psychological states—is entrenched not only in commonsense explanation but in scientific explanation in psychology. There is nothing unnatural or supernatural about such explanation.[28]

Burge appeals to "commonsense" as a guide for what should be considered consistent with naturalism. This is a general feature of liberal naturalism and other forms of what we might call "relaxed" naturalisms. We have good reason independent of empirical scientific inquiry to accept certain entities, methods, or explanations, and this gives us rein to relax naturalistic requirements so as to include these entities, methods, and explanation. Note that this position assumes in its response that *real* naturalism will be a pure physicalism based on the natural sciences alone, and that other considerations lead us to build additional entities and methods into the naturalistic worldview. Burge's explanation also offers us an additional reason for supporting the liberal naturalist move—psychological entities and explanation have been successful, according to him, as scientific explanations, supported by empirical evidence. While we do not get deeply into this issue here, this seems like a more difficult move. Can it really be the case that anything that may figure into a successful empirically based explanation should be considered consistent with naturalism? If so, this makes naturalism such a broad category as to no longer be informative or useful.

Another interesting and telling feature of this explanation is the claim that psychological explanation contains "nothing unnatural or supernatural." This, as explained above, is uniquely uninformative absent a clear meaning of "supernatural" beyond simply "what goes beyond the natural or is otherwise not natural." So there must be something else meant by this idea of the supernatural, the absence of which is supposed to count in the favor of certain positions that physicalists would otherwise reject but which proponents are eager to count as naturalistic.

The entities and methods adopted by most early Chinese philosophers would certainly run afoul of physicalists. However, if we accept a broader conception of naturalism consistent with the kind of liberal naturalism endorsed by a number of philosophers over the past forty years or so,[29] these entities and methods can be understood as consistent with naturalism. What do these philosophers mean by "supernatural" entities of the kind that would rule out a view from counting as naturalist? In each of these cases of seeming relaxation of full-throated naturalism, the reasoning seems mainly to be that these irreducible entities not posited by the physical sciences do lots of philosophical or other work that could not otherwise be done, and that they do not otherwise run afoul of naturalism by requiring adoption of supernatural entities.

What is it to be supernatural in a way that would bar inclusion in a naturalistic system? We see in Liu's quote a link between the supernatural and the transcendent. This is very telling, and she is closer to being explicit about this link than many philosophers who discuss naturalism. As discussed above, the historical development of the idea of naturalism generally took as unacceptable the kind of theistic metaphysics endorsed by medieval philosophers. In their rejection of the "supernatural," these early naturalists understood things such as God, soul, or Platonic realms. Why reject *these* particular entities as supernatural or otherwise non-naturalist, and not other concepts unsupported by scientist commitment? Seeing naturalism as an affiliation claim helps here. In the development of naturalism as a philosophical position in the Western tradition, theism, particularly medieval Christian theism, represented the opposition. Thus, the closer the concepts in consideration approach concepts of central to this theistic tradition, the more supernatural they appear to the naturalist.

This presents an interesting situation for concepts outside of this historical consideration concerning naturalism. What does one who is committed to naturalism say about such concepts as *qi* 氣, *tian* 天, or *dao* 道 in the Chinese tradition; the *atman* of the classical Indian tradition; or similar concepts in a variety of traditions? As we see in scholarship on Chinese philosophy, the way scholars generally proceed is to compare the concepts in question to those in the Western tradition standing within the naturalist-theist opposition, declaring them naturalist or non-naturalist on this basis. But this just shows us that the frame through which we are reading early Chinese philosophy can do little more than tell us which side a thinker or text might be more likely to fall on were we to pluck them from ancient China and place them in post-eighteenth-century Western thought. This can be a useful project of course (in the way any comparative project can be), but it does not tell us much about whether the early Chinese philosophy we engage with was naturalist or not. In essence, the naturalist/non-naturalist distinction, while it can be profitably used in the early Chinese context, cannot definitively tell us whether an early text, thinker, or idea was naturalistic or not. In the similarities of some concepts and arguments to those on the naturalist side of the naturalist-theist opposition in Western thought, there are also differences. And whether we render these concepts naturalist or non-naturalist will generally come down to which side of the modern debate we stand on. We can find parallels between the concept of *qi* (vital essence) and naturalist concepts, but we can also find parallels between this concept and those the naturalist would wish to reject, such as soul (in the theistic sense rather than Aristotle's sense).

We may have many reasons for using certain interpretive frames. The interpretive frame of the naturalist/non-naturalist debate may be useful for determining what in a particular tradition we can accept if we are committed to one side or the other.[30] One who is committed to a naturalist worldview can find in the early Chinese tradition those aspects of concepts and ideas that are compatible with naturalism and adopt or otherwise use those to help construct naturalist systems or make better sense of them. But then reading this naturalism back into the Chinese tradition to make the claim that early Chinese thought was naturalist—this is a mistake. Not only are these same concepts selected as naturalist in fundamental ways similar to non-naturalist concepts, but to maintain that early Chinese positions are either naturalist or non-naturalist is to impose onto the tradition a debate they simply were not having. It would be akin to declaring that certain views in the early Chinese tradition are Christian, Jewish, or Islamic. Certainly, there are concepts and ideas in the early tradition that share much in common with concepts and ideas in one or the other (or all) of these Abrahamic traditions, but it would be absurd on the basis of these similarities to declare early Chinese concepts as Christian, Jewish, or Islamic. An idea simply cannot be a Christian concept, for example, absent the historical and religious context of Christianity.

Thus, our answer to the question, "Is early Chinese concept *x* naturalist?" must be similar to our answer to the question, "Is early Chinese concept *x* Christian?" The most adequate answer to many such questions phrased this way about certain early Chinese concepts is "yes and no." That is, whether a concept *x* can be taken as naturalist, Christian, or fitting any other comparative frame is dependent on what we mean by the claim. The concept of *qi* might be considered naturalist insofar as it can be fit into a naturalist system, on a particular relaxed "liberal naturalist" conception of naturalism, and if we reject some (or much) of what is said about *qi* in early texts and retain only that which does not smack of medieval theism. But no early Chinese thinker ever adopted naturalist ideas in the modern Western sense of the term, nor is the concept of *qi* wholly naturalistically respectable, mainly because early Chinese thinkers were not thinking in terms of a naturalist/non-naturalist distinction. So it can be correct to say that certain early Chinese concepts are naturalist on the basis of their being able to fit into a naturalist system, and at the same time it can be false that these concepts are naturalist, given that they are not part of a naturalistic system, that they have no connection to the historical debate that gave rise to the idea of naturalism, and these concepts are not unproblematically ones that contemporary naturalists might accept.

We show throughout this book that concepts and positions in the early Chinese tradition that are often understood as naturalist also have elements that make them more akin to non-naturalism. We can, that is, use a non-naturalist interpretive frame rather than a naturalist one. When we do this, a very different picture of early Chinese philosophy emerges, which can inform certain non-naturalist commitments in contemporary philosophy, and which perhaps even suggests certain non-naturalist commitments as better responses to certain philosophical problems than naturalistic commitments. In the eagerness among philosophers to read central concepts and positions of the early Chinese philosophical tradition as naturalist, they have overlooked the numerous ways in which these concepts share much in common with non-naturalist positions in the Western tradition. The reading of classical Chinese philosophy in terms of naturalism, we argue, has two sources: (1) the desire to create an *alternative* to earlier, non-naturalist Western philosophy and (2) the desire to legitimize Chinese philosophy among contemporary, overwhelmingly naturalistically leaning "mainstream" philosophers. These represent the "contrastive" and "similarity" approaches discussed in the Introduction.[31]

These two projects are sometimes, but not always, combined. David Hall and Roger Ames, in their well-known work on the Chinese philosophical tradition, for example, pursue (1) independently of (2). Indeed, they seem to take (1) to preclude the possibility of (2). According to Ames and Hall, while Chinese philosophy is naturalist in its orientation, in terms of presenting us with a purely "this world" metaphysics, eschewal of transcendence, and rejection of mind–body dualism, it offers us a naturalism fundamentally different than Western forms of naturalism that emerged from the earlier Greek and medieval European systems.[32]

The concept of transcendence, with which most of this book is concerned, is a hallmark of non-naturalist thought, as connected to the idea of orders of existence outside or above that of the physical world, and the dependence of the world on these transcendent entities. As we discuss below, there are a number of different ways of understanding transcendence (just as with naturalism). Ames and Hall, in *Thinking Through Confucius*, offer a definition of what they call "strict transcendence" that does not rely on ontology, but rather a particular relationship between transcendent and non-transcendent entities. They write,

> A is transcendent with respect to B if the existence, meaning, or import of B cannot be fully accounted for without recourse to A, but the reverse is not true.[33]

Although this, like attempts to offer definitions of naturalism, gives us a vague conception of transcendence, it is enough to work with for present purposes. In the chapters below, we consider a number of different accounts of transcendence, arguing that many of these senses can be found in various early Chinese texts. Ames and Hall make a quite sweeping claim, in *Thinking from the Han*, that transcendence cannot be found in Chinese thought at all. This would, we think, be a shocking and surprising fact if any idea well attested elsewhere in the world could be found *nowhere* in the Chinese tradition. Surely this relies too much on cultural and linguistic determinism of a kind that suggests that even basic structures of the human mind are changed by these features. And if this were so, then why do we see the same basic aspects of culture, language, and other elements of human culture continually duplicated throughout the world? A claim that transcendence does not play a major role in early Chinese thought, or that it plays a much different role than it does in the West, might be defensible (although we argue below that these claims too are largely incorrect). But Ames and Hall make the dramatic and extreme claim that

> one of the most striking features of Chinese intellectual culture from the perspective of the Western interpreter is the absence in any important sense of transcendence in the articulation of its spiritual, moral, and political sensibilities.[34]

Other scholars primarily pursue (2). This often entails (1) of course, given the perceived incompatibility and rejection of non-naturalistic systems in the historical Western tradition. Some examples of this kind of project are Jeeloo Liu's "*qi* naturalism" and Chris Fraser's naturalist reading of the *Mozi*.[35]

Interestingly and perhaps tellingly, much of the push toward reading early Chinese thought in a naturalistic sense is from philosophers. Very few philosophers offer non-naturalist readings of early Chinese thought. Among scholars of religion and history, things are somewhat different. As might be guessed, religious studies scholars are generally more friendly to non-naturalist readings of early Chinese texts. Disciplinary norms may have something to do with this. While naturalism has become nearly a dogma among academic philosophers, among religious studies scholars it is not as popular for perhaps obvious reasons. Especially if we see naturalism as a scientist affiliation claim against religion, as we argue here, we can see the reason naturalism would be less popular among scholars of religion. While one does not have to be a religious believer to study religion, scholars will be much less likely to affiliate with a worldview and camp that takes itself as fundamentally oppositional to the object of their study. Although there are certainly naturalistic readings of religion and some forms of religious expression that are more naturalistic than others (in part because of the rise of the status of naturalism and the desire to associate with it, as in the case of various forms of liberal naturalism), most forms of religion accept at least some non-naturalist entities or methods. This is especially the case considering that naturalism was formed as an alternative or opposing system to particular forms of theism. This also largely explains the appeal of naturalism to certain scholars of Chinese philosophy, who look to early Chinese thought as an alternative to various Western forms of thinking, particularly *theistic* philosophy. Ames and Hall write of Chinese thought as attractive to "students of Chinese culture who … appreciate it as an alternative to Western theism."[36] At one time in the development of Western philosophy, it may have been true that it was hard to find alternatives to theism within the tradition itself, but this is certainly not the case today. Indeed, in the "mainstream" philosophical tradition of the contemporary academy, theism itself is the alternative, as nontheistic and baldly naturalist thought dominates in most institutions. When Ames and Hall wrote their books, things were somewhat (but not *very* much) different, but today the most clearly theistic part of the Western historical tradition, medieval philosophy, has been relegated mainly to parochial institutions. Ancient Greek philosophy still occupies a prominent place in the academy in almost every department of philosophy, but medieval philosophy has been all but erased. Much of the reason for this is likely the inescapably theistic character of medieval thought. Ancient Greek thought, of course, is highly religious as well (at least in many of its proponents), but this religion seems not to offend us as much because it is so distant from modern Western forms of religiosity (generally Christian-inflected). While Plato is certainly a mystic, he cannot be mistaken as an Abrahamic theist.

Ames and Hall argue that numerous scholars read transcendence into the early Chinese tradition in order to render Chinese thought familiar to Western scholars. But this is very curious, given the overwhelming commitment of philosophers and many others in the academy to naturalism, which was as much the case when Ames and Hall wrote *Thinking from the Han* in 1998 as it is today. If the aim is to render Chinese thought familiar and acceptable to current-day Western scholars, one would be much better served reading it as naturalist and materialist—a move we see many scholars indeed make. The early Chinese tradition is not being engaged on its own terms, but in light of its relationship with the West. Neither camp—the "contrastive" scholars who stress Chinese difference or those who stress Chinese similarity—has things completely right. The distance of an early Chinese concept or idea from one of the West cannot be a reason to accept or reject it as authentically part of the early Chinese tradition. If it turns out that many early Chinese thinkers accepted transcendence, substance, and even an Abrahamic conception of God, then they did so, and the similarity of this to certain parts of the historical Western tradition cannot be evidence for ruling it out. It may just turn out that Chinese thought is very similar to medieval Western thought. We do not think that there is such a parallel, of course, but the point here is to show that our preconceived ideas of the similarity or difference of Chinese thought should not play, and cannot legitimately play, any evidentiary role in our interpretation of early Chinese thought. There is no independent reason to think that early Chinese thought must be either similar to or different from the thought of any other time and place in the world.

Naturalism in Early China

Considerations (1) and (2) above can be joined in that they both seem committed to the compatibility of early Chinese philosophical positions and scientistically oriented systems and worldviews. At the heart of both is also a rejection of medieval and certain forms of ancient European philosophy, including the rejection of transcendence, God, souls, mind–body dualism, idealism, dualism about worlds, or any of the other ideas contemporary naturalists would reject.

Part of the reason that naturalism is so difficult to get a handle on is that not only is there disagreement about it among people who appear to be operating with the same general conception of naturalism but there are also very different conceptions of naturalism that have little to do with, although sometimes related to, the conception we focus on here. One commonly invoked conception of naturalism in early Chinese philosophy is the view that important ethical concepts are grounded in views of nature— either human nature or facts about the world itself. This kind of "naturalism" refers not to the character of what exists, but rather the place we ground ethical concepts. We might call this "ethical naturalism" as opposed to "metaphysical naturalism." The problem with this is that there is already a very different view that goes by that name, which has to do with the nature of moral statements as being nonreducible to statements involving entities and properties posited by the natural sciences (in this sense related to metaphysical naturalism).[37] The phrase "moral naturalism" is also sometimes used to refer to the above metaethical view, but perhaps we can use this to refer to the distinct view of an ethical nature described here—one found in the work of philosophers such as Mengzi, Aristotle, Aquinas, and many others.

Consider the question of whether *qi* or *tian* is a naturalistically respectable concept. *Qi* has commonly been read in much of the early Chinese tradition by philosophers as a basic and indivisible unit of the natural world, akin to the concept of the atom in early Greek thought. *Qi* is generally understood as having a conscious or psychological component, and thus it is sometimes translated as "psychophysical stuff."[38] Some other naturalistic-sounding translations Justin Tiwald and Bryan Van Norden note are "material force," "vital energy," and "ether."[39] Jeeloo Liu, as pointed out above, argues that *qi* as basic component of the natural world (necessarily including both physical stuff and consciousness) is naturalistic. There is an inherent difficulty here, however—we still have not agreed on a satisfactory definition of naturalism. Some would claim that any entity that is irreducibly "mental" or "conscious" in nature is fundamentally non-naturalist. Indeed, this is much of what is behind the moves of hardcore physicalists in the philosophy of mind, who attempt to reduce consciousness to physical states. Such reductionists will generally claim that whatever is not ultimately reducible to the entities posited by physics is non-natural.[40] If we can fix whatever definition of naturalism we'd like, then we can make *anything* naturalist. But more importantly, if we extend naturalism to things that most naturalists take themselves as rejecting on other grounds (religious, etc.), then it loses its force. It is no longer either a workable affiliation claim or a substantive doctrine.

It is for this reason that we are suspicious of the "liberal naturalist" move and others like it in Chinese philosophy and other areas. Perhaps the reasons that move us toward rejection of a strict naturalism, such as the acceptance of concepts like *qi*, are reasons for rejecting naturalism *simpliciter*. What is so compelling about the naturalist moniker that we find it necessary to hold onto it even when we no longer accept the doctrine on which it seemed to be founded? The expansionist approach to naturalism is often taken, as in the case of Liu's "*qi* naturalism," when we want to be taken seriously by those who espouse naturalism but we don't want to buy into the full naturalist worldview. But, as pointed out above, if naturalism can be thus relaxed such that anything that can be made consistent with (or does not conflict with) scientific materialism counts as naturalist, then potentially *anything* can be naturalist, and the term loses all meaning.

The early Chinese concept of *tian* 天 is also often read naturalistically, particularly in Daoist texts. The concept of *tian*, like that of *dao*, is very contentious in early China, and understandings of the concept run the gamut from purely naturalistic to openly theistic. While there are certainly some conceptions of *tian* in early Chinese texts that are closer to naturalist views than others (perhaps primarily that of the *Xunzi* and certain parts of the *Zhuangzi*), as we show in later chapters, even the most "naturalistic" of understandings of *tian* in early China is still fairly distant from contemporary scientific naturalism. The concept first developed as a clearly religious, even theistic idea—a concept of a sky deity associated with the early Zhou dynasty.[41] While over the course of the Zhou, into the Warring States and Han periods, the concept of *tian* was "naturalized" by some thinkers in that it came to represent a more diffuse and less personal force, this was neither a universal phenomenon nor a complete one. Just as the Deist conception of God in the West did not completely naturalize a non-naturalist concept, even though the Deist God was clearly not the same as the God of Abraham, the "naturalist" conception of *tian* never completely broke with the early Zhou non-naturalist conception.

As we show through the chapters of this book, reading *tian*, *qi*, *dao*, and other early Chinese concepts as naturalist or through naturalist lenses can be problematic, as it causes us to miss a number of important layers of early Chinese thought. Arguably, even the importance rested on distinctions made between "religious" Confucianism and Daoism (*kongjiao*, *daojiao*) and "philosophical" Confucianism and Daoism (*rujia*, *daojia*) turn on the idea that concepts such as *dao* and *tian* were shorn of any "religious" significance in certain early texts. This, we argue in chapters below, is a mistake.

Indeed, in the case of Daoism, the so-called religious/philosophical distinction between *daojiao* and *daojia* was not discussed in scholarly work until the twentieth century, when Western naturalistic ideas began to gain currency in China. Xu Dishan's 1934 book *Daojiao Shi* (The History of Daojiao) argued for the robust distinction between the two.[42] Thomas Michael further argues that it was Feng Youlan's famous *Zhongguo Zhexue Shi* (History of Chinese Philosophy) that solidified in the West the view that there is a key distinction between these two forms of Daoism. In Derk Bodde's well-known translation of Feng a passage reads,

A (*Daojiao*). Their teachings are not only different; they are contradictory.[43]

This distinction became a common one in Western scholarship on Daoism, but (as we show below) it is a problematic distinction. Feng was wrong that the so-called two forms of Daoism are different and contradictory, and even that they were two forms of Daoism, rather than undifferentiated parts of a single larger tradition. The "non-naturalist" ideas of *Daojiao* are very much part of the texts we deem *Daojia*, which we have determined more rationalist, naturalist, and "this-worldly." We misunderstand these texts when we bar the clear non-naturalism of certain forms of Daoism from consideration as part of the early tradition. It turns out there is no clear line between religious and philosophical Daoism (or Confucianism for that matter). Mysticism, divinity, and the non-natural can be found as much in early philosophical texts as they can in later texts we tend to treat as (and often dismiss as) religious Daoism or Confucianism.[44] Russell Kirkland describes the problem well:

Those who write and teach about Daoism have almost always felt pressed to insist that we should see fundamental discrepancies—even inherent contradictions—between several supposedly different "Daoisms." ... By the end of the twentieth century, the majority of specialists in the study of Daoism, at least in Japan and in the West, seemed to begin to reach agreement that such artificial bifurcations as "philosophical Daoism" and "religious Daoism" do not do real justice to the facts and serve little heuristic purpose.[45]

The influence of scholars like Feng Youlan on this notion of the discrepancies between these two types of Daoism seems clear. Feng, like other well-known Chinese philosophers in the West in the early twentieth century such as Hu Shi, was himself highly influenced by Western naturalist views. Feng wrote his PhD dissertation at Columbia University under the direction of John Dewey, whose pragmatist philosophy grew from a naturalistic conception of the world. Philosophy departments in the United States at the time were also dominated by logical positivism, which clearly made an impression on Feng's work. Feng's *History* can be seen in part as an argument for a certain conception of early Chinese philosophy keeping it in line with Western philosophical thought as it was around the mid-twentieth century.

Hu Shi, also a student of Dewey's at Columbia, was even more explicitly naturalist in his approach. Hu read early Daoism as clearly naturalistic (wrongly, we argue) and focused on what he saw as early Chinese views and concepts consistent with the scientific materialism of the twentieth-century West. In "The Scientific Spirit and Method in Chinese Philosophy," he focuses on the Han Dynasty philosopher Wang Chong and the later neo-Confucians as exemplars of this scientific thinking.[46] Hu's closing remarks offer clear evidence of his desire to locate in the early Chinese tradition something palatable to Western naturalism (also further strengthening the view of naturalism as an affiliation claim). Discussing what he sees as the scientific and naturalistic contributions of Zhu Xi and other neo-Confucians, Hu says,

> Thereby those great Chinese humanists, working with only books, words, and documentary evidences, actually succeeded in leaving to posterity a scientific tradition of dispassionate and disciplined inquiry, of rigorous evidential thinking and evidential research—a great heritage of the scientific spirit and method which makes us, sons and daughters of China, feel not entirely at sea, but, rather, at home, in this new age of modern science.[47]

This kind of appeal for legitimacy to Western audiences is not wholly a thing of the past, especially in the field of philosophy. Nonetheless, we often fail to recognize the influence that this early generation of Chinese philosophers educated in the Western academy had on our readings of early Chinese thought, especially as it pertains to naturalism. Many of the naturalist assumptions we make about the early Chinese tradition can be traced back to them, in combination with a general desire to legitimize our work in the eyes of the overwhelmingly naturalistically leaning field of philosophy. This is also, we contend, why we sometimes find strife between philosophers working on early China and historians, religious studies scholars, and other sinologists. Still, there is less distance between these camps as there may appear. The reason philosophers often read early Chinese texts as naturalist is that they are looking for early Chinese texts as assistance to develop views they take to be *true*. Historians and others are less concerned with the truth of what these early texts claim, and more with understanding what they claimed. Indeed, some historians take it as obvious on its face that most of what was said in early texts was *false*.[48] Most, whether philosophers or historians, however, seem to be committed to some kind of naturalism as *true*. Theologians and other religiously committed scholars, of course, are exceptions to this. This is also part of the reason that the work done by theologians on Asian philosophical texts (what little there is) tends to be very different than that done by philosophers.

The concept of *dao* is a major topic of consideration in the second half of this book. Like *qi* and *tian*, it is understood in very different ways across the variety of early Chinese thinkers. It is especially interesting as it concerns naturalist readings of early China, however, because one of the major issues surrounding interpretation of *dao* is whether early Chinese thinkers understand it as *transcendent* in any important sense. In Chapter 2, we turn to the concept of transcendence, to set the contours that guide us in Part II of the book, when we turn in our argument to early Chinese concepts such as those discussed above.

2

Rethinking Transcendence and Nature

The previous chapter focused upon demonstrating the ambiguity of "naturalism" in modern Western analytical philosophy, and argued it should be taken as an affiliation claim. One common plank in the naturalistic affiliation claim—it seems at times the only one—is the rejection of any entities that are "supernatural" or "transcendent." It is interesting that in naturalistic perspectives, the meaning of "transcendence" is not terribly well defined; most often, it is assumed what is meant by the term. Here, we seize upon this assumption as key, and argue the assumption itself is problematic.

Put simply, our main contention in this chapter is that the naturalistic affiliation claim presupposes a definition of transcendence vis-à-vis nature that is rooted in the early modern European context. Specifically, it presupposes these terms as they were understood and employed by Enlightenment deists. But our aim is not purely descriptive. We also seek to show that this deistic conception of transcendence and nature is, in fact, not representative of how transcendence typically functions in non-naturalistic traditions. Since deism developed out of a Christian context, we will use the Christian theological tradition (here represented by Thomas Aquinas) to show that the deistic conception of transcendence and nature is actually not reflective of how classical Christian theism understands them and their interrelation.

Likely due to the attenuation of premodern thinkers—especially explicitly Christian thinkers—in contemporary analytic philosophy, modern naturalists seem largely unaware that they presuppose a historically unique (even novel) conception of transcendence. Consequently, they also fail to recognize that non-naturalist traditions can and often do articulate transcendence in ways that bear striking similarity to patterns and themes in early Chinese discourse. We therefore provide a concrete example of a non-naturalistic view of transcendence that does not entail what we shall call the "contrastive" conception of transcendence characterizing deism and thus modern naturalism (i.e., the definition of transcendence as set over against nature in mutually exclusive terms).

In terms of procedure, we will first provide a conceptual language for describing contrastive transcendence in general, following the work of Kathryn Tanner. Then, we take up a historical account that articulates how deism reflects such a contrastive conception of transcendence. What we stress, however, is that many orthodox Christian theologians—as representatives of non-naturalism—interpret the deistic turn to contrastive transcendence as itself a departure from a properly Christian understanding of the world. And thus, the final part of our chapter turns to Aquinas to provide an alternative to the deistic conception of transcendence that reflects more what non-naturalist traditions mean by transcendence.

As a brief note, we should mention that our approach in this chapter deals primarily with Christian theological literature on transcendence and nature. This is in part because Christianity is the original context out of which Western discussions of transcendence and nature arise, and thus the context that informs the presupposed content of these claims. However, it is also instructive that much of modern philosophy, including naturalism, is inherently oriented to function as a secular alternative to Christianity in particular and religions more broadly. Consequently, we turn to Christian theology in the concrete as a way of highlighting that modern naturalism actually entails properly theological judgments (though largely negative) that are themselves part of a broader social, political, and variant religious program that founds Western modernity. Unless naturalistic philosophers recognize this fact, they will fail to recognize how the naturalistic interpretation of Chinese thought is, perhaps unwittingly, aimed at supporting and extending a particular a priori worldview, one that is labeled "philosophy" but is as much religious as anything else.

An Initial Footing: Tanner on Theories of Transcendence

As we noted above, most scholars defending a naturalistic interpretation of early Chinese thought do not define the terms "transcendence" or "nature," but treat them as though the idea needs little qualification to be understood. When the ideas are defined, it is usually not to signal a contrast between conceptions of transcendence but merely to express what is held by all those sharing the naturalistic affiliation claim—in other words, it is a pedagogical rather than discursive or polemical definition. Behind both these definitions and the nondefined uses of transcendence in naturalistic readings of early China lie a fundamental agreement that transcendence and nature/immanence are mutually exclusive opposites.

Throughout this book, we will refer to this concept of transcendence versus nature/immanence as a "contrastive" view of transcendence. We take this language from the work of systematic theologian Kathryn Tanner. In this section, we will introduce this concept along the lines of Tanner's use, and demonstrate how extant definitions of transcendence by naturalistic interpreters of Chinese thought—those offered by Hall and Ames and Li and Perkins, specifically—fall within this categorization. The next section will provide a more historical account of how naturalism arises out of such a contrastive view, but our focus in this section is on the concepts themselves.

The term "contrastive transcendence" is developed by Tanner in her book *God and Creation in Christian Theology*.[1] In this book, Tanner identifies two basic approaches to understanding something as "transcendent": contrastive and non-contrastive theories of transcendence. The former refers to a conception of transcendent reality as operating on a fundamentally different realm of reality than the sensible world. Tanner looks to one essential feature that defines the difference between these two models. In contrastive theories of transcendence, "divinity and the rest of the world taken as a whole are viewed as logical contraries within a single spectrum; this forces an a priori separation of the two."[2] Put differently, contrastive models advance precisely by considering what is transcendent as an antithetical contrast to the world.

It is helpful to define contrastive models more closely before defining non-contrastive models, since obviously the latter is based on negating aspects of the former. Tanner argues that the contrastive model of transcendence is represented in classical Greek philosophers such as Plato, Aristotle, and Albinus. These accounts define divinity "oppositionally, as a realm of eternal, changeless intelligibility over and against the world as a whole characterized by the contrary predicates of becoming, uncertainty, and instability."[3] For example, Tanner interprets Aristotle as searching for "intelligibility via a dualistic distinction between an ordering principle and the unordered subject to it."[4] Because Aristotle defines God in this over and against the world manner, Tanner concludes, "Any direct influence of divinity upon the world as a whole must be limited to a final causality which presupposes what it attracts, and preserves to the greatest degree possible the solely self-referential isolation of an indifferent God."[5]

With Albinus, Tanner shows how this dualistic, contrastive conception of divinity versus world has broader effect. She contends that within a contrastive theory of transcendence, the ability for the transcendent deity to be involved with the world becomes difficult to posit. Hence, Albinus develops an indirect account of the divine-world relationship. In this philosophy, she argues, "Intermediate deities of inferior rank are necessary to mediate what is originally formulated as an unmediatable contrast."[6]

At this point, let us bracket off the judgment of whether Tanner's category of contrastive transcendence is fully accurate with regard to classical Greek thought. Instead, let us draw attention to two aspects of Tanner's definition of contrastive theories of transcendence important to our present subject. First, by "contrast," she does not mean merely the *distinction* of divinity as from other types of entities, but rather the definition of the divine or transcendent by means of direct, antithetical contrast to the world. This dialectical contrasting of transcendence versus immanence is key.

Second, we can note that this dialectical contrast is based on a paradoxical proposition. Tanner argues that in contrastive models of transcendence, the divine being conceived as transcendent is actually brought into categorical similarity with the world it is said to be contrasted with. As she puts it, when God is defined through contrastive transcendence, "divinity ... is brought down to the level of the world and the beings within it in virtue of that very opposition: God becomes one being among others within a single order."[7] This is of remarkable importance. According to Tanner, the success of contrastive theories of transcendence requires that what is transcendent is actually understood in terms of ontological univocity with what is immanent. Thus, what is "transcendent" is typologically distinct from non-transcendent reality, but not ontologically distinct—transcendence and non-transcendence are two mutually exclusive species of an ontological genus. Therefore, it is precisely by "immanentizing" the divine or ultimate that it then becomes "transcendent" in a contrastive sense. Put differently, because the divine and the world are placed within the same understanding of ontological reality, this forces them to opposite ends of the ontological spectrum, wherein each is defined by its contrast to the other as two extremes of a continuum.

Conversely, Tanner argues non-contrastive models feature a conception of divine otherness (i.e., distinction) that does not reduce to simple opposition or contrast. In non-contrastive theories of transcendence, that which is transcendent does not compete with the non-transcendent and is not dialectically opposed to it. Rather in non-contrastive theories of transcendence, the sort of difference between "direct contrasts are appropriate for distinguishing beings within the world; if God transcends the world, God must transcend that sort of characterization, too."[8] Perhaps surprisingly, then, because non-contrastive theories of transcendence allow for an ontological distinction between God and the world, they understand the difference between transcendent and non-transcendent reality in terms other than direct opposition, but rather in complementary terms.

This becomes exceedingly important because, as Tanner notes, it is only non-contrastive theories that allow for a closer conception of the encounter between transcendent and non-transcendent reality. As she puts it,

> Far from appearing to be incompatible with it, a non-contrastive transcendence of God suggests an extreme of divine involvement with the world—a divine involvement in the form of a productive agency extending to everything that is in an equally direct manner. Divine involvement with the world need be neither partial, nor mediate, nor simply formative: if divinity is not characterized by contrast with any sort of being, it may be the immediate source of being of every sort.[9]

In sum, contrastive theories of transcendence require mediating steps between the transcendent and non-transcendent—they cannot account for how a transcendent God, for example, is directly involved with the concrete, immanent world because such models define the transcendent in terms of its oppositional contrast to immanence. Non-contrastive theories, on the other hand, define transcendence through a sort of complementary difference between transcendent and non-transcendent reality. There is a difference and distinction to be sure that is a radical and fundamental difference—but it is not the sort of radical and fundamental difference that issues alienation between the transcendent and non-transcendent; rather, it is a difference that unites them.

Our position in this book is that non-naturalist traditions *tend* toward non-contrastive theories of transcendence, whereas naturalism presupposes a strictly contrastive theory of transcendence (which it denies). Put differently, we argue that non-naturalist traditions are more likely than not to be equally suspect about the reality of transcendence when the concept is understood as the naturalist understands it. This doesn't mean, obviously, that non-naturalists either could not or do not hold to contrastive theories of transcendence. We just mean to highlight that not only are there theoretically other ways of articulating transcendence than in contrastive ways, and that more often than not, such accounts are dominant in non-naturalist traditions.

At this stage, however, it is helpful to focus on illustrating how Tanner's term of contrastive theories of transcendence aptly classifies the assumptions about transcendence found in naturalist readings of early China. In order to do so, let us look briefly at two examples of naturalist readings of early China that do define the transcendence that they deny is present in early China. The first is the definition of "strict transcendence" offered by Hall and Ames. They propose that A is transcendent to B if "the existence, meaning or import of B cannot be fully accounted for without recourse to A, but the reverse is not true."[10] With this definition, Hall and Ames seem to conceive of transcendence in clearly contrastive terms. The key to them is that A is seen as transcendent to B in terms of how A acts in non-B-ways, and B is not transcendent because it fails to act in A-ways. In Hall and Ames's picture, A "explains" B as a kind of origin or starting point, but there is no sense that A and B have a kind of relationship such as participation.

A more recent definition of transcendence in an account that presupposes Chinese thought is naturalistic is offered by Chenyang Li and Franklin Perkins. Li and Perkins's account of Chinese metaphysics advances upon both (1) contrasting Chinese thought to the so-called "dualistic" metaphysics of the Greco-Roman tradition and (2) the scientistic presumptions of much of contemporary analytic philosophy.[11] In their discussion of the general framework of Chinese metaphysics, Li and Perkins argue that if metaphysics is taken as "the study of things that do not change" or that metaphysics "concerns only what is super-sensible or transcendent," then there is indeed no Chinese metaphysics.[12] Note how they define this second term in particular: Li and Perkins argue that Chinese thinkers do not hold that there are two radically divided realms of existence (one without forms and one with)—"there is something like a reality-appearance distinction ... but there is no transcendental distinction between the two realms."[13]

One should note that Li and Perkins already have something in mind by "transcendence" and "non-transcendental" that they have not yet defined it at this stage in their work. It is readily apparent that they are presupposing a contrastive view: transcendence is understood in terms of insensible or immutability, or modifying a unique form of "distinction." As they continue, Li and Perkins use a few different phrases to specify what they mean by this "transcendental distinction" they think is absent in early China. On the one hand, they suggest transcendental difference might mean "radically different," though this offers little clarification.[14] More helpful is their contention that within Chinese metaphysics, "the realm of 'what is without (specific) forms' is not like a 'God' who is fundamentally distinct from the physical world ... these two 'realms' are better seen as two conceptions of the same existence."[15]

Ironically, Li and Perkins's transcendence is ruled out inasmuch as it posit "two realms" of existence while suggesting a contrastive collapsing of the ontological distinction between transcendent and immanent. They seem to presume to those holding to transcendence conceive of God or that which is transcendent as another kind or "realm" of existence. But this is precisely what Tanner notes non-contrastive theories of transcendence seek to avoid. Rather, non-contrastive views of transcendence understand transcendence as setting outside the spectrum of existence altogether precisely because the transcendent underlies the entire spectrum of existence. In actuality, what Li and Perkins are suggesting is that there are no *contrastive* conceptions of transcendence in early China—perhaps they are correct in this estimation. But, we stress here that Li and Perkins identify a contrastive understanding of transcendence with transcendence per se, and thus confidently assert that transcendence is completely absent in early China, not merely one kind of transcendence view.

In this way, the presupposition of a contrastive theory of transcendence has clearly impacted Li and Perkins's judgment about whether early Chinese thinkers held to transcendence or not. Because they uncritically—and perhaps unwittingly—presuppose one particular view of transcendence and identify it with *all* views of transcendence, they consequently fail to recognize how early Chinese thought may resonate with other conceptions of transcendence.

This is sufficient to show that naturalistic readings of Chinese thought tend to presuppose contrastive theories of transcendence as the meaning of transcendence per se. In the next section of the chapter, we aim to show (1) that this presupposition is historically derived from Enlightenment deism and (2) that this conception of transcendence *should not* be used as the universal definition of transcendence as this is understood in non-naturalist traditions including from the perspective of classical Christian theism.

A Non-Naturalist Critique of Contrastive Transcendence

If it is readily apparent that scholars such as Hall and Ames or Li and Perkins assume a contrastive conception of transcendence, we can fruitfully ask why is such a conception of transcendence dominant in naturalistic readings of Chinese thought? The reason, we argue, is that naturalism more broadly is a recipient of a presupposed contrastive view of transcendence that became the dominant perspective of scientific-leaning Deists during Western modernity. Although Deists were broadly theistic, the understanding of God that became fashionable in this movement actually led the way for many modern forms of atheism, including those abundant among modern naturalists.

In this section, we seek to present an account of the modern presupposition of contrastive views of transcendence for two reasons. First, to show the historical conditions and contexts of the modern presupposition of a contrastive model of transcendence that underlies naturalistic interpretations of Chinese thought. The second—and more important for our purposes—is to show that this contrastive conception of transcendence should be seen as a departure from, rather than a continuation of, the Christian theological tradition. That is, that the naturalist rejects the existence of transcendence under the definition provided by a contrastive model is *not* exclusive to scientistic thinkers—non-naturalists, such as orthodox Christians, would *also* reject transcendence on these terms.[16] And therefore, we stress that rejecting transcendence on the terms of a contrastive model does not entail a rejection of transcendence per se. Given these goals, we will here present the account of the modern, and ultimately deistic framework of contrastive transcendence by drawing upon historical analyses that take an explicitly theological or religious approach to the narrative.

In his book *The Domestication of Transcendence*, William C. Placher provides a helpful narration and critique of how contrastive models of transcendence rose to prominence in European modernity. Significantly, Placher begins by sounding his disagreement with the suppositions of many that many postmodern thinkers who "attack the Christian tradition, or classical Christian theism, for its picture of a distant, lordly deity, incapable of being affected by the things of the world, standing at the summit of metaphysical hierarchies, and reinforcing their oppressive structures."[17] Placher goes on to argue that this portrayal of a distant, dialectical, and oppressively transcendent God comes from modernity, and is actually not reflective of the classical Christian view of God. Specifically, he writes that "some of the features contemporary critics find most objectionable in so-called traditional Christian theology in fact came to prominence only in the seventeenth century. Some of our current protests ... should not be directed against the Christian tradition, but against what modernity did to it."[18]

In Placher's view, the difference between classical and modern theology lies in epistemology. He argues modernity saw God's transcendence as juxtaposed to the world, and therefore moderns thought they could speak more easily of God's substance. Conversely, Placher contends that classical Christian theology was characterized primarily by an apophatic understanding of God that arose out of a non-contrastive conception of God's transcendence.[19]

At first glance, Placher's argument is counterintuitive: it would seem that the more difference and distance one asserts between the world and transcendent entities, the more that apophaticism would arise. Since this is a term especially associated with Christian theology, and a topic to which we return in Chapters 9 and 10, it is worth briefly defining what apophaticisism is.[20] Derived from the Greek term for "negation," apophaticism is also called the *via negativa* in Latin Christianity, and is differentiated from the *via positiva* or cataphaticism.[21] Apophaticism is a type of discourse about God proceeding upon the basis that one cannot name what God is, only what God is not. That is, one predicates attributes of God by negating that the world we experience is like God's being. Hence, Thomas Aquinas begins his description of God's predicates (derived from reason, rather than revelation) beginning with God's simplicity, but Aquinas does not merely posit "God is simple." Rather, he works through a process of negating God's being composite: God does not having matter, is not composed of soul and body, and so on.[22]

Again, on its face this sort of method would seem to depend upon a contrastive conception of transcendence wherein God is so far beyond the world that nothing of worldly being can be used to name him positively. Placher himself says that "before the seventeenth century, most Christian theologians were struck by the mystery of the wholly otherness of God, and the inadequacy of human categories applied to God."[23] In the seventeenth century, however, "philosophers and theologians increasingly thought they could talk clearly about God."[24] Yet Placher then makes the observation that the seventeenth century "shifted to ... a 'contrastive' understanding of transcendence ... explaining God's difference from created things by saying that God was *transcendent* (distant, unaffected) in *contrast* to *immanent* (close, engaged)."[25]

So how is it that modern discourse that claims God is knowable is more contrastive than classical Christian apophaticism? For Placher, the key is that modern theology thinks of God's transcendence not as a sense of "beyond" human categories but as a point of contrast to the immanent realm of experience. He argues that modern thinkers "increasingly ... thought of God's otherness in terms of distance and remoteness from the world."[26] The problem with this framework is that in a contrastive model, God's transcendence is seen as a proper feature of God's being, rather than naming his otherness. That is, God's being is defined over against the world as its opposite, which has the further effect of making God one other type of being, though a more powerful and vastly different kind of being. As Placher puts it, this contrastive model that arose in the seventeenth century made God "one of the things of the world" and "one agent among others."[27]

For Placher, this is especially evident in the difference between premodern Christian theologians and modern thinkers on the question of evil and suffering. He writes, "If we ask Aquinas or Luther or Calvin, Where is God? or, concerning the tornado or rain that broke the drought, the airplane crash or our neighbor's act of kindness, Who did it? God or some other agent? They refuse to answer the question posed in those terms."[28] He contends each theologian would have attributed a twofold causality: certainly predicating material or temporal causes to a given event (rough winds caused the plane to crash, for example), but that God also caused these events. But, Placher emphasizes that God and other causes are not placed in a total sum relationship—"their accounts do not even permit us to say that God and some other agent collaborated in bringing about events, assigning a percentage of responsibility to each."[29]

At heart, Placher contends this sort of predication of causes to God in the modern period rests upon the collapse of ontological distinctions between God and the world. That is, a world imagined in terms of transcendence and immanence is dualistic because it is monistic. Placher contends that for premodern theology, "God is not one of the beings we can include within any metaphysical system,"[30] which, incidentally, is very reminiscent of the Daoist idea that *dao* is not a *wu* 物, and that it is contrasted with *wu* in a number of ways (see Chapters 8–10 for discussions of this theme). Placher means God is not one of the realities above the physical that is studied in metaphysics according to the Christian tradition; God is really beyond this categorization, and the most metaphysics can study is the effects of God or signs of God's being from created things. Yet at the same time, God is not "beyond" in a sense of distance, for God is said to be "nearer to us than we are to ourselves."[31]

But, of course, a major question for Placher is how did the Enlightenment model of thinking of God as one being among many in the same metaphysical spectrum arise? The usual suspects are there, Descartes, Leibniz, and Spinoza—but Placher lays the blame particularly on the medieval Franciscan theologian John Duns Scotus and the late modern Jesuit Francisco Suárez. This attribution of Scotus and those associated with him as "where things went wrong" has become very popular in Christian theology, though the narrative has also been seriously challenged.[32] For our purposes, it is more significant to see how Placher thinks this shift occurred than to necessarily accept his version of the events, particularly with regard to its genesis. With regard to Scotus, Placher sees the Franciscan friar as initiating a tradition that allows God and human beings to both be attributed "being" in a univocal rather than analogical sense—hence, he is said to promote the teaching of the "univocity of being." With regard to Suárez, Placher argues that he takes Aquinas's analogical conception of God–human relations and reworks analogy so that it actually function as univocity. Thus, according to Placher, the collapse of ontological distinction between God and the world via the turn from analogy to univocity leads to the contrastive model of transcendence found in modernity.

From this, Placher neatly transitions to Rene Descartes. Placher argues that when Descartes arrived at his foundation of *cogito ergo sum*, he then reasoned from this about God's existence. According to Descartes, any idea in the human mind must be caused by something that has at least as much reality as the thing we can attribute to things we experience—the idea of heat must be caused by something as real as when we experience a hot pan. From this, Descartes focuses on the idea of God, and concludes that nothing except God could cause this idea and thus God must exist. This "proof" of God's existence—long debated and often unsatisfying—signals for Placher a radical upheaval in the way God is understood. According to him, God is now explained within the metaphysical universe as having a role to play within it, and thus Descartes can then make stronger (and, in Placher's eyes, more problematic) claims about knowing God.

Demonstrating this point further, Placher turns to Gottfried Leibniz, whom Placher interprets as building upon Descartes.[33] Placher contends that Leibniz turns to talk about God in terms of his perfection, basically understood by Leibniz as the non-contradictory simple qualities that are positive and absolute. Yet, in this move, Leibniz begins to understand God's perfection and simplicity not as obscuring knowledge of God (as it had been for Aquinas) but illuminating knowledge of God. In Placher's reading, Leibniz sees much great access to knowing who God is from the world than his intellectual predecessors. For Aquinas and other premoderns, the lack of a univocal conception of God and the world meant that experiencing good things in the world means we do not know what God's goodness is like in its fullness. However, for Leibniz, "We can recognize the finitude and imperfection of the created world only because we even now have clear and distinct ideas of God's infinity and perfection, so that we can recognize failures to measure up to them."[34]

We do not here wish to defend particular readings of individual thinkers that Placher offers. Rather, we simply wish to emphasize his argument, made with concrete claims, that the modern period initiated a radically new way of understanding the nature of God as the ultimate transcendent subject. Specifically, he points to the move from an analogical to a univocal conception of God and creaturely being led to the collapse of transcendence into a contrastive understanding of transcendence versus immanence. Furthermore, this conception becomes dominant after the Enlightenment, pervading modern philosophy (which, for many Enlightenment thinkers, was at least nominally "Christian" theology) and the presupposed foundations upon which postmodern critics launch their attacks against the metanarratives of Western modernity.

In order to see how naturalism specifically is located in this modern transformation of transcendence, we turn to the work of Louis Dupré. Rather than focus on epistemology and (ultimately) ontology, Dupré interprets the modern shift in terms of an increasingly exclusive focus on efficient causality. According to Dupré, contemporary Western culture is marked by an "absolute distinction between the sacred and the profane" drawn from "an unmitigated separation between divine and earthly reality."[35] This in turn is, in Dupré's words, a "corruption" of Christian ideas of transcendence.[36]

Dupré explains this corruption in two ways. On a general level, he assigns this to a consequence of what he calls "the objectivist attitude" he argues characterizes Western modernity. This attitude is "exclusively object-oriented," a development Dupré attributes to the sixteenth century and forward where "reality became rapidly reduced to its objective, if not its physico-mathematical qualities."[37] In this reduction of the world to *merely* that of experience, one might say, "The world turned into a presence-at-hand, that is, an exclusive object of manipulation, closed to contemplation."[38]

In order to appreciate how this objectivist perspective engenders a transformation of the classical Christian conception of transcendence, it is necessary to understand Dupré's thesis regarding how premodern Christian theology prepares for this turn. Dupré argues that Christianity has always had difficulty striking the balance between God's transcending the world and God's presence in the world, erring on the side of emphasizing how divine Being is distinct from created being.[39] The problem of finding an adequate resolution to this problem eventually begets the objectivist attitude. Dupré's main evidence of this is, significantly, Thomas Aquinas's understanding of the relationship between God and the created order, which we will further explore below. Dupré argues that Aquinas ultimately defines the God-relation as one of causal dependency, which is intrinsically a category of juxtaposition. Hence, he argues that "if God's immanence is restricted to causality"—and Dupré thinks Aquinas makes this proposition—"then in the final analysis his presence to the creature is reduced to the impact of one being upon another."[40]

In brief, Dupré here suggests that Aquinas cannot adequately account for how God is present in the creature. By limiting God's presence to efficient causality, Dupré thinks Aquinas has effectively suggested an account of God as the supreme being whose essence is nonetheless completely separate from and set over against the being-for-one's self that constitutes existents in the created order. Hence, "causality admits of no more intimate union than the one between one being and another," such that God is now *a* being (or at least, in a trajectory toward being understood as one being among others, rather than Being itself) whose relationship to the creature is entirely "objective."[41]

In his book *The Enlightenment and the Intellectual Foundations of Modern Culture*, Dupré offers a similar account that explicitly includes deism in the ambit. Here Dupré expresses his doubt that "any factor has contributed more to the rise of deism and, indeed of atheism in the modern age than the exclusive use of a narrowly defined concept of efficient causality for describing the relation between creation and Creator."[42] Dupré acknowledges the undeniable fact that the conception of God's efficient causality had always been part of Christian discourse (and Aristotelian discourse). But it is vital to note that before modernity, efficient causality was one among many, often simultaneous ways Christianity used to talk about God's relationship with the world. In deism and other modern systems, however, efficient causality becomes the primary and (for all intents and purposes) sole way of articulating this relationship.

As Dupré reminds us, efficient causality is, in essence, "scientific causality," that is, the kind of causality best suited to empirical science and observation.[43] Consequently, within a system that privileges efficient causality to the exclusion of other causal relations, the ability to explain phenomena in terms of natural causes pushes God further and further out of the realm of engagement with the world, and scientific explanation takes God's place, literally. Eventually, we arrive at the Deist conception of God, in which God is mostly associated with the origins of the natural world, the natural law that upholds the world, and the moral law that humans should follow.[44] The shift in Newtonian physics to a mechanistic universe meant God came to be understood as the engineer behind the machine, but the machine itself needed little intervention or maintenance—indeed, if it did, it would point to the imperfection of God as the efficient cause of the cosmos! In this sense, God's transcendence came to be synonymous with His utter and complete *distance* (not just distinction) from the world. Consequently, God's function as creator and guarantor of moral conduct became much more important than any activity of God contemporaneous with that of human beings.

Significantly, Dupré argues that ultimately the deistic conceit of the exclusive preeminence of efficient causality works to usher in modern atheism. For deism had altered the conception of God and world when it had "virtually identified religion with a transcendent promulgation and sanction of moral rules."[45] He notes that as creation particularly came to be understood in terms of efficient causality, disputes on theological questions such as predestination intensified. Given the deistic shift, the dominant solution (Dupré gives the example of Kant) was to turn to nature as "closed" system that is not dependent upon God in any real way apart from establishing the closed system.[46] Once the need to account for a non-natural genesis of the closed system vanished, the need for God disappeared, and so the transition from deism to modern atheism occurred.[47]

Dupré thus contends that traditional Christian theology depends upon a paradox of God's transcendence. There is certainly a sense within Christian doctrine that God is "Wholly Other" and beyond the realm of natural experience. However, at the same time, Christian theology has traditionally resisted contrastive views of God's transcendence that robs the world of significance or likeness to God. As Dupré puts it, "The paradox of divine transcendence is that it can be consistently maintained only as long as God is conceived as fully immanent."[48]

We see this in the impulse of the biblical editors of Genesis, who place side by side two creation narratives: one emphasizing God's otherness and power, the other emphasizing God's intimacy with the created order, indeed identifying human animation with God's very breath (*ruach* or *pneuma*).[49] We see it also in the harsh critiques against Gnosticism by Patristic authors such as Irenaeus of Lyons.[50] The Christian forms of Gnosticism—Irenaeus is set against Valentinism especially—held to a robust dualism, wherein matter was viewed as evil, and the production of lesser emanations from the One (called *aeons*). For Gnostics, the generation of the material world by the Demiurge was a story of loss and evil—a departure from spiritual purity to the prison of the flesh. Gnosticism could not countenance a creator of the material world who was good, and so the God of Christianity was utterly unmoored from the creative act. Against this view, Irenaeus argued that Christian doctrine understood the world to be an immediate gift of God, that is, there were no mediating steps or beings between God and the world. Rather than seeing matter as the product of the evil demiurge, Irenaeus taught the world is the good work of a good creator.

As Irenaeus shows, orthodox Christian non-naturalism requires understanding divine transcendence in non-contrastive ways. Setting God over against the world is simply inadequate to describe what Christian theology teaches about the world. Thus, it is vital to recognize that the kinds of contrastive conceptions of transcendence that arise in European modernity do not represent the standard historical understanding of transcendence in Christian theology. Rather, the deistic and other modern conceptions of transcendence are themselves open to *genuine and wide-ranging critique* from the perspective of Christian non-naturalism.

Therefore, Placher and Dupré's accounts of transcendence in modernity gain us two benefits in particular. First, their accounts show how theologians committed to classical Christianity see modern (and consequently, postmodern) Western thought about God's transcendence as fundamentally disagreeable to classical Christian thought, and this difference lies in the rise of contrastive theories of transcendence. Second, we see that classical Christian theism sees transcendence as allowing for a greater, fuller intimacy between God and the world. In other words, Christian non-naturalism sees divine transcendence not only as a principle of difference from the immanent but also a principle of union.

Consequently, we stress that a non-naturalist tradition—classical Christian orthodoxy for one—has a great many reasons to be critical of the conception of transcendence that is presumed in naturalist readings of China. Put concretely, this means it is possible to affirm with scholars such as Li and Perkins that Chinese thinkers do not speak of transcendent realities that are defined over against the natural order. But this does not consequently mean that Chinese thinkers do not have conception of transcendence at all—we must leave open the possibility that they may simply have non-contrastive theories of transcendence. And, we should add, it seems fair to suggest that such non-contrastive theories are actually more reflective of what non-naturalist traditions mean when they discuss transcendence.

Briefly, we should also attend to another consequence of Placher and Dupré's accounts. Both authors contend that the preeminence of contrastive theories of transcendence in Western thought—at least those relevant to contemporary naturalism—basically began with European modernity. Alongside this fact, one would do well to note that, especially in the United States, the dominance of analytical philosophy has led to the almost universal neglect of premodern thinkers, except by "religious" philosophers. Not only does modern naturalism draw upon a fundamentally modern way of conceiving transcendence and nature, modern naturalists also tend to have very little genuine formation in premodern thought. Consequently, modern naturalists often—wittingly or not—perpetuate the presuppositions of European modernity without understanding whither and how these presuppositions can be legitimately and rationally criticized from the perspective of premodern texts and thinkers.

In this way, the assumption of a contrastive model of transcendence as the sole definition of transcendence is not simply a mistake. It is a sign and consequence of failing to cultivate awareness of the historical myopia that marks much of contemporary philosophy. This ignorance—in some ways planned and in other ways accidental—undermines the description and understanding of Chinese thought. For to interpret

Chinese thought as a priori naturalistic is to subordinate Chinese thought not only to the terminology of the Enlightenment but also to its inner rationale and spirit.

Again, let us be clear that we do not argue in this book that Chinese thought should be universally read as embracing transcendence. What we object to is the claim that Chinese thought is in essence naturalistic and dismissive of transcendence, especially when the terms "nature" and "transcendence" are conceived in limited and, we would say, deeply flawed ways. We might even go so far as to say that naturalism simply provides an inadequate framework for thinking about transcendence as such.

Our position is that non-contrastive views of transcendence provide a better evaluative measure for assessing whether or not Chinese thought includes transcendence. This does not mean that we argue Chinese thought should be universally understood a kind of non-contrastive system. Nor does it mean that we think non-contrastive conceptions of transcendence are inherently harmonious with the inner logic and structure of Chinese philosophy. Ultimately, transcendence in general is so deeply tied to Western theological and philosophical debates that we should only with great caution apply it as a description of Chinese thought. Yet, it seems to us that despite its limitations, assessing whether Chinese philosophers had notions of something like transcendence is still valuable, not least because it has been denied so strongly by naturalist readings. And so, we argue that by thinking of transcendence in non-contrastive ways, we can come to a fairer judgment about whether Chinese thought is naturalistic or not. In order to serve the ends of this assessment, we will now provide a concrete example of a non-contrastive theory of transcendence via the thought of Thomas Aquinas.

A Non-Contrastive Theory of Transcendence: Aquinas

Before turning to Aquinas's account, we wish to be as careful as possible about the implications we intend with this analysis. We do not mean to suggest that thinkers in early China conceive of transcendent reality in ways that Aquinas does. For one, with Aquinas there is still an important sense that God is Wholly Other, which includes doctrinal and philosophical commitments we do not necessarily find among early Chinese thinkers, such as the doctrine of creation from nothing by a personal God. In contrast, early Chinese thinkers most often describe protology in terms of "generation" (*sheng* 生) by *tian* rather than "creation." Even in the *Chunqiu Fanlu*, which uses something closer to creation (the verb *wei* 為, meaning "to make"), we do not find a sufficient interest in underscoring how *tian* is thereby distinct from the cosmos.[51] Still, even as Aquinas understands God as Wholly Other, he does not define this Otherness in terms of radical juxtaposition or a cleavage between God and world. Rather, Aquinas understands the world as analogically related to God, or God as radical ground of the world.

This analogical foundation means that for Aquinas, transcendent reality is not merely distinct from intramundane reality, but the transcendent is the principle of the intramundane order. For Aquinas, the difference between transcendent and non-transcendent reality is expressed in terms of nobility and perfection. At a certain point, the nobility and perfection of God does render human speech and reason incapable of discerning God's nature—in a sense, the transcendent is "beyond" the world. But for Aquinas, this is not a separation of mutually exclusive spheres, but a feature of the intramundane world as being caused by God, and therefore not the same as God. By the same token, however, Aquinas holds that effects bear likeness to their cause—a principle often left out of the modern efficient cause framework—and so the difference between God and world involves a certain likeness. Consequently, Aquinas's analogical conception of the God-world relation—which, we stress against Dupré, always informs his understanding of creation as efficient causation—represents what Tanner calls a non-contrastive conception of transcendence. Within Aquinas's framework, affirming transcendence involves also affirming intrinsic and intimate connections between God and the world.

Aquinas's non-contrastive approach to transcendence entails several presuppositions in his theological and philosophical method. When Aquinas speaks about being and existence, he understands there to be a necessary distinction between ascribing being to God and ascribing being to creatures.[52] One standard way Aquinas describes this difference is that God is self-subsisting being, whereas all other things depend upon God for their existence.[53] This is the logic at work, for example, in the third of Aquinas's well-known proofs of God's existence.[54] Aquinas argues from the principle of contingency that all things that are created were once not, and hence there is no necessity to our existence. Yet, "there must be something whose existence is necessary" that allows all nonnecessary things to be, and this is God.[55]

For Aquinas, however, it is not the case that the difference between God's being and created being is absolute and dialectically opposed. That is, he does not stop at saying human being, for example, is qualitatively different from God's being and dependent upon it as its ground of possibility. Aquinas also argues there is a relationship of similarity between God's mode of being and created being. In the fourth of his famous proofs, Aquinas argues God can be proved to exist from noting that we find gradation in things.[56] He argues that "in things, we find there are some that are more and some good, true, noble, and so on in a like manner."[57] This ability to judge something as "more" or "less" noble, for example, requires something that is the most noble thing that causes this aspect in the thing we judge noble. Here, Aquinas makes use of a favored analogy with heat. To call a piece of iron more or less hot is to note how the iron is caused to be hot by fire and in what way it conforms to fire, the maximum heat. With gradations in things being more or less hot, then, we understand there is a most perfect form of heat—fire—that allows these gradations to be at all. Applying this analogy to ontology, Aquinas holds that the gradations of perfections of being—goodness, truth, nobility, and so on—proves there must be a most perfect form of these perfections that causes them to be in things, and we call this God.[58]

Here, we would call to attention to how Aquinas understands the God-world relationship in these images. For Aquinas, God is certainly qualitatively different in being than are created things, but this is not a dialectical difference. God's being is, rather, the most perfect form of being, and all created things experience a less perfect form of being. Aquinas does not think of this perfection in terms or more or less real, however. When discussing the difference between God's being and created being in terms of simple and composite substances, Aquinas states that "essence is in simple things in a truer and more noble way, according to which they also have a more noble being."[59] Hence, the perfection of God's being is that God is simple—God's being is the same as God's essence—but this does not mean that composite beings such as humans "are" any less way than God "is."

All this is quite significant in light of Aquinas's theological and philosophical method. Aquinas calls theology *sacra doctrina* "holy teaching," and reckons it to be the science or knowledge of God. This is both in an objective and subjective sense. It is objective inasmuch as *sacra doctrina* is the study of God and the things of God. Yet it is subjective inasmuch as *sacra doctrina* advances upon the principles based in God's self-revelation (i.e., what God knows about Himself). Notably, in his description of *sacra doctrina*, Aquinas first uses the verb *transcendere* in the ways we saw above. In the opening question of the *Summa theologiae*, Aquinas argues that because *sacra doctrina* is "in respect to some things is speculative and in respect to others is practical, it transcends (*transcendit*) all other sciences as speculative or practical."[60] Aquinas argues that there is a distinction in nobility or dignity between forms of speculative science on the basis of either certainty or the dignity of the matter studied by a science. Thus, he contends that *sacra doctrina* exceeds other speculative sciences in both of these regards.

We can note already the importance of the concepts Aquinas links with the notion of transcendence. The ideas of possessing a greater dignity (*dignior*) and exceeding suggest a comparison, but not quite contrast in the sense of dialectical juxtaposition we saw in contrastive theories of transcendence. For Aquinas, transcendence does not primarily mean "set against" so much as "a perfection of" or "most excellent." Hence for Aquinas although *sacra doctrina* transcends speculative and practical sciences such as metaphysics and ethics, it nonetheless does not dispense with these. As he sees it, *sacra doctrina* involves speculative science and *sacra doctrina* is a practical science. What distinguishes *sacra doctrina* is that it concerns the most perfect object of the intellect (God's very being on the one hand, human happiness on the other) and has the surest foundation for knowing its object (God's self-revelation). Hence, *sacra doctrina* transcends other philosophical sciences not by being juxtaposed to them but by constituting the perfection of these sciences.

Now we are well prepared to turn to an aspect of Aquinas's thought often criticized in modern theistic philosophy.[61] In *ST* Ia q. 45 art. 3, Aquinas treats the question, "whether creation is something in the real nature of created beings."[62] This is a difficult question to appreciate outside of the Christian and Scholastic context of Aquinas's thought, but with some work, we can show its significance to this chapter's aims. First, we should take note of the context in which Aquinas places this question in the *Summa theologiae*. Aquinas discusses the question of creation being something real in the creature early on within his transition from the doctrine of God's nature to the acts of creation and the created order. Particularly important is the fact that Aquinas discusses this question directly after his treatment of God as the first cause of all things, and in the midst of explaining God's causing all things to be by the mode of emanation.[63]

By appealing to the language of emanation, Aquinas is deliberately borrowing from two philosophical frameworks: the theory of causation taken from Aristotle and the theory of emanation borrowed from Neoplatonism.[64] It is significant that it is precisely this theory of emanation that Tanner points to as evidence of non-contrastive theories of transcendence in early Greece, even if she does not think Plotinus utterly consistent on this score.[65] The key is that by thinking about God as first cause in terms of emanation, Aquinas is emphasizing God's causing all other beings in terms of flowing from God, and not established or made in opposition or distinction to Himself.

When it comes to the question of whether creation posits something real in the creature, we find Aquinas attempting to clarify and refine the Neoplatonist conception of emanation in such a way as to serve the Christian depiction of God. In order to see this at work, we should pay special attention to the first two objections Aquinas deals with. In the first objection of *ST* Ia q. 45 art. 3, we find an argument that creation cannot be anything real in the creature on account of the perfection of God. The objection advances upon the grounds of the Latin verb *creare*, which serves to name both the passive recipient of the creative act (the *creature*) and the active agent (the *creator*). Thus, if "creation" names not merely the act of God to create or the experience of being created, but rather names something real in the thing created, then this would imply (because of the link in the agency of *creare*) that creation is something real in God as well. However, this is impossible from the Christian perspective because God creates *ex nihilo*, without necessity or compulsion. That is, God's act to create is a willed decision to bring about something that is not merely an outgrowth or expression of God's very being. Creation is not an operation that God is compelled to do by his nature, as though it is like human eating or drinking. Since creation, then, is not an eternal act that can be predicated of God, it is clear from the Christian perspective that the creation is not real in God, and thus in the logic of the objection, it cannot be real in the creature, either.[66]

The second objection is a bit more straightforward, at least from the view of traditional Christian theology. This objection argues that creation cannot be something real in the creature because if it were, then this "real creation" would be a mediator between God and the creature. In other words, this objection understands the "real" of Aquinas's article as being something like a principle or force (like the Stoic *Logos* or Plato's *eidos*, perhaps), that God brings about, and which in turn brings about the created things. As we saw with Tanner and Irenaeus above, the Christian tradition rejects any sense in which there is a mediatory agency—that is, intermediary beings such as angels or lesser gods or making the world of matter are untenable for Christianity. In classical Christian theism, there must be a direct causality between God and the creation of the world—God is the true acting subject of creation, on this there can be no doubt. This is also what the second objection of Aquinas's question is getting at: if creation is something real in the creature, this would seem to imply another type of mediatory power meant to create a distance between God and the creature.

It is striking to recognize that Aquinas is sensitive to this concern in his treatment of the question of creation being something real in the creature. Through objection 2, we see that Aquinas is aware of and suspicious of narrations of creation that emphasize the contrast between God and the world. By providing this objection, Aquinas draws attention to how his answer will work within a traditional Christian view of God and the world, in which the world is a product brought about by God and deemed good by

God, and not a view in which God must be protected from the taint of being connected to the world.

With this in mind, we can fruitfully turn to Aquinas's resolution of the question. Those familiar with Aquinas's style know by now that he will indeed defend the claim that creation is something real in the creature. In the first step of his resolution, Aquinas establishes an analogy between creation and generation—that is, the modes of how things come into be either *ex nihilo* (creation) or from the procreative work of species (generation). This is significant because Aquinas is fully aware of the uniqueness of the Christian claim about what it means to create; that is, he knows that the theological sense of creation is a verb that can only have one true subject, God. This action, which consists of bringing existents from nonbeing, is fundamentally different from the acts whereby animals propagate their respective species. Yet despite this overarching difference, Aquinas emphasizes that the relationships appropriate to generating descendants within the species of the world do bear an analogical resemblance to God's creative work. Indeed, Aquinas sees that the generative acts of things in the world are made possible by and are reflective of God's creative agency.

Based on this analogical relationship, Aquinas argues that in generation, something real is posited in the thing generated. By generation, Aquinas especially refers to procreation within a species; let us take father–son generation as an example. When a father generates a son (in this example, we must excuse ourselves from speaking of the necessity of mothers for the sake of brevity), Aquinas would say that this generation posits a real relationship between the father and the son, one that places something real in the son who is generated. What is this something real? In short, it is the fact that the son—who is a living human being—is a son, that is, his very existence bears a relationship to another, his father. In more classical cultures, this can be seen in ways that sons were expected to care for fathers and give them respect, not primarily as a domestic exchange but based on his being a son to his father. Or, in a more modern example, consider paternity tests. The ability to match a father and son based on DNA is a biological statement of this principle since, even if the father and son have no genuine congress, they still have a relationship—the son truly and fully is his father's son and no other's.

Thus, Aquinas then offers the premise that generation has the effect of issuing a real relationship between the generator and generated, yet generation only properly refers to something being made in substantial or accidental form. In creation, however, the entirety of the thing—it's entire substance (*totium substantiam*)—is made. And so, if generation issues a real relationship between the generator and generated, so much more must creation posit something real between the creator and the created.[67]

Aquinas clarifies that what is real between the creator and created is precisely a relationship. He means that creation places within the created thing the fact that it is dependent upon and flows from God—the creature's very existence testifies to God as its principle of being.[68] For the creature, then, creation posits a very real relationship between herself and the creator. Just as a son bears signs of the real relationship he has to his father—often similar physical features—creaturely existence is itself a sign that the created thing has come not from itself or one of its own kind alone, but from God.[69]

In explaining this in his response to the objections, Aquinas makes the fascinating and foundational claims that the relationship between creator and creature is only real in one direction. First, he clarifies that "in God the relation to the creature is not real, but only according to reason."[70] In light of this claim, he states that, "however, the relation of the creature to God is a real relation."[71] One may justly wonder whether Aquinas's position is merely a product of linguistic acrobatics. For surely if a relationship between two things is real, the relationship is real in both terms?

In order to appreciate what Aquinas is up to, we must clearly recognize his reasons for pushing for this distinction. As we saw above, in the first objection of the article on the real relation of creation, the objection suggests that creation cannot be something real in God because it would imply something temporal in God. In his denial that the relation between creator and creature is something real in God, Aquinas is agreeing with this claim. The reason for his agreement is that Christian theology holds that there is no necessity at all to God's creative work, a position dependent upon the thesis that God's existence is perfect and eternal in its self and does not need anything external to God's being to achieve perfection or self-actualization. To posit that creation is something real in God would involve one of the following heretical propositions: (1) that the act of creation asserts a change in God's being or (2) "creator" names an aspect of God's essential being and existence that must be expressed or actualized in creating something outside himself.

Beyond the necessities of Christian doctrine, however, Aquinas has a firm philosophical point. Consider, for example, generation. While a son may bear resemblance and DNA likeness to his father that testifies the son is his father's son, the relationship brought about by generation is not real in the father. That is, generating a son does not bring about a change in the father's ontological reality—he does not bear a resemblance to his son or a likeness with his DNA. We may speak such a way about the father and son, and certainly we would emphasize that the fact the father has generated the son does create a moral obligation on the father's part. But, these assertions would still fall short of positing generation as something real in the father in the same way it is certainly something real in the son.

So the real question is, why does Aquinas stress that the relationship from God to the creature is not something real in God, but the relationship from the creature to God is real? Quite simply, Aquinas is emphasizing the two sides of the creative act of God as he understands it. Although God is not changed or rendered more perfect in the creative act, created things are brought into being in this process. Hence, creaturely existence, purely in its being as it is, is dependent upon and comes from God. This means that creaturely being is truly related to God's being; indeed, our being is subsisting in being given to us by God as an emanation from his own being.

In this view, God's being certainly *transcends* human being—we cannot say created things exist in the same manner God exists. Indeed, we can even say that the difference in how God exists and how human beings exist is fundamentally different such that the limitations of human reason are most evident when we attempt to talk about God's being. Yet, this difference is not the fundamentally different in terms of radical juxtaposition, for human being is created from God and bears a real, true relation to God. For Aquinas, God is really in creatures—we continue to be through God's gift of being, even though we are not really in God (i.e., our being does not add to or enable God's continued being).

For this reason, Aquinas holds that the natural reason of human beings is limited from knowing God, but this is not simply because God is "different" from human beings as though he exists on another level of an ontological spectrum. Rather, for Aquinas, God is the source of the spectrum itself. Thus, it is not that human reason is unable to experience or meet God because he occupies another sphere of existence. For Aquinas, it is like the human inability to look at the sun for prolonged periods of time: our natural rational faculties are simply inadequate to view God's essence in its brightness and truth.

Thus, in his discussion of naming God, Aquinas argues that human beings have the capacity to name God from the exercise of human reason precisely because we can know God as our principle of being.[72] That is, the fact that we are created by God means this real relationship secures an ability to speak about who God is. Yet unlike in the mode of generation—where a son can describe his father's being with great certainty because he experiences the same in kind—in creation we know God as the principle of being as transcendent, or most perfect. Thus, the human knowledge of God based on reason is paradoxical: we can see clearly in this world what God is not, and thus we can speak of God by negation.

But notice the powerful foundation of this *via negativa*—we can only know what is not like God because of the real relationship between creatures and God that grants an awareness of God as not-world. That is, from the fact that this being we possess is from God and a real relationship to him, human beings can know that the various phenomena and wonders in nature are related to, but not equated with, God's being. Indeed, Aquinas's *via negativa* shows that knowing that God is more than the kind of being within in his creation is itself a type of true knowledge about God: in this negation, we certainly recognize God's existence as distinct from created things, yet, in this very movement, testify to the fact of the intimacy between God and world. If it were not for a similarity or relationship in the first place, there would be no risk of confusing the world with God at all! Only in a worldview in which God's transcendence is expressed in the greatest immanence—a testimony held within human existence itself—can God be known through the negative forms Aquinas proposes.

In concluding this brief examination of Aquinas's non-contrastive theory of transcendence, let us summarize the essentials. For Aquinas, God's essence is different from human essence, and fundamentally so. But the term "fundamental" here is meant literally: the difference between God's essence and human essence for Aquinas is that the former is the foundation and ground of the latter. Hence, God certainly does transcend the realm of nature, and indeed the natural world cannot know God perfectly on its own steam. Yet for Aquinas, transcendence means not simply "existing above," but it refers to God's existence as the most perfect and simple being that is the principle of all other forms of being. For this reason, God's relationship to creatures is one of reason, but the relationship between creatures to God is a real relation. All created things, by their very existence, bear an intimate relation to God—indeed, their own being is a participation in God, an emanation from his being, regardless of the rational recognition of this relationship by the creature. For Aquinas, "difference" is inadequate to name the truth of God's transcendence. God transcends the world not in juxtaposing it to himself but precisely in giving it life, being, and sharing in his own life. In short, Aquinas sees God's transcendence *not* as contrast with nature or the immanent world but as present to and within the nature.

The goal of this chapter has been twofold. First, we have sought to show that the standard, presupposed understanding of transcendence and nature that underlies naturalistic readings of Chinese thought is best categorized as a contrastive conception of transcendence. Second, we have sought to show that this is a deeply problematic understanding of transcendence and nature. For one, this view is itself indebted to an immensely historically conditioned view of the world that has its roots in modernity. For another, this contrastive view of transcendence is not representative of how transcendence must be understood, or even typically has been understood in non-naturalist traditions.

Due to the parameters of the naturalistic conception of transcendence, we have appropriately focused on Christianity for an example of a non-naturalist tradition that would (1) heavily criticize how naturalists understand transcendence and (2) defend a non-contrastive view of transcendence. But really, we could easily make a similar case regarding the preference for non-contrastive models of transcendence within almost any of the major theistic traditions (Judaism, Islam, and Hinduism at the least). Consequently, when attempting to assess the presence of absence of transcendence in early Chinese thought, we argue the non-contrastive models are *far* more charitable and effective to produce such a judgment than the contrastive models, which are subject to immense criticism within non-naturalist traditions themselves.

Our argument in favor of non-contrastive models of transcendence need not entail the claim that early Chinese thinkers were practicing non-contrastive theories of transcendence per se. Rather, we simply mean that if we consider transcendence in terms that Aquinas does rather than modern naturalists, it is much harder to conclude that early Chinese thought does not contain transcendence discourse than naturalistic interpreters conclude. This is because, contra the opinion of naturalist interpreters, the fact that one rejects a contrastive conception of transcendence does not entail a rejection of transcendence per se.

3

Naturalism and Non-Naturalism in
the Han Dynasty

Naturalist readings of early Chinese texts often turn out to rely on ideas found not in pre-Qin texts, but in Han texts. While there has been a great deal of philosophical neglect of the Han Dynasty and its key thinkers and texts, much of the evidence presented by scholars for the naturalism of early China comes from ideas found more clearly within Han texts than pre-Han texts. In this chapter, we argue that beginning in the late Warring States and early Han, a move toward a worldview more compatible with contemporary naturalism and the kinds of naturalism that grew out of the project of European modernity can be located. We refer to this as the "naturalistic shift" in the early Han, a phenomenon that manifested itself through correlative cosmology and other aspects of what is often referred to as "Huang-Lao" thought. One reason that the influence of early Han ideas on our readings of the early Chinese tradition has often gone unrecognized is the enormous influence of Song-Ming neo-Confucianism. The neo-Confucians, while explicitly claiming to reject Han thought, were greatly influenced by it, and adopted many of the views of Han thinkers. Contemporary scholars, influenced by the later neo-Confucian tradition that dominated Chinese scholarship after Zhu Xi, tend to read the early (pre-Qin) tradition in neo-Confucian ways, and thus ways consistent with early Han ideas. It is just these Han-derived ideas, however, that serve as the basis for many naturalistic interpretations of pre-Qin texts.

While we argue in this chapter that the "naturalistic shift" in the early Han provides us with something more reminiscent of the types of naturalism that emerged from European modernity, we also show that non-naturalist ideas, including transcendence, can still be found in most Han texts. The Han "naturalistic shift" was not, after all, conceptually identical to the birth of modernity in the West with the late Renaissance through the eighteenth-century Enlightenment. As part of the Han naturalistic shift, the idea of transcendence, as well as the entities thought to be transcendent, while not jettisoned, certainly undergoes a shift. While concepts understood as transcendent in many pre-Qin texts are "naturalized" in the early Han, it is not the case (with exceptions, of course) that transcendence is jettisoned or that a universally naturalistic worldview is developed. Rather, concepts that were previously linked with the transcendent, such as *tian* and *dao*, become naturalized in some respects. Of course, it is important to note that not all early Han texts represent the thought of the

Han "naturalistic shift." New conceptions of transcendence emerge during the Han, as well as philosophical developments unrelated or minimally related to the correlative cosmology and metaphysics of the trends that can be seen as part of the naturalistic shift. The multitude of intellectual trends, traditions, and worldviews of pre-imperial China continues to become more varied and complex during the Han.

The so-called "Huang-Lao" texts of the early Han represent what we might take as the core of the naturalistic shift in this period. There are many points of controversy surrounding Huang-Lao, not least of which concern the identity and integrity of the school (along with the issue of just which texts should be attributed to it). Huang-Lao, like "Daoism" in early China, is a difficult idea to trace. There are no texts that refer to themselves as Huang-Lao texts, and our only references in early texts to the existence of Huang-Lao as a school are in the *Shiji* and the *Han Shu* (the account of which is based on that of the *Shiji* account). It is far from clear whether Huang-Lao was ever a coherent school, trend, or other associative category (such as the *Ru* or Confucians), and most of the texts associated with Huang-Lao today gained this association due to later and contemporary scholars categorizing them as Huang-Lao.[1] Given the difficulties and controversy surrounding the vague notion of Huang-Lao, the category as a whole is not terribly helpful for many purposes, including our purpose here of tracking the naturalistic shift in early Han philosophy. We use the category as a convenient stand-in for a definite trend involving a naturalistic shift and new conceptions of cosmology and metaphysics in the early Han, mainly because of its familiarity and because many of the texts that tend to be classified as Huang-Lao are texts in which we find many of the ideas characteristic of the Han naturalistic shift. We remain neutral here on all other interpretive issues surrounding the category and use of "Huang-Lao" as a school, intellectual trend, or anything else.

R. P. Peerenboom attributes to Huang-Lao texts a "foundational naturalism," holding that in these texts "humans are conceived of as part of the cosmic natural order understood as an organic or holistic system or ecosystem."[2] In their discussion of Huang-Lao, L. K. Chen and Winnie Sung point out that concepts such as *dao* are understood more naturalistically in these texts than in earlier texts. Huang-Lao texts provide a metaphysics meant to enable humans to completely access, understand, and utilize every aspect of the cosmos, in part to explain how the human ruler can have control over all aspects of the world.[3] They write,

> The expression of metaphysical realism is evident—Dao is no longer the unfathomable and undifferentiating state, but has become concretized as some tangible substance in the world. Although Dao for Huang-Lao is also held to be the highest state of existence and also regarded as beyond sensible representation, the realm it covers has clearly shifted from that which is beyond the world to what is in the world.[4]

The concept of *dao* found in numerous Huang-Lao texts can still be considered transcendent in some sense (certainly along the spectrum of non-contrastive forms of transcendence we discuss in Chapter 2), though perhaps in a weaker sense than other early Han texts and pre-Qin texts. In early texts such as the *Zhuangzi*, the way to perfect our action (insofar as this is possible) is to follow the patterns of *tian* (*tian li* 天理), which entails that such patterns are, and thereby *tian* itself is, in some way visible, tangible, and that on which we can model our own activity (even if we cannot fully conceptualize it). *Dao*, on the other hand, is in these early texts a foundational concept, yet not the kind of thing that can be followed, as it is not the kind of thing that can be conceptualized or contain visible patterns.[5] In Huang-Lao and other early Han texts, however, we find the concepts of *dao* and *tian* largely flipped. *Dao* becomes the kind of thing that can be followed, fully manifest in the world, and *tian* becomes the foundation. We move from seeing injunctions to "follow the patterns of *tian*" in early texts to exhortations to "follow *dao*" in early Han texts. Interestingly, the exact same terminology is used here, with the image of "following" (*shun* 順, *xun* 循). We find the construction *shun tian* 順天 in a number of pre-Qin texts, including the *Mengzi, Xunzi, Mozi,*[6] and *Liji*. The constructions *xun dao* 循道 ("follow *dao*") and 順道 *shun dao*, however, are found primarily in Han texts, such as the *Shuoyuan, Huainanzi, Wenzi, Hanshi Waizhuan, Shenjian,* and *Lunheng*. The only place the construction *shun dao* appears to occur in an unproblematically pre-Han text is in the *Hanfeizi*, itself written during the latter part of the Warring States.[7] The construction *xun dao* occurs once in the *Xunzi* and once in the *Zhuangzi*, in the controversial and probably late *Tiandao* ("Way of Heaven") chapter, offering further evidence of this idea of "following *dao*" being a development of the late Warring States and early Han, alongside the development of correlative cosmology, syncretism, and other elements of the naturalistic shift. The construction *cong dao* 從道 is used numerous times in the *Xunzi*, and interestingly also in the *Heshanggong* commentary on the *Daodejing*,[8] though the *Daodejing* itself does not speak in these terms.

In the syncretistic Han text *Chunqiu Fanlu*, we find an interesting combination of ideas of following *dao* and *tian* in chapter 77 (*Xun tian zhi dao*—"Following the *Dao* of *Tian*"), which begins, "follow the *dao* of *tian*—use it to nourish your body—this is called *dao*" (循天之道，以養其身，謂之道也).[9] Here, *dao* is both something to be followed and a feature of *tian*. The notion of following *dao* as a guide, while inherent in early Confucian texts that seem to associate a particular way of living or characteristic activities as *dao*, is interestingly absent in early Daoist texts. While *dao* can be enacted or practiced, *dao* does not appear to be a kind of visible and patterned path one can follow, apparent in the world. The *Zhuangzi* speaks of *dao* being enacted or practiced (*xing* 行),[10] but also as being empty (*xu* 虛) of concepts or "things" (*wu* 物).[11] Insofar as there can, in the earlier Confucian sense, be a *dao* of the sage or a *dao* of any other kind of person, such a *dao* is an essence or substantial characteristic.[12] The *dao* of a sage does not give us any normative content or reveal any patterns inherent in the world or the activity of sages—if it did, it would not make sense to call *dao* "empty" (in the *Zhuangzi*'s terms) or in any way mysterious (in the *Daodejing*'s terms).

Dao in many Han texts (including texts often classified as Huang-Lao) has a transcendent aspect that we see in earlier texts such as *Daodejing*, but a broader account of *dao* is offered by Huang-Lao texts, making *dao* more clearly operative in the world. *Dao* seems also to change its *nature* through its operation in the world. Earlier Daoist texts are marked by their unwillingness to allow *dao* to be of the nature of things in the world even while interacting with these things or in some way forming the basis or ground of these things. Heaven and earth (*tian di* 天地), according to the *Heng*

Xian, are understood to be termed or styled (*zi* 字) as *dao*, although the true name (*ming* 名) of this thing called *dao* is unknown.[13] *Dao*, for numerous chapters of the *Zhuangzi*, remains intangible, hidden, beyond language, even when we become able to recognize and act in concert with it (or alternatively, manifest it through our actions). In Huang-Lao texts, *dao* becomes something more tangible, relatable, the content of which can be both taught and controlled. We find in Han texts in addition to continued discussion of *tian li* 天理 ("patterns of *tian*") a new discussion of *dao li* 道理 ("patterns of *dao*").[14] *Dao* becomes the kind of thing that can have a structure and can properly and fully interact with the world and be conceptualized. Correlative cosmology of the "five phases" (*wu xing* 五行) becomes possible only once we can make sense of all moving parts of the world in terms of their own constitution and internal principles. Thus, we find in Han texts the distinction of the world into the categories of *tian*, earth, and humanity, all comprised of *qi* and governed by the principles of *yin* and *yang*, understood (perhaps) through five phases.

There is a structural difficulty here though. In early texts constructing correlative cosmology, such as the *Chunqiu Fanlu*, we seem to see differing, perhaps competing, accounts of correlative cosmology. One relies on *yin* and *yang* as fundamental principles governing change, while the other relies on the five phases. Even if these two systems can be made consistent, it does not seem like this is done in the *Chunqiu Fanlu*. Instead, it appears that the *yin-yang* and five phases metaphysics were envisioned differently as metaphysical systems roughly connected with this new metaphysics of the Han, both of which rely on making *dao* tangible, or more practically accessible. We can refer to both of these systems, as well as others, as systems of correlative cosmology. Some take correlative cosmology to be a single system or ideology,[15] but in order to do this, we have to make sense of a number of seeming conflicts in the variety of different ways of understanding the correlative system.[16] A better way of understanding correlative cosmology is offered by Erica Brindley, who writes,

> One must be careful ... not to assume "correlative cosmology" to refer to a single cosmology. Rather, it should probably refer to a similar method of explaining the world that subsumed many competing cosmologies.[17]

We can look to the *Chunqiu Fanlu* and other texts for evidence for this position. According to Sarah Queen and John Major, the *Chunqiu Fanlu* was compiled from a diverse group of materials between the middle of the Western Han (mid-second century BCE) and the end of the Eastern Han (220 CE).[18] The text is traditionally attributed to the second century BCE Han court scholar and Gongyang advocate Dong Zhongshu, but according to a number of scholars (including Queen and Major), only a small percentage of the text can be confidently attributed to Dong Zhongshu. The rest was likely written by followers and admirers of Dong, as well as other scholars with systems more or less in line with that of Dong and the Gongyang adherents.[19] In the second half of the *Chunqiu Fanlu*, the authors develop metaphysical views that can roughly be categorized as correlative cosmology, though they do this in different ways. In some chapters of the metaphysical parts of the text, the correlative system is constructed with the concepts of *yin* and *yang* characteristics of *qi* and their changes at its center (this being associated with the parts of the text attributed to Dong Zhongshu).[20] In other parts of the text, "five phases" (*wu xing*) correlative cosmology is developed. Five phases thought is more closely associated with the thought of the *Lushi Chunqiu* and *Huainanzi* than with that of Dong Zhongshu,[21] but there are overlapping explanations between the system, and they share the same approach that we argue in this chapter represents a kind of "naturalizing" of key concepts of the earlier tradition. Of course, this move toward naturalism must be understood in context, in terms of the development of concepts in ways that make them, if understood in a particular interpretive frame, closer to concepts of entities that would be acceptable by the lights of a contemporary naturalist in the Western tradition.

In chapter 41 of the *Chunqiu Fanlu*, the subject under discussion is the nature of *tian* as creator of the human and the nonhuman world. While we see here a conception of *tian* as permanent and not subject to the changes inherent in the world, continuous with views of *tian* in earlier texts, we also find new ways of thinking about the creative power of *tian*. The opening of the chapter reads:

為生不能為人，為人者天也。人之人本於天，天亦人之曾祖父也。

That which can be created cannot create humans. It is *tian* that creates humans. The root of the humanness of humans is in *tian*, and *tian* is also the august ancestor of humans.[22]

Tian itself is not created, according to this passage—a position we do not see in earlier texts, in which *dao* is the primordial and uncreated source from which *tian* emerges. *Tian* has here once again been made the ultimate source of the myriad things, and possesses a key difference from all other things in the cosmos—namely, it is not created. *Tian* appears here as transcendent, in exchange for the *dao* of earlier texts. However, in this context, *tian* does not appear to be the willful, agent-like God or Heaven of the Mohists or even early Confucians, but more akin to the diffuse natural principles governing activity of the rest of nature. It is this latter aspect of *tian* that can make it appear as naturalistic as many other Han concepts. The rest of the chapter explains how human activity is linked to that of *tian* (a theme we also see developed in other early Han texts such as the *Huainanzi*[23]), explaining the mental and physical states at the basis of human agency as having counterparts and causes in states of *tian* that are not associated with agency. Human mental states correspond to seasonal states of nature (*tian*), with characteristic actions of happiness and anger corresponding to hot and cold. It looks as if the *Chunqiu Fanlu* here is setting up a *causal* explanation for the mental states of humans based on these natural features of the world.

人 之 形 體 ，   化 天 數 而 成 。 人 之 血 氣 ， 化 天 誌 而 仁 ； 人 之 德 行 ， 化 天 理 而 義 。 人 之 好 惡 ， 化 天 之 暖 清 ； 人 之 喜怒，化天之寒暑；人之受命，化天之四時。

The shape and body of the human transform according to *tian* and are thereby completed. The blood and *qi* of the human transform according to the stipulations of *tian* and are thereby humane. The virtuous activity of the human transforms according to the patterns of *tian* and is thereby righteous. The likes and dislikes of humans transform according to the warmth and coolness of *tian*. The joy and anger of the human transform according to the cold and hot of *tian*. The reception and allotment of the human transform according to the four seasons of *tian*.[24]

We see here that the features of *tian* are discussed using non-agentive terminology (an issue we return to in Chapter 10). These features of *tian* have a particular causal effect on humans, such that human agency can be causally explained in terms of them, but *tian* itself (considered independently of humanity) does not possess traits such as joy and anger, or reception and allotment. *Tian* creates such states in humans through its natural movements, the alternation of hot and cold, one season after another.

This is further explored in the *Huangdi Neijing*, a medical compilation much of which dates back to the early Han period.[25] In order for the possibility of medicine to arise, particularly in treatment of mental ailments, there must be causal connection between particular properties of nature and mental states or aspects of agency in the human. The *Huangdi Neijing* texts discuss the connections between a variety of mental states and nonmental counterparts in nature that can have a causal effect on these states. Emotional distress, anger, madness, and melancholy, among other states, are due to the movement, quantity, and characteristic (in terms of *yin* and *yang*) of *qi* in the organs. A passage in the *Suwen* section of *Huangdi Neijing* illustrates this, discussing the "five disorders":

邪所亂：邪入於陽則狂，邪入於陰則痺，搏陽則為巔疾，搏陰則為瘖，陽入之陰則靜，陰出之陽則怒，是謂五亂。

That which [evil?] disorders: evil entering *yang* causes *kuang*. Evil entering *yin* causes immobility/paralysis. Attacking *yang* causes *dian* (depression, catatonia) to form. Attacking *yin* causes muteness to form. When *yang* enters, this causes *yin* to [manifest?] silence. When *yin* exits, this causes *yang* to manifest anger. These are called the five disorders.[26]

The text attributes the causes of mental disorders (like physical disorders) with disordered emotions, which are themselves caused by the quality or quantity of *qi* and changes of *yin* and *yang* in the whole body or particular parts of the body. For this reason, operating on one's *qi* can also be treatment for such mental disorders. This is only possible with the development of the kind of metaphysics of correlation we see in the late Warring States and early Han. The patterns of nature, as accessible and tangible (heat and cold, seasonal changes, etc.), are based on movement of *qi*, and cause mental states through their effect on the *qi* of humans.

It is also in this period, in texts like the *Huainanzi*, that we see a focus on the various types and qualities of *qi*. The uniquely human *qi*, according to the *Huainanzi*, is what they call *jingshen* 精神 ("quintessential spirit"), which admits of a certain kind of consciousness as a feature.[27] This *qi* is understood as a more clarified *qi*, suggesting also a collapse of human mental states, consciousness, and agency into the natural world governed by transformation of *qi*. This sets the stage for the possibility of determinism, which is interestingly fairly absent in early Chinese philosophy until the later Han. The discussions of the Eastern Han philosopher Wang Chong (27–100 CE) concerning the allotment or destiny (*ming* 命) of persons assume a strong, nearly determinist view, in which even willful activity has limited effectiveness in altering one's *ming*.[28] It is telling that we do not see such deterministic or nearly deterministic views of human activity in earlier material. This is at least in part because before the correlative cosmology of the early Han, the components of agency such as transformation of mental *qi* and human emotions (among other features) were not explained by internal characteristics linking them to the standard transformative principles of the rest of nature. In texts such as *Zhuangzi*, humans are enjoined to "follow the natural patterns" (*xun tian zhi li* 循天之理),[29] which requires the possibility of failing to follow these patterns and diverging from what appears determined by nature. This requires a conception of non-natural activity or transcendent agency, and engenders the unique early Chinese problem of free will, which appears as a problem to be explained rather than something taken for granted and attempted to salvage.[30]

With *qi* including within itself the dynamic features by which things move and transform, early Han correlative texts establish the ground for a move to understanding the activities in nature, including human activity, as caused by the constitution of things themselves, rather than by the following of some transcendent or supernatural entity or pattern. Chapter 46 of the *Chunqiu Fanlu* states this explicitly in its title: "*Tian's* Distinctions are in Humans". The chapter links human *qi* and the various states of nature, claiming that the features of *tian* can be understood as features of humans, and vice versa.

喜怒之禍，哀樂之義，不獨在人，亦在於天，而春夏之陽，秋冬之陰，不獨在天，亦在於人。人無春氣，何以博愛而容眾？人無秋氣，何以立嚴而成功？人無夏氣，何以盛養而樂生？人無冬氣，何以哀死而恤喪？

The mistakes based on joy and anger and the righteousness based on sorrow and happiness are not in humans alone—they are also in *tian*. The *yang* of spring and summer and the *yin* of autumn and winter are not in *tian* alone—they are also in humans. If humans do not have the *qi* of spring, how can they care broadly and look after the many?[31] If humans do not have the *qi* of autumn, how can they establish their rigidity and complete their accomplishments? If humans do not have the *qi* of summer, how can they nourish abundantly and be happy with life? If humans do not have the *qi* of winter, how can they mourn the dead and have pity on those who grieve?[32]

Passages such as this one link the features of the human on which agency is based and the cyclic features of the natural world such as the seasons. One interesting thing about this passage from the point of view of contemporary naturalism, however, is that the picture it offers is not *reductionist*. That is, the passage denies that the mental states humans possess are reducible to the physical states of *tian*—rather, they are *correlated* with the physical states of *tian*, which enables a co-reduction. The mental states of humans can be explained by the physical states of *tian*, but those physical states can also be explained by the mental states of humans. This is what it means to say that the anger, sorrow, happiness, and so on of humans are in *tian*. And it is on this basis that some translate *qi* as something akin to "psychophysical stuff." For a number of early Han correlative texts, this is exactly right.

This raises the question, however, of whether we can say that early Han correlative metaphysics accepted something like *qi* reductionism. Perhaps they didn't think that everything ultimately reduced to a physical atomic basis, but it does look compatible with the above passage (and others) that both the states of *tian* and the states of humans may be reducible to the basic psychophysical stuff on which they depend. The end of this passage suggests that *qi* in its natural (*tian*-like) guise is the key to understanding various agentive actions of human beings. The *qi* of summer, for example, is responsible for the human ability to "nourish abundantly and be happy with life." A number of other passages throughout the *Chunqiu Fanlu* suggest a *qi* reductionism. A basic statement of this can be found in chapter 58, which also appears to attempt to unify the disparate metaphysical systems of Han correlative metaphysics:

天地之氣，合而為一，分為陰陽，判為四時，列為五行。

The *qi* of heaven and earth—when unified becomes one, when divided becomes *yin* and *yang*, when made distinct becomes the four seasons, and when ordered becomes the five phases.[33]

Here we find an attempt to unify *yin-yang* and five phase accounts of *qi*. There are many other such statements throughout the *Chunqiu Fanlu*, identifying the *qi* of physical categories of nature with the *qi* of mental categories, thus presenting *qi* as a basic psychophysical stuff of which nature and humanity are comprised. A passage from chapter 43 reads:

夫喜怒哀樂之發，與清暖寒暑，其實一貫也。喜氣為暖而當春，怒氣為清而當秋，樂氣為太陽而當夏，哀氣為太陰而當冬。四氣者，天與人所同有也，非人所能蓄也，故可節而不可止也。

As for the expression of happiness, anger, sorrow, and joy and warmth, coolness, heat, and cold, their substance is of a single category. Happy *qi* is warming and corresponds to spring, angry *qi* is cooling and corresponds to autumn, joyful *qi* is Greater Yang and corresponds to summer, sorrowful *qi* is Greater Yin and corresponds to winter. These four aspects of *qi* are what Heaven and humankind can accumulate on its own. Therefore, humankind can regulate these four aspects of *qi*, but it cannot stop them altogether.[34]

We see from these passages that by the early Han, for some thinkers at least, *qi* has become the primary explanation for all activity in the cosmos—rather than patterns inherent in a *dao* that is responsible for the generation of humanity and nature and is in part hidden or inaccessible. *Dao* and *tian* are certainly still discussed in early

Han thought, but both concepts appear as patterned, accessible, and to a large extent naturalized, in that their patterns can be conceptualized, discerned, followed, and (as we see in the case of medicine) the effects of these patterns in objects can be predicted and guided. The patterns of activity are internal principles to objects, based on the nature of the *qi* of these objects. The various changes in *qi* turn out to be related to *yin-yang* and/or five phases, depending on the particular expression. We find instruction in the *Chunqiu Fanlu* to follow the five phases, using the same language that earlier texts such as *Zhuangzi* apply to following the *tian li* (patterns of *tian*). A passage from Chapter 58 reads:

逆之則亂，順之則治。

Turn away from them [the five phases] and there will be disorder, follow them and there will be order.[35]

What we are instructed to follow is not something in any sense external or foundational, but rather the principles manifest internally in our own nature, through activity of *qi*— the psychophysical building blocks of which we and the rest of the cosmos are comprised. Of course, the question of agency and its seeming impossibility arises here just as much as in earlier systems. Given that *qi* determines our activity and that this *qi* contains within itself the principles through which it changes, how can human intention or agency make a difference? How could we "turn away" from the five phases, even if we wanted to? Anything that caused a person to turn away from the five phases would have to be itself understood as the operation of the five phases, in which case the person is not turning away from them at all, but following them. Insofar as every action is a following of the five phases, turning away from them should be impossible. It seems that this requires an explanation of agency as being nondetermined by the principles of change encoded in the five phases and *yin-yang*. But if this is so, then there must be appeal to something outside of the deterministic system of nature, in which everything is explained by the principles of five phases and *yin-yang qi*. That is, there must be appeal to some *transcendent* entity. The early Han texts for the most part do not seem to make this move to the agent as transcendent (although they do retain a conception of the transcendent connected to nature). But it is unclear why they would not have made this move. In the work of Wang Chong (mentioned above), we see an attempt to make sense of agency in an explicitly "naturalistic" way bound by the fundamental principles of nature encoded in *qi*, but Wang is unable to avoid the collapse of this account into a purely deterministic account of human activity.[36]

We see the move toward *qi* and nature-based solutions to the problem of explaining change and patterns in a number of Han texts and systems of correlative thought. For our purposes here, it is not necessary to distinguish the various different systems in early Han metaphysics, but is sufficient to show that the "naturalistic shift" described here can be located in new ways of understanding the relationship between *tian* and *dao*, and the nature of *qi*, linked to *yin-yang* and five phases.

Yin and *yang* were the quintessential principles of change in early China, going back to the earliest texts. The relationship we find between the two in the *Daodejing* typifies standard ways of using the terms.[37] In early Han metaphysics, we begin to see *yin* and *yang* linked more closely with *qi*, as well as with five phases. The "Five Phases" chapter of the *Baihutong* describes one conception of the relationship between these concepts. According to the text, *yang* properties are lofty while *yin* properties are low, and particular phases are associated with one or the other principle. Fire, for example, is associated with *yang* (the text literally says fire *is yang*).[38]

The opening passage of Chapter 58 of the *Chunqiu Fanlu* attempts to unify multiple accounts of correlative metaphysics using *qi*. Certain operations on *qi* create the principles of correspondence and change discussed in correlative texts, according to this passage. We find other passages in the *Chunqiu Fanlu* and other early Han texts that stress one or other of the two positions. We focus here primarily on the *Chunqiu Fanlu*, *Baihutong*, and *Huainanzi*, because these texts include the most wide-ranging and systematic discussion of correlative metaphysics of all early Han texts. We also look at the theories of *qi* and principles of change developed in recently unearthed texts, such as the *Hengxian* 恆先, a text reconstructed from bamboo strips purchased by the Shanghai Museum in 1994, *Taiyi Sheng Shui* 太一生水, a text unearthed in the Guodian tomb excavation in 1993,[39] and parts of the *Huangdi Sijing* 皇帝四經 texts, unearthed in the 1973 Mawangdui excavation. A kind of proto-naturalism can be found as far back as the Warring States, as seen in the *Neiye* chapter of the *Guanzi*.

One of the major themes of the *Hengxian*, especially in the opening passages, is the origin and activity of *qi*.

> 域作 。 有域, 焉有氣; 有氣, 焉有有; 有有, 焉有始; 有始, 焉有往者。 …
> 氣是自生, 恒莫生氣 。 氣是自生自作 。 … 濁氣生地, 清氣生天 。 氣信神哉!
> 芸芸相生, 伸盈天地。 同出而異生, 因生其所欲 。

> Space is created. When there is space, there is then *qi*. When there is *qi*, there is then being. When there is being, there is then beginning. When there is beginning, there is then motion. … *Qi* is generated of itself, constancy (*heng*) does not generate *qi*. *Qi* is generated of itself and created of itself. … Turbid *qi* generates earth, while pure *qi* generates heaven (*tian*). *Qi* is indeed spiritlike! Things mutually generate one another, a process stretching to fill the earth. They emerge the same yet generate differently, thus generating what they desire.

There is a lot packed into these few lines. For our purposes, the central features here are the uses of creation terms such as *zuo* 作, *sheng* 生, and *chu* 出, and the role of *qi* in creation and change.

The opening lines of the *Hengxian* suggest that *hengxian* itself did *not* originate, had nothing in which it was created. It is unclear as to whether *hengxian* should be taken as equivalent to *dao* (although it does seem to play the same role as *dao* in a number of other texts),[40] but regardless of whether we identify it with *dao*, the text clearly holds up the uncaused, uncreated state within which space, *qi*, and ultimately "things" (*wu*) arise. One of the interesting features of *Hengxian* is that it claims that *qi* was self-created (or *spontaneously* created), and not created by *heng*.[41] This has implications for the naturalistic shift in the early Han, even though *Hengxian* was written in the Warring

States period. Franklin Perkins argues that the "cosmogonic shift" characteristic of early Han texts actually began in the late-fourth century BCE,[42] a view with which we take no issue here. Indeed, texts such as *Hengxian* and other recently uncovered texts appear to give us a window onto the origins of this cosmogonic shift, which we also associated with the "naturalistic shift." The cosmogonic/naturalistic emphasis, though originating in the late Warring States, comes to its peak in early Han correlative metaphysics. There are a number of reasons for this, not least of which are concerns about empire, and the issues of accessibility and clarity of standards and principles of change.

The so-called "self-creation" of *qi* according to this passage is particularly relevant. Wu Genyou discusses two possibilities for interpreting the passage: first, that it means that *heng* does not *directly* or on its own produce *qi*.[43] This reading has the virtue of making sense of the following passage that claims that the generation of *qi* does not happen alone (*bu du* 不獨). The other possibility Wu mentions is that the bamboo slips are out of order or missing critical passages. Assuming that the ordering of the text is correct and that no critical clarification is lost, can we make sense of the move of attributing self-creation to *qi*?

The Eastern Han philosopher Wang Chong develops an account of "spontaneous" (*ziran* 自然) generation in his *Lunheng* meant to demonstrate the independent ability of things in the world to arise independently of willful construction. This sense of "self-creation" seems plausible in connection with the *Hengxian*, but there are still problems. The text flatly denies that *heng* generates *qi*, claiming that *qi* is self-generating (*zi sheng*) as well as self-created (*zi zuo*). Later, however, we find claims that certain kinds of *qi* generate the world—turbid *qi* generating the earth and purified *qi* generating heaven (*tian*). If Wang Chong's reading of generation and self-generation here is the correct one, then this would mean that the *Hengxian* accepts a view of *qi* as agentive, offering the position that turbid *qi* intentionally creates the earth, and purified *qi* willfully creates heaven. Given that *qi* is not provided with intentions or such agentive features anywhere in *Hengxian* (or in other texts of the period), this seems highly unlikely.

The move in *Hengxian* is consistent with the "naturalistic shift" we see in late Warring States and early Han texts, in which the internal structure of *qi* and other aspects of the immanent, tangible world are ultimately responsible for both generation and motion of things. The *Hengxian* itself is dated to about 300 BCE,[44] within the final century of the Warring States period. It is during this time that we begin to see the beginnings of the naturalistic shift and other features that become central in early Han thought, such as syncretistic methodologies, in texts such as the *Xunzi*, *Lushi Chunqiu*, and *Shizi*. It looks as if we might place the incipient beginnings of the philosophical trends that culminate in early Han correlative thought during this period.

There are at least two systems of metaphysics we can associate with late Warring States and early Han correlative thought, *yin-yang* and Five Phases systems. The *Han shu* links Dong Zhongshu with *yin-yang* thought, and the scholars Liu Xiang and his son Liu Xin with Five Phases thought.[45] We can see differences between these two systems in the discussions in a number of texts, but in other places we find various attempts to combine the two systems. The main difference between the two systems is the explanatory and grounding emphasis. Five Phase theories make reference to *yin* and *yang qi*, but tend to explain this *qi* in terms of the phases fundamental to them.

We see a reversal of this in *yin-yang* theories. *Yin* and *yang* as principles of *qi* are made fundamental, and the five phases understood on the basis of these principles. We find Five Phases theory clearly put forward in the *Wuxing* (Five Phases) chapter of the early Han text *Baihutong*. In this chapter, the basic structure of the five phases is laid out, as well as their connections to *yin* and *yang qi*. As a preamble to the chapter, before going on to describe the various features of the five phases that explain why things associated with them possess the features they do, the chapter offers a basic overview of the five phases, the *qi* associated with them, and their locations.

五行者，何謂也？謂金、木、水、火、土也。言行者，欲言為天行氣
之義也。地之承天，猶妻之事夫，臣之事君也，謂其位卑。卑者親視
事，故自周於一行，尊於天也。《尚書》：「一曰水，二曰火，三
曰木，四曰金，五曰土。」水位在北方，北方者，陰氣在黃泉之下，
任養萬物；水之為言淮也，陰化沾濡任生木。木在東方。東方者，
陰陽氣始動，萬物始生。木之為言觸也，陽氣動躍，火在南方，
南方者，陽在上，萬物垂枝。火之為言委隨也，言萬物布施；火之為言化
也，陽氣用事，萬物變化也。金在西方，西方者，陰始起，萬物禁止。
金之為言禁也。土在中央者，主吐含萬物。土之為言吐也。

What are the five phases? They are metal, wood, water, fire, and soil. What we call phases are the standards by which *tian* shapes *qi*. Earth is receptive to *tian* just as a wife serves her husband and a minister serves his ruler. This is called establishing the inferior. The inferior desires to look after and serve, and thus its self-motion in this regard constitutes a phase, in order to honor *tian*. The *Shangshu* says: "the first is called water, the second called fire, the third called wood, the fourth called mental, and the fifth called soil." Water is established in the North. In the North, *yin qi* is below the Yellow Springs. It is responsible for nourishing the myriad things. Water runs in rivers, and in this, *yin* transforms things through inundation, which generates wood. Wood is in the East. In the East, *yin* and *yang qi* begin to move, and the myriad things begin their generation. Wood rubs against wood, and *yang qi* is aroused. Fire is in the South. In the South, *yang* is ascendant, and the myriad things extend their branches. Fire follows things, it covers and adorns the myriad things. Fire transforms, and *yang qi* uses affairs to alter and transform the myriad things. Metal is in the West. In the West, *yin* begins to stir, and the myriad things come to a halt. Metal applies a restraint. Soil is in the Center, and governs the sending forth and holding of the myriad things. Earth sends forth.[46]

This is a dense passage, as are those that follow it, associating the seasons with certain characteristic activities as well. We see here a generative conception of the relationship of the Five Phases, a key component of Five Phases theory throughout Han texts. The motion and general activity of objects is understood in terms of the nature of the phases of these objects. Each phase is in self-motion—the phrase used here, *zi zhou* 自周, is reminiscent of the discussion of self-generation and self-creation in the *Hengxian*. Likely the same idea is meant here. The activity of the phases does not come about through the meddling of outside forces, but rather through features internal to the phases themselves are responsible for this motion, and the motion happens without intention or choice. The activity of the phases is not agentive in nature, but natural and regular. We see in the world myriad different kinds of activity, but these can all be explained, according to this view, ultimately by reference to the combinations of phases guiding the activity of *qi*. Notice that the creative ability of the phases themselves is a kind of self-activity that generates on its own the proceeding phase. The analogies drawn between phases and the activity of nature here are part of the naturalistic shift. And there is no part of the chain of five phases that can be understood as unqualifiedly the *first* phase. As the passage describes, water is called first (in the *Shangshu*), but this should be understood in the sense of classification. Following the natural developmental process of phase change described in the above passage, in which analogies are drawn between the activity of a phase and corresponding natural activities, we have an easy connection to draw between the fifth phase, soil, and the first phase, water, built into the description of the activity of water in this passage. What water inundates is soil, and life comes forth from the soil. The transformation of things through inundation described above is the transformation of soil, from which arises wood. Each of the phases can thus be understood as generated through the natural, spontaneous (*ziran* 自然) activity of other phases.

The spontaneous (*ziran*) nature of this process is a crucially important feature as concerns the naturalistic shift in the Han. The way particular entities are constituted plays the central role in explanation of their activity, and this action is attributed to the objects themselves and internal principles at work in them, rather than to distinct previous causes. This understanding of the principles of activity within objects that develops through the correlative thought of the Han period is certainly closer to what contemporary philosophers might consider a naturalistic system, as at the level of explanation of activity, no transcendence or otherwise "supernatural" entities come into play. Indeed, a number of the arguments of current scholars of Chinese philosophy who understand the early Chinese tradition as naturalist rely on understandings of these key concepts that are not fully developed until the early Han. Even then, however, it is somewhat problematic to call early Han thought naturalist. While certain aspects of early Han thought, particularly the correlative metaphysics of texts such as the *Huainanzi* and *Chunqiu Fanlu*, appear more naturalistic than texts of the pre-Han period, we still find conceptions of transcendence in Han texts as well as a conception of substance, which we will come to in later chapters.

The ground of transcendence in early Han texts is twofold: first—in the unnamed and unchanging source of all things, akin to the initial creative nonbeing found in earlier texts, and in the individual agent, as at least partly outside of the deterministic system set forth in correlative texts.

A. C. Graham, in his classic account of correlative thought, understands early Han correlative systems as akin to a form of semiotics, in which comparisons between events and objects are drawn, and the comparisons are systematized in terms of framework concepts such as *yin-yang* and Five Phases.[47] He makes sense of the seeming differences between *yin-yang* and Five Phases thought in that they represent a dual-element comparison in the first case and a five-element comparison in the second case.[48] One problem of this reading is that it unites *yin-yang* and Five Phases thought in a way they were not united in the late Warring States and early Han when they developed. We find stress on different systems across texts, with some, such as the *Baihutong*, focusing on Five Phases as explanation of the activity of objects, and others focusing on *yin-yang*. Although we find both *yin-yang* and Five Phases theory in the *Chunqiu Fanlu*, Sarah Queen and John Major convincingly argue that Dong Zhongshu was associated primarily with *yin-yang* theory, and that the Five Phases sections of the text are associated with a collection of other *Gongyang* tradition scholars (adherents of the *Gongyang* commentary on the *Chunqiu*).[49]

Both *yin-yang* and Five Phase metaphysical theories, which come in a wide variety of specific theories, even within texts, are more amenable to naturalistic readings, and are employed in "naturalistic" ways in Han texts. Looking to the early astronomical and medical texts, we find *yin-yang* and Five Phase thought central to Han attempts to understand the motions of the heavens and treatments for physical and mental disorders and illness in the human being (as briefly discussed above). The sciences, in this sense, take off after *yin-yang* and Five Phase metaphysics is widely adopted in early China. We can make good sense of this if we understand these systems of correlative metaphysics as making claims about the constitution of entities and the ways in which this constitution entails particular changes and patterns of activity in the entities in question.

Two Han texts in which we see the development and expression of the empirical sciences in concert with *yin-yang* and Five Phase correlative thought are the *Tianwen* ("Patterns of the Heavens") chapter of *Huainanzi* on astronomy and the *Huangdi Neijing* on medicine. In both texts, we find accounts of the causal mechanisms behind phenomena such as the motion of the planets or human illness that rely on *yin-yang* and Five Phases in a causal-explanatory way. The Five Phases and *yin-yang* are offered in both texts as explaining why things are as they are observed, and this is critical to know, because knowing how *yin-yang* and Five Phases act generally—that is, the patterns of their actions—will enable us to know how the entities we observe will act in the future. This knowledge is the key to the human ability to treat illness, to undermine the disorders that arise in the human organism, and ultimately to reorder the person in alignment with the proper transformations of the person's *qi*. Of course, in considering this proper ordering, we find non-naturalist ideas like transcendence popping back up in new ways.

A passage from the *Tianwen* makes a connection between *yin* and *yang* characteristics of *qi* and the generation of the days and seasons (mentioned in a chapter on astronomy because of the astronomical significance of the calendar):

二陰一陽成氣二，二陽一陰成氣三，合氣而為音，合陰而為陽，合陽而為律，故曰五音六律。音自倍而為日，律自倍而為辰，故日十而辰十二。

One yin and one yang make two *qi*. Two yang and one yin make three *qi*. Combining these *qi* makes the pentatonic notes. Combining the yin makes yang. Combining this number with the yang makes the pitch pipes. Thus there are five notes and six pitch pipes. The notes double to produce the number of the days. The pitch pipes double to produce the earthly branches. Thus there are ten days and twelve branches.[50]

Just a few lines later, the chapter includes a discussion of Five Phases and their role in production of various components of the heavens (or the sky). Five Phases are discussed throughout the rest of the chapter, as explanation for various changes observed in the skies and the seasons, including the movement of the five visible planets and the progression of the seasons (with their connection to astronomical alignments). Throughout the chapter, and in the two other chapters concerning the earth and seasons in the *Huainanzi*, the Five Phases and *yin-yang* are used as causal explanations for the activities of entities in the world.

An extended passage in the first chapter of the *Suwen* of *Huangdi Neijing* offers what appears to be an account of the emergence of agency in humanity, and an attempt to account for this source of transcendence, in terms of independence of the closed determinism entailed by correlative metaphysics.

黃帝曰：余聞上古有真人者，提挈天地，把握陰陽，呼吸精氣，獨立守神，肌肉若一，故能壽敝天地，無有終時，此其道生。中古之時，有至人者，淳德全道，和於陰陽，調於四時，去世離俗，積精全神，游行天地之間，視聽八達之外，此蓋益其壽命而強者也，亦歸於真人。其次有聖人者，處天地之和，從八風之理，適嗜欲於世俗之間，无恚嗔之心，行不欲離於世，被服章，舉不欲觀於俗，外不勞形於事，內无思想之患，以恬愉為務，以自得為功，形體不敝，精神不散，亦可以百數。其次有賢人者，法則天地，象似日月，辯列星辰，逆從陰陽，分別四時，將從上古合同於道，亦可使益壽而有極時。

Huang Di said, "I have heard that in the greatest antiquity there were true persons (*zhen ren*), guided by heaven and earth, corresponding with *yin* and *yang*. They breathed pure *qi* in and out, standing alone to protect their spirits. Their muscle and flesh was as one, and thus they were able to achieve long life through heaven and earth. Indeed their lives did not have an ending point—like this, their *dao* was generated. In middle antiquity, there were consummate persons (*zhi ren*), uncomplicated in their virtue and maintaining *dao* complete. They harmonized with *yin* and *yang*, transformed with the four seasons, and on leaving the world departed from the vulgar. They accrued purity and maintained their spirit complete. Traveling between heaven and earth, their vision and hearing went beyond the eight reaches. This way, they added to their lifespan and were strong. They, too, may be counted among the true persons. Next, there were the sages. They lived in harmony with heaven and earth and they followed the patterns of the eight winds. They accommodated their cravings and their desires within the world and the common and their heart knew no anger. In their activities they had no desire to disassociate themselves from the world; in their clothing and bearing they had no desire to be observed by the common people. Externally, they did not tax their physical appearance with any affairs; internally, they did not suffer from any pondering. They made every effort to achieve peaceful relaxation and they considered self-realization as success. Their physical body did not deteriorate and their essence and their spirit did not dissipate. They, too, could reach a number of one hundred [years]. Next, there were the exemplary men. They took heaven as law and the earth as rule; their appearance resembled sun and moon. They distinguished among and arranged the stars on the basis of their movements contrary to or following the movements of *yin* and *yang*. They distinguished among the four seasons. They went along with high antiquity and they acted in complete union with the *dao*. They, too, were able to add to their long life and have their full time."[51]

We find similar accounts of the development of persons in texts such as *Huainanzi*, describing the progression from the perfect persons in antiquity who spontaneously acted in accordance with natural patterns to the lesser persons in later times who achieved harmonious yet not perfect lives, and finally to the contemporary age, in which people often radically diverge from the natural patterns, and thus live shorter, more painful, and ultimately less thriving lives. Consider the following passage from Chapter 2 of the *Huainanzi*, discussing the *zhen ren* of ancient times, like the *Huangdi Neijing* passage above. We can take it to (at least in part) be a statement concerning the perfection of the ancients in terms of lack of agency (with such agency seen in many early texts as problematic, as it entails the ability to do otherwise than dictated by the natural patterns):

古之人有處混冥之中，神氣不蕩於外，萬物恬漠以愉靜，攙槍衡杓之氣莫不彌靡，而不能為害。當此之時，萬民倡狂，不知東西，含哺而遊，鼓腹而熙，交被天和，食於地德，不以曲故是非相尤，茫茫沈沈，是謂大治。於是在上位者，左右而使之，毋淫其性；鎮撫而有之，毋遷其德。是故仁義不布而萬物蕃殖，賞罰不施而天下賓服。其道可以大美興，而難以算計舉也。是故日計之不足，而歲計之有餘。夫魚相忘於江湖，人相忘於道術。古之真人，立于天地之本，中至優遊，抱德煬和，而萬物雜累焉，孰肯解構人間之事，以物煩其性命乎？

Among the people of antiquity were some who situated themselves in the chaotic and obscure. Their spirit and vital energy did not leak out to their exteriors. The myriad things were peaceful and dispassionate and so became contented and tranquil. The *qi* of baleful comets such as "magnolias," "lances," "colliders," and "handles" was in every case blocked and dissipated so that they were unable to cause harm. At that time, the myriad peoples were wild and untamed, not knowing east from west; they roamed with their mouths full, drummed on their bellies in contentment. In copulation they followed the harmony of heaven; in eating they accorded with the potency of earth. They did not use minute precedent or "right and wrong" to surpass one another. Vast and boundless, this is what we call "Grand Order". And so those in high station directed ministers on their left and right and did not pervert their natures; possessed and pacified the people and did not compromise their potency. Thus, humaneness and righteousness were not proclaimed, and the myriad things flourished. Rewards and punishments were not deployed, and all in the world were respected. Their *dao* could give rise to great perfection, but it is difficult to find a quantitative measure for it. Thus, calculating by days there is not enough; calculating by years there is surplus. Fish forget themselves in rivers and lakes. Humans forget themselves in the techniques of the *dao.* The true persons (*zhen ren*) of antiquity stood in the foundation of heaven and earth, were centered in uninterrupted roaming, embraced potency, and rested in harmony. The myriad things were to them like smoke piling higher. Which of them would willingly create discord in human affairs or use things to trouble their nature and allotment?[52]

The *Huainanzi*, though it disparages ritual and righteousness (*ren yi* 仁義) in the above passage, goes on to explain that the two, along with ritual (*li* 禮) and a host of other concepts, are necessary today, because of the corrupted and imperfect nature of people, none of whom could hope to achieve the level of the perfect persons of antiquity, in part because of the decline of the human condition in the time since the period of "Grand Purity" (*tai qing* 太清) discussed in numerous chapters in the *Huainanzi*. Grand Purity cannot be reestablished, in part because of the development of agency in humans and the generation of civilization and technologies that, while they aid human life, at the same time create new problems and present obstacles to our natural patterns of action.[53] This process of development can never be undone or unlearned, and thus thinkers like the authors of the *Huainanzi* held that the tools, technologies, and constraints of civilization, particularly ritual, were necessary correctives for a human kind who long ago diverged from harmony with natural propensities. The position is interestingly reminiscent of the Christian doctrine of the fall of humanity and the related doctrine of original sin.[54]

Even though we find a shift in thinking in the early Han about the activity of entities in the world on the basis of their constitution and the generative qualities of *yin-yang* and Five Phases, we can see that transcendence does not disappear from the philosophical scene in the Han. We find a renewed focus on transcendence in a different direction. While *tian* has largely become "naturalized" in Han thought, humanity (*ren* 人) appears to become a source of transcendence. We see the development of something like an undetermined agent, bound in some sense by the inherent structure of the human body and effects of the surrounding world, but not *fully* bound by these. In this way, we see something like the autonomous individual mind or soul that operates on the world, but is not operated on by the world in the same way, in terms of the determinate outcomes specified in correlative metaphysical systems.

In the Chapter 3 of the *Huainanzi* (*Tianwen*) we find an account of the human role in the completion of the cosmos itself, which suggests that not only is the human agent not completely determined by the external world, but in part determines the state of that external world. Humans have, according to the chapter, the ability to "disorder the regularities of nature" (亂其常 *luan qi chang*),[55] which they can do by failing to complete (*cheng* 成) what *tian* provides in the proper way. The *Huainanzi* is clearer about the activity through which humanity completes the cosmos than are earlier texts. The measurements of the heavens are given as examples. Establishing the calendar, the days, and the hours through use of a gnomon, as well as determining the location of the pole, is given as an example of such activity.[56] The transcendence offered through discussion of human agency is something developed to a much greater extent in Han material than in pre-Han material, although certainly the incipient beginnings of these ideas can be found in Warring States and earlier texts.

Numerous contemporary scholars of early China who offer naturalistic readings of early Chinese thought and reject the view that we can find "non-naturalist" concepts such as transcendence or substance at work in these traditions implicitly offer interpretations of key concepts that are much closer to early Han understandings than pre-Han understandings of these concepts. Particularly concepts such as *qi*, *tian*, and *dao* are given Han interpretations and read backward into the tradition in naturalistic ways that not only misrepresent earlier understandings but also take the naturalistic shift of the Han out of its own context. While there is quite a bit of evidence (some of which we have shown above) that new and more naturalistic understandings of key concepts develop in the early Han, it is a mistake to read these back into the earlier tradition, as well as to pluck them out of the context of the rest of Han thought and in doing so reject the non-naturalist elements that can still be found throughout the tradition.

Jeeloo Liu, in discussing what she calls "*qi* naturalism" in early Chinese texts, bases her reading on that of Zhang Dainan, who read *qi* as a basic "primary stuff" out of which all things are created.[57] This atomic reading of *qi* with *yin* and *yang* as properties is perfectly consistent with Han correlative thought, but Liu extends this understanding to early "Daoist" texts such as the *Laozi* and *Zhuangzi*. This, in our view, is part of where things begin to go astray. Liu writes, "Daoist cosmology is fundamentally built on the notion of *qi*. Both Laozi and Zhuangzi appeal to the transformation of *qi* in their speculation of the origin of the world."[58] She then goes on to describe the idea of "primordial *qi*" found in texts such as the *Chunqiu Fanlu* and *Heguanzi*. This is a curious combination. Both of these texts are attributed to the Han or late Warring States, unlike the *Zhuangzi* and *Laozi*. The idea of a primordial *qi* cannot easily be found in either of these earlier texts, nor can Han notions of *qi* as a basic substance with *yin* and *yang* as properties. *Yin* and *yang* are certainly discussed in the *Laozi*, but not as properties of *qi*, but rather as more general categorical concepts. In addition, there is the difficulty here of positing a coherent "Daoist" view of *qi* based on disconnected texts in the Warring States and Han, when it is far from clear we can take Sima Tan's categories as tracking any actual intellectual school or even trend. We find a multitude of different views concerning *qi* in the texts Liu mentions here, but one feature of earlier texts such as *Laozi* and *Zhuangzi* is that the kind of atomic *qi* view found in early Han texts is markedly absent. The closest we come to such a view of *qi* in the *Zhuangzi* is the Chapter 4 discussion of "fasting of the mind" (心齋 *xin zhai*). We do not find the constructs *yin qi* or *yang qi* in texts before the Han Dynasty, with perhaps the earliest use found in the *Liji*.[59]

Going back further, if we look at foundational thinkers in Western Sinology such as Marcel Granet, Frederick Mote, Joseph Needham, Benjamin Schwartz, Feng Youlan, and Hu Shi, whose interpretations influenced more contemporary scholars who endorse naturalistic readings of early Chinese thought, such as Roger Ames, Chris Fraser, Jeeloo Liu, and others, we find reliance on the naturalistic concepts developed in the Han to argue for naturalistic interpretations of early Chinese thought as a whole. Interestingly enough, these scholars generally looked to pre-Han texts to support their positions, but the ideas they offer fit much better with Han conceptions than with those of pre-Han thinkers.

According to Benjamin Schwartz, even in early Daoist texts where he concedes that we do find a form of transcendence in early China, this "most radical expression of transcendence in China" coincides with a naturalistic view that makes the entire cosmos of the same nature and order. The early Daoists, according to Schwartz, "affirm … the world of nature, which abides in and partakes of the essence of the *dao*."[60]

Joseph Needham grounded his naturalist interpretation of early Chinese thought in what he thought was the fact that there was no transcendent entity posited by early Chinese thinkers, and that instead internal patterns within nature determined the development of things. He wrote,

> The harmonious cooperation of all beings arose, not from the orders of a superior authority external to themselves, but from the fact that they were all parts in a hierarchy of wholes forming a cosmic pattern, and what they obeyed were the internal dictates of their own nature.[61]

This idea that the development and behavior of things follow internal principles or patterns rather than being guided or moved by external forces is a development we see most pronounced in Han literature. In particular, the Han understanding of the concept of *ziran* 自然 (spontaneity, nature) developed by thinkers such as Wang Chong, also influential in the thought of *Xuanxue* (neo-Daoist) thinkers such as Wang Bi and Guo Xiang, moves in this direction. The commentaries of *Xuanxue* figures such as Wang and Guo on early Daoist texts play a large role in influencing scholarly readings of these texts to this day. But it is not at all clear that the Han conception of *ziran* can be found in texts such as the *Daodejing* and *Zhuangzi*. Indeed, if we look to pre-Han texts, the best case to be made for something like Needham's interpretation is to look to texts such as the *Mengzi*—but even there, it is not clear that the internalist stance extends beyond the realm of the moral, with which the text is mainly concerned.

The naturalistic shift in the Han toward making sense of the development and activity of things in the world on the basis of internal features and principles led to the development of correlative cosmology, explaining activity in terms of the states of their *qi* and changes of their phase (*xing* 行). From early texts we find a focus on following *tian*'s patterns (*tian li*)[62] or following the way of persons (*ren dao*),[63] which are understood in terms of external principles, accessible by but not inherent within the individual. And for this reason they also require learning (although even for *Mengzi*, we cannot cultivate the internal wellspring of virtue within our nature without some form of learning).

Hyo-Dong Lee discusses the shared tendency among a certain group of scholars to reject transcendence in early China, linking these scholars by what he calls the "cultural-essentialist model." Discussing Sinologists such as Granet, Needham, Graham, Ames, and Hall, Lee writes that they

> see in China the cultural type or pole opposite of the West, dominated by intuitive, organic, and correlative thinking vis-à-vis rational, mechanical, and analytic thinking, and therefore lacking a genuine sense of transcendence (in the sense of a deeper ontological context unconditioned by the world that depends on it).[64]

Lee's insight here connects the organic and correlative to the natural, and thus to lack of transcendence (among other things). If we look more closely at what he calls the "cultural-essentialist" thinkers, we find this organic and correlative approach, which resembles the particular form of thought that develops in the Han, described above, much more closely than it resembles pre-Han ideas. In particular, the idea of *naturalism* as described in Chapter 1 plays a major role in the denial of transcendence, with evidence for naturalist views in early China often taken from Han-inspired interpretation (but often without recognition of Han influence).

Transcendence, on this view, is something linked specifically with the West—a view we think should properly be referred to as "Western Modernity," in which we find a reaction to and rejection of specific types of transcendence themselves created mainly by the project of modernity itself. As we have shown in Chapters 1 and 2, and as we show in later chapters, there are numerous conceptions of transcendence at play in the West, as well as in other traditions, and it is not at all clear that any one of these can be linked with the West as central to its wider tradition of thought. The West, like China, resists essentialization. It, like China, is a moving target. Certain aspects of Han Dynasty philosophy can be found in interpretations of scholars who attribute naturalism and the absence of transcendence to early Chinese thought, but other aspects of Han philosophy (those aspects in which we find non-naturalist elements) are left out.

This attempt to render the early Chinese tradition as naturalist through and through is not limited to Western scholars. Indeed, much of the inspiration for the readings of these scholars came from a group of modern Chinese scholars who advocated for such readings of early Chinese texts. This group of scholars, all educated with a focus on twentieth-century Western philosophy, read the early Chinese texts through this frame, and many of them had the explicit aim to "legitimize" Chinese philosophy with respect to twentieth-century Western Philosophy, or Western thought more generally.

Part Two

4

Transcendence of *Tian*?

The foregoing chapters have admittedly been more programmatic and method-oriented. We have at best made the case that the a priori assumption of naturalism in Chinese thought is problematic. But, we have not yet provided a great deal of evidence that the conclusion of naturalism in early China is inaccurate. Our intention in this book is not to argue Chinese thought is non-naturalistic in a universal way. Rather, we freely admit that some thinkers or texts do fit well within a naturalistic framework. However, we do not think this naturalistic framework is well-suited to most texts or concepts from early China, and that many texts seem to bear a remarkable account of non-contrastive transcendence.

The goal of the remaining chapters in this book is then to offer concrete evidence of our case. We will do so by way of limited, focused analyses of individual texts or groups of texts rather than broad surveys. In this chapter, we seek to assess whether and how transcendence might be at work in one of the most important and ambiguous concepts in early Chinese thought. The concept of *tian* 天 will frustrate both the naturalist and non-naturalist interpreters of early Chinese thought. As Feng Youlan 冯友兰 rightly observed, *tian* had several meanings in pre-Qin Chinese philosophy (Feng identifies five), often appearing to function as "nature" or the celestial cosmos (particularly when used as part of the binomial *tiandi* 天地, meaning "heaven and earth").[1] At other times, such as in *Mengzi* and *Mozi*, *tian* seems divinized as an agent guiding the fortunes of the world (Mengzi) or loving and willing the mutual benefit of all people (Mozi). All told, this situation has led to broad disagreement among scholars of precisely what early Chinese meant by *tian*, or in what way to interpret the "divinity" of *tian*.[2]

Generally speaking, historians tend to see *tian* as the high-god of the Zhou dynasty—perhaps an ancestral deity—whose Mandate was thought to secure and support the dynasty. As the Zhou dynasty bent toward irrecoverable decline, the story goes that Zhou intellectuals lost faith in this previous conception of *tian* and developed an account of *tian* that shed much of the high-god and providential elements.[3] Philosophical scholars who offer naturalist interpretations of Chinese thought tend to either read out or tremendously reduce the religious aspects of *tian*. For example, in *Thinking through Confucius*, Hall and Ames suggest that *tian* was seen as a "non-personal force" very early in the Zhou dynasty.[4] More significantly, while they cannot fully deny the theistic features of *tian*, the authors heavily qualify these features by saying that *tian* is not equivalent to the concept of deity in the West. The inequity of these concepts hinges upon "the contrast between the transcendence of the Western deity and *t'ien* [*tian*] as unqualifiedly immanent."[5]

Without going into a full analysis of philosophical and historical readings of *tian*, it should be at least clear that the naturalist account of Hall and Ames assesses *tian* in terms of a contrastive conception of transcendence. Consequently, the problem of *tian*'s transcendence is for them an either/or proposition: either it is transcendent or it is immanent all the way down. Of course, such a view might be ultimately correct, but there are significant reasons to doubt it. For one, as Hall and Ames note, a great many significant neo-Confucian thinkers have articulated an understanding of *tian* as transcendent, including Tu Weiming and Mou Zongsan.[6]

Additionally, Hall and Ames's conception of *tian* as thoroughly immanent in contrast to the Western deity fails to adequately account for theological debates in later Chinese history. During the Chinese Rites Controversy in the seventeenth to eighteenth centuries, for example, the Kangxi emperor was puzzled why Catholic missionaries would feel the need to use a neologism (*tianzhu* 天主) to describe God, rather than just *tian*. In fact, the emperor appealed to the inherent flexibility of *tian* to claim that a naturalist reading of *tian*—offered by one Vatican representative!—was an inadequate understanding of the term.[7]

Given these reasons to question the naturalist reading of *tian*, we seek in this chapter to assess whether *tian* can be fruitfully interpreted in a non-naturalist way. We have elected to focus on the account of *tian* provided in the *Chunqiu Fanlu* 春秋繁露 (hereafter, *CQFL*), traditionally attributed to Dong Zhongshu 董仲舒 in the Western Han dynasty.[8] We explore whether the *CQFL* provides a non-naturalist account of *tian*, ultimately answering in the affirmative. Due to the importance of the *CQFL* in Chinese intellectual history, the fact that this text seems to provide in part a non-naturalist view of *tian* likely has broader significance for how one reads the Chinese tradition (although recent scholarship has called into question the traditional understanding of how the *CQFL* informed later Confucianism).[9] Here, we will not argue the CQFL's account of *tian* necessarily has consequences for interpreting other texts, but leave open this possibility for a future examination.

As a final introductory word, we should note that on a certain level, the inability to easily identify *tian* as either naturalistic or non-naturalistic is likely an indication of how poorly the naturalism/transcendence problematic serves as a framework for interpreting early Chinese thought. In this respect, it might be best to simply develop another framework for analyzing how early Chinese thinkers were able to balance the diverse aspects of *tian* under a unitive concept (allowing that language allows the same term to function in different ways without necessarily presupposing a unity among all uses of a term). However, in this book, we are attempting to answer those who have dismissed the legitimacy of reading concepts such as *tian* as transcendental and theistic concepts in any measure whatsoever. Thus, our goal in this chapter is to explore whether and how *tian* functions in non-naturalistic ways. Though this does require embracing a framework that may not be ultimately best for interpreting early Chinese thought, this analysis is nonetheless helpful in the specific context of refuting narrowly naturalistic readings of early Chinese thought.

Tian in the Yin-yang Cosmology of the *CQFL*

It is appropriate to begin a non-naturalist analysis of the *CQFL* with the texts most likely to work against such a reading, namely those expositing a cosmology based on the movements of *yin* and *yang*. Before we can fruitfully turn to an assessment of these texts, a word of context is in order. For the better part of the last thirty years at least, many scholars have worked independently to overturn long-held assumptions about the *CQFL* and its purported author, Dong Zhongshu.[10] Most importantly, scholars have demonstrated that large parts of the *CQFL*—especially those based on Five Phases cosmology—are not from Dong's hand or even representative of his thought.[11] For our purposes here, the authorship of the *CQFL* sections is not as important because we are interpreting the text as a canonical whole, and not attempting to articulate the conception of *tian* according to Dong Zhongshu per se.

However, we have attempted to focus as much as possible on the *CQFL*'s account of *tian* in groups of the text that take up a coherent and cooperative position. For example, the present text of the *CQFL* features two cosmological approaches, one based on *yin-yang* and one based on *wuxing*. Scholars have shown that the *yin-yang* approach is reflective of Dong's original position, and certainly precedes the *wuxing* model. Therefore, we have prioritized the *yin-yang* model more so than the *wuxing* model of the *CQFL*, without necessarily assuming Dong's authorship of all of these chapters. That they provide a coherent approach to *tian* is most important for our purposes.

Between the two cosmological approaches contained in the *CQFL*, the *yin-yang* approach contains the most extensive account of *tian*. Thus, one clear necessary locus of assessing the non-naturalist features of *tian* in the *CQFL* (if they are present) is the relationship between *tian* and the principles of *yin-yang*. Notably, the understanding of *yin-yang* in the *CQFL* is rather idiosyncratic, given that the text embraces a much more dualistic, hierarchical understanding of these principles than is typical.[12] For our purposes, it is more notable that the *yin-yang* cosmology at times can seem to reflect a naturalist perspective. However, as we will show below, we do not think the naturalist account does full justice to the *CQFL* description of *tian* even in these chapters, let alone in other parts of the text that do seem to require a non-naturalist reading to understand them well.

There is little need here to describe in full the *CQFL*'s cosmological perspective, including its unique take on *yin-yang*.[13] We need only emphasize that the *CQFL* sees the diverse movements of the cosmos—derived from the principles of *yin-yang* movement—as the Way of Heaven (*tiandao*). This in turn raises a significant question vis-à-vis whether the *CQFL* does or does not provide a non-naturalist account of the world. Does the *CQFL* portray *yin-yang* as constitutive of *tian* itself, or does *tian* exist in ways apart from (indeed, above or beyond) *yin-yang*? In other words, does the *CQFL* use *tian* as a metaphor or term used to describe natural processes per se, or does *tian* have some kind of unique agency that lies behind and causes these processes? Notably, the text shows no signs of great care to clarify this point—it is, rather, a question we raise in light of naturalistic readings of contemporary philosophy. Hence, we should mark well that the *CQFL* author is satisfied with certain ambiguity in the relationship or distinction between *tian* and natural processes.

One concept expressing the apparent conjunction of *tian* and natural processes per se is that of "Heaven's regularities" (*tian shu* 天數). In chapter 43 of the *CQFL*, the regularities of *tian* are described as structured by the number ten. Within the *yin-yang* cosmology of the *CQFL*—in which *yang* activity is especially associated with *tian*'s activity—the number ten is important because it takes ten months for *yang qi* to emerge and complete its achievements.[14] Strikingly, the *CQFL* associates this ten-month cycle of *yang qi* with *tiandao* itself.[15] Ultimately, the *CQFL* uses this association between *tiandao* and the dominance of *yang qi* to argue for the superiority of *yang qi* over *yin* (a notable reversal of the *Daodejing*'s preference for *yin qi*). Yet what is key to recognize here is that it is precisely the identification of *yang qi* with *tiandao* that the *CQFL* author uses to support the conclusion that *yang* is superior to *yin*.

In this context, the movements of *yang qi* are themselves identified with *tian*'s regularities, which have correlates with human beings that constitute principles for ethical behavior. The *CQFL* goes on to describe both human beings and *tian* as possessing four kinds of *qi*: happy, angry, joyful, and sorrowful (*xi nu le ai* 喜怒樂哀). *Tian*'s *qi* qualities correspond to the four seasons (happiness to spring, anger to autumn, joy to summer, and sorrow to winter).[16] For our purposes, it is less important how these four qualities of *qi* are present in humans. More important are the following two claims that can be easily harmonized with a naturalistic reading of the *CQFL*: (1) *tian* has *qi* and (2) the *qi* movement of *tian* is exhibited in the four seasons. This then suggests that the natural processes of the seasons quite simply are convertible with *tian*—*tian* is the processes of *yin* and *yang* that culminate in seasonal transformations. It would therefore follow that, in this framework, *tian* would be a natural rather than transcendent concept.

This all helps explain why *tian* can indeed be observed and *tian*'s way is not inscrutable for the author of the *CQFL*, a theme we return to in Chapter 5 of this book. As chapter 45 puts it, "*tian*'s dao has sequences and is timely."[17] The best explanation of this passage is that the seasonal rhythms of *yin* and *yang* are the *dao* of *tian* and thus "the sage looks to *tian* and then acts."[18] Corresponding with *tian* is straightforward for the author of the *CQFL* because it is evident in the natural processes of the cosmos. And this, by extension, suggests that the *tian* is simply identifiable with these processes. We see this elsewhere in the *CQFL*, when *tian* is said to have transformations (*hua* 化) to which all things respond, and these transformations are more or less exhibited with the changes of the seasons, which as phenomena are caused by or follow the movement of *yin-yang*.[19]

Thus, in its *yin-yang* cosmology—which, we remind is the earlier cosmological framework—the *CQFL* seems to provide an essentially immanent and non-transcendental account of *tian*. Logically, this follows as a consequence upon the text's argument that humanity rehearses or mimics the movement of *tian* in our natural processes. In *tian*, we find "accretion and recension" (*de xing* 德刑) to which human actions should correspond. Human flourishing depends upon discerning the correlates between human beings and *tian* (particularly evident in the latter's relationship to *yin* and *yang*) and imitating *tian* in human action. Consequently, this conception of the anthropological similarities between humanity and *tian* does not suggest a transcendental conception of *tian* as divine, provided that transcendence is understood in a contrastive sense. Additionally, the relationship between *tian* and cosmological processes is even less supportive of a contrastive transcendence, since it is unclear how, if at all, the *CQFL* author sees *tian* as not identical with the cosmological processes per se.

On the surface, these aspects of the *CQFL* seem to support a naturalist interpretation of *tian*, inasmuch as such an interpretation presupposes a contrastive view of transcendence. However, we wish to emphasize that a conclusion that the *yin-yang* cosmology of the *CQFL* is ultimately naturalistic and devoid of transcendence is premature, given that only a contrastive conception of transcendence has been ruled out. Another way to view the issue is to say that there is a naturalist inclination to the *CQFL*'s depiction of *tian* in the *yin-yang* passages surveyed thus far. But this does not mean that other non-naturalist conceptions of *tian* are absent within these same portions of the text.

At the very least, it is apparent that the *CQFL* does not emphasize any distinction or definition between *tian* and nature, but neither does it completely define *tian* in terms of nature. To be accurate, the conclusion that the *CQFL* is naturalistic would require a thorough identification of *tian* and nature. But, just as the clear distinction between *tian* and nature is not forthcoming from the *CQFL*, neither is a clear identification. And we see no reason to presume the must fall on the position of taking *tian* and nature as convertible concepts just because it does not seek to radically equivocate them. This latter refusal to radically distinguish *tian* and nature might be a sign of naturalism, but it could be simply that the distinction between *tian* and nature was not a theological or philosophical problem that arose in the Han context as it did in, say, the Abrahamic traditions in conversation with Near Eastern religions or Greco-Roman paganism.[20]

It is then helpful to ask whether the *CQFL* provides reasons to *not* interpret *tian* in the *yin-yang* passages under a naturalistic framework. In fact, the text does provide such reasons. First, it is true that the text argues that humanity can mimic the processes of *tian* seen in the movement of the seasons and *yin-yang*. However, at the same time, the *CQFL* does not seem to articulate humanity as "merely" a product of *tian*-as-nature. The chapter entitled "*Tian* Is the Maker of Humanity" (*weiren zhe Tian* 為人者天) opens with the argument that "what gives birth is incapable of being the maker of humanity," and the maker of humanity must be *tian*.[21] In this passage, the one giving birth must refer to parents and the natural processes of sexual procreation, and hence the *CQFL* seems to be making the following distinction: propagation of a species is not the same as the generation of a species. The author of the *CQFL* further clarifies that "the roots of humanity's humanness lie in *tian,* and *tian* is the great ancestor of humanity."[22]

From one perspective, it is very possible to read this statement in a naturalistic manner, in a way evocative of Hall and Ames's discussion of the *Zhongyong*. Hall and Ames argue for the following distinction: "The God of the Bible … *created* the world, but *tian* in classical Chinese *is* the world … it is both the single source from which processes and events emerge, and the multivalent field constituted by them."[23] In applying such an account to the *CQFL*, one could argue that by saying *tian* is the great ancestor of human beings and the root of humankind, the *CQFL* author simply means that it is indeed the great primordial processes of nature that give rise to all existence, and humanity in particular.

Granted this possibility, it is not without difficulty. If one were to attempt to interpret *tian* as purely equal to nature, then the *CQFL*'s distinction between human beings propagating the species on the one hand and the generative processes of *tian* on the other is puzzling. If *tian* is simply the name for the cosmological processes of nature alone, it would stand to reason that *tian* would include the natural processes of natural things. It would make much more sense to say that *tian* generates human beings through the natural acts of sexual procreation, or that *tian* is the guarantor of the fact that sex leads to procreation.

However, the author of the CQFL does not seem to interpret the natural processes of human procreation as identifiable with *tian* per se. *Tian* is not understood as similar to humanity, but as its archetype (which itself suggests some kind of transcendence). As archetype, *tian* seems to be the source and cause of human beings in ways that the reverse is not true: human activity does not constitute *tian*, but it is constituted by *tian*. And in this regard, one must conclude that *tian* does indeed transcend the limits of anthropological nature.

But, one may reply this is simply a feature of a distinction within nature. Perhaps the *CQFL* is treating the principles of the cosmos as distinct causes that do in a sense function at a higher level than human actions, but are still natural. An analogy for such a conception of the world can be found in the Aristotelian conception of celestial bodies, which are clearly natural, but are causes of human action and "transcend" in perfection and in some activity the actions of humanity, without being supernatural.[24]

While this would be a creative account of how the *CQFL* understands the cosmos, there are also several complications to it. First, despite seeming to identify *tian* with the cosmic processes including *yin* and *yang*, the *CQFL* employs consequential terms to describe these processes in relation to *tian*. The *CQFL* author says that *tian* "uses" (*yong* 用) or "employs" *yin* and *yang*, or that *yang* "moves in compliance" (*xing yu shun* 行於順) with *tian* whereas *yin* "moves contrary" (*xing yu ni* 行於逆) to *tian*'s way.[25] Certainly, these comments fall short of a systematic position on *tian* and the cosmos, but they are significant as they suggest that *tian* is not simply convertible with the natural processes of *yin* and *yang*. As one who "makes use" of *yin* and *yang*, it stands to reason that *tian* must not only be distinct from *yin-yang* but also superior to them in the sense of being able to cause or use them. Furthermore, this suggests, however ambiguously, a type of agency in *tian* that rises above the limits of *yin-yang*, and consequently, the seasons.[26]

Fortunately, this insight does take on a more systematic character in the *CQFL*, as the author utilizes the functionally synonymous concepts of "*tian*'s will" (*tian zhi zhi* 天之志) and "*tian*'s intention" (*tian zhi yi* 天之意). In the sections of the *CQFL* organized as "Yin-Yang Principles" by Queen and Major, the terms *tian*'s will and *tian*'s intention are primarily used cosmologically, such that the cosmic processes are especially indicative of *tian*'s intention. At times, the link between *tian*'s intention and the cosmos seems one of identification, such as when we find the mutual oppositional movements of *yin* and *yang* are simply called *tian*'s intention.[27] More often, however, the *CQFL* describes *tian*'s will or intention as causing the motion of the cosmos, as actually moving *yin-yang*.[28] Hence the predominant theme of the *CQFL* is that *yin-yang* manifest the *xin* 心 of *tian*, that is, *tian*'s will or intention.[29]

In this light, the theme of *tian*'s will or intention is connected to not simply those cosmological processes *tian* causes but also what *tian* loves, approves of, or even desires. When describing the link between humanity and *tian*, the *CQFL* issues a disagreement with the *Daodejing*, which said, "Heaven and earth are not humane."[30] In contrast, the *CQFL* argues *tian* "loves benevolence and draws near to it."[31] Similarly, it claims that "all that *tian* supports, it bequeaths to humankind. If we examine *tian*'s intentions, we will see that it is inexhaustibly and boundlessly humane."[32] In this way, the *CQFL* does not merely interpret human life as especially resonant of cosmic processes but also interprets *tian* as possessing a special affection and love for humanity and humaneness.[33]

In terms of assessing the naturalism or non-naturalism of the *CQFL*, these observations about the text's depiction of *tian*'s intention are quite significant. For one, these observations suggest that even when the *CQFL* is perhaps at its most naturalistic, *tian* is never fully identified with cosmic processes *simpliciter*. Consistently, though not systematically, the *CQFL* sees *tian* as something distinct from *yin-yang* and the seasons as something moving them and causing them. Consequently, *yin-yang* and the seasons have almost a revelatory role: they tell us what *tian* wills, intends, and loves. Of course, one must keep in mind that explaining the relationship between *tian* and the cosmic processes of *yin-yang* is not the goal of the *CQFL*. Rather, the text is offering these cosmic processes as means of understanding and imitating the way of *tian*. For this reason, there is a strong identification indeed between these natural processes and *tian*, though stopping short of a complete identity or univocation. The author of these passages in the *CQFL* seems to also have in mind that this identification is actually not complete and full, but there is something about *tian* lying behind those processes of *yin-yang* and the seasons that nonetheless manifest *tian*.

So, let us be clear: to this point, we have not argued the *CQFL* presents a clear account of *tian* as transcendent. Rather, we have argued that the *CQFL* presents an account of *Tian* that is not purely naturalistic, and thus is better accounted for in a non-naturalist way. In the cosmology of the *CQFL*, *tian* is understood in terms governed by contrastive transcendence but the text concomitantly embraces what are apparently both naturalistic and transcendental aspects of *tian*. In the remainder of the chapter, we will focus more on a positive account of the transcendental aspects of *tian* that are present in the *CQFL*. This will be in a sense easier because the naturalistic reading of *tian* is at its strongest in the cosmological context. But in the *CQFL*, *tian* is not simply a cosmological concept. When we consider the moral-political and ritual contexts of *tian*, we will find the *CQFL* has even more robust and evident ways of conceiving *tian* in non-naturalistic terms.

Tian and the Ruler Relation in the *CQFL*

For the author of the *CQFL*, the relationship between *tian* and the ruler is of central importance in his conception of the anthropological link between *tian* and humanity.

Interpreting the ruler relationship in the *CQFL* is trickier than it first seems. Historically, many scholars have interpreted Dong Zhongshu as, in the words of Gary Arbuckle, a "subservient tool who prostituted his philosophy to the immediate political requirements of the feudal Han dynasty and its reigning despot."[34] However, Arbuckle himself showed the limits of this understanding, having suggested that the *CQFL* is more subversive than it seems.[35] Specifically, Arbuckle's research suggests that far from providing a convenient account of *tian* and the world to fit the ruler's political needs, the *CQFL* attempts to continue a classical *Ru* instinct to ground worthy ruling in the proper response to *tian*.

From this perspective, the political vision of the *CQFL* offers important resources for understanding *tian* in the text. We argue specifically that, at least according to one conception of ruling in the in the *CQFL*, the non-naturalist contours of *tian* come to special light. As Sarah Queen and others have observed, some chapters of the *CQFL* offer a theory of ruling based on *wuwei*, and in her earlier work she referred to these as "Huang-Lao" chapters.[36] In this section, we focus more on those passages reflecting a conceptual dependence on the triadic relationship between *tian*, earth, and humanity distinctive of *Ru* texts. Since we explore this triadic relationship in more detail via the work of Xunzi in Chapter 6, we will not rehearse the larger context here. It is sufficient, instead, to point out that within the *CQFL* account, the stress falls on the relationship between the ruler and *tian* as that which is most foundational.

Famously, the *CQFL* argues that only the king can truly be the thread that unites *tian*, earth, and humanity.[37] As De Bary et al. once put it, according to the *CQFL*, "The emperor ... is responsible for keeping mankind in harmony with the other members, and of raising all men by the power of his government to the fulfillment of their true human dignity."[38] The key to the *CQFL*'s interpretation of the ruler's role in this triad is to seek to understand how the ruler can gain the wisdom to properly harmonize with *tian* and earth, and how to inspire others to this human dignity.

In explaining the ruler's unique role vis-à-vis *tian*, the *CQFL* develops an intricate conception of *tian* as the model or exemplar for the ruler. One pithy summation of this view is that "the one who would rule other emulates the conduct of *tian*."[39] Of course, the theme of divine emulation can be found at length in non-naturalistic traditions; the traditional Christian doctrine of the image of God is an example of this.[40] Yet in the Christian meaning of it, the emulation of God is found within human nature itself. Most Christian theologians in the tradition have identified being made "in God's image" with the possession of certain perfections that are indicative of divine perfections, such as the use of reason.[41] In a sense, Christian theology can say humans do emulate divine activity, but in the sense that the operations of human nature emulate God, though only analogously and imperfectly.

This raises the fruitful question of what kind of *tian*-activity does the *CQFL* say the ruler emulates? Unlike Christian theology, the *CQFL* does not consider the immaterial capacities of the human person as the ground of imitation of *tian*. Instead, from a certain perspective, the *CQFL* understands the ruler-*tian* relationship in ways that appear quite naturalistic. This is because the *CQFL* explains the ruler's emulation of *tian* in terms of how the ruler observes and mimics cosmological phenomena that are attributed to *tian*.

The text argues that the king "only acts on *tian's* behalf" (*wei tian zhi shi* 唯天之施).[42] Thus, there is a subordination of the king's activity to *tian's*, but this is quickly explained in exemplary terms. As the text says, the king "extends *tian's* seasons and brings them to completion. He emulates (*fa* 法) *tian's* commands and circulates them among the people. He emulates (*fa*) *tian's* numbers and employs them when initiating affairs."[43]In this way, *tian* is not simply a superior of the king whom the latter serves but also a kind of archetype whose activity the king observes and emulates in his own activities of ruling.

One may note, of course, that is precisely those activities associated with ruling and governance that are the foundation of the king's emulation of *tian*. This may implicitly suggest a kind of non-naturalistic conception of *tian* as a ruler-god governing the world. However, when the *CQFL* clarifies the way that *tian* governs, it is clear that any non-naturalistic instinct about *tian* as divine governor must be tempered. For example, the *CQFL* author argues that the sage-kings of old modeled themselves on *tian's* warp (*tian zhi da jing* 天之大經), that is, the schema of cosmological motion and change.[44] More specifically, as we discussed in the previous section, the *CQFL* depicts *tian* as the model of the ruler in terms of the seasons, which are indicative of the four kinds of *qi* of *tian*.[45] In this schema, the king's emulation of *tian* primarily means discerning how to keep his own *qi* in accordance with *tian's qi*.[46] Ultimately, this kind of correspondence with *tian* is, in the political context at least, the definition of rightness (*yi* 義).[47]

The ruler's emulation of *tian* therefore consists primarily in two steps: (1) interpreting lasting principles from *tian* and (2) governing in ways that facilitate accordance with these principles. With regard to the first step, there is ample evidence that this can be understood in a naturalistic sense as we saw in the previous paragraph. Additionally, the text says that "if you trace the circuits of *yin* and *yang* through to the end of the year, you will thereby observe what *tian* draws near to and relies on" (*suo qin er ren* 所親而壬).[48] Put simply, the observation of cosmological phenomena manifests *tian's* will in a manner sufficient to determine principles that the ruler can put into practice.

In terms of putting these principles into practice, in the eyes of the *CQFL* author the ruler's governmental policies should consist in correlating with *tian* in order to bring about a flourishing state. For example, the number of ministers the ruler employs should imitate *tian's* numbers (*tian shu*) and his method of selecting them should follow the seasons of *tian*.[49] This example clearly falls under the more general observation that *tian's* cosmological manifestations are genuinely reliable divisions of space and activity that the ruler can follow. Unlike in Christian and Jewish theology, for example, there is no sense that the *CQFL* sees the application of time to *tian* in purely metaphorical ways. Rather, *tian* is a true and clearly understood model. As the text says, "*tian* and human being possess these principles are therefore unitary. Those who use theme similarly to *tian* will [engender] great order; those who use them differently from *tian* [will engender] great disorder."[50]

All of this evidence helps show that although naturalistic readings of *tian* are not completely baseless, they are also not entirely incorrect. Put simply, such readings fail to make a convincingly complete account of how *tian* was understood in texts such as the *CQFL*. For one, it is important and helpful to return to a point we mentioned above, namely that the emulation of *tian* by the ruler itself is not completely suggestive of a naturalistic reading. For the author of the *CQFL*, *tian* was understood in the context of cosmic order, that is, patterns within the cosmos that can be discerned, articulated, and emulated in order to achieve flourishing. This fact requires, logically speaking, some explanation of the principle of order. In the context of the *CQFL*, *tian* itself is the only possible explanation of this principle. In other words, *tian* is not simply expressive of order, it also seems to be the *cause* of such order in the cosmos.

One reason we think this is the case is the nature of the analogy between the ruler and *tian*. The ruler is meant to employ various policies and selection of ministers as ways of governing and ordering the state. This inherently suggests that the cosmological phenomena that should be followed by the ruler are themselves indicative of governance and order. In other words, *tian*'s numbers and divisions are expressions of *tian*'s own agency. Consequently, the ordering of other phenomena within this agency means that there is one kind of distinction between the seasons, *yin* and *yang*, and so on, and *tian*. Namely, *tian* is the cause of order and intelligibility for these phenomena that grant them their function in the cosmos.

This in itself complicates a thoroughly naturalistic reading of *tian* in the *CQFL*, but we can and should go further. In addition to the exemplarity of *tian*, another key logion informing the *CQFL*'s understanding of the ruler–*tian* relationship is the classical Confucian doctrine of the Mandate of Heaven (*tian ming*). When explaining *tian*'s role in the historical rule of the classical thearchs, the *CQFL* uses significant language to specify *tian*'s agency. Like Mengzi, the *CQFL* argues that *tian* "confers" (*shou* 授) the Mandate to rule on rulers, not those who gave it to their chosen successors.[51]

This aspect of the *tian*–ruler relationship deeply problematizes a thoroughly naturalistic reading of *tian* in the *CQFL*. For here we see *tian* is attributed a kind of agency and will—not in a metaphorical sense of cosmic movement that is indicative of order and governance, but actually choosing and deciding, that is, a willed ordering of things in the political context. Indeed, unlike the patterns of the seasons and *yin-yang*, which are reliable according to the *CQFL*, the text warns that the Mandate of *tian* is not given or taken away in a constant manner (*wu chang* 無常).[52] Clearly, this means that *tian* does not simply bestow the Mandate on a ruler so that this his rule is forevermore legitimized and assured. Rather, *tian* will withdraw the Mandate if the ruler fails to be morally fit to rule.

Notably, the early Han period shows an intense preoccupation with the Mandate of *tian*. This is appropriate given the desire of Han rulers to legitimize Han rule, particularly as contrast to the short-lived Qin. In addition to inspire literature that sought to enumerate the follies of the Qin that resulted in the loss of *tian*'s Mandate, this search for legitimacy led to discussion of signs and omens, and to the development of correlational cosmology in ways that claimed to portend the warp and weft of dynastic epochs.[53] On a cynical reading—which has proliferated among contemporary interpreters of Han thought—the Han rulers were merely interested in the political goal of accruing and legitimizing their own power for their own sake. However, this seems to us to lay decidedly postmodern cynicism about politics onto the intentions of ancient rulers, which is a tricky business indeed. It is just as likely as not that Han rulers really believed that without *tian* or some other transcendent Mandate, the Han would not flourish. Additionally, even if they were merely political strategists, the fact that the

Han rulers sought to *appeal* to an apparently nonpolitical transcendent providence in order to legitimize their rule suggests that a great number of the people they sought to rule *believed* in such a transcendental principle.

Simply put, there are very significant and weighty reasons to think that Han philosophers such as Dong Zhongshu and other authors genuinely saw *tian* as a providential force that must be discerned and not controlled by the ruler. It seems to us that there is no better description for such a view of *tian* in this context than "transcendent." Admittedly, this does not entail transcendence as understood in a contrastive model necessarily, but there is a clear distinction between the ruler and *tian* as a principle. Moreover, in the *CQFL*, it seems to even move toward suggesting the ruler participates uniquely in *tian* as the principle of what we might call headship or rulership. At the very least, the *CQFL* holds that the legitimate ruler is willed by *tian*, and it does not seek in any way to dissuade us from treating this claim as ascribing willing agency to *tian*.

It is worth reminding here that the *CQFL* argues that *tian* provides the Mandate not for the aggrandizement of the ruler, but for the care of the people.[54] Again, one can note in the *CQFL* a kind of acceptance of Mohist principles of *tian*'s love for the people turned to serve Confucian conceptions of the political field of vision. And this is of tremendous importance to note because it means as a consequence that the *CQFL* does not depict *tian* as *merely* an impersonal natural force. Rather, *tian* looks upon the people, desires their flourishing, and moves rulers to act in accord with this principle. Not only is this a robustly theistic conception of *tian* but also non-naturalistic and approaching the transcendent.[55]

According to the Mandate of *tian* portrait provided in the *CQFL*, the ruler's actions and moral dispositions lay open to *tian*'s judgment and discernment. The *CQFL* sees the *Jiao* sacrifice as key within this discernment: the ruler who seeks to rule in the proper way first seeks to give proper worship and sacrifice to *tian*. Consequently, the *CQFL* depicts *tian*'s knowing and responding to the ruler in terms traditionally associated with transcendence, worship, providence, and so on. Moreover, *tian* is not simply a constant principle to which rulers must respond; *tian* also responds in kind to the ruler's actions.

Tian and Worship

Thus far, we have seen sufficient reasons to consider the *CQFL* as possessing a non-naturalist framework through examining those themes philosophers study most. We now turn to a theme often neglected, but of great importance to determining whether a Chinese text such as the *CQFL* should be seen as presupposing naturalism. The fact that *tian* was an object of worship and piety is a fly in the ointment of naturalistic readings of early China. Indeed, Julia Ching argues one way to demonstrate the presence of transcendence in Chinese religions is to "offer evidence for the presence of a strong religiosity in China's antiquity, and then to argue that this religiosity never completely disappeared, even if it was transformed and subsumed by the early development of humanistic culture."[56]

Here we seek to suggest that one finds in the *CQFL* this kind of lingering "religiosity" that refuses to disappear, despite the presence of cosmological systems that would enable the erosion of religious devotion. Alongside the robust political, exegetical, and cosmological treatises of the *CQFL*, one of the dominant themes in the work is arguments in favor of the *Jiao* 郊 Sacrifice, translated by Queen and Major as the "Suburban Sacrifice." The defense of the *Jiao* Sacrifice has great bearing on the complete conception of *tian* in the CQFL. This is because the *Jiao* Sacrifice was that sacrificial practice that took *tian* as its object of worship and request, and therefore the *CQFL's* arguments for the priority of the *Jiao* Sacrifice speak directly to the understanding of *tian* and *tian's* primacy in the text.

During the early Han dynasty, the rulers of the empire were at best inconstant in their piety for specific sacrificial cults. The importance of particular cults was evident not only in the frequency of practice of the rites associated with a certain sacrifice but also in the timing of the sacrifice in light of the calendar. It is clear that Dong Zhongshu himself was deeply invested in convincing the ruler of the need to privilege the *Jiao* Sacrifice by offering it on the first day of the New Year, as an annual practice.[57]

In the *CQFL*, one dominant principle used in arguments defending the primacy of the *Jiao* Sacrifice is the preeminence of *tian* itself. In several places, the text observes a variation of the claim that "*tian* is the lord of the various spirits."[58] This is clear evidence of the phenomenon articulated at length by Michael Puett that the spiritual realm was understood by many early Chinese thinkers to be itself hierarchical.[59] Referring to *tian* as the lord of these spirits means *tian* resides at the top of the hierarchy and influences all the rest. In fact, the *CQFL* goes as far to say that there is a proper sequence of sacrifices so that rulers may sacrifice to lesser spirits, but only after sacrificing to *tian*.[60] Therefore, according to the *CQFL* the sacrificial cult to *Tian* that legitimizes and seems to "activate" the efficacy of lesser cults.

Additionally, the *CQFL* argues the king should have special reverence for the *Jiao* Sacrifice because of the Mandate of *tian* given to rulers. The *CQFL* identifies the *Jiao* Sacrifice as an act that must precede the tasks of ruling.[61] Specifically, the text sees the *Jiao* Sacrifice as partially serving an eucharistic (thanksgiving) purpose, that is, as a recognition of gifts from *tian* that should proceed exercising what given. The eucharistic function of the *Jiao* Sacrifice is therefore connected to the *CQFL's* observation that all things come from *tian* and depend upon *tian* as the supreme ancestor. For these reasons, it is clear that the sacrificial cult to *tian* has a special place in the *CQFL's* reckoning because of the uniqueness of *tian* in terms of creative agency and providential establishment of ruling families.

Taking these two aspects together, the *CQFL's* defense of the *Jiao* Sacrifice holds tremendous importance for the theme of transcendence. Put simply, there is a clear sense that *tian* is not simply one among other spirits but is the highest spirit, worthy of the greatest and prime honor and gratitude. In other terms, we see here a sense in which *tian* transcends the other spiritual beings in power and influence, and certainly *tian* transcends human activity and even that of nature in bringing things into being.

Of course, one might say that in the context of early Chinese cosmology, there can be a naturalistic way of understanding the spiritual realms. As David Pankenier has ably shown, early Chinese culture associated the spirits with astral signs and markers. For example, the deistic concepts of *Shangdi* and *Taiyi* were associated with the celestial poles.[62] Based on this fact, it is tempting to read *tian* and other spirits as essentially metaphors for natural phenomena, which would fit well within a naturalistic interpretation.

However, the rub is that neither the *CQFL* specifically nor early Chinese texts more generally presume that the celestial aspects of the spirits can be interpreted reductively. That is, there is a clear link between the celestial heavens and the spirits, but the spirits are not seen as simply or merely personifications of astral phenomena. We might otherwise state this as meaning the fact that *tian* and other spirits were associated with natural phenomena does not mean that these associations describe the *totality* of how early Chinese understood these concepts. Again, under a non-contrastive conception of transcendence, the need for an either/or definition of *tian* vis-à-vis natural phenomena is diminished. All that is required is some kind of *distinction*, but not necessarily radical difference.

When it comes to the *CQFL*, we can see such distinction without radical difference in defense of the *Jiao* sacrifice. When the *CQFL* speaks of sacrificing to *tian*, it suggests *tian* has sufficient agency to receive and act in light of the sacrifice and worship. Everything about the *Jiao* Sacrifice in the *CQFL* supports a perspective of *tian* as a genuinely theistic reality that is closely associated with, but ultimately somehow distinct from, the celestial bodies. In short, the *CQFL* does not reduce the cosmological or celestial associations of *tian* to claim *tian* is itself purely or merely natural.

Conclusion

In this chapter, we have sought to examine whether *tian* can be said to function in non-naturalistic ways in early Chinese thought. Taking the weighty example of the *CQFL*, we have demonstrated that in some aspects, a naturalistic reading of *tian* can make sense of this text's understanding of *tian*. But we have also demonstrated how a naturalistic reading of *tian* does not *fully* account for how *tian* is conceived in this text. Rather, there are several aspects of *tian* in the *CQFL* that cannot be easily reconciled with a naturalistic framework. While we have not argued the *CQFL* asserts a version of transcendence one finds in the Abrahamic religions, for example, it is difficult to dismiss the presence of genuinely transcendental aspects of *tian* in the text.

Consequently, the depiction of *tian* in the *CQFL* deeply complicates the presupposition that all Chinese thought is naturalistic. Indeed, we argue that such a presupposition actually obscures many of the fascinating aspects of the text, and undermines what the text attempts to say. The presupposition of naturalism in early China would seem to require ignoring significant claims that the *CQFL* both makes and restates from earlier tradition about *tian*. At best, the naturalist presupposition of early Chinese thought would mean it is necessary to consider the *CQFL* as decidedly *not* representative of early Chinese thought, at least in many significant aspects of the text.

5

Does 天 *Tian* Will?

The concept of *tian*, as we have seen in Chapter 4, is at the center of debates on transcendence in early China. Whether *tian* is a transcendent entity or not in early Chinese texts depends on its characteristics, and whether the activity of *tian* is constrained by or otherwise dependent on activity in the world or not. In this chapter, we consider the question of what is meant by appeals to the will of *tian*, whether this is considered in terms of *zhi* 志 (will, intention), *yu* 欲 (desire), *ming* 命 (command),[1] or any of a host of related concepts concerning the disposition of *tian* toward the world.

The issue of the will of *tian* turns out to be important for discerning whether and to what extent transcendence can be found in the early Chinese tradition. The issue here is not that a *tian* that wills must be to some extent anthropomorphic and thus akin to the transcendent God of the Abrahamic tradition. This is because an anthropomorphic deity need not be understood as transcendent. An entity can be responsible for the emergence or creation of the world as well as to some extent anthropomorphic (in that it can be understood as having mental states, intentions, etc.) without being a transcendent entity.[2] Transcendence in the Abrahamic traditions is primarily based on the idea that God must stand in some sense outside of the created order, because God is not bound by the laws of this created order and is not subject to the necessitating effects that activity in the order has. God thus does not age, not because God is undiminished with time but because God is eternal in the sense of being outside of or not subject to time, while all created things are so subject.

Aquinas understands the timelessness or eternality of God in terms of both God's independence of time and God's containment in *all* time.[3] A position like this shows the sense in which the transcendence of God is related to the immanence of God for Aquinas (as for Abrahamic traditions in general). Aquinas holds the same for God's presence in space—God is both beyond space and at the same time omnipresent in *all* space. A number of other medieval Christian philosophers, including Boethius, Anselm, and Duns Scotus (among others), hold roughly such a view of God's eternality. We find different arguments from Islamic philosophers, such as al-Farabi, who argues that since eternality is a feature of God, it must also be a feature of the world, as God's creation.[4]

Whether will or intention requires transcendence will turn on what kind of thing will or intention is. The issue of intention is linked closely with that of agency. For an act to be intended, there must be an agent to intend it, whose acts are understood in terms of choice and ownership of action. Part of the difficulty here is that whether something transcendent is required for will or intention is going to depend on whether will or intention is free, caused, or requires something in any sense outside of the closed causal system of nature. Contemporary naturalist philosophers have to either explain will or intention as consistent with naturalistic determinism (or reject the need for determinism in naturalistic systems) or reject that there is will or intention in the robust sense in which many premodern philosophers understood it.

If we follow the position of medieval philosophers such as Aquinas, will is an element of intellect, and involving some end at which the intellect aims, with intent understood as the intellectual cause of end-directed action with the aim as end.[5]

The key question here for transcendence is whether *tian*, like the Abrahamic conception of God (and other entities), has a will in the sense of an undetermined agency independent of causal states of the world. In contemporary naturalistic systems of thought, scholars have not done away with the notion of will (in terms of entities that can will, such as humans), but this will must be understood as causally constrained by physical facts about genetics, brain states, and other relevant causal information. Philosophers have stumbled for many years over attempts to make free will consistent with a naturalistic view of the world, and the most successful of these explanations is that of the compatibilist, which holds that although human activity is causally determined, free will as we understand it can be accounted for because one's will is free insofar as one has control over one's actions (in terms of agency), and even if agents are so constrained, those agents have control over their own actions, as part of the causally determined chain of events. Desire and activity are linked through will for the compatibilist. In Harry Frankfurt's conception of will, it is just a matter of the efficacy of a desire—that is, a desire causes a person to act in a certain way so as to satisfy the desire can be understood as will. Frankfurt writes,

> It seems to me both natural and useful to construe the question of whether a person's will is free in close analogy to the question of whether an agent enjoys freedom of action. Now freedom of action is (roughly, at least) the freedom to do what one wants to do. Analogously, then. The statement that a person enjoys freedom of the will means (also roughly) that he is free to want what he wants to want.[6]

This conception of will does not require transcendence in terms of the agent's independence from the causal structure of the world, as a libertarian view of the will does. The unconstrained will, on this view, is the freedom not only to want or act consistently with desires but also to be such that one could have done other than what one does, that one is not committed to desiring or acting in a particular way, but chooses in a way that is not caused by elements of the world.[7] Because there is no cause of one's activity (or at least deterministically), the will behind one's action must be unconditioned by the world, not subject to effects of the world in terms of causation—which is just to say that such a will must *transcend* the causal world to this extent.

In a number of early Chinese texts, the issue of the will is discussed independently of the concept of *tian*, and getting clear just what *zhi* entails is a crucial part of discerning the meaning of the will of *tian*, and whether such will requires transcendence. *Zhi* is discussed in numerous chapters of the *Zhuangzi*. For our purposes, perhaps the most important of these uses of *zhi* come in Chapters 4 and 6. In Chapter 4, the Zhuangist version of Confucius and Yan Hui discusses "fasting of the mind" (*xin zhai* 心齋). Confucius explains what he means by such fasting, by first referring to the will (*zhi*). He says,

若一志，无聽之以耳而聽之以心，无聽之以心而聽之以氣。聽止於耳，心止於符。氣也者，虛而待物者也。唯道集虛。虛者，心齋也。

Having a unified will (*zhi*), don't listen with the ears but listen with the mind. Don't listen with the mind but listen with *qi*. Hearing stops at the ear; the mind stops at its signs. Those who use *qi*—they remain empty and wait on things (*wu*). Only *dao* gathers together in emptiness. This emptiness is fasting of the mind.[8]

The unified will here is connected to the operation of the mind described in the process of moving from usual thinking to the fasting of the mind Confucius recommends. Beginning the process requires listening, thinking, and sensing, ultimately engaging in the grasping of the world without concepts—here understood in terms of "signs" (符 *fu*). This situates *zhi* as an agentive and intentional state, and one associated specifically with the mind or mental states.

While *tian* clearly does will according to a number of (though not all) early Chinese thinkers, it is not immediately clear whether this will is the kind of libertarian will that requires transcendence, or whether it is a deterministically compatible will consistent with even the most scientistically oriented of naturalist worldviews. We argue here that a number of thinkers in the Warring States and Han had a conception of the will of *tian* that entails an uncaused or unconstrained libertarian will, associated with agency and mind, and thus we can demonstrate that for at least some early Chinese thinkers, *tian* was understood as transcendent. This can be most clearly demonstrated in the case of the *Mozi*, in which we find a robust conception of *tian* as divine agent, whose will (*zhi*) plays a central role in ethical theory and practice.

While the *Mozi* in particular is important to consult for an account of the will of *tian*, we find the concept discussed in other texts as well, including Han texts such as *Chunqiu Fanlu*, *Lunheng*, as well as earlier texts such as the *Zuo zhuan*. The conception of *tian*'s will in the *Mozi* gives us the strongest (but not the only) case for an agentive *tian* in early China, thus we turn to it here. While it is tempting to read the *Mozi* as offering a view of divine will in line with what we find in numerous transcendent conceptions of God, a number of scholars, most recently Chris Fraser, argue that the Mohist conception of *tian* can be understood naturalistically. To do this, *tian*'s will has to be understood as compatible with the operation of the world and potentially constrained by it—although much of the picture will depend on the extent to which the Mohists have a mechanistic conception of the operation of the world. We argue here that while the Mohists lack such a mechanistic conception, their understanding of *tian*'s will and activity does appear to commit them to a view of *tian* as transcendent.

Chad Hansen has argued that the Mohist *tian* should be understood as "nature," and not as entailing "a form of religious supernaturalism."[9] Chris Fraser argues that the Mohist conceptions of *tian* and the world are naturalistic, resisting the tendency to read *tian* in terms of a transcendent God. The world itself, on Fraser's reading of the Mohists, "manifests fixed, recognizable patterns."[10] This sounds like the kind of mechanistic world posited by naturalistic/scientistic thinkers, and this is intentional on Fraser's part. Part of his overarching project is to show that the Mohist claims and system are not as radical or unintuitive as they are often made out to be, taking the perspective of contemporary naturalistic philosophers as the key intuitions. Indeed, he takes the *Mozi* to represent the earliest naturalist system in the Chinese tradition.[11] He writes,

> The *Mozi* presents the earliest explicit version of what I will call Chinese metaphysical and metaethical "naturalism." The brand of naturalism I am referring to here involves two interrelated claims. One Is that reality just is the world of nature and observable phenomena, and accordingly whatever exists is to be explained as part of nature. Ultimate reality is not an abstract realm of ideal forms, nor one of a supernatural, transcendent deity or spirits. Instead, it is simply "the stuff of people's ears and eyes," as the *Mozi* phrases it. This conception of reality as the observable natural world has been widely shared by thinkers throughout the Chinese tradition.[12]

Whether Fraser is right about this will largely turn on the Mohist conception of *tian* and its relationship to the world. If the Mohist view on *tian* and *tian*'s will is properly compatible with a naturalistic account of the world of the type Fraser posits, then we should be unable to find libertarian, transcendence-entailing understandings of *tian*'s will, desires, or other states. Fraser recognizes that the very theistic sounding way in which the Mohists write about *tian* requires some explanation, and he argues that for the Mohists, *tian* should not be understood as a transcendent divine agent, but instead as a "semi-personified concept of nature—in effect, 'Nature' with a capital 'N.' Although their conception of nature is what we might call … an 'enchanted' one, *tian* for them still refers to nature, and not, for instance to a deity that transcends or exists beyond the natural world."[13] This is a bold claim, given the ways Mohists speak about *tian* throughout the *Mozi*, the intentions and activities they attribute to it, and the account they offer of the interaction between *tian* and the world. Given that these ways are so similar to theistic accounts of God, Fraser certainly owes us some evidence that we should not take claims of the *Mozi* that appear as such at face value.

Fraser argues that the Mohist *tian* can be distinguished from the Abrahamic conception of God in part through the considerations of epistemic access to the will of *tian*. Fraser claims that rather than discerning *tian*'s desires through "revelation" by *tian*, humans must discover its desires on their own through observation of *tian*'s behavior.[14] This fact, along with other disanalogies to Abrahamic religion such as lack of similar kinds of devotion and prayer, leads Fraser to reject "spiritual transcendence" as part of the Mohist conception of *tian*. It is important to note here that the claims of disanalogy to Abrahamic conceptions of God are misleading. First, as we note elsewhere, it is problematic to take Abrahamic conceptions of God as the hallmark of transcendence, then claiming that insofar as a concept diverges from that of Abrahamic conceptions of God, it is thereby not a concept of a transcendent entity. As we have argued, this would deny transcendence to concepts such as the Platonic Forms or the One of Plotinus, the *Brahman* of Advaita Vedanta, and many other concepts of clearly transcendent entities. Second, the view that one discerns *tian*'s will or desires through observation of nature is neither distant from Abrahamic conceptions of God nor in fundamental conflict with the notion of revelation. Indeed, numerous theologians in Abrahamic traditions understand such access to God's nature as itself part of revelation. For Aquinas, this is the role of natural theology. Aquinas argues that humanity can access a number of truths about God's nature through natural reason, and that revelation is necessary for accessing those truths about God that cannot be discerned using natural reason. The first twelve chapters of Book One of Aquinas's *Summa Contra Gentiles* covers just this topic. At the beginning of chapter 3, Aquinas writes,

> There is a twofold mode of truth in what we profess about God. Some truths exceed all the ability of the human reason. Such is the truth that God is triune. But there are some truths which the natural reason also is able to reach. Such are that God exists, that He is one, and the like. In fact, such truths about God have been proved demonstratively by the philosophers, guided by the light of the natural reason.[15]

In the Islamic tradition, we find an even stronger position concerning natural theology in the view of the Mu'tazilites, adherents of *kalam* thought, who held that God's nature could be fully discerned through natural reason, thus collapsing the two modes of truth of Aquinas into a single rational mode. Thus, we see that the idea of the human need to discern truths about God's nature or desires via nature or natural capacities cannot be taken as itself inconsistent with the view of God as transcendent. God plays a necessary role in nature, according to most accounts, and as such can be discerned in nature (at least to some extent) using natural reason.

The desire (*yu* 欲) of *tian* is discussed in a number of passages in the *Mozi*. In the *Fayi* chapter, *tian* is described as desiring that people universally care for and benefit one another, with the argument that we can know that *tian* desires this because *tian* itself universally cares for and benefits all humans, which we can know through observation of the way it responds similarly and universally to all. The sameness of *tian*'s activity toward all demonstrates, for the Mohists, not that *tian* should be understood as having impersonal, regular, or mechanistic patterns—rather, it demonstrates features of *tian*'s character, *tian*'s care for all. According to the *Mozi*, the way we discern the desires and intentions of *tian* is through observation of the activity of *tian*.[16] Following *tian* and using it as a standard (*fa*) is a reliable guide to following the desires of *tian*, as in the case of *tian* there is nothing stopping its desires and intentions from issuing in manifest activity, as may be the case for humans. The fact that we can know the desire or the will of *tian* by observing *tian*'s activity at least demonstrates that there is no possible barrier between *tian*'s desire, will, and activity. *Tian* simply always acts as it desires. The fact that we can reliably know *tian*'s desire and will through observing of its actions does not mean that we must see *tian* as mechanistic or naturalistic; rather, it entails only that there is no possible gap or barrier between *tian*'s will and *tian*'s action, which is just what we should expect if *tian* is lawgiver and divine agent. While *we* may diverge from *tian*'s activity (and thus *tian*'s desire or will), *tian* itself never does. *Tian* does nothing that *tian* itself does not will.

Part of what seems at issue here is the nature of *tian*'s action and will or desire. The Mohists cannot have seen the action of *tian* as identical to its desire or will—we know the latter through observing the former not because they are identical but because *tian*'s will is always necessarily realized in action. If the two were identical, there would be no reason to distinguish them, no explanation of *tian*'s activity on the basis of desire or will, and the knowledge access argument that the Mohists make would become trivial. If what *tian* desires and what *tian* does are in fact the same, while conceptually distinct, then we can make sense of *desire* as grounding of action, as well as the claims the Mohists make concerning the correspondence of the two. If the two are conceptually identical, on the other hand, as they would have to be for the naturalist move to work, such that *tian*'s will is nothing other than, is reducible to, or otherwise somehow conceptually reliant on the regularity or mechanistic nature of *tian*'s activity, then the Mohist discussion should be a reductive or eliminitivist one like that of the Eastern Han philosopher Wang Chong, who denies that *tian* has either will or desires.

The most extensive and technical discussion of *tian* in the *Mozi* comes in the *Tianzhi* ("*Tian*'s Will") chapters. In the first of these chapters, the *Mozi* discusses the distinction between what *tian* desires (*yu* 欲) and what it hates (*wu* 惡).[17] According to the text, *tian* desires righteousness (*yi* 義) and hates unrighteousness. The Mohists here argue that if we follow the desires of *tian*, in treating others consistently with righteousness, then *tian* will satisfy our own desires, which are distinct from those of *tian*, in that we desire fortune and hate misfortune. Righteous action then becomes a way to ensure fortune. Later in the chapter,[18] we see additional claims about *tian*, holding that *tian* is superior (*shang* 上) to humans, and as the superior provides them with a standard (*fa* 法), in the same way that a ruler provides the standard or law for the people to follow. *Tian* then is a lawgiver that possesses desire and a will, and that rewards humanity for acting in ways consistent with its will.[19] *Tian* is also said to care about or love (*ai* 愛) the people, which can be known through its impartial or universal activity of enlightening (*ming* 明), possessing (*you* 有), as well as through the fact that it sends misfortune upon those who commit evil acts such as murder.[20] The *Tianzhi* chapters continually stress that *tian* punishes humans for activity inconsistent with the desires or will of *tian* and rewards humans for activity consistent with them. In *Tianzhi* 2, the Mohists even compare *tian*'s relationship with the world to a ruler's relationship to his ministers.[21] If the doctrine of *tian*'s will is merely a naturalistic account of the patterns or regular activities of nature, it is unclear what this comparison could mean. A ruler creates laws and enforces them, rewards and punishes, and acts on the basis of his desires and will. *Tian* as part of the world or pattern within the world could not have a similar kind of relationship with things in the world.

In the first *Tianzhi* chapter, the Mohists describe the relationship between the intentions (*yi* 意) of *tian* and righteousness (*yi* 義):

順天意者，義政也。反天意者，力政也。

Those who follow the intention of heaven govern through righteousness. Those who turn away from the intention of heaven govern through power.[22]

For the Mohists, the link between righteousness and the will of *tian* is established by the reward of *tian* for righteousness. In the case of the state, this can be demonstrated by the fate of righteous states. The Mohists claim that such states will be harmonious, wealthy, with plentiful resources so that the people are properly clothed and fed, peaceful, and without anxiety.[23] The unrighteous state that rules through power, attacks weaker states, and does not aim for the well-being of its people will be the opposite. This, we might think, is a bizarre claim, as it is an empirical claim for which one can seemingly find plenty of contrary evidence, even during Mozi's own time. What would the Mohists say about unrighteous states that have power and employ it in non-benevolent ways, yet still enjoy wealth and the other benefits the Mohists claim come from only righteous action? The Mohists, like other religious and philosophical systems tying moral action to divine reward, had to have recognize that bad things happen to good people (as Thrasymachus and Glaucon argue in Plato's *Republic*). If this is the case, then how do the Mohists avoid the conclusion that *tian* does not reliably punish the wicked and reward the righteous after all? The Mohists could have made the move that some other systems (like Plato's) do, in tying the reward for good action to features independent of its practical results, tying it to overall human thriving, or building in motivational features such that righteousness is its own reward (a move similar to the one *Mengzi* makes). But the Mohists never do this—they argue for the identification of righteousness with the will of *tian* on the basis of its purported practical effects for the individual, state, or ruler.

The purposive nature of *tian*'s activity is stressed in *Tianzhi* 2.6. The Mohists claim that *tian* has the kind of care for humans that it enjoins humans to have for one another—caring for all people universally and impartially. This can be seen through *tian*'s supportive activity. *Tian* creates what it does, according to the passage, for the benefit of humans. This is a key passage, as the Mohists claim here that *tian* is what creates, guides, and orders the entities and patterns of nature, rather than being identifiable with those patterns themselves. The Mohists appeal to *tian* here, and *tian*'s intention (namely, to benefit humans) as *explanation* of entities and patterns in the world. If *tian* is simply these patterns themselves, the "capital 'N' nature" Fraser claims, then this appeal can have no force—*tian* as nature itself, the entirety of the patterns and entities, can have no power of guidance or be used as the explanatory ground for itself in this way. The passage reads,

且吾所以知天之愛民之厚者有矣，曰以磨為日月星辰，以昭道之；制為四時春秋冬夏，以紀綱之；雷降雪霜雨露，以長遂五穀麻絲，使民得而財利之；列為山川谿谷，播賦百事，以臨司民之善否；為王公侯伯，使之賞賢而罰暴；賊金木鳥獸，從事乎五穀麻絲，以為民衣食之財。自古及今，未嘗不有此也。

Now there is that though which we know that *tian* cares broadly for the people. *Tian* spoke and created the sun, moon, and stars to light the road for the people. *Tian* instituted the four seasons—spring, autumn, winter, and summer—to arrange and organize the people. *Tian* sent down thunder, snow, frost, rain, and dew, to grow the five grains [for the people to eat] and hemp and silk [for people to wear]—all so that the people could obtain these and benefit from them. *Tian* arranged the mountains, rivers, and valleys, and spread within them many things, in order to administer good and evil to the people. *Tian* created the institutions of the kingship, dukedom, marquises, and lords, using them to reward the worthy and punish the wicked. *Tian* provided metal, wood, birds, and beasts, to follow and assist in cultivating the five grains, hemp, and silk, to provide valuables to the people in the form of clothing and food. From ancient times down to the present, things have never failed to be this way.[24]

The language used here to describe *tian*'s activity is important. *Tian* spoke (曰 *yue*) to make the celestial bodies offer light to order the path for humans, it established (or instituted, 制 *zhi*) the four seasons, and caused (使 *shi*) the people to benefit from its providing of grains, hemp, and silk. *Tian* arranged (列 *lie*) the geological features of the world such as mountains, valleys, and rivers, and created (為 *wei*) the institution of kingship and the lords, to carry out *tian*'s own reward and punishment. The language here suggests something more than mere identification of *tian* with these features of nature. If *tian* is itself nature, as Fraser argues, then appealing to *tian* as instituting, creating, or causing aspects of nature is doing nothing more than to point out these aspects of nature themselves. But this passage is certainly doing more than that—it is not merely pointing out that these aspects of the world attributed to *tian* do in fact benefit humans (which presumably all parties to the argument recognize, and would be a trivial point), but that the fact they so benefit humans demonstrates some additional fact that not all parties would initially recognize or accept—that is, that some agency must be behind all of this, intentionally making it the case that things beneficial for humans are brought about.

In this way, the Mohist argument is very much like the so-called "teleological argument" for God's existence, offered by numerous theistic philosophers through history, such as Thomas Aquinas and al-Ghazali (among a host of others), and which can be found in numerous places throughout Abrahamic scriptures themselves, such as in the Christian New Testament (*Acts* 14:17[25]) and the *Quran* (80:24–32[26]). The difference from the standard forms of the argument connected to Abrahamic religions, however, is that here it is an argument not for *tian*'s existence (which the Mohists take as a given) but rather for the position that *tian* cares for humans. The Mohists work from the fact that things in the world are so as to benefit humans to the conclusion that they were designed so as to benefit humans, which not only entails a designer but also a benevolent intention on the part of that designer. The naturalistic criticism of this argument, made by Wang Chong hundreds of years later during the Eastern Han period, is a forebear to modern objections to the teleological argument. We eat the five grains and wear silk and hemp, according to Wang, not because these things are designed for us but because they, of all the myriad things in nature, fulfill the needs we have for food and clothing.[27] The Mohist teleological argument for *tian*'s benevolence fails to take into account that most things in nature do not have any beneficial function for humans at all, and thus we do not use those things. For what purpose were these things then created? If in a world of millions of things, we find a few that are useful to satisfy our needs, this does not so clearly support the position that these things were designed with our use in mind. Of course, Wang and other early Chinese dissenters did not have access to modern evolutionary arguments that offer a more satisfying explanation of why we are able to survive by making use of things in our natural environment. Still, the availability of Wang's response suggests that if the Mohists were naturalists of this stripe, there would be little sense in appealing to *tian* in the way they do. If *tian* were only nature in its whole for the Mohists, then they could have (and should have) had a similar conclusion to that of Wang Chong concerning desires and intentions. The activity of nature is 自然 *ziran* (spontaneous) according to Wang, where this spontaneity entails lack of will or intention, lack of agency. If no early Chinese thinkers understood such agency in terms of independence of a deterministically bound world and its patterns, then Wang Chong's response would be inexplicable.

The variety of ways the Mohists speak about *tian* in the *Tianzhi* chapters—that it is responsible for features of the world beneficial to humans, governs humans like a ruler governs the people, rewards and punishes, cares for the people universally and impartially, wills and desires, and determines laws by which humans should live— suggest a view of *tian* as a divine transcendent agent in the same vein as the God of the Abrahamic traditions.

Chris Fraser's primary reason for understanding the Mohist *tian* as naturalistic is that it acts consistently with intelligible patterns, according to the Mohists. For this reason, we can know *tian*'s will simply by observing nature. Fraser writes,

> Generally, we discern [*tian*'s] intent by observing and interpreting its conduct, which for the Mohists amounts to a conception of regular, reliable patterns of nature. ... The Mohists see Heaven, and thus nature, as fundamentally intelligible, consistent, and predictable. If we act in line with its intent, it will reliably support and reward us; if we do not, it will discipline us. Consistent with the idea of Heaven as nature itself, the Mohists see Heaven's interactions with people as largely reactive, like the operation of regular natural patterns, albeit natural patterns that include moral and political norms. Throw a stone in the air, and it falls. Do good, and Heaven will support you; commit crimes, and it will punish you.[28]

This is a curious argument. Fraser here links nature with regularity and intelligibility, but fails to consider distinctions between kinds of and reasons for regularity and intelligibility. Not everything that is regular and intelligible can be associated with natural patterns or lack of agency. Natural patterns are always regular and intelligible, but the regular and intelligible are not always so because of natural patterns. Almost every system of metaphysics recognizes aspects of the world as regular and intelligible— this would be impossible to deny. But different metaphysical systems give us different explanations of that regularity and intelligibility. Naturalistic systems will offer something like patterns or laws of nature as explanation, while non-naturalist systems will offer a host of other explanations. In Platonic non-naturalism, the regularity and intelligibility of the world is explained by the resemblance between things in the world and those originals in the realm of the Forms that they resemble or partake in.[29] The fact of regularity and intelligibility here surely does not show that Plato's account is naturalistic—he explicitly appeals to a non-natural principle to explain such regularity. And if we turn to theistic systems within the Abrahamic traditions, with which Fraser contrasts the Mohist conception of *tian*, we find much the same. These traditions reject neither the regularity and intelligibility of the world nor the regularity and intelligibility of God's activity and will. Indeed, if we are expected to adhere to God's will, this will must be in some sense regular and intelligible. In most Abrahamic religions, for example, God's will is codified in laws contained in scripture. This certainly makes them intelligible, and their regularity is also assumed from the fact that the scriptures do not change, and the system of reward and punishment is determined on the basis of one's following of these regular and intelligible laws. It is not their grounding of regular and intelligible laws or patterns that determines whether God, *tian*, or nature represent naturalistic or transcendent entities. Rather, it is the ways they determine these regular and intelligible patterns or laws that make the difference.

Consider the issue of the goodness of God's nature and activity in the philosophy of religion in the Abrahamic traditions. God's will, according to nonvoluntarist thinkers, is immutable because God is fully good, and thus always acts consistently with the good. The voluntarist position (that God is literally omnipotent) is rejected here, because the idea is that God could not make good actions bad ones, and also (because of God's completely good nature) God will never act in bad ways. Thus, God acts in ways that are regular, intelligible, and seemingly patterned. This does not, however, undermine God's free will or transcendence—neither capriciousness nor action contrary to a pattern is necessary for such will—it is only necessary that one *could* act in alternative ways, not that one *does*. A number of medieval philosophers of religion, such as Aquinas and Ibn Rushd, argue for such a position.[30]

But *can* God act contrary to the good? God's will, that is, seems constrained if God's nature or character is such that he will always choose the good. Even such constraint, however, may be worked around. As long as the constraint is not a *metaphysical* constraint—that is, what keeps God from acting contrary to the good is his own nature, rather than his inability to choose—freedom of will seems salvaged. God can (in the relevant sense of "can") act contrary to the good, but because of God's nature as fully good, God will never in fact do so.

This is all relevant to the discussion of *tian* in the *Mozi* as it shows that the failure of the patterns and activity of *tian* to diverge from a regular, duplicable, and intelligible pattern and the recognition of the action of *tian*, as so regularized, does not in itself entail that the Mohists held a naturalistic view, that they saw *tian* as the embodiment of nature in the way Fraser claims. And given that the ways they speak about *tian* in general mirror those of theists in other traditions, we need a strong reason for understanding this view of *tian* as radically different from theistic appeals in other traditions. Independently of some reason to think that the Mohists could not have accepted a transcendent *tian* (perhaps because the concept of transcendence was absent from early Chinese discourse—which we suspect is behind Fraser's position[31]), we should then take *tian* as transcendent for the Mohists.

Fraser avoids the difficult question of how we can understand *tian* as a natural principle if it has something like a will, by claiming that 志 *zhi* and 意 *yi* "refer to the aim or object at which one's thoughts are directed,"[32] rather than a cognitive process themselves involving choices and desires. If then the "intent" of *tian* is understood in terms of aim, we need not attribute beliefs or any other propositional attitude to *tian*. This cannot, however, account for desires (欲 *yu*), which are also attributed to *tian* in the *Mozi*, along with a number of other mental states.[33] It may of course be possible to make sense of mental states on a naturalistic account of the world, as many naturalist philosophers of mind attempt today, but it is not clear that Mohists attempt such a move, given the way they describe the activity of *tian* as similar to that of a human agent.

The concept of *zhi, pace* Fraser, had agentive and mental associations in much of early Chinese thought. We find in numerous texts, association of *zhi* with mental states. The *Huangdi Neijing* discusses the "five physical and mental states" (*wu xing zhi* 五形志),[34] while Du Yu's commentary on the *Zuo zhuan* speaks of *zhi* as categorizing particular emotional states, such as hate, joy, anger, sadness, and happiness.[35] The agentive and mental association of *zhi* is not limited to Han texts, but reaches back to early uses. Chapter 6 of the *Zhuangzi* contains a passage that presents *zhi* as a property of the mind (*xin*).[36] *Zhi* is defined as *yi* 意 in the *Shuowen Jiezi* (and vice versa), a concept that is also connected closely with mind and agency in early Chinese texts. The two terms are occasionally used together, in the construction *zhi yi* 志意. The clearest association of *zhi* with the mental is found in the *Huangdi Neijing*, where *zhi* is contrasted with *xing* (physical, form), in something like a traditional mind/body distinction.[37]

While the most robust consideration of the will and desires of *tian* is found in the *Mozi*, other early Chinese texts address the issue to varying degrees as well. Agentive language applied to *tian* can be found in numerous other early Chinese texts outside of the Mohist tradition. In the *Zuozhuan* we find mention of the "desires of *tian*" (*tian yu* 天欲), in a discussion of the desire of *tian* to kill (*sha* 殺) plants in a case of drought. The facts of drought are here explained by the state of desire in *tian*, rather than a regular pattern. Indeed, the desire explanation here seems to be a way to explain activities of *tian* that do not seem to follow a regular or orderly pattern. While droughts happened on occasion, they generally could not be predicted—they did not happen in any regular pattern people could discern, as did the seasons or the motions of the stars and planets. Thus, the agency of *tian* could be invoked to explain such seeming divergences from the regularities of nature. The agentive activity of *tian* in this way was often seen in terms of reward or punishment for human activity—in this case, for divergence from proper norms of human activity.[38]

The *Hanshu* also mentions a case of the desire of *tian* to send rain[39]—another unpredictable (or less predictable) aspect of natural activity. This activity of *tian* does not seem to have been understood in these texts as a kind of automatic natural or mechanistic response to human activity or disorder, but rather in terms of reward and punishment by *tian*, drawing a parallel to the way a ruler can reward and punish. A number of texts speak of reward and punishment by *tian*, including *Zhuangzi*,[40] *Guanzi*,[41] and *Lushi Chunqiu*, among others. The parallel language used for the states and activities of an agentive ruler and *tian*—terms such as will (*zhi*), desire (*yu*), appeal to affective states such as anger (*nu* 怒), love or care (*ai* 愛), and agentive activity such as reward (*shang* 賞), punishment (*xing* 刑)—strongly suggests an agentive view of *tian*. And we should expect as much, given the explicit parallels drawn between humanity and *tian* in a number of texts, particularly in the late Warring States and early Han. If there is an anthropomorphic *tian* in early Chinese texts, it is as much because humanity resembles *tian* as it is that *tian* resembles humanity. In the next chapter, we offer our interpretation of a dominant conception of the relationship between humanity and *tian* in early China, one that provides further evidence for numerous forms of transcendence.

6

Transcendence in Relation: Humanity and *Tian* in Early Chinese Thought

Introduction

As we have seen, the *topos* of *tian* makes for fertile soil for analyzing non-naturalist themes in early Chinese thought. In this chapter, we seek to explore the possibility of non-naturalist readings of Chinese philosophy by examining an important locus in all non-naturalist traditions: the relationship between humanity and that which is (possibly) transcendent. One slogan that naturalistic readings of early China seize upon is *tian ren he yi* 天人合一, "*tian* and humanity form a union," interpreting this as a theme of the identification of *tian* and humanity on the same "natural" scale.[1] But even if we grant that this meaning is accurate and universal across early philosophers who invoke the concept, should such a view be taken as genuinely representative of *all* early Chinese thinkers?

In this chapter, we seek to problematize such an assumption by focusing on the relationship between *tian* and humanity as presented in the *Xunzi*, though with context provided by other early texts. *Xunzi* might seem an odd choice for such a reading, as many—most notably Kurtis Hagen and Janghee Lee—perceive Xunzi as a somewhat paradigmatic naturalist in early China.[2] Though we do not deny there are compelling reasons to provide a naturalist explanation of *Xunzi*, our goal here is to show it is plausible to also offer a non-naturalist reading of the text by closely examining Xunzi's understanding of the relationship between *tian* and humanity.

Our thesis is straightforward: if the standard account of early Chinese thought is to assert a unity between *tian* and humanity, Xunzi can be seen as either challenging or greatly qualifying this assertion. Instead, Xunzi emphasizes the distinctions between *tian* and humanity to such a degree that *tian* begins to seem very transcendent in his account. We believe that attending to how the *Xunzi* offers a kind of non-naturalism is helpful for resolving interpretative problems in the text. One main issue is easily visible when one sets Xunzi in contrast to popular conceptions of the correlative cosmology of the Han period. A fundamental conviction or presupposition of Han philosophers who developed concepts such as the *wuxing* and *yin-yang* as a cosmological framework was that the natural course of the world revealed important information about human affairs, especially the rise and fall of rulers. In this sense, the Han cosmology can be said to believe in "the book of nature" that can be examined, known, and drawn upon to make predictions about proper action.

Xunzi, on the other hand, teaches that "it is only the sage who does not seek to know *tian*."[3] Here we reach a problem: If the naturalistic assumption that, for Xunzi, *tian*=nature is correct, then why does Xunzi not think nature should be known and studied? If *tian* is really just nature and nothing transcendent whatsoever, one would expect the same kind of scientistic inclination as one finds in Western naturalism, wherein the "sage" (in this case, the naturalist) is the only one who really seeks to know nature and thereby explain all things according to nature. This is especially difficult given Xunzi's general confidence in human learning—unlike the *Zhuangzi* and *Daodejing*, Xunzi not only defends human learning as key to moral formation, he also goes as far as to attack pseudo-science and errors in his contemporaries.[4] Hence it is puzzling why such an ostensibly scientific and rigorous defender of knowledge would suddenly advocate ignorance of *tian* if all Xunzi understood *tian* to be is nature pure and simple.

Of course, our reading is not isolated. Other scholars have labored to show how Xunzi is, in fact, as deeply "religious philosopher."[5] While we do not explore Xunzi's approach to religion per se, we do think these scholars have a better starting point for understanding Xunzi's thought. But again, we should stress that this does not mean that the naturalist reading of Xunzi is entirely fruitless. In fact, it has quite a ring of truth that is helpful for comparative analyses. Compared with God in the Abrahamic traditions or even some accounts of Brahman in Hinduism, Xunzi's *tian* seems much more naturalistic indeed. Thus, our contention is not that a naturalist reading of Xunzi is wholly inaccurate, but that it is incomplete: we do not think that the naturalist presupposition fully accounts for the concept of *tian* found in the *Xunzi*.

The focus of the chapter lies on another important formula in early Chinese thought: that there is a triadic relationship (*can* 參) between *tian*, earth, and humanity.[6] We contend that in Xunzi's treatment of the triad formula, the relationship between *tian* and humanity is structured in a way that is analogous to transcendence. Specifically, we argue Xunzi exhorts the triad as a proper form of *relating* to *tian* in its otherness precisely because he does not think it proper or possible for humanity to emulate or model *tian*. This latter option—one we saw explicitly at work in the *CQFL*, for example—was that *tian* or the ultimate was the proper archetype of human action. In this chapter, we argue Xunzi's insistence on relation amid difference can and should be read as an attribution of some manner of transcendence to *tian*.

Transcendence through Difference: The Triad Trope in Xunzi's Tianlun

This chapter focuses on one particular theme in Xunzi's discourse on *tian* (*Tianlun*) that we will examine for its transcendence possibilities. The key passage for our examination in this chapter is as follows:

天有其時，地有其財，人有其治，夫是之謂能參.

Tian has its seasons, the earth has its resources, and humanity has its governance, and this is what is called being able to form a triad.[7]

In order to understand this passage in light of an assessment of transcendence in Xunzi's thought, two main questions must be answered. First, how does Xunzi understand *tian* as a term of relation to the earth and humanity? Second, what does he consider the proper relative concept for human beings that forms an appropriate triadic relationship with *tian* and earth?

Some scholars contend that Xunzi's position should be interpreted in a naturalistic framework. Kurtis Hagen interprets *tian* and earth as meaning "the forces of nature" and argues Xunzi means that "anyone who has sufficiently developed his or her moral character and intellect can contribute to the ongoing creation and renewal of culture."[8] Importantly, this naturalistic interpretation has broader justification than many naturalistic readings of early China. For one, as Hagen's text shows well, the naturalist interpretation of Xunzi (or at least something bearing a great likeness to naturalism) can be found in Japanese scholarship.[9] Also, there is evidence of naturalistic-friendly interpretations of *Xunzi* in the Chinese tradition well before the modern period. For example, the Tang-era scholar Yang Jing 楊倞 interpreted the passage as meaning "humanity is able to govern *tian's* seasons and earth's resources, and employ them, and this is making a triad with *tian* and earth."[10]

These interpretations all seem to share a common theme in that they use one ostensibly known variable (what *tian* is) to interpret the unknown (how to relate to *tian*). Thus, reading 天有其時 as a completely naturalized reading of *tian*, the term of human relation becomes apparent: simply look upon nature and use it to your ability. We would like to question if this has got it right, though. When he says *tian* has its seasons, does Xunzi mean to assert that *tian* means and only means "forces of nature"? If one presupposes a contrastive theory of transcendence, the answer must be yes. But does Xunzi presuppose such a vision of things that identifying *tian* with the seasons is a complete and utter naturalization of *tian*? And, therefore, does he really mean that the triadic relationship with *tian* comes down to the proper use of these natural forces?

Unfortunately, the broader appearance of the triad trope in especially Confucian literature is not as helpful in answering this problem. Primarily this is because it seems that Xunzi was the first in the *Ru* tradition to employ the triad trope in an explicit way referring to *tian*, earth, and humanity.[11] In the *Liji*, the *Kongzi Xian Ju* chapter includes a dialogue between Kongzi 孔子 and Zixia 子夏 that mentions the triad in this way, but this is not evidence of terminology preceding Xunzi.[12] Consequently, later Confucian uses of the triad likely not only draw upon Xunzi but also can be read as a response to his conception of the matter. For example, later in this chapter, we introduce a later interpretation of the triad that can even be taken as criticizing Xunzi's view of *tian* as overly naturalistic itself. We don't, of course, think this later interpretation seems to correctly understand Xunzi's account. But the point for now is that it is difficult to depend upon later texts of the early Confucian tradition to clarify Xunzi's position when they did not always seem to agree with his perspective.

What is needed, then, is an analysis of the text itself to determine whether Xunzi thinks *tian* does simply and entirely mean "nature" or whether there is something else to his account of the concept. Thankfully, the *Tianlun* provides an excellent starting point for such an analysis. One reason the naturalist reading of Xunzi seems to nicely fit the text is due to the rather strong criticisms Xunzi levies against what one might call "religious" interpretations of *tian*. As the *Tianlun* opens, Xunzi harshly opposes those who would associate *tian* with directly causing fortune or poverty, or health or illness. According to Xunzi, "the actions of *tian* are constant—they cannot cause a Yao to flourish as ruler or cause a Jie to be overthrown."[13] This means that *tian* is not an agent who brings about these occurrences through direct intervention. Xunzi goes on to say that "if one holds firmly to the basic matter, and uses it well, then *tian* cannot make him poor; if one nourishes what he is given and acts in accordance with the proper seasons, *tian* cannot make him sick."[14] Xunzi continues in this manner, restating his essential point in various ways: human beings can neither blame nor praise *tian* as the cause of their fortune or misfortune, but bring about these states themselves.

Clearly these critiques are aimed at certain religious perspectives, likely forms of shamanism that exhort ritual performance as a way of manipulating *tian* to act for one's benefit.[15] But are these signs of a religious critic as such, whereby we should conclude that Xunzi means to reject *all* religious interpretations of *tian* as problematic? Edward Machle has helpfully observed what is self-evident to non-naturalist traditions: criticisms such as those Xunzi offers in the *Tianlun* can be asserted by a thoroughgoing naturalist or a robustly theistic thinker.[16] At most, these criticisms point out that there are views of *tian* that Xunzi finds inaccurate and distasteful, namely a conception of *tian* that is swayed and won over by ritual acts and supplications. Interestingly, one can conclude from this that for Xunzi, it is precisely the attempt to "employ" (*yong* 用) or "order" (*zhi* 治) *tian* that is problematic in propitiatory rites. In the naturalist interpretation, then, Xunzi is portrayed as simply shifting the mode of use or governance from religious to rational means.

Upon such a naturalistic reading of Xunzi, the misuse of relationship with *tian* that Xunzi critiques is actually cast aside. Rather, the naturalist reading uses this critique as a fulcrum to argue that Xunzi is really arguing about *tian* being something different than his adversaries. Namely, such readings see Xunzi as not just attacking certain religious uses of *tian*, but the religious conception of *tian* altogether. We, on the other hand, are not convinced it is right to see Xunzi as taking out, root and branch, the religious understanding of *tian*. Rather, it seems to us that his critique of manipulative religion and turn to the triadic formula is actually meant to assert the transcendence of *tian* and so clarify the real role religion plays in moral virtue and social flourishing.

Let us test this thesis. At the heart of Xunzi's critique of ritual manipulation of *tian* lies his contentions that there is a fixed constancy (*chang* 常) to *tian*. Consequently, this constancy means *tian* does not directly cause the fall or rise of a particular ruler. Similarly, Xunzi rejects a link between *tian*'s movements and the enrichment or impoverishment of people, or health or illness. Xunzi argues that *tian* "is unable" (*bu neng* 不能) to augment or change such things. Hence, ritual methods such as auguries, oracles, and religious sacrifices meant to manipulate *tian* to act in a certain way (e.g., give rain) or bring about a particular blessing do not properly recognize the fixed quality of *tian*.

The fact that Xunzi focuses on the fixed qualities of *tian* in his essay is deeply significant. Whenever one views natural phenomena in themselves, it is evident they are not "consistent," except in broadest terms possible. There are seasons in which one should expect snow or great heat, but many important phenomena are not tied to specific temporal periods. Rain, for example, *qua* phenomenon will appear quite randomly without any fixed or constant causes. If we are to assert a fixed quality to ostensibly random phenomena such as rain, what we mean is there is some cause X that is constant and out of which arise the speciously random phenomena in question. We can then explain cause X in one of two ways: either active or legal. That is, cause X can be an acting agent (such as a god) who moves the phenomena to happen or a law of nature, which represents the proposition that under conditions Y, one will always or most often have phenomena P.

This raises an interesting and helpful problem for considering transcendence in the *Xunzi*. For at least in one regard, Xunzi clearly acknowledges there is some kind of fixed ordering principle that is not subject to the kind of mutability and inconstancy that mark many aspects of human life. Might he mean this is a "transcendent" principle? Inasmuch as this ordering principle is distinct from the mutable and inconstant world of phenomena, and is the principle of order of this world of phenomena, the ordering principle must *in some sense* transcend the world of phenomena. Of course, the naturalist perspective can concede this point and merely respond that the "transcendence" mentioned here is still within the "natural" order. But this seems to beg the question. For it is unclear that law of nature L is actually part of the natural order. One need not be a metaphysical realist to see that a law governing things is not exactly the same as the things it governs, and thus unless one understands "nature" as "anything not God" (which naturalists implicitly often do, it seems), then it is not at all clear that even a view of cause X as a law of nature is still "natural."

At this stage, it is helpful to note that Paul R. Goldin sees Xunzi's position on the fixed quality of *tian* as bearing remarkable similarity not to modern naturalism, but to Modern deism. As Goldin puts it, for Xunzi, "Heaven has established its works, but thereafter, like an absentee god, plays no active role in terrestrial affairs. Instead, heaven has bestowed upon us the faculties by which we may apprehend the patterns of nature and act in such a way as to make these work for our benefit."[17] Goldin goes on to make an extended comparison between Xunzi and the English deist William Tindal to support his suggestion that Xunzi's position sounds like eighteenth-century deism.[18]

Goldin's comparison of Xunzi to eighteenth-century deism is helpful indeed when set alongside naturalist interpretations to the *tian*–human relationship for Xunzi. In *Xunzi and Early Chinese Naturalism*, Janghee Lee attempts a thoroughly naturalistic interpretation of *tian* according to Xunzi. Lee recognizes that Xunzi emphasizes the distinction between humanity and *tian*, but argues it can be interpreted naturalistically as follows: "*tian*, for Xunzi … is a spontaneous, nonintervening nature whose magical working manner is totally different from the arduous, voluntary manner of humans."[19] This conception of *tian* raises several problems. First, if *tian* equals Nature (as Lee asserts), then what does it mean to say nature does not intervene? That is, if *tian* is the order of nature itself, then how can we possibly say that this order of nature does not intervene in itself? Part of what Lee means is that *tian*-as-nature has no will—does the nonintervention of *tian* according to Lee, then, simply mean the lack of willed intervention?

More importantly, if *tian* is meant to equal nature as the naturalist understands it, then what can possibly justify the kind of distinction Xunzi is making between nature and humanity? Anne Cheng once described Xunzi as desiring to "clearly dissociate the cosmological domain of *tian* from the ethico-political domain of man."[20] Under a naturalist paradigm, however, this dissociation makes little sense. For surely if the cosmological facets of nature are simply natural, they are not "magical" or "totally different" as Lee suggests, but knowable and predictable. A naturalist perspective would seem to warrant a *closer union* of these two domains rather than dissociation, precisely because human beings are part of the natural process of the cosmos.

Put simply, Xunzi's insistence on the fixed qualities of *tian* is no clear conceit to a naturalist perspective. In fact, it can be aligned with a robust theistic account of things. In fact, following Goldin's suggestion, we might even consider whether Xunzi represents an affirmation of transcendence precisely in a contrastive model. In other words, we must continue to analyze Xunzi's fuller conception of *tian* in order to see what, if any, transcendence is there for him.

If we follow Xunzi's lead and contrast the tractable, manipulative views of *tian* with Xunzi's own, what we soon find is not just a disagreement about whether *tian* is fixed or not, but how humans should properly respond (*ying* 應) to *tian*. Following this logic of Xunzi, we argue he can be readily seen as defending the transcendent mystery of *tian* that is surrendered in tractable accounts of *tian*. After stating his initial critiques against tractable views of *tian*, Xunzi concludes, "thus, having insight into the distinction (*fen* 分) between *tian* and humanity, this can be called 'extending the human' (*zhi ren* 至人)."[21] For Xunzi, the proper response to *tian* depends upon a proper understanding of the difference and distinction between what *tian* is and what humanity is, and only then can human action be genuine and fulfill human agency.

What, then, is the nature of this distinction? Xunzi first describes the distinction in terms of *tian* having an "office" or "duty" (*zhi* 職). Significantly, he chooses to describe this office or duty in negative terms, saying *tian's* office is to act in the following ways: "without acting, it is complete; without seeking, it finds."[22] In this sense, *tian's* office or place is marked by a kind of action human beings do not instinctively perform ourselves. For this reason, *tian's* office is something that human beings "cannot increase" (*bu jia* 不加) through contemplation, ability, or investigation. In fact, Xunzi argues that such human endeavors to augment or understand *tian* are "contending with *tian's* position."[23]

For Xunzi *tian's* position is covered in a certain ineffability, and therefore *tian* cannot be manipulated or controlled, nor can it be imitated as such. Rather, proper human response to *tian* must be through "triangulating" (*can* 參) with *tian* and the earth.[24] But, there is a lingering warning here from Xunzi: if one were to cease to live out this triad and rather desire to obtain that with which one makes the triad (*yuan qi suo can* 願其所參), this would be a grave confusion (*huo* 惑).[25] In other words, triangulating with *tian* properly involves recognizing that I as a human cannot desire to be like *tian*. Rather, I can only respond and relate to *tian* properly when I understand the fundamental distinction (*fen*) between *tian* and my human existence. In other words, I must recognize that *tian* is not human (or subject to human will), and that I as a human am not like *tian* in order to maintain the proper triadic relationship with *tian* and the earth.

Here we come to a vital point in Xunzi's account of *tian* that decisively inclines toward a non-naturalist view of things. As we saw above, Xunzi holds that *tian* is fixed and constant. If *tian* simply meant the forces of nature, as Hagen suggests, then one would expect Xunzi to argue that the scientific (or analogous) study of *tian* is conducive to learning how to flourish. Indeed, for Xunzi, there does seem in nature the kind of basic book of moral virtue necessary to begin to flourish, and so we can expect him to hold something like the following: the more one seeks to know and understand *tian*, the more one understands humanity and undergoes proper self-cultivation leading to sagehood.

However, Xunzi does not hold such a position. Rather, he makes the paradoxical claim that "only the sage does not seek to know *tian*."[26] But, what precisely does Xunzi mean with this observation? Yang Jing argued for the following interpretation: "the *tian dao* is difficult to comprehend, and thus the sage only seeks to cultivate human affairs, and does not labor to worry about or know *tian*."[27] If these interpretations are right, it is difficult to see how to square Xunzi with a naturalist vision of things. For if *tian* is simply "nature" pure and simple, then the difficulty of comprehending the *tian dao* cannot be insurmountable; it would just require someone of extraordinary mental capacity to do it. And wouldn't the sage be precisely that person? Moreover, if *tian* means "nature" then how can Xunzi justify a severe caesura between the world of nature and that of human affairs? As a naturalist, one must read Xunzi as arguing that nonhuman nature is mysterious and unknowable, and only the sage knows to keep his mind focused on human affairs. Maybe Xunzi means this, but if so, it is a shockingly antirational position for him to take, given his robust defense of learning elsewhere in the *Xunzi*.

Kurtis Hagen offers a variation on this theme: "*Tian*, in this case, stands for propensities of nature which are outside people's power to influence. This statement does not imply that the sage does not have a sophisticated appreciation for these propensities, but knowing the workings of nature are not what Xunzi's *junzi* seek."[28] This reading dovetails with Hagen's interpretation of *tian* in the *Xunzi* as "merely provid[ing] us with a starting point, a natural world with regularities in which to operate."[29] In such a portrayal of things, human response is to build up culture and society building upon these natural regularities. This would mean, then, that the sage would not seek to know *tian* because *tian* can provide no information telling humans what we need to do to flourish—there is nothing in *tian* that the sage can really know to help flourishing.

The benefit of Hagen's position is that it limits Xunzi's claim here to one of practical wisdom: the sage seeks how to flourish as a human being and, thus, does not concern himself with things he cannot change. On the surface, this is an attractive solution, but it brings its own difficulties. For one, how does one square such a reading of "practical wisdom" according to Xunzi with the models of sages in Chinese antiquity? Xunzi's own favorite sage, King Yu, gained fame through redirecting the flood waters through irrigation systems. Doesn't Yu's example show us that sagely governance in particular requires responding to natural propensities one cannot *control* or *change*, but to which we might adapt? Can we take Xunzi seriously to suggest that practical wisdom does not involve seeking to know *tian* if all *tian* means are propensities of nature out of our control? At least, if Xunzi does mean this, it seems we should not take him as a helpful authority for learning how to flourish in a world in which humans are inundated by natural propensities over which we exercise absolutely no control or influence.

Another issue is that if *tian* simply means nature, that seems to make Xunzi inconsistent. After all, according to most Xunzi scholars, the creative function of human culture is about building upon what are the beginning points of nature. If this is true of Xunzi, it should be fairly clear that knowing *tian* should be important for him. The practical wisdom argument Hagen makes does not resolve this problem because for Xunzi, the practical wisdom of being human and creating conditions for human flourishing depends upon knowing *tian* if all *tian* means is nature pure and simple.

What can make sense of this position is to interpret Xunzi as meaning something more like what Goldin proposes: that there is a transcendental and theistic conception of *tian* at work, even if the deity of *tian* is not providentially involved in the work of human culture. On this reading, it is simple enough to explain the sage's ignorance of *tian* as a kind of "respect for the mystery" of *tian*. And because in this reading *tian* is not simply identifiable with natural forces, it is a consistent position: for Xunzi, a theistic *tian* can be convincingly unimportant to practical wisdom, but a naturalistic *tian* cannot be as convincing.

The text does, in fact, seem to develop just such an account of the "mystery" of *tian*. Later on in the *Tianlun*, Xunzi returns to the foundational cosmological motion: the movement of the stars, of the four seasons, and the bringing fourth and nourishing life, among other things. He labels each movement as an "achievement" (*gong* 功) and distinguishes this achievement from the labor or work that produces it (*shi* 事). In this distinction, Xunzi argues that daimonic (or perhaps, theistic?) knowledge (*shen* 神) is that whereby one does not observe the work, but only observes the achievement.[30] Thus, Xunzi means to describe some sort of action that lies behind cosmic motion that is, in itself, indiscernible (*bu jian* 不見), but which is nonetheless observable from what it produces vis-à-vis cosmic motion.

This premise allows Xunzi to observe that "all know what it brings to completion, none know what it is without form—this is what is called 'the achievement of *tian*.'"[31] Here, Xunzi shifts from the result side of the issue to the cause. In this passage, *tian* is presented as a genus of action and motion that cannot be known in itself—indeed, it is "without form" (*wu xing* 無形) that would enable it to be described. All human beings have the ability to perceive the results of *tian*'s actions, but Xunzi emphasizes we do not see the movement itself. Hence, attempts to control or manipulate this action would necessarily fail; the best we can do is become good observers of what *tian* achieves and respond to it properly.

It makes sense to map Xunzi's comment that *only* the sage does not seek to know *tian* according to this difference between achievements and activities. Only the truly wise understand that *tian* in itself ("without form") cannot be known, but only its achievements. Thus, the sage seeks to know *tian's* achievements alone, because that alone is what he is capable of knowing. He knows *tian* by seeking to not "know" *tian* as it is, and rather knows *tian* in the way proper to the human intellect—by intuiting the distinction between *tian* without form and *tian's* achievements.

Briefly, it is worth noting that something like Xunzi's achievements–activities distinction is commonly found in non-naturalist theistic traditions. In Hinduism, one can see an analogous theme in the distinction between *saguna* and *nirguna* Brahman, that is, Brahman "without form" (*nirguna*) and "with form" (*saguna*), the latter of which is revealed through avatars.[32] In Byzantine Orthodox Christianity, there is a tradition going back to Gregory Palamas that makes a clear distinction between God's energies and God's essence, the latter of which can never be known by the human intellect, even in paradise.[33] In more contemporary Christian thought, Karl Rahner is often credited with formalizing a distinction between the "immanent trinity" (the inner life of the trinity) and the "economic trinity" (the trinity acting toward the world).[34]

Given this "family resemblance" to non-naturalistic theism, we suggest it is fruitful to read Xunzi as offering a theistic and not utterly naturalized conception of *tian*. This is because in Xunzi's account, the sensible world of cosmic motion can indeed offer a connection with *tian* and is the work of *tian*. But there is also a sense in which *tian's* proper action lies behind or perhaps beyond the realm of sensible experience. For Xunzi there is a paradox of *tian*. On the one hand, the sage can know something about *tian* and relate to it properly, but this does not seem to be positive knowledge (i.e., knowledge of what *tian* is in itself). Moreover, seeking such positive knowledge is dangerous for human flourishing, according to Xunzi. The idea that we can discern the fullness of *tian*, manipulate it or imitate it, would mean that human flourishing would lie in performing Heavenly sort of agency, rather than the unique parameters of human agency. For Xunzi, the apophatic conception of *tian* is part of helping human beings recognize that human agency is unique and distinct (*fen*) from *tian's* agency, and that we must seek to harmonize and triangulate with *tian* rather than grasp at "contending" with *tian's* office (*zhi*).

Driving home this point, in a later passage of the *Tianlun*, Xunzi asserts a distinction between the *junzi* 君子 and *xiaoren* 小人 along these lines. Here, Xunzi describes the *junzi* as follows: "for the *junzi* reveres his own place, and does not have ambition for that of *tian*."[35] We suggest Xunzi means here that the *junzi* has a reverent and accurate understanding of his own "place" in the cosmic scheme and does not look to take up that which belongs to *tian*. On the contrary, the *xiaoren* "erroneously" (*cuo* 錯) understands his place in the cosmic scheme and does nurse an "ambitious desire" (*mu* 慕) for the place of *tian*. In this context, taking *zai tian* 在天 as the "place" of *tian* does not primarily mean spatial location, but should be understood in terms of *tian's* "position" or "office" (*zhi* 職). For Xunzi, the *junzi* is distinct from the *xiaoren* in that the former understands the fundamental distinction between *tian* and humanity and, for this reason, respects the unique human agency he must enact as part of a triadic relationship with *tian*. However, the *xiaoren* seeks to know *tian* as it is, he "longingly looks at" (*mu*) *tian* and would seek to imitate or perhaps usurp *tian's* position (*zhi*) in the cosmos.[36]

It seems that for Xunzi, true human flourishing involves this mysterious reverence for *tian* and *tian's* otherness. Human beings can know *tian's* office in some ways by the sensible world, particularly by the results and achievements of *tian*. But we cannot know this position in itself, nor should we try. Human intellectual efforts are misplaced if we desire or have ambition to know *tian* and imitate its position in the cosmos.

For this reason, we can conclude that for Xunzi, human flourishing requires discerning not how to control *tian* but how to relate well to *tian* through what can be known of *tian*. Ultimately, we argue that there is at least some measure of non-naturalism or transcendence at work in Xunzi's understanding of *tian*. For if Xunzi takes *tian* as simply natural forces, it is unclear why the proper relation to *tian* rests upon mystery as such. Here we should recall once again that Paul Goldin has felicitously likened Xunzi to an eighteenth-century deist. Indeed, this is a compelling similarity that explains well how the relational distinctions Xunzi makes cooperate with his exhortation that the sage does not seek to know *tian*. Like the deist, it seems for Xunzi that *tian* is not simply distinct, but radically distinct from human life. The natural phenomena are signs of *tian*—its achievements, perhaps—but not identifiable with *tian* as such. And this is key because due to the distinction between *tian's* activity and its achievements, *tian* is also beyond the range of human supplication or manipulation. We can *only* respond to *tian* and *tian's* achievements because they are at a remove from us.

Before moving to the next stage of our analysis, there is a significant benefit of turning to a theistic reading of Xunzi, apart from the arguments we make above. Homer Dubs once made the influential observation that Xunzi initiated a sort of decline in Confucianism, moving away from the "high theism" of Confucius.[37] This conception of Xunzi as the ruination of earlier themes in Confucianism has taken several forms over the centuries, most of which have been revealed to be less convincing than originally thought. Is it ultimately fair or accurate to see Xunzi as a kind of iconoclast who sought to radically alter the vision of Confucius that, as many would admit, did have a theistic conception of *tian*? We would argue that given the way Xunzi sought to identify his thought with the proper continuation of Confucius' way, reading his defense of *tian* as a theistic concept—indeed, even a "higher" theism perhaps than Confucius imagined— seems to square better with Xunzi's motivations and methods as a thinker than does a thoroughly naturalistic interpretation.

At the very least, we think there is perhaps a compelling albeit ironic case to be made that the *Xunzi* features one of the strongest transcendence frameworks in early China. We don't seek to make that particular case here and are not convinced the thesis is accurate, but the sheer possibility of making such a thesis is notable. For it suggests that the general assumption of many scholars that Xunzi is a thorough and clear naturalist should be questioned and analyzed further for its accuracy.

Comparing the Xunzi and Liyun

In this last section of this chapter, we seek to show that our reading of *tian* as transcendent in the *Xunzi* is not simply a possible reading, but helps make sense of later Confucian conceptions of the triadic trope. To be clear, we do not argue that later Confucians read Xunzi explicitly in the way we describe him above (which is a heuristic analysis at best). Rather, our aim is to show that the transcendence of *tian*—in some degree—was an issue in the way the triad was interpreted or employed in other early Confucian texts. Specifically, we propose reading the *Xunzi* on the triadic formula in conversation with the *Li Yun* 禮運 chapter of the *Liji* 禮記.

Liyun, 14 includes a passage that makes for notable comparison and contrast with Xunzi's teaching on the triad. And, as Michael Puett has shown, the chapter also provides a robust metaphysical perspective in which this triadic formula operates.[38] The citation of the triad formula is as follows:

故 聖 人 參 與 天 地 ， 并 於 鬼 神 ， 以 治 政 也 。 處 其 所 存 ， 禮 之 序 也 ； 玩 其 所 樂 ， 民 之 治 也 。 故 天 生 時 而 地 生 財 ， 人其父生而師教之：四者，君以正用之，故君者立於無過之地也[39]

Only the sage can form a triad with *tian* and earth, and join with the ghosts and spirits in order to govern rightly. Residing in what endures, he follows the rites; enjoying what is to be enjoyed, he governs the people. Thus, *tian* produces the seasons and the earth produces resources, while man is produced by his father and educated by his teacher. These four the lord may rightly use and thus establishes himself in a place without error.

Of the points of contrast with the *Xunzi* passage, there are three that are most notable. First, in the *Liyun* passage, the focus has shifted from *humanity* forming a triad with *tian* and earth to the sage in particular. This is significant because for Xunzi, the human triad with *tian* and earth is in a sense ontological—humans (such as the *xiaoren*) can work against the relationship, but humankind as such stands in a kind of relationship to *tian* and earth that then leads to the human development of ritual as moral cultivation. However, the *Liyun* formulation suggests the relationship is more primarily a kind of moral relationship, perfected by the sage in ritual activity. We should note that in the *Wang Zhi* chapter of the *Xunzi*, Xunzi notes it is the *junzi* that forms a triad with *tian* and earth.[40] Thus the moral relationship in the *Liyun* is not absolutely different from Xunzi's perspective, but it is different from the presentation on *tian* in the *Tianlun*.

Second, it is notable that the triadic relationship is supplemented with other human relations. The text specifies that triangulation is how humans relate to *tian* and earth, whereas humans "stand by the side" of ghosts and spirits. This suggests a more technical meaning of the triadic relationship than one finds in the *Xunzi*. More importantly for our purposes here, the inclusion of ghosts and spirits broadens the cosmological scope and meaning of the relational proposals at work in the *Liyun*. A third notable difference is in the change of verbs in the second description of the triadic activities. In the *Xunzi*, we find the following: 天有其時，地有其財，人有其治. In the *Liyun*, the similar passage removes the verb of possession (*you* 有) for one of production (*sheng* 生).

It is difficult to imagine the *Xunzi* and *Liyun* versions of the triadic formula were composed in complete isolation. Since there are reasons we discuss below to assign a late Warring States date to the *Liyun* passage, we hypothesize that the *Liyun* was composed with knowledge of the *Xunzi*. Working under this hypothesis, we can ask *why* does the *Liyun* alter the shape of Xunzi's formula in significant ways? The answer undoubtedly lies in the *Liyun*'s different framework of the world and ritual's place in the world. What we propose here is that the transcendence of *tian* seems to be part of the framework difference in these texts.

Let us take the descriptions of *tian* vis-à-vis the seasons in these passages as a point of departure. Setting the passages side by side, we have one account (Xunzi) holding that *tian* has or possesses the seasons and one account (*Liyun*) holding that *tian* produces the seasons. Just looking at the level of grammar, there is a qualitative difference between conceiving of *tian* and the seasons in these ways. In classical Chinese, *you* 有 suggests more of identity than just ownership, and from this perspective Xunzi's formulation could suggest a close identification of *tian* with the seasons. One could readily speculate that a shift from using the verb 有 to using 生 is aimed—in part—at having the effect of distinguishing *tian* from the seasons, that is, suggesting the transcendence of *tian* more strongly.

Ultimately, the shift from *you* to *sheng* can only be understood in light of the context of the texts in question. To be fair, the grammar only suggests it is *possible* that transcendence is part of the consideration in the difference between the two passages and need not actually play a real role. In order to ascertain whether transcendence is actually a concern of the *Liyun* passage, we must first provide more context in which to understand the passage.

Above, we noted that we are operating under the assumption that the *Liyun* was composed with knowledge of the *Xunzi*. Our rationale for this assumption is based on the research of Wang E 王锷.[41] Wang considers the *Liyun* one of three texts in the *Liji* that began to be composed in the early Warring States period and completed in the late Warring States period. Specifically, he believes the *Liyun* began as the writing of Confucius' disciple Ziyou 子游 and completed by later thinkers influenced by the Yin-yang School and the nascent Five Elements philosophy.[42] While Wang does not cite *Liyun*, 14 in his evidence, this passage occurs alongside those passages he cites to support his case, and it seems to function in keeping with this cosmological framework. Even if the *Liyun*'s triadic formula is older (which we think is unlikely due to its positioning), it likely comes from a Zi You-inspired branch of Ruism, which Xunzi criticized in his *Fei Shi-er Zi* chapter.[43] But, as we noted, it is more plausible to read *Liyun*, 14 in light of the cosmological schools to which Wang attributes partial authorship of the text.

It is not coincidental that the Yin-yang and Five Forces metaphysics became associated with genuine naturalistic or naturalistic-analogous movements in early China. Therefore, if *Liyun*, 14 interprets the triad formula in light of the development of Yin-yang and Five Forces cosmology, this can helpfully explain the criticisms the text might imply about Xunzi's use of the triad in the *Tianlun*. Simply put, in the context of the broader concerns of the *Liyun* that develop in the direction of Yin-yang and Five Forces cosmology, the overarching theme is that human rituals arise out of being able to have masterful knowledge of nature and respond to nature with this knowledge. In this view, the cosmological correlates provide an accurate means of interpreting events and predicting their impact. Unlike Xunzi's sage who does not seek to know *tian*, the sage of the *Liyun* seems much more focused on knowing *tian*.

For the author of the *Liyun*, in other words, it is plausible to infer that Xunzi is *too* transcendental. By asserting again the productive agency of *tian* and the earth, the *Liyun* more clearly locates *tian* within the natural cosmological movements. In this way, *tian's* production is brought into frame as part of natural cosmic drama that can be interpreted and utilized. This interpretation is bolstered by a later passage of the *Liyun*, especially indicative of the Yin-yang and Five Forces cosmology strain. In *Liyun*, 21, the text has it that

> thus the sage created standards, undoubtedly by means of establishing them in *tian* and earth, rooting them in *yin* and *yang*, controlling them with the four seasons, to mark them with the sun and stars, the moon as the measure, the spirits and ghosts as companions, the Five Forces as their substance, rites and righteousness as their instruments, the human emotions as their file, and the four intelligent creatures as something to be cared for.[44]

The importance of this passage is not simply that *tian* is brought within the ambit of *yin-yang* cosmology, but that it is subjected to the knowledge and use of sagely rulers.

Whereas for Xunzi there is a mysterious otherness to *tian*, the *Liyun* sees *tian* in a rather perspicacious light. Even if the *Liyun* author would not have considered the text's position in these terms, one can justly say that from the view of the *Liyun*, Xunzi's *tian* is excessively transcendent.

Conclusion

In recent scholarship, the portrayal of Xunzi as a naturalistic thinker has become popular. In this chapter, however, we have sought to show that this portrait raises a significant problem for the assumption that all early Chinese thinkers presupposed naturalism. For one thing, we have given arguments that Xunzi himself is not as naturalistic as some of his interpreters would have us believe, namely that there are ways his thought seems to work contrary to naturalistic values. On the other hand, even if one assumes Xunzi is a naturalist, his very argument suggests this naturalism could not have been presupposed by all Chinese thinkers. After all, if the *Tianlun* of Xunzi is articulating a naturalistic perspective, it does so *by way of criticizing* other views of *tian* that apparently *do not* conform to this naturalistic view. And, indeed, texts such as the *Liyun* suggest that, if it is accurate to read Xunzi as a naturalist, then it is not at all clear that other Chinese thinkers accepted this naturalism as the right way to conceive of *tian*.

All that said, the analysis in this chapter would lead us to conclude that Xunzi was not a naturalist. Rather, we think it is fair and accurate to interpret the *Tianlun* as defending some aspects of *tian's* transcendence by shifting from an emulation or manipulation model to a relation-in-difference model of *tian*. Consequently, far from seeing Xunzi as a poor naturalist, we think it is better to interpret him as a very unique and interesting non-naturalist, whose conception of *tian* should be placed in conversation with other non-naturalist conceptions of the world and the divine.

7

天理 *Tian li*—The Patterns of *Tian* and *Dao*

The discussion of *tian li* 天理 (patterns of *tian*) or *li* 理 (pattern) in early Chinese texts, we argue, demonstrates a conception of transcendence on which the discussion relies in a number of texts. While *li* is a more familiar concept in Song-Ming neo-Confucianism, the development of the concept of *li* in early texts of the Warring States and Han demonstrates a relationship between the pattern and *dao*, as well as a more general conception of the relationship between *tian* and *dao*, that demonstrates transcendence. Consideration of the relationship between *li*, *tian*, and *dao* is complicated by the fact that we find a number of positions in early texts—in particular, we find differences between thinkers who take *tian* as foundational and those who take *dao* as foundational. Some of these differences can be traced to widespread intellectual trends or even schools, while others are due to more individual differences.

In this chapter, we look to the concept of *li* and its development in Warring States and Han texts, particularly the *Zhuangzi* and *Huainanzi*, which offer the most clearly metaphysically realist and transcendence-based accounts of *li*.

The topic of *tian li* links to that of transcendence in a number of ways. First, the debate concerning the nature of *li*—whether it is something found in the world mind-independently or whether it is (at least in part) dependent on human construction—turns out to have implications for transcendence. This is because *li* has both a nominal and a verbal sense in classical Chinese—it is not only pattern but also *patterning*. It is a kind of activity that things in the world—things such as agents—engage in. This leads some to the view that *li* must then be at least partly of human construction, as there can be no natural agency outside of human agency. If *li* is mind-independent and an aspect of (nonhuman) nature, then there must be a patterning agent responsible for the patterns observed in the world, whether this agent is transcendent or not. Our position here is that such an agent, given the views we find on *tian li* in early texts, is understood as transcendent by at least some early Chinese traditions. The link between the concepts of patterns (*li*) and *dao* that we begin to see in late Warring States and early Han texts strengthens this view. Second, the idea of "following" *tian li* that we see developed in the *Zhuangzi* and *Huainanzi*, both in the case of humans and natural objects, suggests that *li* is not understood as contained within the nature of things that can follow *li*, but rather is closer to an archetype grounded in *dao*. The use of the concept of *dao* in connection with this following of *li* in the *Zhuangzi* is crucial here.

In the final section of this chapter, we consider the concept of *dao* discussed in the *Zhuangzi* and related texts, transitioning to the topic of the last part of our book in the following three chapters. *Dao*, as the ground of *li*, is understood in a way suggesting transcendence. While the case is made more difficult by the fact that early Daoist thinkers generally discuss *dao* in negative terms (consistent with the apophatic theology we discuss in later chapters), we argue that considering features of Daoist discussions of *dao*, especially in comparison with apophatic thinkers of other traditions, a conception of a clearly transcendent *dao* emerges.

We consider a variety of different views on *tian* and *dao* in early texts, including the shift in the early Han toward making *dao* foundational in Huang-Lao texts (which we touched on in Chapter 3). In many early Chinese texts, the concept of *li* is that of a pattern inherent in (although not clearly identifiable with) nature or heaven, discernable or discoverable by humans but not fully independent of or external to humans (in part because the patterns are inherent in all things, including humans), and grounded in a transcendent source (whether *tian* or *dao*, depending on the text in question). While the natural patterns enable organization of human life and the activity of nature, these patterns are such that they are discerned or discovered, rather than created. That is, the *li* are not mind-dependent, conceptual constructions of humans. Indeed, the *li* are the necessary grounds for effective conceptual construction—that is, only through understanding the *li* can humans create effective guiding concepts, teachings, plans of actions, objects, etc. Effective action, for many early texts, is action that is responsive to the *li*, organized on the basis of the *li*. Critically for the case for transcendence, these mind-independent patterns precede the physical stuff of the cosmos, emerging from *dao* and seemingly forming the precondition for the emergence and operation of things (*wu* 物) in the world and their characteristic behaviors. This serves as an important difference between *li* and something like the laws of physics in contemporary scientific naturalism. In the contemporary naturalist view, features of physical stuff itself determine the patterns of activity. The laws of nature are not prearranged patterns or patterning grounded in a fundamental agent or entity. Rather, they are simply descriptions of the regularities of interactions between objects based on the physical features of those objects.[1] For a number of early Chinese thinkers discussed here, particularly during the late Warring States and early Han, the patterns themselves are prior and determinative. They are not grounded in natural properties of the world, of the cosmos of things (*wu*), but rather are prior to things, such that the activities and features of things are determined via their following of these patterns. This makes the *li* transcendent in a way that physical laws of nature in contemporary scientific materialism are not. This understanding of the concept of *li* represents a shift away from one that appears to have initially been much more naturalistic. This shows that not only do transcendence and other "non-naturalist" positions continue to emerge even through what we call the "naturalistic shift" of the early Han, but also the development of concepts does not (as we often think) always move from early non-naturalistic senses to naturalistic senses. Here we see an example of the development of a crucial concept moving in the other direction.

The Concept of Li 理

Li is a difficult concept in early Chinese texts, in part because thinkers use it in a variety of ways, all specifying an organizational principle of some kind. Brook Ziporyn, in the first of his two books on the concept in early Chinese and later neo-Confucian thought, distinguishes between "ironic" and "non-ironic" uses of *li*, which he translates as "coherence," the former of which he associates with the *Laozi* and the inner chapters of the *Zhuangzi*, and the latter of which he associates with early Confucianism, specifically the *Analects* and the *Mengzi*.[2] Ziporyn argues that *li* concerns the intelligibility of things, writing that "*li* is in most cases precisely something to be cognized, and something that is capable of being discerned."[3] Ziporyn argues that *li* should be understood not as contained in the world or grounded in nature or some transcendent source, but rather *constructed* by agents.

Harold Roth discusses the origins of the term and its early meanings, connected to patterns found in rock. The *Shuowen Jiezi* supports this, defining *li* as "the order within jade" (治玉也).[4] Roth explains: "the *li* are patterns inherent to a block of uncut jade that permit it to be split or cut along regular lines. … veins along which the material will fracture in a predictable way."[5] This suggests a realist view of *li*, as something found in the world, the discernment of which one can use to facilitate effective action. At least in this oldest sense, *li* is very much something in the world, an organizational feature of things. It is still a possibility that later texts or thinkers within the tradition modified this definition or understood *li* in very different ways. But the evidence suggests that most early texts offer a conception of *li* very much in line with this older sense of inherent patterns.

When we look at early philosophical uses of the term, it appears most accurate to say that *li* is primarily something capable of being *followed*. Independently of the metaphysical status of *li*, most early thinkers discussing it were concerned with the issue of following *li*, with the assumption that somehow activity that followed the *li* would thereby be skillful, effective, or otherwise advantageous. Being cognized is perhaps an element of this in many cases, but is not necessarily so, particularly according to texts like the *Zhuangzi*, which is suspicious of conceptualization. Responsiveness to the *li* is critical and explains how the developed person, according to early Daoist views, is able to act in a spontaneous and "non-active" (*wu wei*) manner while still hitting on the right way of acting. Discerning the *li* is thus not always (or perhaps even not *often*) a matter of cognizing *li*. Ziporyn's claim about cognizing is necessary on his reading, because he ultimately holds that *li* are constructed in part by human activity—the concept he reads as "coherence" is one heavily dependent on the human mind to make sense of and understand the coherence of things.

There are important aspects of *li* that cannot be captured on a conventionalist account like Ziporyn's, and a model in which *following* is the primary way humans respond to *li* makes better sense of many of the early uses of the term. The sense in which early texts understand the following of *li* requires a mind-independent *li* discernible in nature that humans do not construct, but rather discover and respond to. This is not to say that early texts leave no role for convention and human conceptualization of the world—the Zhuangists in particular have a robust understanding of these aspects of the world. Even on these views, however, *li* is understood in a realist fashion, anchoring the human to the world. The *Zhuangzi* and the *Huainanzi* offer, in our opinion, the most complex view of *li* and its relationship to the world, one we refer to as a "quasi-realist" view—thus we spend most time in this section focusing on the Zhuangist/Huainanist position.

Li is a relatively common term in early Chinese texts, and we find it in a number of contexts. In Confucian literature, it can be found throughout the *Mengzi* and *Xunzi*, as well as other early texts in the Warring States and Han. In these texts, it appears to often have the sense of "rules," "principles," or "determinations," with a shared feature of all of these being the sense in which *li* are things *to be followed*, or that specify or demand certain kinds of action.[6] *Li* can be commanded or ordered, linked with *ming* 命 (mandate, allotment) in the *Yueling* chapter of *Liji*.[7] In this sense, *li* appear as something like "injunction," which we can link with other early uses, such as those in the *Mengzi* and *Xunzi*. The *Mengzi* partners *li* with *yi* 義 (righteousness) in 6A7, claiming that it is *li* and *yi* that all minds agree in valuing, just as all eyes agree in valuing beauty and all ears agree in valuing sounds. Here, it seems that the *Mengzi* makes *li* something necessarily intelligible, something that can be tracked and/or sensed with the mind. Following the parallel between the claims about the eyes, ears, and mind, *li* and *yi* would seem to be necessarily the kinds of things that the mind can access. But in this accessing of *li* by the mind (*xin*), is it necessary that it be *cognized* as such? Much of this depends on the understanding of *xin* found in the *Mengzi*. It seems right that in the *Mengzi* (or at least in this passage), *li* is accessed by the mind and cognizable, but this does not entail that *li* is always or necessarily such. Following the parallel in the passage, just as we might say that while the eyes can view beautiful things, not all things that are beautiful are visible to the eyes, we can also say that while the mind can cognize *li*, perhaps not all *li* is cognizable by the mind.

What primarily characterizes *li*, in a sense shared across texts, is that things follow or respond to *li*—something like "order" or "ordering" captures multiple related senses of *li*. *Li* can be an ordering in a nominal sense, a structure of objects or things in the world—this is the reason it is often translated as "pattern."[8] It can also signify order in the verbal sense—the act of patterning or putting into order. The combination of *li* with *yi* 義[9] is seen in a number of texts, such as the *Mengzi*,[10] *Zhuangzi*, *Guanzi*, and *Lushi Chunqiu*, with the idea here seemingly that *li* is structural and plays a role in making the thing what it is.

While the idea of *tian li* 天理 (the patterns of *tian*) is most prominently discussed in the *Zhuangzi*, it can also be found in a host of other early texts, including the *Liji*, *Hanfeizi*, *Chunqiu Fanlu*, *Hanshi Waizhuan*, *Baihutong*, and others. The construction appears only once in the *Huainanzi*, in a passage from the first chapter (*Yuandao* 原道), claiming that the *tian li* can be extinguished (*mie*) based on failures of human activity. The *Huainanzi*'s conception of *tian li* and the human role in the creation of the cosmos are discussed further below, as it offers us another source of transcendence in early texts, one connected to human agency.

Most scholarship on *li* in recent years focuses on its use in the neo-Confucianism of the tenth–twelfth centuries CE, as the concept occupied a far more central role in neo-Confucian than in early Chinese thought.[11] Some scholars have traced the development of the concept from early uses to later neo-Confucian uses, such as the early twentieth-century Chinese scholars Tang Junyi and Feng Youlan, Western sinologists A. C. Graham and Joseph Needham, and in more recent scholarship, Roger Ames and David Hall, Brook Ziporyn, among others. Of these, only Tang, Ziporyn, and Ames and Hall discussed *li* in early texts, with the others focusing mainly on neo-Confucian understandings of *li*. Tang Junyi's understanding of *li* tracked early uses in Confucian and other texts. He argued that in the earliest uses, such as that of the *Shijing*, *li* is action based, understood in the verbal sense, a patterning or ordering, concerned with dividing or organizing material.[12] This division or ordering aims at some end, with a suggested link to ordering in the sense of the mandate from a ruler. One interesting and important feature of Tang's reading of *li* in early texts is the connection of *li* to both activity and to intention. *Li* is an intentional dividing or ordering process guided by particular aims or intentions, tied then to the will or intention of an agent. Tang refers to this conception of *li* as 文理 *wenli* ("cultural *li*"), in the sense of *li* as the activity of culture in determining, conceptualizing, and distinguishing things for particular purposes.[13]

While Tang's claim here is modest, focusing on the sense in which *li* is connected to ordered and purposive activity of human beings, other scholars, particularly Joseph Needham, A. C. Graham, and Brook Ziporyn, moved to the claim that *li* is a conventional, mind-dependent human activity, rather than something found in nature independently of humans and that makes things what they are. *Li*, for them, is constructed rather than discovered. According to Ziporyn, Needham's rejection of externalist or realist readings of *li* was based on his rejection of transcendence in early China:

> for Needham, [translations of *li* such as "form", "reason", or "law of nature"] are misleading in that they suggest an external source of order, either form as imposed upon passive matter, or natural law as enforced by God as legislator, in both cases implying a transcendent source of order standing outside the things which are ordered, bearing a different ontological status.[14]

Here we see an example of the kind of explanatory circle at the root of some interpretations of early Chinese thought. *Li* cannot be external or, in the world, mind-independently because this would suggest transcendence, a concept early Chinese thinkers didn't have. But there are a couple of interesting questions here. First, why think that "an external source of order" requires transcendence? Are there not "laws of nature" on naturalistic views of the world? Second, what is the reason scholars like Needham have for rejecting transcendence, especially if transcendence appears in such a metaphysically modest form as that required to make sense of something like "laws of nature"? Presumably, their reason is that concepts such as *li*, as well as the others discussed in this book in which we might expect to find transcendence, do not actually entail transcendence. It is very similar to the circularity implicit in Chris Fraser's argument for reading the Mohist *tian* as naturalistic: *tian* should be understood naturalistically because early Chinese thinkers did not accept transcendent entities, but the evidence for the claim that they did not accept transcendent entities can only come from analysis of their concepts such as that of *tian*, *dao*, etc. as naturalistic. Thus, we can respond to both of these moves in the same way. One cannot use the supposed lack of transcendence in early China as a reason for rejecting a transcendence-entailing reading of a key concept if the nature of those very concepts constitutes the evidence for the claim that early Chinese thought lacked a concept of transcendence. If concepts such as *li*, *tian*, *dao*, and others do not entail transcendence, there must be independent evidence for this.

It is unclear if Needham is right that an external source of order corresponding to *li* would require transcendence. If *li* is something akin to laws of nature or natural patterns inherent in things, such patterns might be understood in terms of the inherent nature of things absent an ordering entity. Indeed, this is just the way that contemporary scientific naturalists think of natural laws such as the basic laws of physics. The patterns or principles that guide and/or constrain the activities of things are based on the kinds of things they are and the features these things have—that is, the laws governing the activity and interactions of things are dependent on features of the entities making up the constitution of these things themselves. To that extent, entities in the world do not follow some *externally imposed* order, on a "laws of nature" view. So why not think that *li* in early Chinese texts refers to the same kind of constitutionally grounded order or pattern, such that *li* can be understood as a mind-independent or "external" source of order, such as entailed by "laws of nature," without entailing transcendent entities?

Part of what is going on here involves the link between the nominal and verbal senses of *li*. It is understood not only as the orderly pattern inherent in things that explains their activity but also as an active patterning or ordering—a willful distinction making or patterning, as Tang Junyi pointed out. If *li* in this second sense is mind-independent, then it seems that there must be some other entity that can will, intend, and act in such ways as to pattern or order entities in the world and their activity. Can we understand such an entity in a non-transcendent manner? It depends. Insofar as we can make sense of human agency without transcendence, we can also make sense of the agency of something like *tian* without transcendence (this point is part of what Chris Fraser relies on in his reading of the Mohist *tian* as naturalistic). But just because we *can* make sense of such agency without transcendence doesn't mean that we *should*. There are independent reasons to understand the agency and activity involved in the ordering of the world via *li* as involving transcendence (independent of but related to the reasons for seeing *tian*'s will as involving transcendence).

The construction 天理 *tian li* (patterns of *tian*)[15] is for our purposes most important. A critical issue for us is the relationship between this construction and that of 道理 *dao li* (patterns of *dao*), which can also be found in early texts (with the two sometimes found in the same texts). Investigating these structures uncovers important features of *li* as well as of *tian* and *dao* in early texts. The construction *tian li* is found and discussed mostly in the *Zhuangzi* and *Chunqiu Fanlu*, as well as a mention in the *Huainanzi*.[16] The *Hanfeizi* and *Shenzi* also have much to say about *dao li*, which proves useful given the connection of *li* to the verbal sense of ordering.

In the *Zhuangzi*, most of the passages including discussion of *tian li* involve issues surrounding the *following* of *tian li*—the need for such following and its results. In chapter 14 (天運 *Tianyun*), chapter 15 (刻意 *Keyi*), and chapter 29 (盜跖 *Daozhi*), we find discussion of the following of *tian li*. All of these chapters, it is interesting to note, fall outside of the traditional "inner chapters" section of the text, with the first two instances in the "outer chapters" and the third in the "miscellaneous chapters."[17] We find two other mentions of *tian li* in the *Zhuangzi*—in the *Yufu* chapter as well as a single instance in the inner chapters, from chapter 3 (養生主 *Yangshengzhu*). While the second of these passages does not explicitly speak of following the *tian li*, the same sense of the *tian li* as that on which the effective agent relies is used. This comes during the famous monologue of Cook Ding in chapter 3. Ding explains his ability to carve oxen without ever his blade becoming dulled, while others do not cut as well and their blades are dulled after time. Ding's response is useful here in coming to grips with the issue of what is meant by *tian li*:

臣之所好者道也，進乎技矣。始臣之解牛之時，所見无非牛者。三年之後，未嘗見全牛也。方今之時，臣以神遇，而不以目視，官知止而神欲行。依乎天理，批大郤，導大窾，因其固然。

What I am fond of is the *dao*, which goes beyond skill. When I first began carving oxen, I could see nothing but oxen. After three years, I stopped seeing oxen in their entirety. And today, I encounter the ox with my spirit, and do not use the eyes to observe. My knowledge stops and my spirit takes over. I rely on the patterns of *tian* (*tian li*), making use of the openings, guided by the empty spaces—by this my action is effective.[18]

We see here that reliance on *tian li* is what enables Cook Ding to follow the openings and natural empty spaces within the ox, which can only happen, the passage suggests, when one sees without the concept of *ox* guiding (and limiting) one's actions. Reliance on *tian li* is an alternative to reliance on the eyes and even on the mind. Cook Ding says that his knowledge (*zhi*) stops when the spirit (*shen*) takes over, and reliance on the *tian li* happens through this operation with the spirit. By "spirit" here, the author seems to have in mind a kind of egoless and unconceptualized state of action in direct response to the world—a kind of instinctual activity that might be considered responding to the world on the information from one's senses alone, or even from nature itself.[19] The use of *shen* in other passages in the *Zhuangzi* suggests this, including the text's discussion of the *shen ren* (spirit person) as one without a self-conception and the kinds of goals accompanying such a conception.[20] Reliance on the *tian li*, then, is not the reliance on something that is cognized in the usual way (which issues in knowledge) or that humans construct or impose on objects through conceptualization or goal-directed activity. The spirit, in following *tian li*, makes use of inherent features of the object itself to guide its activity, with the associated suggestion that *tian li* is a matter of these features of objects, rather than features of the agent or based on activity of the agent. Relying on the *tian li*, according to this passage, is to a large extent a *passive* activity, allowing direct responses based on mind-independent features inherent to objects themselves. If *tian li* in this passage is understood in terms of a human construction, something like "the coherences humans construct from *tian*," or the activity of this construction, then relying on the *tian li* would in essence be reliance on one's own discriminative or ordering ability and activity, which conflicts with the claims made earlier in the passage that knowledge stops in the reliance on *tian li*, and that concepts such as that of "an ox" or "oxen," on which we normally rely, are superseded.

Some later neo-Confucian usage of the term, while different in numerous ways from the early uses of the Han and pre-Han period, also suggests that *tian li* is something mind-independent and found in the world. Cheng Hao (1032–1085 CE) contrasted *tian li* with 人欲 *ren yu* (human desires), suggestive of *li* as properties of *tian* independent of humans.[21]

A number of contemporary scholars share a similar interpretation of *li* in early Chinese texts. Chenyang Li's characterization of *tian li* comes close to the one we endorse and entails a kind of transcendence: "The real thing to know is not the myriad things themselves, but the '*li*' or '*tian li*'—the principle of Heaven—which is present in myriad things."[22] Though we ultimately understand the sense in which *li* can be said to be *within* things in a way suggestive of transcendence, Li's position mirrors our own insofar as we take the *tian li* to be manifest within things, rather than constructed by the activity of things.

It is possible to take *li* to be inherent within objects in the world, yet understand it in a non-transcendent way. Kim-chong Chong, for example, understands the *tian li* of *Zhuangzi* chapter 3 as referring not to something broad or universal, but to features of particular objects. He writes: "there are no overarching principles to be discerned from it and that should serve as the basis of any normative order."[23] Chong resists thinking of the *tian li* in this context as orderly, however, in the sense of a codifiable principle that can guide action through rules. This much seems right, as following the *tian li* involved in the carving of oxen, according to Cook Ding, enables him to follow the natural openings and joints. Where such openings and joints are will be a matter of the individual ox before him. Thus, chapter 3 of the *Zhuangzi* does seem to suggest that *tian li* are not universal principles. This does not show, however, that *tian li* should be understood simply as features of an object. The empty spaces and joints on one ox may be different from those on another—this is why relying on the *tian li* is often inconsistent with "seeing an ox." When one carves following a conception of an ox, one carves according to not what is before one but according to a template or rule concerning what is supposed to be before one, a rule based on definition and disallowing of the natural differences between actual things in the world. The concept of an ox is that of a thing uniform in its features. Any actual ox will differ from any other, such that a single concept that is meant to capture what they all share will exactly resemble none of them. Chong stresses the sense in which the construction "*tian li*" is meant to suggest that the *li* in question are mind-independent and "in the world" in a real sense, as *tian* is used in the *Zhuangzi* (as well as in other texts, as we saw above with the much later work of Cheng Hao) as an oppositional concept to *ren* (humanity).[24] He explains:

In the *Zhuangzi* as a whole, binomials involving *tian*, such as *tian jun* (天鈞) and *tian ni* (天倪), are used in opposition to any artificially fixed conception of things, or as imposed by human beings. The same can be said about the notion of *tian li*.[25]

This cuts against a reading of *li* in early texts as constructive activity of the human mind in organizing the world in certain ways. The concept of *tian li* becomes even more revealing when we consider the verb sense of *li*—not only as pattern or order but the patterning and ordering activity of an agent. *Tian li*, as a feature of *tian*, is both an order or pattern of *tian* and an order or pattern *by tian*. That is, *tian* as the world itself, the creative agent behind the world, or nature (depending on the conception of *tian* under consideration) actively patterns the world. Even though, as mentioned above, individual objects such as oxen are patterned differently, the pattern inherent within each object is not such based solely on the nature of the object itself, but rather is such based on the nature of *tian*. This does not, of course, entail that every thinker or school who discussed *tian li* had a Mozi-like theistic conception of *tian*. Certainly no such conception of *tian* can be found in the *Zhuangzi*. It does show, however, that *tian* is understood as a distinct entity with creative capacity to order and pattern the world, and that these patterns in the activity of *tian* are grasped through a kind of intuitive response rather than constructed through discursive or conceptual cognitive activity.

Following and Patterning

While there is a tendency among philosophers to look only at the "inner chapters" of the *Zhuangzi*, the vast majority of the text, which falls outside this division, is certainly of use. While we believe that the traditional inner/outer/miscellaneous distinction is problematic, and both masks different strands of thought within each of the groupings and grounds an incorrect view of the inner chapters as most authentic, oldest, or associated with a single author/school, nothing here turns on this view.[26] It is enough to show that the views found in the outer and miscellaneous chapters are authentic early Chinese, pre-Han views and were not imported from some later source from years during which Chinese philosophers had a conception of transcendence.

We find a relevant discussion of *tian li* in chapter 14 (*Tianyun*) of the *Zhuangzi*. This instance, like that in *Zhuangzi* chapter 3, concerns following the *tian li*, an account of the reasons for and the effects of following these *li*. A common refrain concerning *li* in the *Zhuangzi* and in other texts is that *li* are primarily understood in terms of following. In the verbal sense of "ordering," the imperative mode is built into the notion of an order. The focus on *li* as guiding or understood in terms of following similarly suggests an imperative built into the concept of *li*. *Li*, that is, is not only the kind of thing that *can* be followed—as one can follow the path of a car along the road—but it is the kind of thing that *should* be followed, with this normativity built into what it is as *li*. An order, for example, is different than a general statement of behavior (or even a suggestion?). In the latter cases, one may follow a behavior without the behavior itself or the statement of it having any prescriptive force. In the case of an order, on the other hand, the prescription is part of what it is to be an order. *Tian li* can in this way be understood as normative and descriptive patterns in the world and of the world.

In the passage in question in *Zhuangzi* chapter 14, the mythical Huang Di (Yellow Emperor) is discussing the perfection of music in explaining the power of a performance of [Xianchi] music:

夫至樂者，先應之以人事，順之以天理，行之以五德，應之以自然   The most summative music first responds (*ying*) within the affairs of humans, follows via the *tian li*, practices using the five virtues, and then responds using spontaneity.[27]

We see here consistency with the passage on *tian li* from Chapter 3 discussed above. In Chapter 3, following natural patterns (in humans) is done with the spirit (*shen*) rather than knowledge (*zhi*), and this passage extends that message. Following the natural patterns is a matter of responding (*ying*) to things in a spontaneous (*ziran*) manner. The concept of *ziran* is discussed throughout the *Zhuangzi*, linked to an automatic, intuitive, and non-conceptual kind of activity.[28] This sense of *ziran* is similar to the *wuwei* (non-action) discussed more often in the *Laozi*.[29] In the *Zhuangzi*, it is primarily associated with a particular characteristic of activity, but this association brings about an understanding of the term as akin to something like "nature" in later years. The work of the Eastern Han philosopher Wang Chong represents a large step in this direction—Wang argues that the activity of nature (as opposed to human agents) is *ziran*, that is, without intention, will, or the other characteristics of acts that make them intentional acts of an agent. What characterizes nature or the world as distinct from the human is the *ziran* quality of its activity—thus, *ziran* becomes a stand-in for the entirety of the processes and entities of nature itself.[30]

Another important concept here is that of *ying* (response), a concept developed to much greater extent in the *Huainanzi*, to which this chapter (and others in the *Zhuangzi*) may be linked.[31] The concept of *ganying* (resonance) developed there explains this resonant response in terms of automatic movement given stimulus from things that cause movement in the object based on their similarity to it. A key example given of this is the vibration of nearby strings of a stringed instrument like a *guqin* (or the ancient *se*) when one string is plucked.[32] Charles Le Blanc argues that the concept of *ganying* is the central concern of the *Huainanzi*, writing that "it was around the idea of [*ganying*] that the philosophy of *Huainanzi* was elaborated."[33] As in the case of *tian li* in the *Zhuangzi*, regardless of whether it is the central or the most fundamental concept in the *Huainanzi*,[34] it is certainly an important concept, and one tied to the following (*shun*) of *tian li* and behavior (*xing*) in concert with the five virtues. Perfect music itself, according to Huang Di in the passage, responds and resonates (*ying*) with the affairs of humans, a process suggested by the end of this passage that ideally happens spontaneously. Thus we see again evidence in the *Zhuangzi* of the *tian li* as mind-independent, inherent in the world as well as associated with the activity of the world, to be discovered and responded to rather than constructed or even known in the usual way.[35] The sentence after the above quoted passage from *Zhuangzi* 14 claims that the four seasons were *li* (patterned, ordered), presumably by *tian* (although the passage leaves the agent unnamed).

The discussion of *tian li* in chapter 15 (*Keyi*) also stresses the extent to which following the *tian li* is something not just outside of the realm of knowledge, but in opposition to knowledge. In following the *tian li*, one eschews reliance on the (discursive) mind and on the concepts through which the discursive mind operates. The relevant passage reads:

去知與故，循天之理，故無天災，無物累，無人非，無鬼責。

[The sage] moves away from knowledge and conceptualization, follows the patterns of nature, and thus does not encounter calamities of nature, is not harmed by things, is not blamed by people, and is not chided by the ghosts.[36]

This passage also suggests that the *tian li* are not grasped through knowledge and conceptualization, but they are also not created by human processes of ordering or distinguishing (entailed in conceptualization). The language of *following* is always used in the *Zhuangzi* to describe the proper human activity as connected to *tian li*, never creating, engendering, or enacting in any way. The terms *shun* 順 or *xun* 循 are often used in concert with *li* to describe this following. The *Heshanggong* commentary on *Laozi* describes the "great following" (*da shun*) of *Laozi* 65 as a following of the discerned *tian li*, as we find it in passages in the *Zhuangzi* and elsewhere.[37]

A passage in the *Tiandi* chapter claims that *li* comes about at the completion (*cheng*) of things (*wu cheng sheng li* 物成生理—"things being completed, *li* is generated"). While this "completion" in some contexts suggests a human activity or reliance on prior material,[38] in this passage it seems to be disconnected from the human context, as it comes in a description of how the various features of the world arose, with no reference to the specifically human. What could be meant here by the generation of *li* upon the completion of things?

We find discussion of *tian li* in other early texts that seems to echo this characteristic accepted by the Zhuangist authors. The *Yueji* chapter of *Liji* mentions the possibility of the *tian li* being "extinguished" or "destroyed." The *tian li* is an aspect of the human, according to the chapter, insofar as it is an aspect of anything in nature, including the human. The full discussion is useful for our purposes here:

人生而靜，天之性也；感於物而動，性之欲也。物至知知，然後好惡形焉。好惡無節於內，知誘於外，不能反躬，天理滅矣。

Humans when they are generated are at peace—this is a matter of the inborn characteristics (*xing*) they receive from *tian*. Things in the world (*wu*) create emotions and move the person—this is a matter of the desires of their inborn characteristics. Knowledge of things in the world reaches its summit, and after this likes and dislikes take shape. When likes and dislikes are not controlled within, knowledge is tempted to focus on the external. One then becomes unable to return to the self, and the *tian li* are extinguished.[39]

This passage explains the *tian li* as opposed to desires, or at least uncontrolled or unruly desires, and associates the *tian li* with the internal rather than the external.

This would seem to suggest that *tian li* are in the mind or dependent on the mind rather than in the world mind-independently. While this is the case, the *tian li* in this passage do not seem dependent on or constructed by the conceptualization or distinction making that amounts to patterning or ordering things in the world. Rather, it appears to be something inherent in the self based on its nature, linked to inborn characteristics (*xing*) that can be disrupted. Inborn characteristics, as mentioned in the first part of the passage, are fixed or created by *tian*, and thus if the *tian li* are part of these inborn characteristics, then they should also be fixed or created by *tian*.[40] But desires are also attributed to our inborn characteristics according to the above passage, and these various features of human inborn characteristics can come into conflict with one another. Thus, while the passage attributes the original peace of humans to inborn characteristics, it is the response of inborn characteristics to "things" and "knowledge" that creates problematic desires. These desires in themselves, according to this passage, may not be taken as altogether bad things, but they create the possibility for *tian li* being undermined, as their becoming out of control causes problems.

Clearly, *things* (物 *wu*) play an important role in derailing the human ability to follow *tian li* or to contain *tian li* (the *li* are spoken of in these different ways across texts). In discussions in the *Zhuangzi*, this is generally because "things" are at least in part constructs of human conceptualization (*shi-fei* 是非), which require value judgments based on desires, and obscure the *tian li*. The construction of "things" is connected to valuation, according to *Zhuangzi* chapter 2:

古之人，其知有所至矣。惡乎至？有以為未始有物者，至矣盡矣，不可以加矣。其次以為有物矣，而未始有封也。其次以為有封焉，而未始有是非也。是非之彰也，道之所以虧也。道之所以虧，愛之所以成。

The ancients had that in which their knowledge reached its limit. How did it reach its limit? They took it to be such that there had not yet begun to be things (*wu*)—this is the summative limit. It is impossible to go beyond this. The next level of people took there to be things, but such that there had not yet begun to be signs of them. The next level of people took there to be signs, but such that there had not yet begun to be "this" and "not-this" (*shi fei*). When "this" and "not-this" become manifest, the *dao* becomes obscured. When *dao* is obscured, emotional commitment (*ai*) is completed.[41]

The process that ends with valuing and devaluing begins with the distinction of the world into discrete things (*wu*). It is possible to engage in some level of this without damaging oneself, injuring *dao*. But the person with the greatest knowledge (like that of the ancients) is one for whom there are not things to begin with. Clearly, this does not here mean a certain kind of discrimination of things in the world. The Zhuangist sage would understand "tree," "cup," etc., just as well as the rest of us do and be able to see the world in terms of trees and cups. If the sage were not able to do this, they would be unable to make sense of the language of others and unable to interact with the world in an effective way. Why, for example, would such a person expect the body of the cup to come along when grabbing the handle?[42]

So what is it then that the person for whom there has not even begun to be things (*wu*) does? We might understand this as referring to varying (deeper to more superficial) ways of eliminating value boundaries.[43] The last and the lowest level of person this passage discusses, the one who makes distinctions between things but does not take things in terms of right or wrong (*shi fei*), is able to understand the distinction between ox and non-ox, for example, or between a sharp and a dull blade, but does not attach particular value to one over the other—does not see one state as the "to be had" state and the other as the "to be rejected" state.[44] According to chapter 2 of the *Zhuangzi*, such a person has still achieved the perfected state, as they rely on conceptualized distinctions. The perfected person relies on *tian li* alone, like Cook Ding in chapter 3, which is, as the *Liji* passage above suggests, independent of the process of construction of "things." While *li* are thus independent of "things," they also seem to determine the way "things" manifest, behave, and are organized in the world. That is, "things" seem to rely on *li*, according to a number of passages across texts.[45] Later in the *Yueji* chapter of *Liji* (cited above), there is a discussion of the "*li* of the myriad things" (萬物之理), again suggesting a connection between "things" and pattern—though it is not altogether clear whether the pattern or the things are ontologically prior in this relationship. That is, are patterns metaphysically dependent on things, such that pattern only exists when there are things to be patterned, or do things instead follow preexistent or foundational patterns?[46]

There is evidence across early texts to show that at least a number of thinkers take *li* to have ontological priority, and that "things" and indeed the world itself, along with the patterns, are reliant on a transcendent principle, *dao* for some texts and *tian* for others. Before the Han, *tian* tended to be the transcendent entity in which pattern (*li*) and things are grounded (although pattern seems to have ontological priority over things), and in early Han texts, we find a widespread move toward *dao* as the fundamental transcendent entity. There are certainly texts in both periods that do not follow these general features, but we can take them to offer a general picture.

In the *Chunqiu Fanlu*, *tian li* is connected to moral behavior, with a kind of specified activity recalling the active sense of *li* as something like "ordering." Here, it appears as something like "moral imperative." In one passage from chapter 26, the text explains that when state possessing the Way (in the Confucian sense—that is, a righteous state) attacks a state lacking the Way (an unrighteous state), this is *tian li*.[47] Here, *tian li* is prescriptive, the kind of thing that should be followed, inherent in the world. To describe certain actions of a state as *tian li* is to associate those actions with the activity of *tian* or the favor of *tian* in some way. The text explains that the Qin attacked and defeated the Zhou because the Zhou lacked the Way, and then the Han attacked and defeated the Qin because the Qin lacked the Way. This suggests a kind of natural progression linked with *tian*—a state is attacked and overcome when it loses the Way, and this is a matter not of contingent human decisions but rather is a matter of *tian* itself. If a state with the Way attacking and defeating one lacking the Way follows or constitutes the *tian li*, then such activity can be construed as the action of *tian* itself— the patterns inherent in the world that make things such that one state that defeats another in this manner makes the actions, whoever else's they might also be, properly understood as actions of *tian*, consistent with *tian*'s patterns. The passage goes on to explain that had the Qin failed to conquer Zhou or the Han failed to conquer Qin, then this would have constituted failure to follow or understand the *tian li*, which would then obscure people's ability to understand ritual (禮 *li*).[48]

In chapter 41 ("What Creates Humanity Is *Tian*" 為人者天), the states of humans are likened to states of *tian* that they mirror and from which they are ultimately drawn. The passage reads:

人之人本於天，天亦人之曾祖父也。人之形體，化天數而成；人之血氣，化天誌而仁；人之德行，化天理而義。

The origin of humans is *tian*—*tian* is thus the ancestor of humans. The form and body of humans is completed via the transformation of the parts of *tian*. The blood and *qi* of humans is made humane via the transformation of the testaments (*zhi*) of *tian*. The virtuous activity of humans is made righteous via the transformation of the patterns of *tian* (*tian li*).[49]

The passage goes on in the same vein to describe the origins of a number of other human characteristics in transformation of features of *tian*. We see from this passage the continued emphasis in *Chunqiu Fanlu* on *tian li* as somehow prescriptive or moral in nature. Here, it is linked to the creation of "virtuous activity" (*de xing* 德行) in humans. Given the nature of the other comparisons made in this passage, this suggests that *tian li* has a generally prescriptive character, that it roughly plays the role within *tian* that human moral action plays for humans. This would be consistent with the previously mentioned passage from chapter 26 of the *Chunqiu Fanlu*. We also find support for this connection by looking carefully at the other connections between *tian* and humanity drawn in this passage. The first clause in particular, that the form and body of humans are completed (*cheng* 成) via the transformations of the parts of *tian*, echoes a view recounted throughout the *Huainanzi*, with perhaps its clearest statement in chapter 3 of the *Huainanzi*. In explaining the resonant effects of *tian* on humanity and vice versa,[50] the chapter describes the similarities between *tian* and humanity. In order for two things to have a resonant effect on one another, they must, according to the *Huainanzi*, be of the same kind. *Tian* and humanity, the text argues, are of the same kind, and humanity is modeled on *tian*. We can find numerous features of the human that map onto those of *tian* and can thus make sense of the resonance between the two, such that activities of *tian* have an effect in the human world, and human activities have an effect on *tian*.

Tian, according to *Huainanzi* chapter 3, has features matching those of humans, who are presumably modeled on the former.[51] *Tian* has nine layers (*zhong*), likewise humans have nine openings.[52] *Tian* has four seasons organized via the twelve months, likewise humans have four limbs organized via twelve joints. *Tian* has twelve months organized via 360 days,[53] and humans likewise have twelve limbs[54] organized via 360 nodes/joints. We find connection between the four seasons and features of humans in the *Chunqiu Fanlu* chapter 41 as well. A somewhat different connection is made here, though. It is not the four limbs likened to the four seasons, but rather mental or emotional states. Just as *tian* has spring, autumn, winter, and summer, humans have likes, aversions, sadness, and joy. The *Chunqiu Fanlu* passage further provides explanation of this similarity in the human origination in *tian*. It is because *tian* is the ancestor and origin of humanity that humans have the features they do, which can be seen as modifications of underlying features of the originating entity—just as children of two parents have modifications of features of the parents (including recessive traits that may not have been apparent in the parents but were in their ancestors).

Given this modification of features of *tian*, the identification of *tian li* with virtuous action and potency (the term *de* here suggesting a kind of active ability in some ways akin to the Aristotelian "virtue," but not limited to moral features[55]) suggests that the *tian li* is linked to (or identifiable with) the inherent disposition of *tian* in terms of normative distinction-making and distinctions. We use "disposition" here in the sense of the possession of a property that makes it the case that *tian* acts and makes distinctions in particular ways, but does not necessitate *tian* acting in such ways—thus also overlapping again with the Aristotelian conception of virtue as disposition of character.

Whatever else we can take from the *Chunqiu Fanlu* passage above, it serves as clear evidence that at least for some early Chinese texts, *li* is in the world mind-independently and is the basis for the activity of objects. If we can establish that *tian li* is properly understood in a number of early Chinese texts, however, the question still arises as to whether these *li* are transcendent in any of the senses we outlined in previous chapters. The *tian li* can be understood as the ontologically distinct ground of the world in a number of early Chinese texts. This is part of the reason these same texts often offer an apophatic understanding of *li* and of the relationship between *li*, *tian*, and *dao*, which we discuss in Chapters 9 and 10. It is to the connection with *dao* that we now turn.

Tian Li and Dao

In the *Zhuangzi*, we find a variety of views concerning *li* and its relationship to *tian* and *dao*. The *Zhuangzi* is a difficult text for a number of reasons, and we clearly find in it a number of sometimes deeply contrasting philosophical positions. Part of the difficulty inherent in understanding the text is that we do not know the reasons behind its compilation. While we may be able to isolate and describe different strains of thought in the text, it is difficult to know what it was about these different views, if anything, that led the compilers to combine them in the existing text. While we are skeptical about the adequacy of the traditional inner/outer/miscellaneous chapters distinction (as discussed above), it is clear that there are a number of disparate materials compiled in the *Zhuangzi*. While we make no claim about the organization of these materials and which chapters are linked to one another, we can find evidence of two distinct views concerning *li* in the text. On one of these views, *li* is linked with a transcendent *dao* only accessible apophatically—that is, through expression of that which is *not* predicable of *dao*—and via activity. Interestingly, the alternative view we also find in the *Zhuangzi* takes *li* to be secondary and a result *of* things and their organization.

The clearest statement of the first view in the *Zhuangzi* can be found in chapter 16 (*Shanxing*). A passage at the beginning of the chapter identifies *li* with *dao*. The same passage, however, seems to take *dao* in the non-metaphysical sense, as a way of acting or living, rather than the metaphysical *dao* as "ground of being" found in other places in the text. It is helpful here to cite the extended passage:

古之治道者，以恬養知；知生而無以知為也，謂之以知養恬。知與恬交相養，而和理出其性。夫德，和也；道，理也。德無不容，仁也；道無不理，義也；義明而物親，忠也；中純實而反乎情，樂也；信行容體而順乎文，禮也。

> Those of the ancients who brought order to the *dao* used tranquility to nourish their knowledge. Knowledge was generated and they did not use their knowledge to forcefully act/create. This is called using knowledge to nourish tranquility. Knowledge and tranquility communicate and mutually nourish one another—harmonizing and patterning (*li*) come forth from their inborn characteristics/nature. Their potency (*de*) is harmonized, while their way (*dao*) is patterned (*li*). When potency is nowhere unformed, there is humaneness (*ren*). When *dao* is nowhere unpatterned, there is righteousness (*yi*). When righteousness is clarified and things (*wu*) are in relation, there is loyalty. When at the core there is purity and substantiality and return to essence, there is music. When there is honest conduct in form and body, and following of culture, there is ritual.[56]

There are a few odd and interesting things about this passage. First, the sense of *dao* used here in the beginning suggests that it is not something ontologically prior to the myriad things or even persons, but rather something that persons, such as the ancients, can organize, shape, or order. *Dao* is not here used in the sense of the "ground of being" we find elsewhere in the *Zhuangzi* as well as in related texts. While there does seem to be a distinction between a general or universal *dao* in the first part of the passage (that which the ancients brought order to) and a particular *dao* later in the passage (the *dao* of knowledge and tranquility), both senses of *dao* here diverge from the ontological ground of being we see elsewhere. Here, we find *dao* in the sense discussed by scholars such as Hansen, Fraser, Ziporyn, Ames (among others).[57] The association of *li* with *dao* in this passage also seems to use *li* in the verbal sense, of a patterning, related to the ordering (*zhi* 治) attributed to the ancients at the beginning of the passage. While the link initially seems to be a definition (道理也), when read along with the following sentences, we see that it must be a general statement of activity, where *li* is not pattern but a patterning activity that operates on *dao*. The *dao* is, and can be, patterned. This is the most interesting result of this passage—this echoes the beginning of the passage claiming that *dao* can be ordered.

The pressing question here is whether *dao* in the sense of ontological ground of being shares this feature with the active individual *dao* discussed in this passage. Is *dao* as such ordered via the patterning of *li*? As we see in a number of other passages in the *Zhuangzi*, much of the text thinks of *li* (in particular the *li* of *tian*) as something for humans to follow (*shun, xun*) rather than create. It is not clear whether *li* is understood the same way in this passage. We can note that what is attributed to the ancients is not the patterning (*li*) of *dao* but the ordering (*zhi*) of *dao*—this may suggest that *li* is not the kind of activity humans can engage in with respect to *dao*.

In this passage, the patterns (*li*) are associated with *dao* rather than with *tian* as they are in some other chapters of the text. It is unclear if this patterning of *dao* is the same as the patterning of *tian*, and whether this happens independently of human activity. While the *tian li* discussed in other passages in the *Zhuangzi* (discussed above) appear to take such *li* as preexistent or given patterns to be followed by humans, the *li* associated with *dao* in this passage from chapter 16 seem to be understood as connected with human activity and intention—a patterning by the sage. In this patterning (along with harmonizing), sages brought order (*zhi*) to *dao*.

A crucial point here is the issue of the nature of *dao* itself in these texts. For years, there has been a debate between scholars concerning the nature of *dao*, with some (such as Ames, Hansen, Ziporyn, etc.) arguing that it should be understood primarily as dynamic, active, or fixed through activity. We find such translations as "way-making,"[58] "course"[59] offered by these scholars, while more static or singular translations such as "way," often prefaced with the definite descriptor "the," are preferred by other scholars. This debate has calmed in recent years, as we find instances across and within texts of multiple uses of the term *dao*, corresponding to each of these senses. The sense we are most concerned with in this book, however, is the metaphysical sense of *dao*, which is relatively neglected within philosophy on account of the primarily ethical focus of most of the texts in which philosophers currently tend to be most interested. Even in these texts, however, we find the metaphysical sense of *dao*—particularly in texts such as the *Daodejing* and *Zhuangzi*. When we expand our focus outside of the commonly read Warring States texts, however (common among philosophers in particular), we find a much more robust use of the metaphysical sense of *dao*, which becomes prevalent in so-called "Huang-Lao" texts in the Warring States and early Han. That these texts tend to be neglected by philosophers is not a surprise, given the historical tendency to focus on certain canonical early "school" (*jia* 家) texts. As a number of scholars have argued, the traditional "school" divisions created by Sima Tan in the Han Dynasty misconstrue the actual relationships between texts and thinkers in the Warring States and before.[60] Thus, it is a fruitless task to try to discover a uniquely "Daoist" or "Confucian" sense of *dao*, and statements in texts deemed "Daoist" to support a non-transcendent conception of *dao* cannot be taken as evidence of the views of a so-called Daoist tradition.[61]

The discussion of *dao* in terms of the language of absence or non-being (*wu*) in texts such as *Laozi*, *Neiye*, and *Huainanzi* does not entail that *dao* is a non-transcendent principle or active feature of the world. Indeed, on a mystical reading of such texts, *dao* can be seen as playing the same role as transcendent entities in other mystical traditions, including Abrahamic, Brahmanist, and Buddhist traditions. A number of scholars, including Harold Roth, Livia Kohn,[62] Benjamin Schwartz, and Louis Komjathy,[63] have read texts such as the *Zhuangzi*, where they discuss perspective, freedom, and undermining of the "self" as mystical in nature. The aim, according to these mystical readings, is to achieve unity with *dao* itself, which is expressed in terms of absence or nothingness because of its transcendent nature. Moeller and D'Ambrosio call this the "religious" as opposed to the "secular" reading,[64] although we think a better characterization of this is a "transcendent" as opposed to a "naturalist" reading. While the transcendent reading seems to have had cache among scholars of religion, philosophers (especially in the last decade or so) have tended to lean toward naturalist readings of *dao*.[65] Chris Fraser, Hans-Georg Moeller, Paul D'Ambrosio, Brook Ziporyn, and numerous others have offered naturalistic readings.

Moeller and D'Ambrosio argue that transcendent or "religious" readings of the *Zhuangzi* are influenced by so-called *daojiao*, or "religious Daoism" interpretations,[66] through the lenses of later Daoist movements that we are more inclined to term as "religious" in distinction from the "philosophical" Daoism of Warring States texts. We are hesitant to make this distinction in the Daoist tradition. It is the relic more of Western and later attempts to make distinctions between the meditative, ritual, and devotional practices of particular Daoist groups and texts that could be seen as co-opted for secular or independent purposes. The *daojia–daojiao* distinction as different phenomena was not made until modern times.[67] While the term *daojiao* was used as early as the Wei-Jin period, mainly as a term to distinguish Daoism from Buddhism (*fojiao*), there was no understanding that *daojiao* represented anything different from the *daojia* of Sima Tan. Thomas Michael notes: "in the long period of traditional Chinese history, the terms *daojia* and *daojiao* were applied interchangeably (together with the term *daozhe* as a third entrant that is not often attended to in modern scholarship)."[68] The distinction between religious and secular thought is very much one of Western modernity, and not of early China. When we attempt to understand early Chinese texts such as *Laozi*, *Zhuangzi*, or any other, we might use a frame of religious or secular thought according to our purposes, but we will not find, and should not expect to find, particular texts to align with one or the other side of this distinction. Almost always we will find some elements of any early Chinese texts that fit better with religion and other elements that fit better with secular thought. Offering a transcendent interpretation of early texts need not be tied to other aspects of early Chinese thought or contemporary philosophy marked as "religious"—that is, the issue of transcendence does not reduce to the issue of religion. The idea of transcendence in the discussions of Western modernity (such as the work of Immanuel Kant) grew largely out of consideration of religion, but the idea of transcendence is separable from, and should be separated from, that debate. The transcendent interpretation of *dao* in early texts is certainly *compatible* with religious readings or the understanding of Daoist texts as religious, but does necessitate neither. Nor can "religious" *daojiao* understandings influence mystical or transcendent readings of early texts, absent an acceptance of a distinction between religious and secular thought.

Transcendence, mysticism, and techniques for development of the spirit such as meditation are not simply later relics of a "religious" Daoism distinct from the philosophical form of early texts. These can be found in early texts as well. Harold Roth argues that a number of the passages from early "Daoist"[69] texts such as *Laozi* and *Zhuangzi* contain explanations of and instructions for mystical forms of meditation or self-cultivation practice he refers to as "apophatic" meditation.[70] The first stage of this apophatic practice, according to Roth, is the undermining or elimination of reliance on the senses. Roth points to chapters 12, 52, and 56 of the *Laozi* as demonstration of this. We might also look to the discussion between Confucius and Yan Hui in chapter 4 of the *Zhuangzi*. This kind of meditative practice aimed at moving the mind away from the senses can help to focus attention as well as to eliminate desires, according to Roth.

This is reminiscent of similar practices in Buddhist and Brahmanist traditions, with much the same aims. An additional aim of Daoist forms of meditation that we do not find in these other traditions, however, is that retention of *qi* 氣 (vital energy) is fostered by mental disconnection from sense perception. *Qi*, as a necessary component of life, is responsible for one's vitality and effectiveness in general. When *qi* is reduced, one's health, general ability, and effectiveness are reduced.

A result of this meditation is that one "obtains the empty *dao*" (*de xu dao* 得虛道), according to the *Xinshushang* chapter of the *Guanzi*.[71] Only the developed person, understood here in terms of the sage (*sheng ren* 聖人), obtains *dao*. A similar claim about emptiness and *dao* is made in *Zhuangzi* chapter 4, in the discussion between Confucius and Yan Hui. *Dao* and *xu* (emptiness) are characterized as similar and brought together in both of these passages. *Dao* appears at least in part as a kind of "nothingness" or non-being. Another passage from *Xinshushang* describes *dao* as empty and silent:

天之道虛，地之道靜，虛則不屈，靜則不變，不變則無過，故曰不伐。

The dao of tian is empty, the dao of earth is silent. Empty, and thus it does not bend—silent, and thus it does not change. It does not change, and thus it is without transgression. For this reason it is said that it does not harm.[72]

The emptiness spoken of here and in *Zhuangzi* chapter 4 associated with *Dao* is generally also understood as only possible to obtain when one undermines or eliminates the "self" or the discriminating mind. The text shows us a clear version of this, in the discussion of "fasting of the mind."

仲尼曰：「齋，吾將語若！有而為之，其易邪？易之者，皞天不宜。」顏回曰：「回之家貧，唯不飲酒、不茹葷者數月矣。若此，則可以為齋乎？」曰：「是祭祀之齋，非心齋也。」回曰：「敢問心齋。」仲尼曰：「若一志，无聽之以耳而聽之以心，无聽之以心而聽之以氣。聽止於耳，心止於符。氣也者，虛而待物者也。唯道集虛。虛者，心齋也。」

Confucius said: "Fasting—I will tell you about it! To have an idea and then enact it, is this easy? Glorious *tian* does not approve of it." Yan Hui replied: "My family is so poor that we can't afford to drink wine, and we go for months without rich vegetables or meat! Given that this is the case, how could I possibly fast?" Confucius said: "But that is the fasting of ritual sacrifices, not the fasting of the mind." Yan Hui asked: "might I ask—what is this fasting of the mind?" Confucius said: "Having a unified will, don't listen with the ears but listen with the mind. Don't listen with the mind but listen with *qi*. Hearing stops at the ear; the mind stops at its signs. Those who use *qi*—they remain empty and wait on things (*wu*). Only *dao* gathers together in emptiness. This emptiness is the fasting of the mind."[73]

Directly after this explanation of "fasting of the mind," Yan Hui says that he can now enter a state in which there is no more self, no more Yan Hui—that there has indeed never *begun* to be a Yan Hui (*wei shi you hui ye* 未始有回也). The connection here between emptiness and the *dao* is reminiscent of the *Guanzi* passages discussed above. *Dao* collects emptiness, according to the text, and it is *qi*, rather than the senses, that is able to be empty, thus like the *dao* itself, and wait on things (*dai wu*). The "fasting of the mind" discussed here leads to this emptiness. This "fasting" is likely connected to the apophatic meditation practices discussed by Roth.

Identifying *dao* with emptiness and recommending emptying of the self, through processes such as "fasting of the mind" or the *zuo wang* 坐忘 (sitting and forgetting) of *Zhuangzi* chapter 6, suggests that when the practitioner attains this state of emptiness, relying only on *qi* (as in the above passage), he or she attains a kind of unity with *dao* itself, allowing the practitioner's actions to be like (or literally *be*) the actions of *dao* itself. The empty, nonbeing, silent quality of the *dao* makes it the case that *dao*'s actions are very different than the actions of persons or things (*wu*) in the world. Numerous passages from early "Daoist" texts, however, explain that *dao*, even in its characterization of non-being, has an irresistible effective power. The very title of *Daodejing* suggests as much—the potency (*de*) that comes from the *dao*. The various discussions in that text of the efficacy of "non-action" (*wu wei*) attest to the potency of this empty source. According to chapter 48, the person who has cultivated the emptiness of *dao* gains an unstoppable potency, itself characterized by non-action. "They do nothing, yet there is nothing undone" (*wu wei er wu bu wei* 無為而無不為).[74]

Given that this non-action associated with the creative activity of *dao* is what plays the agentive role in the case of the most effective action, which comes with the merging of self with *dao* (or alternatively the *dissolution* of self in *dao*), there must be a key connection between *dao* and the *tian li* that other passages of the *Zhuangzi* enjoin the individual to follow. Following *tian li* and elimination of the self both issue in effective action, according to numerous passages of the text. It is plausible that these are not two distinct methods of achieving effective action, as each is explained in terms that captures the other. Thus, the one who engages in fasting of the mind "waits on things (*wu*)," allowing the natural activities and dispositions of objects to guide action. "Things" (*wu*), as seen in the *Tiandi* passage discussed above, is understood in some places as playing a role in the generation of *li* (*wu cheng sheng li* 物成生理—"things being completed, *li* is generated"). The "waiting on things" of chapter 2, given this and additional connections, is, then, most plausibly understood as an appeal to following *tian li*, something we find in numerous places in the *Zhuangzi* and elsewhere.

The relationship between the transcendent *dao* and *tian li* in at least parts of the *Zhuangzi* and related texts, then, is if not one of identity then one of coextension. The same activity enables one to follow *tian li* and merge with *dao*. This activity, according to the passages discussed here, involves the elimination of at least some aspects of the person we often see as necessary to the self. It is in part for this reason, we think, that we find a Zhuangist rejection of traditional conceptions of personhood in numerous parts of the *Zhuangzi*, particularly chapter 4.[75]

The ability of humans through certain kinds of self-cultivation (or negation) to follow the *tian li* and/or merge with *dao* is discussed by Michael Puett, who reads a number of texts of the early Chinese tradition as offering self-cultivation techniques through which humans might become gods or spirits with the robust efficacy over events in the world this suggests. Puett writes of the *Jingshen* chapter of the early Han text *Huainanzi*,[76] which considers a human role in the construction of the cosmos:[77]

> Why would the authors of the *Huainanzi* passage utilize such loaded terms to characterize the actions of the spirits before the emergence of the cosmos? Why do spirits have to align the cosmos before it is spontaneously formed? The answer… has little to do with early Chinese assumptions about the cosmos. […] The authors of the chapter discuss programs of self-cultivation that enable the adept to become a spirit. Spirits first aligned and oriented the cosmos, and humans can then become spirits and exercise control of the cosmos as well.[78]

This transformation of the human to the spiritlike or godlike Puett discusses is linked to the practices of "Daoist" texts such as the *Zhuangzi*. Indeed, the *Jingshen* chapter of *Huainanzi* was connected to the Daoist movement behind the Yellow Turban rebellion at the end of the Eastern Han. Insofar as texts such as the *Huainanzi* proclaim the human ability to attain a spiritlike state through cultivation of activity corresponding to *dao* or to *tian li*, they appeal to a transcendent source not identifiable fully with nature as such, but grounding nature and ultimately enabling its operation.

Conclusion

In this chapter, we have argued that the patterns or propensities (*li* 理) associated with *tian* or *dao* (depending on text and tradition) demonstrate a view of transcendence in numerous early Chinese texts. The changing meaning of *li* over time and across texts has been discussed by a number of scholars,[79] but the ways in which these various senses of *li* are linked to transcendence has not until now been extensively considered. The association of *li* with both *tian* and *dao* in different texts, as well as its seeming ontological priority over things (a view taken up later in Chinese history by neo-Confucians such as Zhu Xi and Wang Yangming[80]), is highly suggestive of a transcendent source of *li*. Its close connection to the concept of *tian*, which we have shown above and in previous chapters was understood as transcendent by a number of early Chinese thinkers, as well as its connection to *dao*, demonstrates the ways in which *li* can be better understood by using a framework of transcendence. In the following chapters, our discussion shifts more fully to consideration of the concept of *dao* in early Chinese texts.

8

Changing without Change: *Dao* and Causation in Early Daoism

Introduction and Some Key Prolegomena

In this chapter, we complete the turn from analyses of non-naturalism and transcendence in early Chinese thought that focus on *tian*, to analyses focused on the central concept of *dao*. Our goal is to assess whether or not *dao* should be interpreted in naturalistic terms. As with our preceding studies of *tian*, we find that attempting to speak for "the" Chinese view of *dao* is, in general, a difficult proposition. Given the diversity of texts and opinions on *dao* in early China, not to mention the difficulty of defining the "original meaning" of texts such as the *Daodejing* (hereafter, *DDJ*), it is best to limit the scope of one's analysis and claims regarding the naturalism of *dao*. In this chapter, then, we assess whether *dao* seems to be a naturalistic conception in the *DDJ* and other early Daoist texts drawing upon themes in the *DDJ*.

Specifically, we approach the concept of *dao* in this chapter via an analysis of the ways in which *dao* is and is not immutable in the view of early Daoists. This theme is appropriate for two reasons. First, because change and causation are key aspects of *dao*-theory in the *DDJ* and other texts inspired by the *DDJ*. Second, because immutability is a classical feature of divine transcendence in Abrahamic theologies. Thus, the way early Chinese thinkers articulated *dao* vis-à-vis change is likely to furnish excellent grounds for interpreting whether or not these thinkers mean to attribute some form of transcendence to *dao*.

Before turning to our analysis and providing the particulars of our assessment, we should first deal with an aspect of our analysis that requires adequate explanation. As we have noted, immutability is a classical attribute of God in Abrahamic traditions, and therefore our comparison of *dao* vis-à-vis change would seem to presuppose our assumption that *dao* is or can be read in a theistic or divinized sense. Without qualifying our reasons for attempting such a reading of *dao*-change, one might justly charge us with begging the question by presupposing a non-naturalist account of *dao* in our assessment of the concept precisely on naturalist–non-naturalist grounds.

In fact, we readily acknowledge there is little evidence that *dao* functioned as a theistic or deistic concept in early China, particularly if one means by this a personal god. In terms of the root concepts at play, then, we find it inappropriate to prima facie equate *dao* with "God" as G. G. Alexander suggests in describing the *DDJ* as "thoughts on the nature and manifestations of God."[1] However, at the same time, it is notable that even Alexander did not *simply* equate *dao* with God. Rather, Alexander explained *dao* to mean God in the following specific ways: "the great everlasting infinite First Cause from whom all things in heaven and earth proceed."[2]

One can fairly say, we think, that Alexander erred in conceptually equating *dao* with God, yet also note that he struck at something both appropriate and compelling. Namely, there simply are several aspects of how God is understood—particularly in the Abrahamic traditions—that resonate with how Daoists understand *dao*, especially those aspects concerning *dao* as generative principle of the world. For example, in the *Hanfeizi*, we find *dao* defined as follows: "the beginning of the myriad things and the principle that regulates truth and falsehood."[3] These claims resonate with classical Christian theism, for example, that understands God not only as the subsistent act of Being in all things participate but also as the basis of all moral law (both as the ultimate Good and as the giver of divine and natural law that provides moral guidance for human beings). This should not diminish the importance of key differences between *dao* and God, of course. Unlike God, *dao* does not "speak" the world into existence (see Genesis 1:3–31 or Quran 41:11), issue revealed truth, or have a creative agency or will in its generative capacities.

Now, one might argue that precisely what ultimately distinguishes *dao* from theistic analogues is that Daoists in particular see *dao* as a thoroughly non-transcendental principle of generation. In other words, it may be that the differences between *dao* and God just mentioned are consequences of a fundamental disagreement about the generative principle of the world being transcendent. Perhaps this is so, but we would like to usher a caution about too hastily coming to such a conclusion.

If we were to attempt to account for *dao* in theistic terms, the best we would do would likely be to describe it as a kind of panentheistic principle, as others have already done.[4] This suggestion helpfully reveals the complications of attempting to ask whether something like *dao* is transcendent. In the Western philosophical tradition, "panentheism" often carries a presupposed theological judgment. Christian theologians, for example, have criticized panentheistic conceptions of God precisely on the problem of how they fail to account for divine transcendence, and likewise many Western panentheistic concepts arise out of frustration with the conception of transcendence in the Christian framework.[5] And this, in turn, depends upon the concrete ways in which transcendence is understood at a given time.

The most famous and influential defenses of panentheism (or analogues to it) in modern Western though arise out of the contrastive framework of transcendence we describe in Chapter 2. This, then, gives rise to an ironic situation. Those who deny the *dao* is transcendent do so on the basis of an a priori theological judgment about what counts as an adequate account of divine transcendence. One should add to this fact that Western philosophy inherently depends upon the Christian account of revelation and divine transcendence to define what "counts" as transcendence and what does not. Therefore, if one says the *dao* is not transcendent, what this means is that the *dao* is not transcendent in ways that adequately describe the divine as understood and described in Christian (or Jewish or Muslim) scriptures. We would like to here suggest this is an inappropriate attribution because the Christian account of transcendence is the dominant one in the West, but it need not be the only possible version of transcendence. Indeed, theologians can argue the Abrahamic conception of transcendence is superior to a panentheistic mode, but more often than not, this will be precisely a *theological* argument attempting to describe God as He is.

In short, to presuppose a priori that the *dao* is utterly absent of transcendence is to rashly make a theological judgment about the *dao*—that is an inadequate theistic concept—without a properly theological analysis that assesses the question. Philosophically, it seems fairer to hold that the *dao* might provide a different account of transcendence. We argue that if we allow for the possibility that *dao* functions in transcendent ways not limited to a contrastive theory of transcendence, it is then clear that there are several aspects of *dao* that do indeed function in transcendent ways. This and the following chapters are attempts to articulate these aspects, beginning with the theme of immutability.

Aquinas on Divine Immutability

Classical Christian thought—as opposed to modern process or neoclassical thought—holds that the divine nature is unchanging or immutable.[6] Modern theologians who have articulated a viewpoint of the divine nature that involves change within God are often charged with diluting divine transcendence. This points to the fact that in Western theology at least, the immutability of God is a classical and important doctrinal anchor in the understanding of God as "transcendent." But what exactly is meant by holding that God is immutable and, therefore, transcendent? Most modern critics of immutability hold that there is a weakness in traditional theism to clarify how God could genuinely respond to the world if the divine nature was truly immutable.[7] For neoclassical philosophy, for example, divine immutability signals a kind of contrastive account of transcendence in which God is set over against the world, rather than a kind of genuine interrelationship or interdependence between God and the world.[8] Crucially, however, as we discussed in Chapter 2, classical theism in the Christian tradition did not presuppose such contrastive theories of transcendence as that which marks modern Western philosophy and theology. Therefore, thinkers such as Augustine of Hippo and Aquinas held to divine immutability as a perfection of God that did not presuppose a contrastive relationship with the world.

Consequently, before turning to inquire whether Daoist texts hold some account of the transcendent *dao* vis-à-vis change, it is helpful to revisit what immutability means about divine transcendence in the Christian tradition (through which the categories of transcendence and immutability are primarily mediated to modern philosophy). For this purpose, we will first revisit Aquinas's theology. The choice is felicitous, for we argue Aquinas allows us to make a helpful distinction within the immutability claim. For him, we contend, to say God is immutable means holding two subordinate positions: 1) that God is not subject to change via extrinsic causes and 2) God is not subject to intrinsic change, that is, God does not cause himself to change. This distinction will be important in our analysis of Daoist texts, since we hold that early Daoists seem to hold that *dao* is immutable in the sense of 1, but not in the sense of 2.

At its simplest, the claim that the divine nature is immutable is to assert that God does not change or undergo *mutare*. For Aquinas, who was heavily influenced by Aristotelian physics, *mutare* was, generally speaking, an intrinsic feature of the created order. God, on the other hand, is above this drama of change and transformation and always is as He has been. If this were all there was to the doctrine of divine immutability and transcendence within it, there would be little to see as transcendent in early Daoism. For these authors, as we will show, the *dao* is itself change; one might say *dao* is defined precisely as *mutare*. Thus, on its face, it seems early Daoists' accounts of *dao* bear no resemblance to accounts of divine immutability. Upon a more sophisticated reading, however, there are multiple aspects of divine immutability needing distinction that open up the possibility that Daoism is not quite so opposed to immutable transcendence as one might assume.

For the sake of this chapter, we will limit our analysis here to Aquinas's position on divine immutability as it appears in the *Summa theologiae*.[9] In the *ST*, Aquinas poses the question of divine immutability in terms of whether God is "in anyway changeable" (*est Deum aliquo modo mutari*). His negative answer to this question draws upon other predicates of the divine nature he discussed in preceding questions and articles. Aquinas provides two types of reasons why God cannot change in anyway. First are three "intrinsic" reasons: because God is pure act, because God is simple (that is not composed of parts, but is His act of being), and because of God's infinite nature.

It is difficult to grasp the meaning of these intrinsic reasons for divine immutability outside of the technical framework of act-potency Aquinas takes from Aristotle.[10] When Aquinas says that God cannot change because He is pure act, this is for Aquinas a really apophatic claim that God is not subjective to passive potency.[11] Following the terms of Aristotelian physics, Aquinas considers change marking creaturely life in terms of the reduction from potency to act, that is, the transition from being or having a property in potentiality to the actual being or possession of it. To make an analogy from modern physics, we can look to the fact that the ball at the top of the stairs has the potential to begin to roll down the stairs, pick up speed, and ruin the cat's day. Now, it is clear that it is only when something (or someone, more likely) pushes it, and the ball begins to move that it has kinetic energy. But for now we will not focus as much on the fact that change must be caused by something, and instead simply note that mutation concerns this shift from a state of "could be" to "is." To deny such potency is to say that there is no transition in God from one state of what God could be to a state in which God has fulfilled his possibility. God cannot be reduced from potency to act, but must always be in act.

To appreciate why this is so, one must see that Aquinas would hold that creaturely life is constantly beset by processes of reducing potencies to act, that is, change. Some changes are necessary due to limitations of our bodies, and some involve willing the change we undergo (i.e., I cannot play baseball and sit on the couch simultaneously) or our wills (e.g., I am sitting on the couch now, but desire to play baseball later). Beyond such changes, the entire course of human life and other creatures is constantly best by *mutare*. As infants, we come into the world in a great deal of potency: we do not yet speak meaningful words, our bones have not fully conjoined, and we have no concepts of caring for others, empathy, etc. As we age we grow taller, our vocal chords change, we begin to form sounds dictated by our native language, and we develop emotional intelligence as well as the use of reason. In short, we change as a means of enacting what humans typically do. By the same stroke, we experience change as decay, as in diseases that remove health from us. We are constantly changing, growing, and/ or decaying.

For Aquinas, the *mutare* of creation can also be expressed in ontological terms. Aquinas holds that there is a distinction in all created things between our concrete existence and our act of being (called the real distinction in being). Even if one assumes Aristotle's thesis on the eternality of matter (which Aquinas doesn't for theological reasons, but holds it is not erroneous on philosophical grounds per se), I have not always existed in the form I am now, as a man. Therefore, my concrete existence as a man was precipitated by a change that caused my substantial form to be.[12] For this reason, all created life—which does not give rise to itself—is a result of a specific instance of *mutare* that Aquinas calls generation or, when God is the subject of generation of such life, creation.

In speaking of God as immutable, Aquinas therefore means a number of things. For one, it means that God is not like creatures in the sense that He does not experience the distinction between being and existence—rather, God is Himself a subsistent being who was not caused to be via an act of generation.[13] In the same vein, Aquinas means to claim that the kind of potency or potentiality marking created life does not obtain in God: God is not subject to the growth or decay of *mutare* because He already enacts what He is in perpetuity. For there are no faculties in God that can become more perfect than they already are, nor any capacities God has that can decay or diminish.

Admittedly, Aquinas is primarily concerned with these intrinsic definitions of immutability, whereby he argues that the divine nature cannot be changed because it already is what it can ever be and thus protects the perfection of the divine nature. Yet the intrinsic kinds of immutability are also tied to an extrinsic conception, often described as the doctrine of divine impassibility. Impassibility is often translated as "the inability to suffer"; taken in an emotional sense, it more precisely means the inability to be the patient or object of the actions of another agent.[14] In Aquinas's terminology, the transformation seen in the reduction of potency to act is a caused motion. For X to be reduced from potency to act, some cause Y must act upon X to bring about this change. And this means that X must "suffer" or receive the action of cause Y in order to move from potency to act.

Some natural examples that Aquinas often draws upon are helpful in illustrating his point. How does the iron become shaped into a sword? It is thrown in the fire, taking on the properties of heat, therefore becoming malleable. For human beings, we become language users because we hear our parents speak it and they and others speak to us. We go outside and the sun's rays make our skin turn red. We become able to grow taller (and perhaps wider) because we eat nutrients that fuel our natural processes. All of these changes are caused in that something besides ourselves brings them about, or perhaps some principle within us beyond our control brings them about.

For Aquinas, God could not possibly change in this way. If God could become an object or patient of change—that is, be reduced from potency to act by another cause that moves God in this way—then God could not be God. For then God would be put in motion or caused to change by something that precedes Him as a cause, and thus He would not be God, but rather the causing thing would be. Thus, God's intrinsic and extrinsic immutability coincide, because God cannot *suffer* change caused by something outside of Him. To put it more specifically in terms Aquinas offers, if God were not impassible, then God's causing agency that brings the world from potency to act would not be His own, but rather He would be participating in a greater or more perfect cause.[15]

Thus, Aquinas provides two ways of understanding divine immutability: one way is based on the "intrinsic" perfections of God, such as His being pure act, which do not allow change to be a property of the divine nature.[16] The other concerns an extrinsic kind of mutability, holding that nothing can relate to God in such a way as to cause Him to change. Many interpreters have overlooked this distinction in Aquinas's thought because for him, they are cooperating claims. In part, this is because Aquinas is concerned with the God of Christian revelation, who is a personal God and not an impersonal transcendent principle. Hence, Aquinas denies that God can grow more perfect in intellect, experience emotions (the passions), or have an end outside himself. Notice that each of these intrinsic changes would be caused by extrinsic causes, and thus God's perfection for Aquinas is intimately connected with his being unable to be moved by another agent.

For our purposes here, we stress that although Aquinas holds these claims together, it is not necessary to hold both in order to affirm transcendence per se. Independently, either claim suggests a kind of transcendence on the part of the nature of whom these claims are predicated. In other words, early Daoists do not need to claim both the intrinsic and extrinsic immutability of *dao* in order for a scholar to judge their account of *dao* to be genuinely transcendent in some manner.

Indeed, in the remainder of this chapter, we do not claim that early Daoists hold with an intrinsic account of the *dao* as immutable. That is, early Daoists do see the *Dao* as mutable inasmuch as the *Dao* is perpetual change; we might say the "inner life" of the *Dao* is characterized by *mutare*. However, we think early Daoists seem to agree with Aquinas's extrinsic view of immutability. That is, these texts conceive of the *dao* as not subject to or caused to change by anything else. Rather, the *dao* causes change and is not caused to change. And in this way, the *dao* has transcendent characteristics. Namely, the *dao* is "above" or "beyond"—or at least distinct from the natural world—inasmuch as natural change is caused by the *dao*, but *dao*-change is not caused by the natural world.

Change and Changelessness of the Dao

In this part of the chapter, we will analyze the theme of *dao* vis-à-vis immutability in three texts of the early Daoist tradition: the *Daodejing* (*DDJ*), the *Heshanggong Laozi*, and *Huainanzi*. We will also draw upon the *Liezi*, which purports to be an early text, but in its current form is often assumed to be of a much later date.[17] In this context, we are reading these texts as an extended and ongoing dialogue over the course of several centuries about *dao* and change, with the *DDJ* having a justifiable place of prominence. Briefly, we should note that we have selected to draw upon the *Heshanggong* commentary to the *DDJ* more often than that of Wang Bi. While the latter is more influential historically, the former seems to us more helpful for understanding how the *DDJ* was read in the early Chinese context.[18] In a different way, the *Liezi* is valuable as a later text for showing the persistence of themes concerning *dao*-change across Daoist tradition.

Our goal here is to delineate how these texts articulate a conception of *dao* as transcendent in terms of extrinsic change. We argue *dao* is described as transcendent in terms of extrinsic change in three ways. First, these texts (especially commentaries to the *DDJ*) develop a terminological framework to distinguish between what we have called intrinsic and extrinsic change, and deny the latter applies to *dao*. Second, we show that these texts see *dao* as the root to which all things return through change, while the *dao* itself is not subject to this type of change. Third, we show that in early Daoist cosmogony, *dao* is seen to cause the changes occurring through *yin* and *yang* movement, whereas *dao* is not caused to change by *yin* and *yang*.

Therefore, our analyses focus on what Bryan W. Van Norden has called "causal transcendence" rather than what he terms "normative transcendence," that is, how the *Dao* functions as an exemplar for the human sage.[19] The latter is worthy of analysis, of course, but it is easier to square normative transcendence with naturalist presuppositions. In such a reading, *dao* can be seen as metaphorically transcendent as a moral archetype of naturalness or spontaneity, but not necessarily genuinely transcendent in ways naturalism uses the term. Thus, by focusing on causal transcendence themes in these texts, we can better show the presence of "genuine" transcendence in them.

The first thing we stress in our analysis is that, again, we are making a very specific claim about these texts vis-à-vis the immutability of *dao*. We do not argue that early Daoism sees *dao* as immutable in terms of intrinsic change. This is evident from the textual tradition. On the one hand, there is a tension in the Daoist tradition about the *dao* in relationship to the world of form (*xing* 形). As the *DDJ* puts it, the *dao* is "nothing" (*wu*), formless, and nameless, whereas the world is "something" (*you*), formal, and comes from that which can be named (i.e., *tian* and earth). Importantly, Daoist texts tend to assert a distinction in kind between the generative agency of the *dao* and that of *tian* and earth—the *dao* is a more remote cause of things that begin the cosmological processes, and *tian* and earth are more proximate causes that directly produce the myriad things. Hence, the *dao* is on this view very much unlike the world of form.

At the same time, *dao* is also the great principle of fecundity and life present in all things. In the view of early Daoists, *dao* is empty and formless precisely because it can or does fill all the diverse forms of the myriad things. The *dao* is in perpetual use (*yong*) as all things exist, and so it cannot be exhausted. In this sense, the *Dao* is "nothing" because it is "everything": it is without definition and distinction because it pervades all categories and realities. And thus, one can say that *dao* causes things to be in an immanent fashion, being present in and through their existence.

On this view of *dao* in which it pervades all, fills all, and is constantly "being employed," it follows necessarily that *dao* is in a state of perpetual intrinsic change. An

Aristotelian or Thomist might say that *dao* must be in a state of perfect potentiality, otherwise *dao* would simply be one thing among others and not the principle of all things. If it were not in a persistent state of change, *dao* would have a self (*zi*) and could not exemplify the purity of selfless action (*wuwei*). Consequently, *dao* is the primal model of spontaneity or naturalness because it is change in itself.

As a concrete example, one sees this conception of *dao* at work in the "mysterious feminine" (*xuan pin* 玄牝) concept from *DDJ* 6. This passage uses the mysterious feminine to articulate *dao* as a principle of perpetual fecundity, as the "gateway" (*men* 門) through which all things come into being, as the "root" (*gen* 根) of *Tian* and earth.[20] Whereas *Tian* and earth are considered the nameable "mother" of all things, *dao* is cloaked in mystery as the principle of fecundity that nevertheless continues to act in and through all existing things. And so *dao* is subject to intrinsic change, that is, it "moves itself" in Aristotelian terms. Consequently, *dao* is not immutable in terms of pure act, which we saw to be the case with the Christian God in the view of Aquinas.

However, early Daoist texts do not hold the *dao* is completely, utterly mutable. These texts distinguish—though not systematically, to be true—between intrinsic mutability (or *dao*-change), which they affirm, and extrinsic mutability (the changed *dao*), which they do not. *DDJ* 25 features the most important instance of distinguishing these kinds of change, as well as the consequent suggestion that *dao* is extrinsically immutable. This passage tells of a primordial age (before the production of *tian* and earth) in which things were possessed in "confused completeness." In describing this primordial state, the text says it is "silent and void, it has its position for itself and does not change."[21] When the *DDJ* says *dao* does not change, it uses the phrase *bu gai* 不改.

Notably, significant scholars have understood this passage as a denial of mutability in some respect on the part of *dao*. For example, Chen Guying argues the negation of *gai* "describes the absoluteness and eternal nature of the Tao. It is in perpetual motion and is the source of all change in the universe, but itself does not change."[22] But it is also helpful to walk through why such a reading is compelling and appropriate. In this light, one may fruitfully ask what exactly is the referent of *bu gai* in *DDJ* 25? If, as seems clear from context and according to the commentarial tradition, *dao* is the mysterious subject of the chapter's opening lines, it would seem there are two options: either *bu gai* refers to *dao* as such or it is modifying the "solitary position" (*du li* 獨立) of *dao*.

If it is the latter, then it might be the case that *bu gai* is not taken as a predicate of *dao* at all, merely its "position." It would be possible, though difficult, to take the "solitary position" of *dao* as unchanging in ways that would not really predicate a sort of substantial immutability of *dao* itself. For example, taking the metaphor of the empty center in *DDJ* 11, one might take the "position" of the *dao* in the negative center of all things, and that *dao* is *bu gai* in respect of never failing to be in that central position. However, the weaknesses of such an interpretation are readily apparent. For if the *dao* is the empty center that never shifts from that position, this would seem to also suggest something substantial about *dao* vis-à-vis immutability. The linguistic metaphor of an "unchanging position" soon gives way to needing to discern on what basis the metaphor is possible and whether the metaphor turns out to be something descriptive of *dao* itself, even if indirectly.

For our purposes, we will merely note that the early *DDJ* commentaries did not shy away from making a substantial reading of *bu gai* in *DDJ* 25. Regarding the "solitary position" of the *dao*, the *Heshanggong* commentary treats this as meaning "the *dao* has no companion or complement."[23] Wang Bi offers a similar interpretation that "the *dao* is not the companion of any creature."[24] In this sense, both commentaries take the "solitary position" of *dao* as a description of the uniqueness of *dao* as generative principle, since the context of the passage is clearly cosmogonic or protological.

Moreover, both Wang Bi and the *Heshanggong* commentary take *bu gai* to be a distinctive rather than subordinate claim to the solitary position. In taking *bu gai* this way, both *Heshanggong* and Wang Bi utilize a more technical (though far from "systematic") terminology. This is necessary because, as both commentators knew, the *DDJ* has a robust account of *dao* as subject to intrinsic change. Therefore, in what sense can it be "without change" as a consistent description of *dao*? One might argue, of course, that the *DDJ* does not mean to be consistent about *dao*. Perhaps, but both of these early commentaries assume there must be some consistency in *dao* description.

Both the *Heshanggong* and Wang Bi offer different versions of the following essential claim: *dao* is the sole principle of change that acts through constant change (*hua* 化) but it does so in immutable perpetuity, and thus the *dao* suffers no alteration (*gai* 改). Specifically, *Heshanggong* interprets *DDJ* 25 as meaning that *dao* "is the unaltering one whose changes are perpetual (*bu gai zhe hua you chang* 不改者化有常) ... the *dao* pervades and travels through *Tian* and earth, and there is nothing it fails to enter."[25] Wang Bi has it as meaning "*dao* constantly returns and changes, as beginning and end, but without losing its perpetuity (*bu shi qi chang* 不失其常), and thus it is said to be 'without alteration' (*bu gai*)."[26]

In these comments on *DDJ* 25, then, *hua* and *gai* take on the task of referring to different conceptions of change. Inasmuch as *hua* refers to the transformations of things and transformation as a property of something, *dao* is said to be *hua*. But as the same time, the *dao* does not develop, grow, or become something else than this principle and agent of *hua*. Therefore, its intrinsic character of *hua* is immutable, and it is not subject to *gai* change in anyway.

As our analysis moves forward in this chapter, we argue that one way of appropriately mapping the *hua/gai* distinction is the difference between intrinsic and extrinsic change. However, at this stage, we should be clear that neither the *DDJ* nor the commentaries we have cited develop this distinction enough to fully integrate it into the intrinsic–extrinsic distinction we are proposing. Primarily, this is because the term *gai* is a *hapax legomenon* in the received text of the *DDJ* and does not appear at all in the *Guodian* versions (including the *Taiyi Sheng Shui*, which Sarah Allan has argued is an early cosmological appendix to the *DDJ* by another author).[27] On the other hand, *hua* appears more often. *DDJ* 57 associates *hua* with *wuwei* action, that is, the kind of natural changes that will occur when one harmonizes with the *dao*.[28] In this light, *hua* seems to mean *dao*-change either in the *dao* itself or when things morally participate in *dao* to allow *dao*-change.

From this context, we can surmise that *gai* can mean deviation from *dao*-change and perhaps associate it as a kind of change stemming from "intentioned action" rather than *wuwei*. If this is accurate, then *gai* can—albeit indirectly—suggest extrinsic change. For when we act for something with intentions, we act with desires for that thing: hence the Daoist understanding of *wuwei* as "desireless" activity.[29] Inasmuch as these desires are *qing* 情, the Daoist tradition would recognize that they are akin to what Western tradition describes as the *passiones*, namely that they are bodily responses to external stimuli. In this sense, if *gai* implies at least in one meaning change or deviation based in emotional desire, then *gai* involves extrinsic causation, that is, being moved by a thing in such a way as to alter my course of life to pursue it.

In this way, saying *dao* is *bu gai* is to associate *dao* with extrinsic immutability, indeed an impassibility in the sense of not being swayed or altered by other things or better, and moreover, no particular desires for particular things. And this way of speaking is, we should note, perfectly compatible with explicit *dao* descriptions in these texts. In the *DDJ* in particular, *dao* is undoubtedly seen as being free from the need or desire to strategize so as to obtain particular ends. It is *hua* without desire or plans to accomplish anything—it just is change.[30] Because *dao* is without desire for anything outside of *hua*-change, it is completely unaffected by other things—nothing else can act upon the *dao* to manipulate its activity or have it alter its course through intercessory prayer, for example. The *dao* is, in an extrinsic sense, immutable or even impassible if one prefers.

Notably, this observation suggests that the popular opinion that *dao* concerns "becoming" *rather than* "being" is an inaccurate comparison meant to establish foils between China and Western thought. In one sense, the *dao* is in a constant state of "becoming" if we mean by this *hua*-change. But in an equally important sense, the *dao* is not at all becoming. For the *dao* is not less *hua*-change at one point, and later more *hua*-change, nor is its *hua*-change dependent upon what the myriad creatures do. In this sense the *dao* is as "static" as any of the "timeless" and "essential" categories in Western thought that are subject to popular derision in postmodernity.

As our analysis proceeds, we emphasize that one of the clearest ways the immutability of *dao* is present in early Daoist discourse regards cosmogony. While Daoist thought does, as we show above, hold to the intrinsic mutability of *dao* as inherent in its generative causing all things to be, this also testifies to a fundamental distinction between *dao* and things. Namely, *dao*-change generates the world, but worldly change does not generate *dao*. This cosmogonic or protological framework is, we think, ultimately the most appropriate context in which to read the *hua-gai* distinction we describe above. That is, *dao*'s extrinsic mutability (*bu gai*) follows upon the Daoist account of *dao* as generative cause (through *hua*-change).

Briefly, it is noteworthy that this trajectory can be found elsewhere in the early Daoist tradition. The *Huainanzi* speaks similarly about *dao* causing things to be in a way fundamentally distinct from the myriad things. In *Huainanzi* chapter 1, we find a discussion of the "diffusion of the One" that generates *tian* and earth. The One pervades *tian* and earth, and disperses into becoming the myriad things, which the text says pass through it as a "portal."[31] This is the intrinsic mutability of *dao* as *hua*-change. This is because the One here is not simply the cause of the Many, but in a sense the "becoming" of the Many, truly pervading and existing through these things.

However, at the same time, one should note the One is diffused and dispersed, and *not* the reverse. Nothing is added to the One, and nothing is taken away. Rather, the One causes and becomes the Many in a way fundamentally different from the Many, who cannot cause or become the One through diffusion or dispersion. In short, if *dao* is the One in this passage of the *Huainanzi*, then it is immutable in an extrinsic way. The generative cause of *dao* only works in one direction—nothing generates *dao*.

It should be evident that this kind of extrinsic immutability of *dao* signifies a kind of transcendence.[32] Inasmuch as it cannot be affected by things, *dao* is "above the fray" and quite apart from the things it generates. Indeed, this is not merely a moral transcendence, but a substantial one. For *dao* generates things in a way that is completely unlike how things act on *dao*; in some sense, things cannot act on *dao* at all. For early Daoists, the sage strives to harmonize with *dao*-change to be sure, but this is simply cooperating with, following, and participating in it. The sage does not act *upon dao* to bring about a desideratum—rather he works to free himself from desire because *dao* will not be swayed or affected at all. Thus, even if *dao*-change is the intrinsic principle in all things, it is still (and even for this reason) transcendent in some respect in that it is beyond our capacity to affect, and ultimately understand.

Dao-Immutability and Decay

One of the most famous (perhaps infamous) preoccupations of the so-called "religious Daoism" was death and the possibility of extending life. Indeed, some scholars have argued this preoccupation is a primary marker of the fundamental difference between religious and philosophical Daoism, the latter of which accepted death as natural. For our purposes here, it is most important that both accounts of death point to the fact that Daoist texts wrestled at length with one of the brute facts of life: the phenomenal world is always in a state of growth and decay. In this section, we examine the theme of growth and decay in early Daoist cosmology and argue that this theme is useful for seeing how early Daoist texts describe *dao*'s immutability and transcendence in one regard. Concretely, we argue that early Daoist texts see *dao* as the principle of this growth and decay, but without undergoing this growth and decay itself. That is, unlike formal things, *dao* does not diminish or mature. Its cycle of change is, in this sense, constant and immutable, and radically different from the ways formal creatures exist in the world.

DDJ 40 states that "returning (*fan* 反) is the movement of *dao* and the fragility (*ruo* 弱) of *dao* is its utility."[33] *Heshanggong* interprets the first clause to mean the following: "as the root, *dao* is the source of all motion, for its movement produces the myriad things and when it ceases this movement, there is death."[34] *Heshanggong* thus most basically sees *dao* as the root upon which all activity returns inasmuch as it is activity. The notion of *dao*'s ceasing its movement (*bei* 背) is best interpreted as meaning when *dao* is no longer active in a thing, rather than meaning *dao* intends a withdrawal of life-giving action to things.

This interpretation by the *Heshanggong* holds much that is of interest to our analysis. First, there is the position that *dao* is the principle of generation and decay for all things. That the *DDJ* calls this movement "returning" suggests this is a result of the *dao*'s intrinsic mutability. That is, *dao* is constantly in *hua*-change motion in pervading all things that not only generates them but also moves them to decay.

Here we can benefit from a comparison to the classical Christian theological framework of creation as an *exitus-reditus*, a coming from and returning to God.[35] In Christian theology, God is the act of Being, through which all beings come into being. Yet God is also the Good and thus the proper end of all things, that is, that to which creation returns, like pilgrims coming home. However, in Christianity, God is seen as the cause of this movement of exit and return, and is present throughout the movement in existent things—yet God is not identified with the process of movement itself. It seems fair to say that the early Daoist tradition contrasts with Christianity when it sees *dao* not only as the principle from which things come and return but also as the immanent principle in the motion itself, that is, as perpetual *hua*-change that brings about generation and decay.

At the same time, however, the *Heshanggong* commentary suggests that *dao* as principle of generation and decay of all things is still distinct from these processes in significant ways. Of foremost importance is the fact that *dao* is the principle of all motion and activity. This suggests that all things that are generated out of *dao* participate in its motion and activity when they act. But the *Heshanggong* also suggests this participation is limited, or at least not identical to *dao*-activity. This is because the *Heshanggong* describes death in terms of the cessation of *dao* activity. It is not that *dao* itself has ceased to move and cause, but that an individual thing has ceased to participate in or enact *dao*-activity. Hence, the *dao*-activity that generates and underlies all things does not appear to be itself subject to the processes of growth and decay that *dao*-activity engenders in the myriad things.

Upon further inspection, the immutability of *dao* vis-à-vis growth and decay seems to be a natural corollary to the generative mutability of *dao* found in Daoist texts. Again in commentary on *DDJ* 40, the *Heshangong* interprets the "fragility" of *dao* as meaning it is "constantly in use" (*chang yong* 常用).[36] The "utility" or "employment" of *dao* functions in most early Daoist texts as a description of *dao* as the immanent principle that fills and pervades all things. Closely related to the notion of the "suppleness" (*rou* 柔) of *dao*, Daoist texts such as the *Heshanggong* use fragility to articulate how *dao* is always the principle of things and changing phenomena, and thus it is always "in use."[37]

Lying behind this conception of *dao* as employed in all things is that *dao* is not permanently defined, possessing clear boundaries and distinctions. In the preferred terminology of Daoist texts, it is in itself formless (*wu xing*).[38] On the contrary, *dao* is fluid, filling out spaces of things that are defined in and by material form and limits.[39] Hence, *dao*'s lack of formal definition is why it can be constantly used and this in turn renders *dao* capable of "persisting in perpetuity" (*gu neng chang jiu* 故能常久).[40]

On the one hand, the fragility means *dao* is essentially change in itself: it can be in all things (*you* 有) because it is nothing (*wu* 無).[41] As "nothing," *dao* is not identifiable as this or that, but is the change leading to and through which this or that persists. However, this also means that *dao* is not "a thing." *Dao* is not a *wu* 物 that has been brought into existence, will grow, consume, and eventually decay.[42] The *dao* does not need to pursue practices to extend its life or make itself harmonious with itself, but *dao* has no real "self." Whereas defined things are born, grow, and decay, *dao* is for all intents and purposes everlasting (as *jiu* 久 signifies lasting for a long period of time).

Admittedly, this reading of *dao* as a constant principle is not universal within Daoist interpretations. On the basis of a distinction between Huang-Lao and "pure" Daoist thought, one might even associate our interpretation with the "logical" order interpretation of the world that Randall Perenboom has argued is particularly characteristic of Huang-Lao texts.[43] But, we should stress, even if this is so, it does not undermine our main thesis in this book. For even if the Huang-Lao interpretation of the constancy of the *dao* is not universal to all so-called Daoist thinkers, it was still a genuine option and approach among some early Chinese thinkers. Hence, inasmuch as this interpretation entails transcendence, it demonstrates the presence of transcendence in some respect in early China.

Indeed, it is difficult to imagine how the constancy of *dao* as principle does not require *some* account of *dao* as transcendent. From the perspective of early Daoist texts, it seems evident that it must follow that *dao* is change, but it does not *experience* change the way formal things do. Specifically, as "nothing," *dao* can be the agent or subject of change, but not an object of change, otherwise it would also be subject to growth and decay, and thus not perpetually employed, but only employed within the limits of a particular thing or species of material being. And in this sense, the *Dao* transcends the type of change seen in the material world of nature, even as it is the ground and principle of this change.

This is a very important point. Even if we stress that in the Daoist perspective *dao* does pervade all as the principle of growth and decay, and is therefore immanent in all things as this principle, this does not remove the immutability and transcendence of *dao*. This is because inasmuch as it signifies this constant principle of intrinsic change that anchors processes of growth and decay, *dao* necessarily stands apart in some way from the things themselves that undergo this process. Indeed, the more immanent one makes *dao* as a principle of change, the more necessary it is to affirm *dao*'s transcendence in the same movement. For if *dao* is that principle of growth and decay in a given thing A, then there must be something apart from *dao* that is being acted upon or caused to change by *dao*. If that principle is immanent to thing A, then it must be distinguished from the parts of thing A that do undergo growth and decay, such as parts of the body. If the principle immanent to A that underlies A's growth and decay is not itself subject to growth and decay, but is constant, then it must be distinct from and thus transcend *in some respect* thing A.

One way to clearly see this kind of necessary link really at work in the Daoist tradition is the theme of elongating life. If *dao* is perpetual or long-lasting and humans are apparently not, how might we close the gap? If *dao* was considered a purely immanent principle of change that itself could be altered or changed by the human subject, then we would respond to this problem with strategies of alteration. That is, we would search for ways to isolate *dao* principle and change its properties.

Significantly, Daoist tradition does not presume that such actions are possible. Rather, from the *DDJ* on, the tradition enjoins practices that allow for a harmony with *dao*.[44] Consider the following passage from the *Huainanzi*: "Tranquility and calmness are that by which the nature is nourished. Harmony and vacuity are that by which Potency is nurtured. When what is external does not disturb what is internal, then our nature attains what is suitable to it."[45] Note here that nourishing one's nature is understood in terms of cultivating attitudes that the *DDJ* associates with *dao* itself, namely tranquility (*jing*) and vacuity (*xu*). We see here, then, the extension of Daoist thought, which holds that the key to flourishing is not in attempting to alter *dao*, but understand, harmonize, and imitate it. If one wishes to nourish one's nature, one must seek to follow the model of *dao*-activity. The implication we'd stress here is that this strategy is necessary precisely because *dao*-activity—which directs all life—cannot itself be altered or changed by human will or whim. It is, in this view, immutable, and something to be imitated rather than transformed.

This kind of spiritual practice approach is explicitly connected to the drama of life and death in the *Liezi*, wherein we can indirectly find the theme of the immutable mutability of the *dao*.[46] Broadly speaking, the *Liezi* exhorts the acceptance of death as the natural complement or end (*zhong* 終) of life. The text variously describes death as a state of rest (*xi* 息), a "return to the ultimate" (*fan qi ji* 反其極), or "humanity in the state of returning" (*gui ren* 歸人).[47] But the text also carefully associates the continual generation of life (*sheng* 生) with *tian*, in a typically Daoist fashion that restricts the theistic interpretation of *tian* favored by Confucians and Mohists.[48] In the *Liezi*, *tian* causes the change of life, and then other changes are brought about by earth, and the movements of *yin* and *yang*.

Effectively, then, the *Liezi* identifies *tian* and earth more immanently with the cycle of growth and decay that is inherent in the natural processes of the myriad things. Within this view of things, there is an implicit distinction between a) these processes of production and decay and b) *dao* that underlies them and explains these processes, but is ultimately not identical with them. This is because the "return" schema of the *Liezi* ultimately involves reference to *dao* as a principle distinct from the processes of returning itself: "that which is produced returns to the unproduced, and that which has form returns to what is without form."[49] All things that have been caused to be (produced) and that have been caused to have form have a root in that which is without these qualities. However, that which is not produced and without form is said to not have the unproduced or formless as its root. In other words, that which is not brought about through the generation of *tian* and that which has no form provided by earth or impacted by *yin* and *yang* has no root. Such an unproduced and formless entity—that is, *dao*—therefore returns to nothing: it simply is what it is.

We can conclude, then, that in the *Liezi*'s view *dao* is not produced and does not decay. It transcends these processes that are characteristic of material life because it is not caused in the same way the material world is caused, that is, by the "forming cause" (*xing*) of *tian*. This is the case even when the *Liezi* attributes death to *dao*. In the *Zhongni* chapter of the *Liezi*, the *dao* is described as a paradox of life and death. On the one hand, it is "without source and perpetually living" (*wu suo you er chang sheng* 无所由而常生), while yet it also "has a source and is perpetually dead" (*you suo you er chang si* 有所由而常死).[50] For the *Liezi*, the point of this is not to say *dao* does grow and decay, but to precisely show how *dao* transcends the dichotomy of living and dying. According to the *Liezi*, *dao* is perpetually living inasmuch as it "brings about life and lives itself, for if something reaches its *terminus* without perishing (*gu sui zhong er bu wang* 故雖終而不亡) it is perpetual."⁵¹ It is perpetually dying inasmuch as "it brings about death and dies, and if something has no *terminus* and perishes to itself (*wei zhong er zi wang* 未終而自亡), it is also perpetual."⁵²

Put differently, the *Liezi* holds that the process of life and death depends in many respects upon our own formal (*xing*) definition: it is by our material and immaterial existence inasmuch as we are distinct from others (i.e., inasmuch as we have something identifiably our own or *zi* 自) that we live and we die. But by virtue of having a self, we do not persist in the same way *dao* does. *Dao* has its *terminus* in its own spontaneity as principle of generation, but this is not an intention or goal *dao* must set for itself: it merely *is* this. In contrast, as we age and eventually die, we know our body will transform, becoming once again part of the earth. But *dao* does not undergo the dissolution of the self as a return of its source, because it does not exist as an identifiable self, and it does not have a source outside of itself. In this sense, *dao* is already and perpetually the dissolution of the self, the perpetual experience of death as return.

Thus, we see that even or perhaps precisely because the Daoist tradition stresses the immanence of *dao*-change as underlying the natural processes of growth and decay, it also testifies to *dao*'s transcendence of this process. Even if one wishes to stress that *dao* is coextensive with this process, we must admit that the process of growth and decay is not itself subject to the process of growth and decay. Therefore, it seems difficult to escape the fact that early Daoist texts suggest that *dao* serves as the root and source of the phenomenal world, in such a way as to transcend the world in certain respects.

Dao Immutability and *Yin-Yang*

In this final section of the chapter, we turn to a final topic of the mutable immutability of *dao* in early Daoist texts. Here, we focus on showing how early Daoists considered *dao* as transcendent vis-à-vis *yin-yang* cause or change. What we mean by this is that early Daoist texts articulate a distinction between *dao*-change and *yin-yang* change such that *dao*-change is not affected by or subject to *yin-yang* change. Our premise here is that *yin-yang* change in these texts refers to change in the phenomenal world caused by the motion of *yin-yang*, which are themselves caused by *dao*. Thus, *yin-yang* change is a mode of *dao*-change or even a result of *dao*-change. The key is we argue this relationship only works in one direction, meaning that *dao* is not caused to change by *yin-yang*.

Even at this initial stage, we have reached a point of contention worth noting. Many scholars may question whether the distinction between *yin-yang* and *dao* is appropriate in light of how these concepts function in Chinese texts. Specifically, one may ask whether *yin* and *yang* were truly considered to be *causes* of change in early China. Did early Chinese see *yin* and *yang* as acting upon the world to bring about phenomenal change or are there merely the metaphysical proof or expression of these changes?

Those who doubt the aptness of our distinction have a case based on significant texts in the tradition. For example, in the *Xici* commentary to the *Yijing*, we find it said that "the one (movement of) *yin* and one (movement of) *yang* is called *dao*."[53] This suggests that *dao* simply is *yin* and *yang*: the latter are not distinct agents from *dao*, but how *dao* acts in the phenomenal world. Similarly, the art of divination and augury so important in ancient China interprets the movement of *yin* and *yang* as signs of changes already underway, and thus humans can respond to them. From one important perspective of Chinese thought, then, we might say *yin* and *yang* are not causes of change at all, at least not in any way distinct from *dao*-change, expect perhaps notionally.

However, correlational cosmological models in pre-Qin and Han China do portray *yin* and *yang* as in motion, often associated with the seasons and cardinal directions. It may not be the case that there is a distinction in priority of time, that is, that *yin* and *yang* first move and then other things are caused to move, but there is a priority in the sense that the movements of *yin* and *yang* impact or control the movements of the myriad things. They act in accord with *yin* and *yang* and not the reverse. In a sense, *yin* and *yang* function similarly to Aristotle's and Aquinas's conception of celestial bodies: by virtue of their motion, they are causes of motion in other things, even if contemporaneously. It is striking that *DDJ* 42, for example, speaks of the myriad things in carrying *yin* and embracing *yang*, as though *yin* and *yang* underlie the fundamental action of all things.[54] From this perspective, we can say that *yin* and *yang* are causes of change in the material world. As Robin R. Wang has put, "yinyang is the cause of things as becoming and is also embedded in all things as their structure."[55]

Our emphasis for the purposes of this analysis is that regardless of how one formulates *yin-yang* vis-à-vis change, the following seems indisputable: for early Daoists, *yin* and *yang* are associated with phenomenal change that is in harmony with and expressive of *dao* and *dao*-change, but *dao* is not itself characterized by or subject to *yin-yang* change. That is, *dao* is not subject to the movement either signified by or caused by *yin* and *yang*; *yin* and *yang* are only efficacious in the phenomenal world. And so, there are two ways of stating our claim here that emphasize different aspects. One is that we mean to argue *dao* is not moved by *yin* and *yang* as are formal things. A second is that *yin* and *yang* are terms used to describe the change flowing from *dao* as it functions in the phenomenal world, and thus one can predicate *yin* and *yang* change of the phenomenal world, but *dao* is not characterized by this kind of change, except inasmuch as it itself causes such change.

With these clarifications in place, let us turn to the texts. The first place we can look to find *dao* distinct from *yin-yang* change is *DDJ* 42, which teaches that "*dao* produced the One, the One produced the Two, and the Two produced the Three."[56] The original meaning of the text is debated, of course, but the *Heshanggong* helpfully incorporates *yin* and *yang* into this arrangement. According to the *Heshanggong*, the One produced by *dao* is life (*dao shi suo sheng* 道使所生) and the Two refers to "the One producing *yin* and *yang*" (*yi sheng yin yu yang* 一生陰與陽).[57] Significantly, then, *yin* and *yang* are generated by the *dao*, though removed one step in causation, and are therefore effects of *dao*, even if they are not to be seen as wholly alien from *dao* (as indeed everything is still in *dao*).

What this means is that *yin* and *yang* appear as part of *dao*'s generation of things, but, as source of *yin* and *yang*, *dao* is not an object of *yin* and *yang* activity. According to *Heshanggong*'s perspective, *yin* and *yang* move and produce the Three (*tian*, earth, and humanity).[58] Thus, the action of *yin* and *yang* is toward the phenomenal world or the world of form: they are how *dao* maintains the generation of the phenomenal world, but the process does not work in reverse. The Two do not generate or cause change in *dao* for *dao* cannot change in the same way things can when "carrying" or "embracing" *yin* and *yang*.

Robin Wang's understanding of *dao* and *yin-yang* in terms of the cyclical view of the cosmos in early China is helpful in elucidating this point. Citing the *Zhuangzi*, Wang likens *dao* to the axis of the cosmos—"what happens inside the circle"—and *yin-yang* is apparently meant to fall in the place of what enables the circle to remain a circle, that is, "what sustains that movement."[59] In this sense *yin* and *yang* are centrifugal forces that carry motion and change from the center to the extremes of the cosmos. But, crucially, they do not act as centripetal forces that work back upon the center.

Another important perspective on *dao* vis-à-vis *yin-yang* change is found in the well-known cosmogonic passages in the *Chu Zhen* 俶真 chapter of the *Huainanzi*.[60] The chapter opens with a cosmogonic or protological interpretation of the *Zhuangzi's* famous riddle on *wuyou* 無有. The *Huainanzi* associates "the beginning" (*shi* 始) with the concept of confused completeness found in *DDJ* 25.[61] That is, it interprets the beginning to mean that things are inchoately present in *dao*, but are "indistinct and not yet dispatched" (*fanfen wei fa* 繁憤未發).[62] The second stage in the origins of the cosmos is when the *qi* of *tian* and earth begin to ascend and descend, respectively, and when *yin* and *yang* begin to mix and meet (*cuo he* 錯合).[63] While *yin* and *yang* appear early in the cosmic process, they are here still introduced within the context of the initial movements of *qi* in *tian* and earth, that is, the beginning of formal existence from the confused and undifferentiated state preceding it.

Additionally, when the *Huainanzi* comments on Zhuangzi's clause that "there was not yet beginning to have 'there was not yet beginning to have 'there was nothing,'" the text associates this with another description of the nascent cosmos. In this time, "*tian* and earth were not yet divided, *yin* and *yang* were not yet distinct (*wei pan* 未判), the four seasons were not yet separated, and the myriad things were not yet produced."[64] What seems clear from this comment is that *yin* and *yang* are forces of change that are only extant as the cosmos moves toward formal existence. From this, we must conclude that not only is *dao* the source of *yin* and *yang*, but also that *yin* and *yang* are causes of change vis-à-vis formal, material existents.

It is worth noting that because the *Huainanzi* is a text worked out among diverse authors with at times competing perspective, the text sometimes has moments of disagreement. One such instance is in the *Tian Wen* 天文 chapter, wherein we find a narrative of cosmic origins that diverges from that of the *Chu Zhen* chapter.[65] This chapter of the text focuses on the beginning of space and time, which it says produced *qi*. This *qi* then divided into two: the pure and bright ascended to become *tian*, while the heavy and turbid descended to form earth. We then find that *tian* was completed first and then earth because the types of *qi* they contain differ and were difficult to unify. Only then, after these processes of *qi*-converging, do we find *yin* and *yang*: "the conjoined essences of *tian* and earth produced *yin* and *yang*. The supersessive essences of *yin* and *yang* caused the four seasons."[66] In this version of cosmic origins, *yin-yang* are explicitly invoked as causes of inner-worldly phenomenon that seem to only act once *tian* and earth are formed. This makes good sense in light of the correlational cosmology of the *Huainanzi*, which articulates how the movements of *yin* and *yang* produce the five elements, which in turn permeate all things.

In short, in two different perspectives, the *Huainanzi* has *yin* and *yang* explicitly in terms of phenomenal processes and change that works out the change of *dao* and harmonizes with it. Because of this association of *yin-yang* with formal things, it is implicit that *dao* is therefore not caused or moved by *yin-yang*. For in the *Huainanzi* as in other Daoist-leaning texts, *dao* is primal "nothing" in contrast to the world of something and form. Inasmuch as *yin-yang* are associated with and active in the "something" side, they do not act upon *dao*, for *dao* is not the sort of object upon which *yin-yang* act. Put differently, one might say that *yin* and *yang* are key to how the cosmos "resonates" (*ganying* 感應) with *dao*.[67] But, clearly *dao* does not need to resonate with itself in the same way, and so *dao* produces *yin* and *yang* but is not produced or affected by *yin-yang* change as a patient of that change. It very much transcends the effects of *yin* and *yang*, even as these movements mimic and mediate *dao*-change to the phenomenal world.

We would be remiss not to mention briefly the protological passages of the *Liezi* that also distinguish *dao* from the objects of *yin-yang* movement. Generally speaking, the *Liezi* rarely speaks of *yin-yang* in the context of *dao*, but primarily associates them with *tian* and earth.[68] For example, in the *Tian Rui* chapter, we find, "in ancient times the sages employed (*yin* 因) *yin-yang* in order to (*yi* 以) govern *tian* and earth."[69] This shows that the *Liezi* emphasizes that *yin-yang* changes are so deeply tied to the phenomenal world that the sage can employ them as a direct means of (*yi* 以) governing *tian* and earth and bring order to cosmic chaos.

Furthering this association of *yin-yang* with *tian* and earth, the *Liezi* says that, "the *dao* of *tian* and earth is neither *yin* nor *yang*."[70] In context, this means that *tian* and earth bear fundamental roles: *tian* produces life (*sheng* 生) and earth endows with form (*xing* 形). Moreover, they perform these roles as an office (*zhi* 職) that requires a standard of fittingness (*yi* 宜) as they carry out their proper operations. The *Liezi* then associates *yin* and *yang* with the fittingness of the offices of *tian* and earth; that is, *yin* and *yang* establish what the proper office of *tian* and earth are, almost as though *yin-yang* are the internal logic and coherence of *tian* and earth. Due to *yin* and *yang*, then, *tian* and earth must simply follow these standards and maintain their respective offices.[71] Again, the key here is that *yin* and *yang* are associated particularly with the movement from *dao* to *tian* and earth. They mediate *dao*-change, expressing and communicating it perhaps, but only in one direction: toward the phenomenal world, never in regression to the center.

Indeed, it is notable that the *Liezi* locates this description of *yin-yang* within a catena of capacities for opposite states found in things. Many of these do evoke the emptiness or flexibility of *dao*: the ability to be soft or firm (*rou gang* 柔剛), to be hot or cold, to be mysterious or august, and so on.[72] One conclusion that seems appropriate from this is to see *yin-yang* as the means by which things become like *dao*. As causes of change, *yin-yang* allow us to have the same kind of softness and hardness of *dao*, the same mysteriousness and profundity found in *dao* itself. Thus, it does seem that *yin-yang* are imitative of *dao* as changeless change. However, even in this portrayal of things, *dao* is still not subject to *yin* and *yang*. At best, *yin* and *yang* allow the myriad things to be harmonious with *dao*, but in itself, the *dao* does not experience the effects of *yin* and *yang* to have the properties of change it is.

Conclusion

In the foregoing, we have admittedly not offered exhaustive evidence for the immutable mutability of *dao*. However, we believe the evidence we have brought forward is indisputable in regard to demonstrating that early Daoist texts do find *dao* to be not subject to change in important ways. Even though *dao* is internally perpetual change (i.e., intrinsically mutable), it cannot lose its nature as perpetual change or be caused to change, grow, or decay by any other thing (therefore it is extrinsically immutable). It is difficult, then, to avoid the conclusion that Daoist texts argue that *dao* indeed transcends the world in some respects, while not denying it is, at the same time, the immanent principle of all things. Specifically, early Daoist texts portray *dao* as transcending the extrinsic mutability that characterizes the world of form. While this is clearly not a position equivalent to the "absolute transcendence" of Aquinas, for example, it is still a robust vision of transcendence that, in our opinion, cannot be gainsaid.

9

Transcendence and Generation: Pseudo-Dionysius and the Daodejing

One of the classical tropes of transcendence discourse concerns generative causality, which is also one of the thorniest tropes of transcendence to understand properly. After European deism, most intellectuals articulate transcendence in terms of efficient causality, wherein A generates B through means not natural or inherent in B.[1] Consequently, A is not only external to B but also acts to generate B in ways that transcend the natural capacities of B or the natural means of procession and generation that allow B to arise spontaneously. Such a conception of generative causation can function as a type of transcendence, of course, but it is not the only form. Georges Lemaître, SJ, for example, stands as a historical example of being able to hold to the transcendent divine creation of the world alongside a view of the immanent processes of efficient causality in the early cosmos. Therefore, we argue that in assessing transcendence in a given tradition one should grant—in agreement with most non-naturalist traditions—that generation by a transcendent cause does not negate or diminish the reality of immanent process that brings about and sustains life.

With this clarification, we now turn to analyze the presence of transcendence in early Chinese thought focusing on the topic of protological generation. Specifically, in this chapter we argue that the *DDJ*, at least, features a robust account of *dao*-transcendence in understanding *dao* as the origin of all things. In order to articulate this schema, we find it helpful to focus on the relationship between the cosmology of the *DDJ* and the form of apophatic discourse found in the text.[2]

Apophatic, or negative, frameworks are often but not universally indicative of transcendence. In theistic apophatic systems such as that offered by Plotinus, language fails to name the ultimate because of substantial properties of the ultimate. In non-theistic apophatic systems, such as Jacques Derrida's deconstructionism, the stress falls on the frailty of human language or cognition, regardless of objects of knowledge. These distinctions have also been applied in Chinese philosophy, wherein scholars often treat the *Zhuangzi* as offering the latter form of apophaticism, though this needs qualification.[3] When it comes to the *DDJ*, however, not all scholars agree as to what motivates the apophaticism of the text. For example, D. C. Lau and A. C. Graham supported a linguistic interpretation of apophaticism, whereas Benjamin Schwartz and A. T. Nuyen tend to a substantial reading.[4]

It is self-evident that how one resolves this question of what kind of apophaticism is in the *DDJ* will go a long way toward interpreting transcendence as either active or absent in the text. That said, instead of rehashing the language/substance debate here, we take an alternative approach. Here we analyze the *DDJ* in comparison with an apophatic text that provides a classic model of transcendence discourse, the Christian treatises of Pseudo-Dionysius.[5] Specifically, we analyze the *DDJ* in comparison primarily with the *Divine Names* (hereafter *DN*) and secondarily with the *Mystical Theology* (hereafter, *MT*).

A complication to this comparison is that Pseudo-Dionysius purposefully and frequently uses terms that are often translated as "transcendence" explicitly in his corpus, while the *DDJ* does not. This is in part not only due to the Christian context of Pseudo-Dionysius but also due to his appropriation of the Neoplatonic discourse on the One to discussing God as Christians understand him.[6] Thus, in comparing Pseudo-Dionysius and the *DDJ*, what is most important is not the explicit claims about the transcendence of the One in the former, but the kind of characteristics, images, and other signifiers of the meaning of transcendence. It also means that perceiving the presence or absence of transcendence in the *DDJ* is not a linguistic, propositional problem, but rather one of images or consequences of certain descriptions of the *dao*.

Transcendental Apophaticism: Pseudo-Dionysius

The goal of this section is not to provide a full account of the Dionysian concept of apophaticism and its role in Dionysian spirituality, but rather to focus on a specific aspect of this account: how the transcendence of God fits in this framework. Although the *MT* provides a more directly apophatic approach than the *DN*, the latter is much more extensive in length and development of the ideas of the text. For Pseudo-Dionysius, the *DN*, which discusses how language can talk about God, is balanced by the apophaticism of the *MT*; but we can also press this relationship in the opposite direction. This is important because there is a tendency to interpret apophaticism as testifying to transcendence because it would seem to work within a contrastive conception of transcendence. However, for Pseudo-Dionysius, the transcendence of God grounds *both* the limits and the possibilities of language to describe who He is.

As we noted, the *MT* is more properly apophatic than the *DN*.[7] Following the model of Neoplatonic apophaticism, the *MT* focuses on the negation of attributes meant to be applied to God, a process that is described as a kind of ladder of intellectual ascent. In this ascent, one is exhorted to "strive upward as much as you can toward union with him who is beyond all being and knowledge."[8] This ascent is apophatic inasmuch as it necessarily involves stripping away what is known or thought to find union with the ultimate. The *MT* likens the apophatic ascent to the work of a sculptor: "they remove every obstacle to the pure view of the hidden image, and simply by this act of clearing aside they show up the beauty which is hidden."[9]

Within the schema of apophatic spirituality, what must be "cleared aside" are the positive conceptions one might apply to the divine being, even the perfections of being. For this reason, some scholars have argued we should take Pseudo-Dionysius as offering an essentially meontological account of God, inasmuch as God is "no-thing" and no "being."[10] Yet even such claims must be somewhat tempered. The *MT* indeed argues that one should negate even affirmations of perfection about the divine, but not because it is untrue as such to say the divine is perfect in these ways. Rather, the text states that "we should not conclude that the negations [of affirmations] are simply the opposites of affirmations, but rather that the cause of all is considerably prior to this, beyond privations, beyond every denial, beyond every assertion."[11] The affirmations we can make of God can be genuinely true, but they also fall short of what is truly being described.[12]

Here we may transition to the *DN* by posing a guiding question: If God is indeed beyond even affirmations and perfections, why is this so? The above quote from the *MT* suggests the answer is in one sense very simple: because God is transcendent. But what precisely does Pseudo-Dionysius mean by this? A contrastive conception of transcendence would hold that God's Otherness is so total and comprehensive that He can in no way be grasped, understood, or conceived by the human intellect. But then, if such a transcendent God is purely contrasted with the world, then it is entirely unclear what kind of union or ascent is genuinely possible with God, save some kind of eradication of finite being, which we do not find in Pseudo-Dionysius.

We submit that for Pseudo-Dionysius, the divine transcendence works in two directions. The first and most easily recognizable is that transcendence describes the difference between God and the world. However, at the same time, this conception of divine transcendence is paired with the understanding of the divine as present in and through all things. Both ways of articulating divine transcendence are founded upon the recognition of God as the cause of all things. On the one hand, this means nothing can be like God in any way (direction 1). On the other hand, it means that all things exist only by and through God, and hence all things participate in God and testify to Him (direction 2). Thus, for Dionysius, God's transcendence means both a radical difference from the world *and* concomitantly a God as the radical foundation of all existence, the ever-present and indeed immanent source of all perfections and goodness found in creation.

We would argue that these "directions" of transcendence are interdependent in the Dionysian corpus. This is apparent in the principal term Pseudo-Dionysius uses to articulate divine transcendence, the Greek term *hyperousios*.[13] The term itself is of Neoplatonic origins and is difficult to render precisely in other language. The Latin translation of the Dionysian corpus renders the term as *supersubstantiliatis*.[14] Colm Lubheid treats it on occasion as "that which transcends being." The essential difficulty is that *hyper* has a sense of meaning "beyond" (as in differentiation) but also "more extensively or complete." At the same time, then, the *DN* describes the divine being as "beyond" the category of substantial being (*ousia*) and also a "hyper" or intensified kind of *ousia*. As the Dionysius scholar Paul Rorem puts it, "that God is existent and yet also beyond existent is a particularly Dionysian form of simultaneous affirmation and negation, all in the prefix *hyper-*."[15]

This double meaning of *hyperousia* is important because it suggests the interdependence of the two "directions" of transcendence we are here seeking to elucidate. That is, it suggests that divine transcendence is not *solely* a principle of differentiation from the world, but also some positive account of the God–world relationship. In order to see this, however, it is helpful to treat the negative and affirmative aspects separately.

In terms of the transcendence describing the difference between God and world, Pseudo-Dionysius uses *hyperousia* to elucidate how God exists in a way beyond and radically departing from the world of created things. For example, the *DN* speaks of God as "that which lies hidden beyond thought and beyond being" (*hyper logon kai hyper noun kai ousion*).[16] In this context, *hyper* seems to mean a "beyond" relationship in the mode of discontinuity. For this reason, the *DN* points to an initial spiritual response to such *hyperousia*, which is to stand in "wise silence" that honors the ineffable God.[17]

Importantly, this description of God occurs in the first chapter of the *DN*, which provides a description of how it is possible to even speak of divine names. Pseudo-Dionysius is emphatic that the "natural words" of the human intellect are unfit for the task of naming God. It is only through the Scriptures of the Bible that this becomes possible.[18] And this in turn is because Christians understand the Bible not merely as a product of human authorship (though it is) but also divine authorship that, in part, illuminates the intellects of the authors who compose the scriptures.[19] Hence, Pseudo-Dionysius emphasizes that the Holy Spirit (one of the Persons of the Trinity in Christian doctrine) grants a certain power to the writers of Scripture "by which, in a manner surpassing speech and knowledge, we reach a union superior to anything available to us by way of our own abilities or activities in the realm of discourse or of intellect."[20]

Consequently, for Pseudo-Dionysius it is only through God's activity to make himself known in revelation that speaking of the divine names becomes genuinely possible and fruitful. Hence, he exhorts that "we must not dare to resort to words or conceptions concerning the hidden divinity which transcends being, apart from what the sacred scriptures have divinely revealed."[21] These descriptions of scripture are very helpful for delineating one of the primary meanings of thinking of God as *hyper-ousia*. In this sense, *hyper-* truly does mean a radical difference between God and nature, in this case seen in the incapability of the human intellect to grasp God. Those resources or capacities for speech and knowledge that are purely and solely connatural to the human intellect are seen to be deficient for naming God who lies "beyond" (*hyper*) them, or above them in the imagery of the *MT*.

Strengthening this conception of divine transcendence-as-distinction is the ongoing tension between natural capacities of the human intellect and scripture that are present as the *DN* discusses the names of God that are revealed. Lest one believes that revelation has given human intelligence genuine access to the *hyperousia* that God is as an object of intellectual mastery, Pseudo-Dionysius reminds that even in revelation, the names of God are analogies meant to raise those who contemplate them "upward." In this ascent, "we leave behind us all our own notions of the divine. We call a halt to the activities of our minds and, to the extent that it is proper, we approach the ray which transcends being."[22] Thus, the ascent on the basis of revelation still requires a form of apophatic abandonment. It seems what Pseudo-Dionysius means is that one can apply words to God on the basis of revelation, but one cannot simply rely upon these words to signify on the basis of sense knowledge. Instead, the love of God expressed in the action of self-revelation must "enclose," "wrap around," and "cover" the truth the mind knows through sense-knowledge, thereby lifting up this knowledge to new heights.

The crucial point to keep in mind, of course, is that this sort of ascent structure and account of the shortcomings of the human intellect are not due to a despondent anthropology but due to an understanding of the *hyper*-existence of God. As Pseudo-Dionysius says,

> with regard to the super-essential [*hyperousia*] being of God … no lover of the truth which is above all truth will seek to praise it as word or power or mind or life or being. No. It is at a total remove from every condition, movement, life, imagination, conjecture, name, discourse, thought, conception, being, rest, dwelling, unity, limit, infinity, the totality of existence.[23]

Undoubtedly, Pseudo-Dionysius means that whatever human beings have in mind with these various concepts or realities we encounter, God lies beyond the scope of these terms. In this sense, it is fair and accurate to read the phrase "total remove" in a strong manner, highlighting the discontinuity between God and the world humans experience. This is supported by the fact that the Greek term Pseudo-Dionysius uses—*hyperochikos*—can be understood as a contrast to *synochikos*, typically meaning something that concerns or brings about continuity.[24]

Here we find an excellent place to transition to the second "direction" of transcendence in the *DN*. For with *hyperochikos*, Pseudo-Dionysius uses the ambiguity of *hyper-* to contrast with continuity. Does he mean, then, to argue *hyper* is the negation of continuity between God and the world? Assuming Pseudo-Dionysius means that God is "beyond" continuity with the world we experience, it is unclear if Pseudo-Dionysius means this is an absolute beyond or simply a state of intense degree. The Latin text of the *DN* is instructive here, for it renders *hyperochikos* as *superlate*, from which modern English derives the term superlative.[25] From this perspective, *hyperochikos* can suggest a discontinuity in one respect, namely in the distinctive perfections of God vis-à-vis creation. At the same time, this would not suggest *absolute* discontinuity or difference, but rather a kind of continuity of perfection of excellence of one subject over another.[26]

We argue that for Pseudo-Dionysius, taking God as *hyperousia* does not solely mean God is contrasted with created being, but also serves to explain how God is immanent in all created beings.[27] In speaking of the name "being" applied to God, Pseudo-Dionysius argues there is indeed a tremendous disparity between divine ontology (if we can even speak of God in these terms) and creaturely ontology, not least because God is simple, One, etc. But, Pseudo-Dionysius also says that in terms of the world, God becomes "differentiated in a unified way."[28] On the one hand, Pseudo-Dionysius means by this that God is the One who is the source of the plurality of created things. On the other hand, Pseudo-Dionysius means to emphasize that God in His Oneness shares Himself with the differentiated things. He does not suffer division and distinction in this sharing, and thus He is "unified" even as He "differentiates" through the existence of His creation.

Andrew Louth has observed that although creation per se is not a central theme in the *DN*, nevertheless the Dionysian presupposition of the Christian account of creation helps distinguish his work from his Neoplatonic influences.[29] According to Louth, in Procline Neoplatonism, the emanation of all things from the One was understood in terms of mediating being through a hierarchy of creation. That is, the One emanated the henads (the gods, for Proclus), which ultimately are the source of the Many. In other words, the One is the source of all things, but only through mediated steps of emanation. Against this conception of things, Louth argues Pseudo-Dionysius is committed to the Christian understanding of God, which results in two alterations Pseudo-Dionysius makes to the Neoplatonic framework of emanation. First, Pseudo-Dionysius "qualifies the notion of emanation by insisting that being is derived from God alone."[30] Second, "he turns the doctrine of divine names into a doctrine of divine attributes (that is, attributes of God, the one God)."[31]

In other words, because of his belief in the Christian doctrine of God as the genuine, intentional creator of all things, Pseudo-Dionysius cannot merely hold to the absolute transcendence of the One as Neoplatonists could. Rather, he must find a way to assert a genuine continuity between the creator God and the created order. And thus, the apophaticism of Pseudo-Dionysius is fundamentally paired with a cataphatic movement, that is, speaking positively about the divine. And this is crucial because in the Neoplatonic tradition, apophaticism was how one could approach the One, whereas cataphaticism was appropriate with the emanations from the One that exceeded human being, such as the henads or other manifestations. But, as Louth puts it, for Pseudo-Dionysius, "the reference of both apophatic and cataphatic theology is the one God … it is of the same God that we are to make both affirmations and denials."[32]

One important place we find this kind of paradoxical cooperation of apophaticism and cataphaticism is in the Dionysian discussion of the integrity of the many. In the *DN*, Pseudo-Dionysius writes of the fact that the entire world is constituted by united things (e.g., a man is an irreducible unity, as is a tree). Whence comes their unity? According to Pseudo-Dionysius, these differentiated unities exist in participation with the divine unity, which actively and perpetually persists in them, making them individual unities. In the words of Pseudo-Dionysius, "He is one and dispenses his oneness to every part of the universe as well as to its totality, to the single as well as the multiple."[33]

What is key to emphasize here is that for Pseudo-Dionysius, the immanent presence of the divine unity is immanently present in the plurality, though differentiated from it (i.e., not reducible to it). And this presence is not a quality in addition to God's transcendence, but a quality *of* God's transcendence as such. This is clear when Pseudo-Dionysius writes that God "is nothing less than the archetypal God, the supra-divine transcendentally one God who dwells indivisibly in every individual and who is in himself undifferentiated unity with no commixture and no multiplication arising out of his presence among the many."[34] The dwelling presence among the many is thus possible as an act of divine transcendence, not in addition to it.

Similarly, Pseudo-Dionysius clarifies how it is that God is called good, or Goodness itself. On the one hand, God is "above" or "beyond" all created goodness as its source.

In God, goodness is "undivided" and "far above" any examples we might give for understanding it, such as the sun.[35] Yet at the same time, God shares His undivided goodness with all things that are called good. This Goodness, then, which is above all and the source of all things, "is…really an excess of being. It is not *a* life, but is, rather, superabundant Life. It is not *a* mind, but is, rather, superabundant Life. It is not *a* mind, but is superabundant Wisdom."[36] In all of these descriptions of God as *super*— where *super* translates to *hyper*—it is clear that God is not classed as one form among others in a species. But at the same time, God is not merely differentiated from the classification itself—God's Goodness underlies the classification of species of being, life and wisdom as the overflowing abundance and perfection of these. And so God is both "above" and "within":

> The goodness of the transcendent God reaches from the highest and most perfect forms of being to the very lowest. And yet It remains above and beyond them all, superior to the highest and yet stretching out to the lowliest. It gives light to everything capable of receiving it, it creates them, keeps them alive, preserves and perfect them. Everything looks to it for measure, eternity, number, order. It is the power which embraces the universe. It is the cause of the universe and its end.[37]

Describing the Good God as the end (*telos*) of all things adds a final dimension to the understanding of transcendence in Pseudo-Dionysius's account. God is certainly "beyond" all things, but is so precisely in and by God's being the source, maintaining principle, and culmination of all things. Just as all things come from God (*exitus*), Pseudo-Dionysius emphasizes the movement of return (*reditus*) that underlies all existence: "the Good returns all things to itself and gathers together whatever may be scattered."[38] And now it should be clear why God is for Pseudo-Dionysius truly beyond the grasp of human knowing. For God is the principle that brings forth all things, that is immanent in them as the continual principle of their being and the *terminus* to which all things tend. God's being is *hyper* not simply in a sense of differentiation, but in terms of the grades of perfection and greater intensity of being. God exists in Himself in ways that humans cannot claim to know or explicate accurately, but not as merely an "other" apart from us. Rather, God cannot be known in His fullness because we owe our being to Him, at the time of our generation, in our present, and in the utter shape of all our desires and aims.

To summarize, what we see in Pseudo-Dionysius is an account of divine transcendence that explicitly understands the supernatural existence of God to mean much more than simply juxtaposed to nature. God's transcendence is not juxtaposed to His immanence, but the latter is constitutive of the former. In this way, God's omnipresence as the principle of being means that He is not identical with any one thing or the class of beings we encounter. For all of them at once testify to their same principle, the "formless" which brings forth "form."[39] God brings forth all things as the immanent principle within them, which is part of what it means to say God is transcendent.

The *Dao* as Formless Source of Form: Intelligibility and Transcendence

There is no great controversy in the simple yet instructive observation that the Neoplatonic and Christian conceptions of God found in Pseudo-Dionysius are quite different from the *dao* in the *DDJ*. We do not intend to overlook such differences, as we show below. However, our task here is not to compare the conceptions of God and *dao* per se, but rather to examine whether the apophatic tendencies of both texts show evidence of an idea of God or *dao* as transcendent. In other words, is transcendence a similarity bound up within the differences between these concepts about the ultimate? We have seen with Pseudo-Dionysius that the transcendence of God is not simply about utter difference with the world, but also about God as source of the world's perfections. Might similar non-contrastive forms of transcendence characterize the *DDJ*? It is the task of this chapter to make such a determination.

It is inarguable that the *DDJ* draws heavily upon negative concepts in its articulation of *dao*. The primary terms are the *dao* as "formless" (*wu xing*), "nameless" (*wu ming* 無名), "simple" (*pu*), or "nothing" (*wu* 無).[40] Thus, the dominant terms are primarily aesthetic, though the *DDJ* also uses quantitative terms such as the profound or deep (*shen* 深) that function in negative ways.[41] In what follows, we focus more on the imagery of *dao* as "formless" as a matter of convenience. While the meaning of *you* (something) and *wu* (nothing) are intensely debated by scholars, one clear theme of the text is that the myriad things possess form (*xing*) and *dao* does not.[42] As we demonstrate in this section, this formal distinction between *dao* and things is partially explained in terms of generative causation.

It is helpful to first highlight the general apophatic tendencies of the *DDJ*.[43] One thing that is clear is that in the *DDJ* there is a clear sense *dao* lies beyond—that is, it transcends—human capacities to grasp it. We might say that for the *DDJ*, the limitations of grasping *dao* are almost entirely intellectual, since imitating and harmonizing with *dao* are achievable goals in the text. But knowledge of *dao* is clearly elusive. Even the name "*dao*" is admitted to be an imperfect attempt to say what this reality is.[44] A vital question, then, as we noted in the introduction to this chapter above is why does the *DDJ* portray the *dao* as so beyond the grasp of human understanding?

In the Daoist trajectory set by the *DDJ*, the answer to this question has a great deal to do with the cosmogonic structure of causality.[45] According to the *Heshanggong* at least, the *DDJ* has a tiered theory of causation. One of *DDJ*'s most intriguing and ambiguous claims is that "the *Dao* produced the one, the one produced the two, the two produced the three, and the three produced the myriad creatures."[46] According to *Heshanggong*, the claim that "the *dao* produced the one" means "the *dao* caused what has life to be."[47] Presumably, this means then that the *dao* produces life itself as the one. The two, according to *Heshanggong*, refers to the principles of *yin* 陰 and *yang* 陽, which in their activity produce forces that create the distinction between *Tian*, the earth, and humanity (*fen wei tian di ren* 分為天地人).[48] It is notable that the same verb—producing life or "birthing" (*sheng* 生)—is used to describe the chain of causation.[49] In the eyes of *Heshanggong*, the *DDJ* argues for a univocity between the ways in which inner-worldly causes generate life, and the *dao*.

However, if there is univocity in the activity of generation, the productions are still distinct. Indeed, there is a hierarchical difference between these productions such that some are more immediate or immanent, and others more distant. The oft-cited opening passage of the *DDJ* is noted for its claim that "the *dao* that can be known is not the perpetual *dao* and the name that can be named is not the perpetual name."[50] The subsequent claim offers an interpretive key, stating that "that which is without name is the source of *Tian* and earth; that which has name is the mother of the myriad creatures."[51]Clearly from the perspective of the *DDJ*, the cosmos as we know it is produced from the agency of *tian* and earth. As the passage cited above demonstrates, these powers are seen as the most proximate or immediate causes of generation, and this immediacy grants them an intelligibility. According to the framework of the *DDJ*, the human intellect can know *tian* and earth are its source, naming them as proper entities (as *tian* and earth) and recognizing it as the world's "mother."

At the same time, however, *tian* and earth are also subordinate powers and causes, themselves caused by *dao*. Consequently, whereas the *DDJ* steadfastly interprets *dao* as "formless" (*wu xing* 無形), *tian* and earth are identified as possessing form (*you xing* 有形). This latter claim is extrapolated by *Heshanggong* in commentary on *DDJ* 40.[52] The original text claims a characteristic relation of generation between something and nothing: "the myriad things are born from something (*you* 有), and something is itself born from nothing (*wu* 無)."[53] *Heshanggong* interprets this difficult passage in terms of the tiered cosmological generation, arguing the something–nothing distinction refers to the generative differences of *tian*/earth and *dao*. According to *Heshanggong*, when the *DDJ* says all things come from "something" it is referring to the proximate generative cause of *tian* and earth, which themselves possess form and embodiment (*xing wei* 形位) and communicate this to creatures. But this generative cause that is with form itself comes from the *dao* that is formless, and thus it is "nothing" in the schema of form and intelligibility.[54]

The *DDJ*'s comparative rather than ontological use of nothingness as a point of contrast to the generative capacities of *tian* and the earth is imitated in the *Huainanzi*, chapter 2. As we saw in the previous chapter, the *Huainanzi* takes the famous puzzle of *Zhuangzi* 2.2 as an earnest attempt at protology. The text associates the claim "there was a beginning" (*you shi* 有始) with a primordial "un-emanated confusion" (*fanfen wei fa* 繁憤未發) in which the incipient beginnings of life were still "not yet possessing form, distinction, or definition" (*wei you xing lei yin* 未有垺垠).[55] The next step in the cosmogonic process, as the *Huainanzi* portrays it, is the descent and ascent of *tian-qi* and earth-*qi* and the apparent beginning of the movement of *yin-yang*. In this stage, there is a desire (*yu* 欲) to have all things connect, even though there is still not the completion (*cheng* 成) of form and definitions.[56] The third major cosmogonic stage, then, is when *tian* and earth possess *qi* but do not yet communicate it. Once *tian* and earth begin to communicate *qi*, then there is "something" (*you* 有), that is, the myriad creatures that are concrete and formed (*xing* 形) things.

This cosmogonic interpretation by the *Huainanzi* helps illustrate the extent to which early Daoism connects *dao* with formless generation. In the very beginning where there is naught but *dao*, one might say there is "existence" in the abstract, but it is uncommunicated, undifferentiated. It is only as *tian* and earth emerge from *dao* that the cosmos begins to move toward material existence. Even if *tian* and earth can in a sense from the view of the *Huainanzi* be seen to participate in the formless nothingness of *dao*, *tian* and earth are also closer to "something" than is *dao*. Hence, *tian* and earth are "swaddled" (*bao guo* 包裹) by the nothingness of *dao*: these generative forces are more proximate and knowable than the ultimate generative source of the cosmos, the *dao*, which remains "expansively deep, of remarkable breadth, incapable of having anything outside of it; it is also minutely fine, sharp as a point, incapable of having anything inside of it."[57]

When one looks carefully at the distinctions between *dao* and *tian*/earth as generative causes, the deeply "transcendental" features of Daoist cosmogonic discourse become quite evident. At the most basic level, the apophatic descriptions of *dao* seem derived from a conception of *dao* as remote cause. *Dao* produces several mechanisms of the world that lead to the human intellectual being, and thus the human intellectual being cannot grasp and understand the *dao* in itself. From the perspective of the corporeal and form-bound human intellect, *dao* is really nothing, it is "empty" of the sort of distinguishing characteristics we encounter in the phenomenal objects of the world. In short, *dao* transcends the intellectual and phenomenological faculties of the human person to grasp it as it is because it is the nonformal source of the form needed to know objects as we do.[58]

Inasmuch as the *Huainanzi* is evoking a Laoist interpretation of *dao* (one might argue, even a Laoist interpretation of the *Zhuangzi*), it seems clear that the *DDJ* and those who follow it mean to ascribe to the *dao* a type of generative causality that includes unavoidably "transcendental" features.[59] Most evidently, *dao* seems to transcend the categories of the material world. But this is not merely an intellectual weakness of human beings to not know or describe *dao*. Rather, *dao* also is "transcendent" inasmuch as it lies "beyond" what the material world knows as the structure of cause and generation. Certainly Daoists in early China do not mean that the *dao* is not active in the ongoing work of and generation as immanent in all things—far from it. However, there is a strong sense that *dao* underlies all cause and generation in such a way as to lie "beyond" the world as a perfect nothingness or formlessness.

Moreover, there is something significant at work in the juxtaposition of causality between *dao* and *tian* and earth. Given the theistic-leanings of Confucians and Mohists regarding *tian*, it is possible that the cosmogonic contrast between *dao* as remote, primordial and formless cause on the one hand, and *tian* and earth as proximate and secondary cause on the other, is part of a Daoist strategy to undermine the philosophical principles of opposing perspectives.[60] By making *tian* subordinate to *dao* and (to borrow an image from Neoplatonism) further down in the "chain of being," the *DDJ* stands in a better position to claim understanding of the truly most fundamental things of the cosmos. Moreover, the political aspect of the Daoist interpretation of *wu wei* is bolstered by such a contrast between *dao* and *tian*, because early Daoism more completely "immanentizes" the activity of *tian* (including *tian's* mandate), so that the *dao's* spontaneous fecundity can become the supreme model for human life, rather than the more proximate cause of *tian*.

We admit that this reading of *dao–tian* comparison is somewhat speculative, but it is illustrative as a heuristic device. Put simply, in the cosmogonic comparison between *dao* and *tian* in texts such as the *Daodejing*, there are compelling reasons to interpret these texts as intending to limit the impact of *tian* as a conceptual anchor for Confucians and Mohists precisely by suggesting *tian* is more immanent or immediate to the material world than is *dao* in terms of generative causation.

From analysis of the relationship between causality and unknowability of *dao* in the *Daodejing*, one can see that something analogous to transcendence is at work here. *Dao* is conceived as something like the *primum ens*, which does "rise above" material existence in the sense that it cannot be seen as the proximate, but only the remote cause of material existence. Because the material world is more immediately produced by the agency of *tian* and earth, these can be known and properly named. As more remote cause, the *dao* is epistemologically more elusive.

However, there are important qualifications to this vision of transcendence of the *dao*. One of the major points of disagreement between the Christian account of creation and the *DDJ* regards the sort of causality in forming the material world. To use Aristotle's language, both Christian theology and the *DDJ* would ascribe to God or *dao* a kind of remote efficient causality and thus share this mark of transcendence. However, the *DDJ* adds to this a conception of the *dao* as the material cause of the world, as the source and principle of *qi* 氣. Since we discuss this theme more below, for now we simply point out that Christian theology rejects thinking of God as the material cause of the world, a position that in Christian history has often been faulted for diminishing the nature of God's distinction from the world.

And so, ascribing transcendence to the theme of remote causality in the *DDJ* should not be taken to imply a conception of transcendence that neatly aligns with dominant Western models, even non-contrastive ones such as that found in classical Christian theism. Since *dao* is the material cause of the world, it is indeed immanent as principle of existence. Yet in the *DDJ*, *dao* is simultaneously transcendent as remote cause. For our purposes here, we are not presently concerned about whether these two ideas can be held in harmony, or if one governs the other—that is, we do not mean to assess the quality of the position either for or against. Rather, our goal is to simply point out that transcendence is part of the *DDJ* and early Daoist discourse, though in a different context than Western readers might expect for such ideas and claims.

To summarize our position, then, for the *DDJ*, *dao* is at once remote cause but also the principle of life intrinsic to all things. Certainly the *dao* is the paradigm of spontaneity or "naturalness" and it is undoubtedly the cause and principle of nature that is interiorly present in it. However, the *dao* is also categorically distinct from the world in terms of intelligibility and articulation. Although it is not "beyond" nature in the sense that the *dao* can be uncovered and emulated by stripping away self-interest and intentioned action, the *dao* does transcend the world.[61]

Conclusions

The analyses of Dionysian texts and the *DDJ* show clearly that there are two different conceptions of apophaticism and generation at play here. Yet despite the massive and significant differences between the two traditions, both can be classified as conceiving of God or *dao*, respectively, as transcendent. In order to substantiate this conclusion, let us make some observations about these commonalities and differences gleaned from the foregoing analyses.

First, to the important differences. One of the most significant differences between the *DDJ* and Pseudo-Dionysius concerns the "direction" of transcendence. In the *MT*, Pseudo-Dionysius speaks of the journey to God in a conventionally Christian way, that is, ensconced in a journey upward. Indeed, the pervasiveness of the Greek prefix *ana* (meaning to go up) in Pseudo-Dionysius's terminology for the apophatic journey to God is distinctively indicative of this point. For Pseudo-Dionysius, as well as for the broader Christian tradition, speaking of God as "transcendent" does mean looking up to the heights. God is, in this sense, clearly "above" the world in the Christian meaning of the phrase.

Contrast this to *dao* that, many others have noted, prefers a kind of negative imagery of *dao* as source. *Dao* is more like the valley, the empty space cleft between the positive. It is emptiness, like the bellows emptied of air. In this sense, the *Laozi* tradition has no anagogical movement as does the Christian theology of Pseudo-Dionysius. There is no ascent to *dao*. Rather *dao* is found "within," perhaps even "below," the manifestations of form. Thus, in this regard, David Hall is quite right when he contrasts the "ecstasy" (going out) mysticism of Christianity with what he calls the "constasy" (going with) mysticism of Daoism.[62] Unlike Hall, however, we do not conclude this means the Daoist tradition dispenses with transcendence per se, rather only a particular kind of transcendence. The emphasis of needing practices to go "with" the *dao* highlights the fact that though it is immediate in some respects, it is not in others and, hence, transcendent.

Additionally, it is vital to note that Pseudo-Dionysius speaks of God as transcendent not only as source and constant principle of being in all things but also as end (*telos*) of all things. This is clearest in Pseudo-Dionysius' position that God is the ultimate good that all things seek. He is the source of all goodness and the highest good that is to be loved and desired above all else. And God therefore gathers things into Himself precisely as the good. For this reason, the apophaticism of Pseudo-Dionysius and the Christian tradition is, in a sense, restricted to the normal course of life. For after death, there is the final return to the One Goodness involving a sufficient retention of consciousness such that the human being may know and love God as the terms of this return. That is, there is no dissolution into God, but an eternal sharing in God (*apotheosis* in the Patristic formulation).

The *DDJ* is not entirely void of such notions as returning to *dao*. However, it seems one must say that the Daoist conception of returning (*gui* 歸) to *dao* is dramatically different from Christian eschatology. For one, it is not clear Daoists would speak of *dao* in proper terms as the end or Good (in the sense of a teleological good).[63] Surely *dao* is the source of all things, but *dao* does not love the goodness of all things or despise their corruption as Christians claim God does. Rather, the *dao* has no desire, no *telos* to its own action and does bestow itself as a proper end or *telos* of the myriad things. At best, Daoists suggest we must imitate *dao* and seek the emptiness that will harmonize with *dao*, but this strikes us as a kind of liberation from teleology rather than its embrace. Moreover, the Daoist conception of death does not result in the conquering of ignorance of *dao* found in life. Rather, the return to the *dao* seems to consist precisely of a kind of dissolution of the self or ego.

Hence, the fact that the practices of apophaticism in Christian theology and Daoism have different goals seems dependent upon the different conceptions of transcendence the traditions have of God and the *dao*, respectively. Harold Roth neatly captures the difference in his description of the ends of Daoist meditation:

> The classical Daoist adept practiced apophatic mediation not only for its own sake but for the practical transformative benefits it brought to her in everyday life. These goals were self-reinforcing and directly experiential; they were not thought of as conducive to some future distant soteriological goal of liberation or of going to a better place after death.[64]

From this perspective, we can justly refer to Daoist mediation as a "this-worldly" practice. But, we should not mistake this kind of concern with a dismissal of the genuine ways the *dao* functions as a transcendent concept in these same texts.

Of course, it may be that these differences are not as severe as we have suggested, but we maintain a strong reading of these differences for a rhetorical purpose. Even if one accepts there are vast and essential differences in the conceptions of God and *dao* in Pseudo-Dionysius and the *DDJ*, one must also admit profound points of agreement. For one, both texts see God/*dao* as the ultimate principle that causes all things to be and that is present in all things. More importantly, both texts see these aspects of God/*dao* as key to the necessity of apophatic approach to this principle. In other words, it is precisely the fact that God/*dao* underlies all forms that the ultimate is seen as formless in itself. It is precisely inasmuch as God/*dao* causes things to be in a different and higher manner than procreation within species that the ultimate cannot be known in itself.

In this sense, both the *DDJ* and Pseudo-Dionysius can be said to agree about a certain kind of transcendence that must be applied to *dao*/God. Both perspectives would hold that human beings do not connaturally know the nature of that which has caused us to be as the ultimate or prime cause of generation. What has caused us to be exists differently from us, in such a way that we cannot simply reason our way into an adequate understanding of it. At the same time, what has caused us to be is not simply different from our being, but it explains our being as an intrinsic principle: for both Christianity and Daoism, the ultimate is simultaneously within and without us. That is, human beings can recognize that we subsist in the ultimate and the ultimate subsists in us. But we also recognize that our being is not coextensive with the ultimate. Rather, the ultimate reaches beyond the limits of our own being to be in all other things. And for this reason, we cannot know or understand that principle as we understand the world of things. God/*dao* is not the sum total of what may be experienced phenomenally, but somehow is to be differentiated from them; in this way, the ultimate necessarily transcends the things that participate in the ultimate for their being.

Indeed, it is instructive to note that in comparison with Pseudo-Dionysius, one might even argue that the *DDJ* tradition has a stronger conception of transcendence than the Christian text. For in Pseudo-Dionysius, God is the ever-present cause and principle of all things. God's *hyper*-being is the full perfection of being in which all things participate without mediation. However, much like the Neoplatonists Pseudo-Dionysius attempted to correct, the *DDJ* conceives of intermediaries in the order of causation. The *dao* gives birth to *yin* and *yang*, which then give birth to *tian* and earth, which in their turn can be called the mother of all things. But *dao* is a more aloof, more distal cause than is the God of Pseudo-Dionysius. Of course, the Daoist tradition softens this by connecting *dao* with something approaching material causality (but not quite), but it never denies the remote/immediate structure of *dao* generation. In this view, Christianity sees God's causation of the world as perpetual—His transcendence is seen in His perpetual immanence that maintains and guards all things. The *dao*, in comparison, brings about things in a more remote way and thus is a more distant and harder-to-conceive cause than God is according to Christianity.

As a concluding note, we should say we are not offering any of these reflections as a final word about how to interpret the *DDJ* (or Pseudo-Dionysius for that matter). Rather, these reflections serve our larger point, which is simply this: If one approaches the textual corpus of early Daoism assuming a priori that it rejects transcendence, then this obscures very striking and indeed important features of the text. The foregoing analyses at the very least demonstrate that if Pseudo-Dionysius's account of God can be uncontroversially called transcendent—which it can—then this gives us good reason to say some conception of transcendence is at work in the *DDJ*. What is remarkable is not that the *DDJ* dismisses transcendence, but that it utilizes transcendence in interesting and at times puzzling ways. We submit that it is fairer to let the *DDJ* and other Daoist texts be part of a robust dialogue about transcendence—about which it seems to have unique and important things to say—rather than dismiss its relevance to such discourse out of hand.

10

You and *Wu*: Cataphasis and Apophasis

Dao in Cataphatic and Apophatic Mode

As shown in the last chapter, early Daoist texts such as *Daodejing* offer a conception of *dao* as generatively linked to things, accessed (at least in part) apophatically, standing apart in a transcendence similar to that found in the work of Pseudo-Dionysius. In this chapter, we look to the debate concerning creation and agency both in early Chinese texts and among contemporary interpreters. We argue that in early Daoist texts, particularly the *Zhuangzi* and *Daodejing*, *dao* is understood both cataphatically and apophatically, captured by discussions of *dao* as associated with both *you* 有 (being; having) and *wu* 無 (nonbeing; lacking). While Daoist texts seem to privilege and center the apophatic with respect to *dao*, with Han texts such as *Huainanzi* going even further and taking nonbeing as central and the root of being,[1] there is also a cataphatic mode in these texts, pointing to the sense in which the transcendent is not fully inaccessible or beyond understanding. The cataphatic and apophatic modes, concerning *you* and *wu*, give a variety of ways of speaking about the properties of transcendent entities, including in consideration of creation and generation. In the second part of the chapter, we look to the debate concerning creation and agency, arguing that in early China, creative power and agency were not linked in the same way as in a number of other traditions, and that the agency is not a central feature of transcendent creative entities for most early Chinese thinkers. We argue against views of transcendence associated with creative agency. Both in the early Chinese tradition and in a number of others, we find views of transcendence that do not require agency. We look particularly to the views of the Neoplatonists for a comparative example outside of early China. We look to an interpretive debate concerning creation and agency in contemporary scholarship on early China and argue that we find conceptions of transcendent creative entities both with and without agency in early China, but that such agency is not a requirement for transcendence. We conclude the chapter by arguing that we find both agentive and non-agentive conceptions of transcendent creative entities in early Chinese thought, and that claims that early Chinese thought as a whole lacks certain conceptions found in other traditions should be viewed with suspicion.

Discussion of the transcendent in terms of "nothingness," as expression of its intrinsic difference from accessibly existent or fully knowable things, can be found in the work of a number of philosophers of the early medieval period prior to the rise to dominance of Aristotelianism in the Scholastic period. As discussed in the previous chapter, the writings of Pseudo-Dionysius develop this type of apophatic theology. Similar positions can also be found in the work of the ninth-century CE Irish philosopher and theologian John Scotus Eriugena, who developed a vocabulary meant to capture properties of the transcendent God derived from Pseudo-Dionysius, and reminiscent of Daoist language about *dao* itself. While earlier Neoplatonists and the numerous thinkers influenced by them often use apophatic language to capture transcendence, Eriugena's categories in particular are useful in helping us make sense of what is going on in Daoist texts such as *Zhuangzi* and *Daodejing*.

For Eriugena, the omnipresence and omnipotence of God entails that God is present or immanent in all things, even while God at the same time transcends all things. Eriugena, like Pseudo-Dionysius before him, uses the language of absence and "nothingness" to describe God, who is said to be beyond all categories and created things in the world. Though Eriugena places God in *natura*, this category is not meant to include all and only things completely open to a single set of laws of interaction. God is the single aspect of *natura* that creates but is not created, according to Eriugena.[2] Eriugena understands God in two distinct ways, however. All of nature can be understood as a manifestation of God,[3] with different categories of nature understood in terms of different divine theophanies. In consideration of God's creative capacity, God can be understood as that which creates but is not created. But God in another mode is that which is not created and does not create. The critical move Eriugena makes here is to attribute the existence of all things to the divine nature, and thus also hold that God is manifest in all things. Things can only exist, he argues, insofar as they participate in the divine nature—a view reminiscent of Platonism and Neoplatonism. Since this is the case, he concludes that "all things that are from [God] can be predicated of [God]."[4] It is at least in part this predictability that accounts for God's transcendence. To God, we must predicate both a thing and its opposite. Of this, Eriugena says:

> If therefore the aforesaid divine names refer to other names directly opposed to themselves, necessarily also the things that are properly signified by them are understood to possess contrarieties opposite to each other, and through this they cannot properly be predicated of God, to whom nothing [is] opposed, or with whom nothing is observed differing coeternally in nature.[5]

For this reason, Eriugena refers to God's attributes with the addition of the term *hyper*. God is not essence, but *superessence* (*hyperousios*), not goodness, but *supergood* (*hyperagathos*).[6] Explaining this qualification and addition, Eriugena writes:

> All these things that are predicated of God by the addition of the particles *super* or *more than*, as [for example that] he is superessential, more than truth, more than wisdom, and similar things, are most fully comprehended *in se* in the two aforesaid parts of Theology [the cataphatic and apophatic]; so that they may obtain the form of the affirmative in enunciation, but the power of the abdicative in meaning.[7]

We find that mystical thinkers in Abrahamic traditions have a conception of transcendence and access to the transcendence that very much echoes what we find in certain corners of the broader early Chinese tradition, particularly in the work of Daoist thinkers. The "nothingness" language of early Daoist texts echoes that of Eriugena, but Daoist texts generally do not offer the kind of explanation of this negative language that we find in theologians like Pseudo-Dionysius, Eriugena, or Ibn Arabi. What should we make of this reticence on part of the Daoists? While the *Daodejing* is perhaps a special case due to the poetic and spare nature of the text, much of what we find in other Daoist texts such as *Zhuangzi*, *Huainanzi* (not itself a Daoist text but certainly Daoist-influenced), and even the commentaries on *Daodejing* seem to give more explanation of what they are after, even if this explanation is itself couched in ironic language in texts like the *Zhuangzi*.

The Zhuangist conception of *dao*, like Eriugena's conception of God, is that of a transcendent entity in which all existing things are grounded, but which itself surpasses all of the categories applicable to existing things. For Eriugena, the two categories of claims about God, the cataphatic and the apophatic, are meant to capture this. We can speak about God using human language and concepts, and even approximate truths about God's features, as long as we understand that what we are doing is limited and contingent, subject to clarification that undermines it, because of the inability of our concepts to fully capture God's essence (thus superessence). Daoist discussions of the nature of *dao* display the same dual modes. While the fact that Daoist thinkers discuss *dao* in two often very different and conflicting ways does not in itself show that they are making something like the cataphatic/apophatic distinction found in Eriugena's work as a way to capture transcendence, the nature of the distinction as discussed particularly in the *Zhuangzi* does help make this case.

There may be many reasons behind the need for two distinct (and sometimes inconsistent) modes of discussion concerning particular entities or the world as a whole. Different linguistic or social contexts might call for different ways of speaking about particular things, attributing properties to these things in one context that one does not in another, or even positing the existence of things in certain modes of discussion that one does not in another. Some examples of this are relatively metaphysically benign. We discuss the same objects in very different ways in practical and theoretical contexts, for example. The features we may ascribe to a glass of water in one context (ability to quench my thirst) we may fail to ascribe in another context (clear liquid). Of course, in the case of different contexts in this sense, there is no *incompatibility* or contradiction of the features we ascribe in different contexts. We can correctly say that water has the properties of being a clear liquid *and* being able to quench my thirst, and many other besides these. In the case of the cataphatic/apophatic distinction, properties are attributed in one context that are denied in the other.

One such system that gives us incompatible or contradictory properties in different modes of discussion is the early Buddhist philosophical account of what is called the "two truths." Distinguishing between conventional truth and ultimate truth, Buddhist philosophers such as those of the Abhidharma school argue that only claims about irreducible entities such as the momentary psychophysical events (*dharmas*) that make up experience can be *ultimately* true, while we can still say conventionally true things about entities that correspond only to mental formations involving the association of ultimately real objects.[8] For the Buddhists, this distinction is meant to (among other things) make sense of how one can truly make claims involving self-reference when they at the same time reject the existence of a self. Ultimately no selves exist, but we can refer to collections of aggregates and their interactions conventionally using the concept of self.

Notice that here what differs in the two modes is explanatory specificity. On the level of conventional truth, what one truly says is reducible to what is ultimately true. This does not seem to be a case of transcendence, though. Conventionally real entities do not transcend ultimate reality, and ultimately real entities do not transcend conventional reality. There is no transcendent entity being discussed here, but rather a fundamentally existing world (described most accurately on the level of ultimate truth) that can be accessed via reducible conventions as well. While there is some structural similarity between this distinction and that of the cataphatic and apophatic for Eriugena, the apophatic (the level of "ultimate truth" for purposes of comparison) involves a kind of denial of the ability to capture or express truths about God and God's nature using our concepts or language at all, while the cataphatic can be understood as the sense in which we can grasp God's nature through God's effects—in this case, all of nature. Thus for Eriugena, even cataphatic theology will express God's transcendent nature: God is not goodness but *supergoodness*, and so on. In one mode, we express God's transcendence through the conjunction of all properties, and in the other we express it through the negation of all properties.

Some of what we find in chapter 2 (*Qiwulun*) of the *Zhuangzi* concerning language and *dao*, and the distinction between the apparent or effable *dao* and the great *dao* (*da dao* 大道), seems to fit with a cataphatic/apophatic distinction in the attempt to describe the transcendent. A passage from the chapter considers the differences between how the sage thinks about the world using concepts and categories, and how the sage thinks about it outside of these bounds:

六合之外，聖人存而不論；六合之內，聖人論而不議。春秋經世，先王之志，聖人議而不辯。故分也者，有不分也；辯也者，有不辯也。曰：何也？聖人懷之，眾人辯之以相示也。故曰：辯也者，有不見也。夫大道不稱，大辯不言，大仁不仁，大廉不嗛，大勇不忮。道昭而不道，言辯而不及，仁常而不成，廉清而不信，勇忮而不成。五者園而幾向方矣。故知止其所不知，至矣。

Outside of the limits of society, the sage simply exists and does not discourse. Within the limits of society, the sage discourses but does not declare. In the age of the *Chunqiu*, the annals of the former kings, the sage declared but did not argue. Thus in making distinctions there is that which is not distinguished. In arguing, there is that which is not argued. One might ask—how is this so? The sage keeps it within, while the multitude argue about it in order to show one another up. Thus we can say that those who argue have something they are missing. The great *dao* can't be discussed. The great argument can't be spoken. The great humaneness is not humane. The great honesty is not self-satisfied. The great bravery is not haughty. When *dao* is apparent it is not truly *dao*. When words are used to argue they do not truly hit the mark. When humaneness is enduring it is not completed. When honesty is pure it is not genuine. When bravery is haughty it is not completed. These five are round yet they tend toward becoming square. Thus the knowledge that stops at what it does not know is the summative knowledge.[9]

The sage accesses the world in two distinct ways, one corresponding to the world (*liu he zhi nei*) and one corresponding to considerations outside of the world or normal categories (*liu he zhi wai*). The fact that the sage is able to access *dao* at all outside of the normal categories suggests that there is an alternative means of knowledge of *dao*, different than the "lesser knowledge" involving conceptualization, distinction making, and language. In considerations outside the world or normal categories, according to this passage, the sage does not engage in discussion (*lun*), but just exists alone (*cun*). *Dao* itself is captured primarily in negative language akin to the apophatic language of Eriugena and others. *Dao* contains no signs (*feng*), nothing through which it can be distinguished as a *thing* (*wu*). Other passages from *Zhuangzi* chapter 2 extend this idea—*dao* becomes hidden (*yin*) when the concepts of genuine and artificial (*zhen wei*) are applied to it (道惡乎隱而有真偽？).[10]

It is telling that the concept of *zhen* (genuine, true) is used in this passage. Elsewhere in chapter 2 and in other chapters of the *Zhuangzi*, the author(s) describe *zhen* in ways that seem to associate it closely with *dao*. Chapter 6 (*Dazongshi*) remarks at length on the *zhen ren* 真人 (true person) and the true knowledge (*zhen zhi* 真知) that such a person possesses. A passage from chapter 6 describes the *zhen ren* as one who is able to ascend to the *dao* as a result of their resemblance of this conceptless (signless) *dao*:

何謂真人？古之真人，不逆寡，不雄成，不謨士。若然者，過而弗悔，當而不自得也。若然者，登高不慄，入水不濡，入火不熱。是知之能登假於道也若此。

What is it that we call a true person? The true person of ancient times did not turn away from the unpopular, did not attempt to become heroes, and did not make elaborate plans. Being like this, they could make mistakes without regret, and accomplish things without being self-satisfied. Being like this, they could ascend higher without fear and trembling, enter the water without being inundated, enter the fire without being burned. It is this knowledge that enables one to ascend to *dao*.[11]

Dao itself does not contain genuine (*zhen*) and artificial (*wei*) when considered in itself, but considered from the perspective of the individual agent, when one becomes like *dao* one becomes genuine or true (*zhen*). These two ways of discussing *dao* and the properties of *dao* are reminiscent of Eriugena's discussions of God in cataphatic and apophatic modes. We can attribute features to *dao* as manifest in human activity that we cannot attribute to *dao* in itself, as *dao* in itself transcends all categories and features we might ascribe to it. Although Daoist texts are not explicit in making this distinction, we can attribute to these texts different modes: a mode in the discussion of *dao* as immanent, discussion of *dao* using concepts and words—a mode to which we can attribute *zhen* and other properties; and a mode in discussion of *dao* as fully transcendent—a mode in which we must say that *dao* contains neither *zhen* nor *wei*, and nothing can be predicated of it using concepts. *Dao* in this sense is not a thing (*wu*). It is this apophatic conception of *dao* that seems to be behind the negative claims in texts such as the *Zhuangzi*.

In this light, we can make sense of some of the discussion of "things" (*wu*) and their association with *dao* in chapter 2 of the *Zhuangzi*, such as the following passage:

可乎可，不可乎不可。道行之而成，物謂之而然。惡乎然？然於然。惡乎不然？不然於不然。物固有所然，物固有所可。無物不然，無物不可。故為是舉莛與楹，厲與西施，恢恑憰怪，道通為一。

If there can be there can be—if there can't be there can't be. When the *dao* is enacted, it is thereby completed. When things are named, they thereby become so. How is this so? It is so from it being so. How is this not so? It is not so from being not so. Each thing has that in which it is so. Each thing has that in which it can be such as it is. There is no thing that is not so. There is no thing that cannot be such as it is. Thus whether we have a blade of grass or a pillar, a rock or the beautiful Xi Shi, the vast and changed, or the wily and strange—*dao* makes these all as one.[12]

We also find here a critical distinction between *dao* and *wu* on the basis of action and speech. What fundamentally reveals certain features of *dao* is non-linguistic practice (*xing*), while things (*wu*) gain their existence from concepts and language. This is part of the reason that things are transformable and constantly transforming (*wu hua* or *wanwu zhi hua*),[13] given that the creatures on which "things" depend occupy different perspectives and themselves transform. At the end of chapter 2, the author offers the famous butterfly story as an example of the "transformation of things."

昔者莊周夢為胡蝶，栩栩然胡蝶也，自喻適志與！不知周也。俄然覺，則蘧蘧然周也。不知周之夢為胡蝶與，胡蝶之夢為周與？周與胡蝶，則必有分矣。此之謂物化。

Some time ago, I dreamed that I was a butterfly, happily acting as a butterfly, going about what it wished. I knew nothing about being Zhuang Zhou. Suddenly I woke up, and just then I was Zhuang Zhou. And I didn't know whether I was Zhuang Zhou who had been previously dreaming that I was a butterfly, or whether I was a butterfly now dreaming I was Zhuang Zhou. But mustn't there be a difference between Zhuang Zhou and a butterfly? We can call this the transformation of things.[14]

The "things" that transform in this case are Zhuang Zhou himself, the butterfly, and the experience of each subject. All perspectives, which can be captured in terms of *shi-fei* conceptualization, distinction, creation, and reference, can be understood as involving (or bringing about) "things." While these things may change and thus transform our experience (one may find oneself to be Zhuang Zhou at some times and a butterfly at others), understanding of *dao* (the "greater knowledge" discussed throughout the text) enables one to retain one's bearings in the face of transformation.[15] This is because the person who understands *dao* recognizes that there are no uniquely privileged perspectives in *dao*, that although *dao* is the basis of the myriad things, it is not itself ultimately *one more* of these things.

A number of scholars argue for an apophatic reading of Zhuangist and other Daoist views on *dao*. David Chai, Louis Komjathy, William Franke, Francois Jullien, and others present views of the *Zhuangzi* and related texts as offering apophatic accounts of *dao*.[16] Franke writes, in his study of apophaticism across the globe, about the concept of "the pivot of the *dao*" in the *Zhuangzi*:

> What is needed, then, is a word that can divest itself of all its particularities so as to metamorphose potentially into other words without limit and hypothetically into all other words, overcoming their ostensible mutual exclusivity. [...] This mobility, though remaining open to and responding to all occasions, is an image of the global vision that corresponds to the *Dao* and lies beyond language, with its distinctions and differential logic and restrictions, and with its inevitably enclosed point of view.[17]

While focusing on apophatic language can help us make sense of Daoist discussions of *dao* as non-conceptual, ineffable, and fully transcendent, the discussion of *dao* in these texts also has a positive element closer to Eriugena's sense of the cataphatic, in which properties can be attributed to *dao* using language, with the caveat that such conceptualization of *dao* gives us a limited conception of *dao*. If we are not fooled by language into thinking that this conceptualization gives us a unique and privileged perspective or uniquely true claims about *dao* based on attribution of properties to *dao* (in itself), we can use this positive language to make sense of *dao*. We can understand the claims about *dao* that do not appear in apophatic mode in this way. We find seemingly contradictory claims about *dao* that attribute features to it only to later deny those same features of it.[18] And these seeming contradictions come within chapters and even passages of Zhuangist and other Daoist texts as well. The first chapter of the *Daodejing* is filled with such movement between apophatic and cataphatic modes. That without name (*dao*) is the origin of heaven and earth, according to the chapter. At the same time, it (*dao*) is the mystery that goes beyond mystery (*xuan zhi you xuan*).[19]

When positing transcendent entities, one generally has to make some distinction between the accessible and inaccessible aspects or the transcendent entities in question, because these transcendent entities, such as God, soul, noumena, or *dao*, maintain some necessary connection with the visible, accessible, immanent cosmos. Often, a transcendent entity will be understood as the creative source of the cosmos and sometimes as continually active in the cosmos. In order for there to be such relationship between the immanent cosmos and transcendent entities, there must be some way the transcendent entity in question enters or is manifest in the immanent world—otherwise such an entity must remain causally inert and potentially fully unknowable and inaccessible, even through apophatic means.

We find numerous ways of making this connection in different texts and traditions. A particularly influential general way of doing this in traditions linked to the ancient Greek (including European and Middle Eastern philosophy) is the roughly *Platonic* solution. A general Platonic view holds that immanent entities in the accessible cosmos are related to transcendent ideal forms (of some kind) in which they are grounded—that is, which are their creative source and on which their essential features rely. Plato himself understood this relation between Forms and the individual things in the world grounded in them in terms of resemblance[20] in some places and in other places in terms of the "partaking" of individual things in their related Forms.[21] A perhaps more influential updating of the Platonist view (and one more useful for drawing parallels to early Chinese forms of transcendence) was that of Plotinus, who understood the relationship between a transcendent One and the numerous things in the world as a kind of illumination or emanation from the One, serving as both creative source and underlying nature of individual things. Plotinus, recognizing the One as transcendent and thus inaccessible in itself, argued that there are two other manifestations (or hypostases) of this essential being, the intellectual principle (*nous*) and soul.[22] The One, though fully transcendent, can never be completely inaccessible, as it is the foundation and source of all things, and that in which they have their nature (the other two hypostases likewise linked to the One).

A key connection is made here between the immanent stuff of the cosmos and the transcendent in the form of the hypostases. The immanent can be understood as an illumination of, partaking in the same nature of, but lesser manifestation of, the fully transcendent One. And as we see in the work of Eriugena, using "immanentist" language to describe the transcendent (cataphatic access) cannot be understood as incompatible with apophatic description of the transcendent.

The immanentist language that can be found in Daoists texts is used by some scholars to justify a reading of *dao* as completely immanent and manifest.[23] But use of this language alone, as we see in the case of Eriugena, does not commit a thinker to an immanentist conception of the concept discussed. If Daoist thinkers discussed *only dao* using this immanentist language, this would certainly be evidence that they held the view of *dao* as immanent and not transcendent. But we find both immanentist and seemingly transcendentist language, both cataphatic and apophatic language, concerning *dao* within Daoist texts. Both sides in the immanence–transcendence debate have passages to which they can point. But what is required here that we can make sense of are the numerous varying (and sometimes seemingly contradictory) claims in these texts as demonstrating a particular view. That is, an interpretation that explains the seeming contradictions is more powerful than one that explains only one or the other conjunct. We have seen that at least some thinkers, such as Eriugena or Plotinus, who accept transcendent entities, have reason to posit multiple modes of access to such entities. This is generally because in transcendent entities discussed in particular philosophical or theological systems, there is some crucial connection to the world. There would be no reason for us (and ultimately no way for us) to discuss transcendent entities that did not interact with, manifest themselves in, or somehow otherwise have accessible relationship with the immanent world. Yonghua Ge, discussing this aspect of transcendence in Christianity, writes:

> It is true that the *Dao* is characterized by a strong sense of immanence in relation to the world, but its immanence does not necessarily preclude its transcendence. In the Christian tradition, God's immanence is consistent with his transcendence. If this is the case, it is possible that the immanent *Dao* can be simultaneously transcendent.[24]

Eriugena's cataphatic/apophatic distinction can help to capture this idea, and the way *dao* is discussed in numerous early Daoist texts suggests that something like this distinction is in play. Ge points out that the distinction between the "nameable *dao*" and the "nameless *dao*" in early Daoist texts shows that *dao* should not be understood as solely immanent.[25] While Daoist texts do not explicitly draw a nameable/nameless distinction with regard to *dao*, we can make the best sense of the seemingly contradictory claims about *dao* in these texts by attributing such a distinction to them. Such a distinction also makes sense of the distinction between knowable and unknown, and that with features and without features. This makes most sense if we see something like Eriugena's distinction concerning God in the case of *dao*. Below, we look at a number of passages in the *Daodejing*, *Zhuangzi*, and other *dao*-oriented texts to demonstrate that a cataphatic and apophatic distinction as applied to *dao* is at work in at least some Daoist texts.[26]

First, let's look at passages that proponents of an immanentist view of *dao* point to in support of their view. While one often finds the claim that *dao* is understood as an immanent concept in early Chinese texts, this is less often supported by textual evidence.

Bin Song, in his recent work on transcendence in the Confucian tradition, points out that the claims of *dao* as origin in the *Daodejing* do not necessarily distinguish between *dao* as having "ontological priority" and *dao* as "cosmologically preceding" the rest of the world.[27] It is only in the case of the first, he argues, that *dao* can be taken as transcendent (at least in a sense shared with the transcendent creative God of the Abrahamic traditions). Scholars who argue for an immanent *dao* generally point out the apparent continuity between *dao* and the world that emerges from *dao*.[28] The spontaneous emergence of the world from *dao* itself does not entail a naturalistic or non-transcendent picture of *dao*. Song points out that *dao* in the *Daodejing* is taken as temporally prior to the cosmos, which spontaneously emerges from the *dao*,[29] and that prior to the emergence of the cosmos, *dao* is formless, "invisible, inaudible, and intangible."[30]

One problem with this view is that although the *Daodejing* does seem to suggest a temporal priority of *dao*, it also asserts *dao*'s continued existence, and the formlessness of *dao* even alongside of the formed myriad things. *Dao* is something accessible (in some way) to us, something we can use (*yong* 用),[31] something we can obtain (*de* 得),[32] and something we can lose (*shi* 失).[33]

The temporal priority of *dao* and the emergence of things from *dao* (rather than separately created from an ontologically distinct God) also do not entail lack of transcendence. Numerous scholars take this disanalogy from the Abrahamic notion of divine creation as definitive proof of the immanence of *dao*. The notion of *creation ex nihilo* is necessary for transcendence in this sense, according to these scholars. The doctrine of creation from nothing, however, is a development in later Abrahamic thought that itself builds on earlier conceptions of transcendence (the Latin origin of the phrase should tip us off to its late development). There is no evidence of the doctrine in the Hebrew scriptures or the Greek New Testament, and it was not until the early Church period that we see the doctrine emerge. Ian Barbour wrote that "Genesis portrays the creation of order from chaos, and … the *ex nihilo* doctrine was formulated later by the church fathers to defend theism against an ultimate dualism or a monistic pantheism."[34] Philosophers such as Augustine in the Christian tradition attempted to make sense of the absolute superiority of God by distancing God from the creation to such an extent that the creative power of God became problematic. For Augustine, knowledge of God is only possible through Christian faith (unlike the rationalist approach of Aquinas which entails traces of God's effective power in the world).[35] Willful creation as another mark of transcendence is also due to quirks of the development of philosophy and theology in Abrahamic traditions. The idea that a spontaneous and non-willed emergence of the cosmos from some original ground-of-being or principle must be understood as non-transcendent or naturalistic requires the view that only an entity possessing agency can be ontologically distinct (enough) from the cosmos to ground transcendence. But agency in itself does not get us the required ontological difference—most would admit that agency in the human case (if we have it) is part of the world and non-transcendent.

Older conceptions of transcendence in the West, including that of Platonists, look much closer to what we find in Daoist texts such as the *Daodejing*. Notice (as we pointed out in previous chapters) that the grounds on which scholars reject transcendence in Daoist texts—the continuity with and emergence from *dao* of the world, and the natural and spontaneous emergence of things from *dao*—would also entail that Platonists, such as Plotinus, do not accept transcendence. Plotinus gives us a key example of a thinker who accepts such a view, yet clearly has a transcendent conception of his central concept, the One, and the divine hypostases. For Plotinus, transcendence is understood in terms of the One's independence, existence as ground of being, and the entrance of lower orders of being into the world with emanation from the One that brings all things in the cosmos into being.[36] It is also true of the One that it creates not willfully, but in virtue of what it is—the emanation of the things of the cosmos (including the hypostases) from the One happens *naturally*, that is, on the basis of the pure act of the One that happens as a result of its nature, not as a result of its agency.[37] In this sense, its creation is natural and spontaneous, just as that emanating from the *dao*, in passages like *Daodejing* 42.[38] Scholars have adopted the term "emanation" to explain Plotinus' doctrine of the One's creative power. While Plotinus does not himself use such a term, later philosophers influenced by Neoplatonism use terms similar to this, including the *ishraq* ("illumination") of the twelfth-century CE Persian philosopher Yahya ibn Habash Suhrawardi. While Plotinus' doctrine of emanation is understood not in terms of temporal priority but rather in terms of ontological priority, it is still the case that the things in the world, including the other hypostases, come to be from and on the basis of the act of the One, and share in its nature.[39] In this way, the numerous things in the world can be said to partake in the One in the sense that they are constituted by, are modifications of, and in some sense *are* the One.

At the same time, the One is clearly transcendent, both beyond being and ineffable. For strikingly similar reasons to those found in the *Zhuangzi*, the One cannot be conceptualized in the normal way. The One fails to be a thing, or substance (*ousia*), because every substance is both limited and multiple (as possessing qualities).[40] As thus no thing, the One transcends all things in the cosmos. It is unnameable and ineffable, for even the act of attributing a name to the One would introduce multiplicity. As Plotinus writes:

> If one must bring in these names of what we are looking for, let it be said again that it was not correct to use them, because one must not make it two even for the sake of forming an idea of it.[41]

The creative capacity of the One (and other parts of nature) is also explained in terms similar to those used by *Dao*-oriented texts. The nature of things leads to emanation or creation of new things. In performing their own characteristic activities, existing things bring about new creation, and this creation proceeds from the essence of the creating thing. Plotinus writes:

> All existences, as long as they retain their character, produce—about themselves, from their essence, in virtue of the power which must be in them—some necessary, outward-facing hypostasis continuously attached to them and representing in image the engendering archetypes: thus fire gives out its heat; snow is cold not merely to itself; fragrant substances are a notable instance; for, as long as they last, something is diffused from them and perceived wherever they are present.[42]

This seemingly spontaneous and automatic creation from the essence of a thing accounts also for the creation of the two other hypostases, *nous* (intellect) and *psyche* (soul), from the One, and thereby the creation of the entire cosmos of things. This creative act of the One is explained in terms of its essence and its perfection,[43] and the created hypostases themselves create on the same basis, until the proliferation ultimately results in the creation of the sensible world. Transcendence, in Plotinus' system, is understood in terms of the ontological dependence, higher level of "being," and conceptual inaccessibility of the One.[44]

This shows that the fact that the myriad things of the cosmos are discussed in Daoist texts as emerging from and continuous with *dao* does not in itself show that these texts do not offer a transcendent conception of *dao*. And such readings of *dao* as immanent also struggle to make sense of the claims of ineffability and inapplicability of concepts to *dao* we find in Daoist texts right alongside claims about the origin of the myriad things from *dao*.

Roger Ames argues that passages of Daoist texts such as *Daodejing* chapters 1 and 25, that sound to many (including us) like a discussion of a transcendent and ineffable entity responsible for the generation of the myriad things, should instead be understood as discussion of determinate and indeterminate aspects of human experience. Part of the evidence he offers for this is what he argues to be the meaning of terms *you* 有 (existence; having) and *wu* 無 (not existing; not having). Ames claims that these terms do not concern existence, but rather "having at hand." He writes:

> Since the classical Chinese language does not employ a copulative verb that predicates "existence per se" as an essential being, the terms usually used to stand in for and translate the alien notions of "being" and "not-being" have been *you* and *wu*, respectively. But in fact, *you* means not something that "is" (*esse* in Latin) in the sense that it exists in some essential way; it means rather "having present-to-hand."[45]

There are a number of problems with this view. While Ames is right that *you* can have the sense of "having present-to-hand" or simply "having," it is simply incorrect of *any* language to say that every sense of a word comes along with every use of it. In classical Chinese, as in English, the same word can be used in different senses, and senses can be independent of one another. For example, the English term "work" has a number of different senses, but it is not the case for every use that each of those senses is in use. If I say "he doesn't have any work," it means that the person in consideration is not employed. If I say "this computer doesn't work," it means that the computer is not operational. These two senses are certainly related, but do not mean the same thing, and when I say of my friend that he hasn't found work, I do *not* also mean that my friend has not found operational capacity. One does not get all the senses of a word with one use. This is the reason that we can (and must!) translate the same word differently given different contexts.

This is the case for terms like *you* and *wu*. We cannot deny that these terms sometimes do have the sense of "having" and "not-having." But it is simply implausible to deny that they also can have the sense of "existing" and "not-existing." Indeed, there are a number of uses of the terms in classical Chinese texts that simply do not make sense if we read *you* and *wu* in this way. Let's look at a couple of examples. In the discussion of ghosts in the *Mozi*, the consideration is whether ghosts *you* or *wu*.[46] The author considers the question: 鬼神可謂有乎? (Can ghosts and spirits be said to -*you*-?) Now, if the author here is discussing the question of whether ghosts are or are not available or "present-to-hand," the discussion becomes far more trivial as well as seems to assume the existence of ghosts. An even more difficult case for Ames's reading is the discussion of the generation of things at the beginning of chapter 2 of the *Huainanzi*. Here, *you* and *wu* are used to develop a cosmogony describing the arising of the myriad things from an initial state devoid of *you* (existence). If *you* and *wu* in this context are read as "having-at-hand" and "not-having-at-hand," then it makes no sense that the authors of the chapter would understand this coming to be in terms of the generation of things. As the chapter describes part of the process:

天氣始下，地氣始上，陰陽錯合

The vital energy of *tian* began to descend, the vital energy of earth began to rise— and *yin and yang* were unified.[47]

To read *you* and *wu* as *always* having the sense of "having-at-hand" and "not-having-at-hand" is to deny that classical Chinese has the expressive power of other languages in which numerous senses of words are possible, which is also an implausible view concerning classical Chinese. We see clearly that technical terms such as *dao, tian, qi* and other contentious terms are used in variety of ways across (and within) texts, and myriad other more ordinary terms are also used with different senses in different contexts. Just to name a few: the term *zhi* 之, which is most often used as a possessive— as in *xian wang zhi dao* 先往之道 (the way of the former kings)—but can also be used as a verb, with the sense "to go." These two senses are not related and never coincide. The term *yu* 與 can be both a conjunctive "and" as well as the verb "to give." Which one is meant is generally clear from the context, but there are never contexts in which *both* senses are meant (outside of poetry or plays on words). A language in which there was no ability to determine multiple senses of terms based on context would be impoverished, and certainly one in which it would be impossible to engage in wordplay, literature, or philosophy. Indeed, chapter 1 of the *Daodejing* seems to require that key terms such as *dao* and *ming* have numerous senses—otherwise the basic negations established in that chapter would be almost literally incoherent. If the *dao* that can be *dao* is not the constant *dao*, and the name that can be name is not the constant name, then there can be neither *dao* nor name. Clearly one of the uses of *dao* and *ming* must refer to something different than the other, because the presumption here is that there *is* a constant *dao* and a constant *ming*. Otherwise, what is the point of discussing the conditions for their lacking constancy?

The upshot here of reading Daoist texts alongside Neoplatonism and later apophatic theologies such as that found in Eriugena's work is that this gives us key examples of traditions of transcendence in which we find the very features in virtue of which immanentist scholars deny transcendence to the concept of *dao* in Daoist texts (and early Chinese texts in general). Anyone who discusses transcendent entities, on pain of incoherence, must have some way of accessing, knowing, and describing the transcendent entities in question. And any tradition in which a transcendent entity is held to be responsible for creation and/or maintenance of the world, and that can otherwise interact with that created world, must have some aspects through which it is conceptually or otherwise accessible to inhabitants of that world. Otherwise, the transcendent would literally be nothing to us, in the sense that we would not even be able to (nor would it occur to us to) conceive of it.

This seems to account for the two modes of discussion of *dao* in Daoist texts, along the lines of the two modes of discussion of God in the work of Eriugena. William Franke writes: "…the *Dao* has at least two faces, one manifest and one hidden, like the moon, although more deeply or inwardly, it remains still one and the same."[48] Cataphatic and apophatic access to *dao* are both necessary, because *dao* is a transcendent entity that nonetheless interacts with and at the same time in an important sense is immanent within the world.

Taiji and the Source of Creation

Much of the transcendence debate among contemporary scholars surrounds the issue of creation and Chinese cosmogony. In this section, we expand a particular point we made in the last chapter concerning the *Daodejing* to a broader consideration of creation and transcendence, as it connects to the issue of *you* and *wu*. One debate involving the concept of *creation ex nihilo* has been precipitated largely by the comparative work of Robert Neville on this topic.[49] Bin Song argues for transcendence in the Chinese tradition, focusing on the issue of creation in Christian thought and Confucianism.[50] The contemporary discussion of transcendence in early Chinese texts, according to Song, traces back to Julia Ching's *Confucianism and Christianity,* in which she rejects the notion of metaphysical transcendence in early Chinese texts on the basis of the absence of a notion of *creation ex nihilo* in the Chinese tradition. While Ching's study is focused on Confucianism in particular, the adoption of Dao-tradition positions in Han and later "Confucian" texts problematizes this claim.

Paulos Huang focuses on the concept of *taiji* in his consideration of creation, arguing that the concept of *taiji* 太極 represents the fundamental creative principle for Confucianism (neo-Confucianism in particular, as *taiji* is absent from early Confucian texts), and that while there may be a kind of transcendence represented by *taiji*, it is not the same kind of transcendence found in theistic systems like that of Christianity.[51] Huang distinguishes between two kinds of transcendence: transcendence as "objective-lying-beyond-the-limits" and transcendence as "actively to go beyond some limit." Huang argues that we find in Confucianism the second type of transcendence, particularly connected with self-development and ethical considerations, but not the first. He rejects the first on the basis of the absence of a "personality" on the part of *taiji* (arguing that "creation" rather than "production" requires a personality for the creator), and the absence of the view that the source of the world is a different substance than the world that is produced or created. Frederick Mote made a similar claim about early Chinese texts in general, claiming that:

> The Chinese have regarded the world and man as uncreated, as constituting the central features of a spontaneously self-generating cosmos having no creator, god, ultimate cause, or will external to itself.[52]

There are a number of problems with this view. One of them is that Huang is unclear on what he means by "personality" and just why this is necessary for creation rather than production. What he could have in mind is intention or agency—we might want to say that causal efficacy is insufficient for attribution of creative power, but that something more such as intention, choice, or agency is necessary to distinguish between mere causation (what Huang calls "production") and creation. One of the key features of intentional creation is that the created thing is connected to a chain of reasons and has some purposive end. A created thing is something created *for* some particular purpose. The particular purpose is inessential here—a thing might be created to help the creator achieve some practical end, such as a tool, or it might be created simply to satisfy the desire of the creator to create and have no practical end. But it makes sense to distinguish the act of creation as intentional to contrast it with non-intentional action or non-agentive causation. If agency makes the difference between creation and production (a view we will see a number of early Chinese thinkers themselves actually take up), and creation in this sense is necessary for transcendence, this bars any conception of "objective-lying-beyond-the-limits" transcendence to views of creation that do not rely on divine agents. It turns out then that Platonist and Neoplatonist conceptions of creation like those of Plotinus (among others) are not properly transcendent.

Why think that a causal principle or creative being must be an *agent* to be objectively beyond the limits and different in substance from what it creates? For Plotinus, the One is completely transcendent, such that it cannot be understood or accessed in itself but only through what it creates, yet the relationship between the One and the created world is not that between an agent and its intentional creation. The created world (including the other two hypostases of the divine) is created automatically and from the nature of the One itself, not through any agentive decision making or action. Perhaps one sympathetic to Huang's view could simply deny that views like the Neoplatonist view hold an "objective-lying-beyond-the-limits" transcendence, but then it seems like we are conceiving of such transcendence far too narrowly, such that it only applies to (some) Abrahamic theistic conceptions of God. And if this is the case, then the answer to the transcendence question in early China (or anywhere else) is trivial—that is, anyone who does not hold a view of a divine agent responsible for creation does not accept transcendence. Transcendence, on this view, just reduces to divine creative agency. This is an unsatisfying move for a number of reasons. Concepts of transcendence are meant to capture the idea that there are different orders of existence, some of which are outside of or in important ways not subject to the states and conditions of the order(s) of existence we and the rest of the sensible world are subject to. It is for this reason that we generally take Platonism, for example, to unproblematically represent a worldview in which we find transcendence. Or the view of the Advaita Vedanta school in India, in which the sensible world, including the "material mind," can be understood as forming one (ultimately illusory) order of reality to which the true self (or pure consciousness) is not subject—it is also natural to see this as a kind of transcendence.[53] Or even the Buddhist *nirvana*, which is always negatively (apophatically) characterized because it is (explicitly) understood to be unconditioned (while all things in the world are conditioned) and clearly thus "beyond the limits." If transcendence is narrowed to only theistic "lying beyond the limits" in terms of divine agency, then we must reject these other systems as offering transcendence, which seems to narrow the term beyond its usefulness and its intended sense.

Indeed, packed into Huang's own description of this form of transcendence, "objective-lying-beyond-the-limits" is just such a description as the broad conception we outline above. And if this is the case, it seems implausible to think there is no other way for a system to accept something objectively lying beyond the limits of the sensible or mundane world without that thing being a divine agent. Indeed, the Neoplatonists give us good evidence that this is false on its face, as Plotinus' One is explicitly defined (insofar as it can be captured in concepts or definition) as beyond the limits of attribution, conceptualization, or even being and non-being.[54] Indeed, anything to which we could attribute agency would have to be something *less* transcendent than Plotinus' One, as such a being would necessarily contain multiplicity and traits of created things.[55]

Another difficulty with Huang's view is his reliance on the concept of *taiji* 太極 as demonstrating that what creates the world is same in substance as the world itself. The concept of *taiji* developed prior to its use in neo-Confucianism to describe the accessible and manifest aspects of the formation and changes of the world. This use is retained in the work of certain neo-Confucian thinkers. Zhu Xi, for example, took *taiji* as central, but it is unclear that even he understood *taiji* to be the fundamental creative principle rather than a principle of patterning or ordering the world.[56] *Taiji* for Zhu Xi does not seem to be ontologically foundational in the way transcendent creative entities are, and perhaps thus not the best concept to look to for evaluating whether we can find transcendence in neo-Confucian or any other Chinese tradition. In addition, Zhu Xi's use of *taiji* must be understood in terms of the historical development of the concept and the connotations it would have already had by the time he adopted it. Zhou Dunyi (1017–1073 CE) was probably the most important immediate predecessor of Zhu Xi to discuss *taiji*. And when we look to Zhou's account of *taiji*, it is not at all clear that *taiji* is continuous with the world in terms of substance as Huang claims. Indeed, for Zhou, it would not be correct to call *taiji* a substance at all, as it is beyond being and non-being (much more similar to Plotinus' One or the *dao* of the *Daodejing* than to either an Abrahamic divine agent or a natural principle). A passage concerning the creation or generation of things at the beginning of Zhou's *Taijitu shuo* ("A Discussion of the *Taiji* Diagram") reads:

自無極而為太極。太極動而生陽，動極而靜，靜而生陰，靜極復動。一動一靜，互為其根；分陰分陽，兩儀立焉。陽變陰合，而生水、火、木、金、土。五氣順布，四時行焉。五行，一陰陽也；陰陽，一太極也；太極，本無極也。

Emerging from *wuji* and becoming *taiji*—*taiji* moves and generates *yang*. This moves *ji* and there is stillness, and from stillness *yin* is generated. Stilling *ji* returns to movement. One movement, one stillness, these are mutually the root. Distinguishing *yin* and *yang*, the two modes are established. *Yang* transforms and *yin* unifies—this generates water, fire, wood, metal, and earth. The five *qi* following these come to fruition, and the four seasons progress. The five phases (*wu xing*) are one *yin yang*. *Yin yang* are one *taiji*. *Taiji* has its root in *wuji*.[57]

Here, we see that not only does *taiji* not seem to be a generative principle continuous with or of the same substance as things in the world, but we also see that the root (*ben*) of *taiji* itself lies in *wuji*. Thus pointing to *taiji* as a supreme creative principle, even for neo-Confucians, is problematic. And given that Zhu Xi adopts Zhou Dunyi's system, it is also unlikely that Zhu Xi envisions *taiji* to play the transcendent "objective-lying-beyond-the-limits" role. So if Huang finds that the concept of *taiji* does not represent such a transcendent entity, this does not in itself show that Zhou Dunyi, Zhu Xi, or any other neo-Confucian (let alone other Chinese thinkers) did not have a concept of such "objective" transcendence, merely that if they did, the concept of *taiji* did not represent such a transcendent entity. But perhaps Huang is simply looking in the wrong place. Given that the centrally transcendent entity in Abrahamic traditions is the divine agent, Huang seems to look for the closest parallel in Chinese traditions to the concept of the Abrahamic God. But this is to conflate all of the features of the Abrahamic divine agent with transcendent entities or even with divine agents *as such*.

Insofar as one is looking for something as close as possible to the Abrahamic divine agent, then *taiji* may appear to be the best available concept. But when we are asking the question of whether we can find transcendence in a given tradition or text, we should attend only to the features relevant to transcendence *as such*. That is, if we recognize that transcendence does not reduce to divine creative agency (as indeed it can't if Platonists, Advaitins, and anyone other than divine agent theists have concepts of transcendence), and that one could accept a transcendent entity lacking many of the features of a divine agent, then looking for a concept parallel to that of a divine agent will not be very helpful. Another premise is needed here, of course. Not only is it the case that one can accept transcendent entities without a divine agent, but one can also accept a divine agent without transcendence. The Greek pantheon and the gods of the Vedas and Avestas, for example, are clearly divine agents, but lack the difference in substance and unconditioned existence "beyond the limits" that would qualify them for transcendence on either Huang's view or that of most others. If being a divine agent, then, is neither a necessary nor a sufficient condition for being a transcendent entity, then searching for parallels to the Abrahamic divine agent in other traditions will not be a reliable guide for discerning whether the tradition in question has a conception of transcendence.

Bin Song points out an additional problem with Huang's view—it is unclear whether he is right about *taiji*. Even if we do take *taiji* as the best case for transcendence in neo-Confucian texts, it is textually problematic to claim that *taiji* is continuous with (in terms of having the sameness of substance as) the created world. The passage above from the *Taijitu shuo* offers evidence that this reading of *taiji* is incorrect. First, *taiji* emerges spontaneously (*zi* 自—more on this concept below) from *wuji*, and the movement (*dong*) of *taiji* brings about the generation of *yang* and (through an extension of the process) *yin*. It is the operation of *yin* and *yang* that brings about the five phases (*wu xing*) and from there the myriad things. Given this process, it seems simply incorrect to claim that the myriad created things are of the same substance as *taiji*. *Taiji* is not yet even a principle (as are *yin* and *yang*), so how could *taiji* be understood as substantially the same as the myriad things?

We also see that in Zhou Dunyi's explanation, *taiji* is not the fundamental ground of being out of which everything emerges, because *taiji* itself emerges from *wuji*. We need not read Zhou's *wuji* as "nothing," such that *taiji* is understood as created ex nihilo (or rather spontaneously emerging ex nihilo), as we have seen that there was already by Zhou's time (early eleventh century CE) an established sense of apophatic description of central transcendent principles, such as *dao* in early Daoist texts, that render the ineffable (because transcendent) entity or principle foundational to the world in terms of negation or absence (the term *wu* 無 being particularly prevalent in this application).[58]

Taiji is discussed as far back as the *Zhuangzi*, in which it also appears as an important but not foundational concept. Zhou Dunyi's claim that *taiji* emerges from *wuji* finds a parallel in the *Zhuangzi* chapter 6 claim that dao is prior (*xian* 先) to *taiji*. We see that *dao* in this passage of the *Zhuangzi* is described in negative terminology, following the apophatic technique described above in numerous early Daoist texts. But this does not entail that *dao* is literally nothing, that it is the inert and empty nothingness from which things (including *taiji*) emerge in a kind of ex nihilo fashion. Rather, *dao* is described in terms of nothingness because of the essential ineffability of *dao*, because, as in the apophatic theologies we have considered above, since *dao* lies "beyond the limits" (to use Huang's terminology), it cannot ultimately be captured using the concepts and terms that themselves are derived from conditioned experience of the created world. The passage from *Zhuangzi* chapter 6 in question, describing the *dao* in apophatic manner, reads:

夫道，有情有信，無為無形；可傳而不可受，可得而不可見；自本自根，未有天地，自古以固存；神鬼神帝，生天生地；在太極之先而不為高，在六極之下而不為深；先天地生而不為久，長於上古而不為老。

Dao has its essence and has its legitimacy—it lacks activity (*wei*) and shape (*xing*). It can be transmitted but it cannot be received, it can be obtained but it cannot be seen. It is self-originating and self-rooted. Before the existence of heaven and earth, it was of itself solidified and existent, from time immemorial. The spirits and deities emerged from it. It generated heaven and generated earth. It is prior to *taiji* yet not lofty, it is below all locations yet not deep. It is prior to the generation of heaven and earth yet never aging, reaching further back than time immemorial yet never old.[59]

It is the formative *dao* that is both prior to and somehow generates *taiji* as well as all other things in the cosmos, yet this *dao* cannot be straightforwardly captured with words, recalling the ineffability claims of the *Daodejing* as well as the apophatic theology of figures like Eriugena and Pseudo-Dionysius, and the transcendent conception of the One of Plotinus. Zhou Dunyi's, and also thus Zhu Xi's, conception of *taiji* cannot be considered historically disconnected from these older senses of *taiji*. Indeed, Zhou's discussion of *taiji* in the *Taijitu shuo* is wholly consistent with what we find in the *Zhuangzi* chapter 6 discussion. And, just as in the *Zhuangzi* case, the concept of *taiji* turns out to simply be the wrong place to look for transcendence. Based on what we have shown, Huang is indeed right that the concept of *taiji* is not that of a transcendent entity. But this does not show that the neo-Confucians (or other Chinese thinkers) did not have a conception of transcendence. Many did. For the Zhuangists (of Chapter 6 at least), this concept was *dao*. For Zhou Dunyi, it was *wuji* (which might be linked with *dao*).

The issue of creation and reliance on agency is actually one we can find in early Chinese texts themselves. While the debate concerning the creation or generation of the cosmos in Han and Wei-Jin period philosophy does not concern the issue of transcendence directly, the related issues discussed there are relevant to the current debate among scholars concerning transcendence in early China. Particularly in the debate surrounding transcendence as linked to creation, the views of Han and Wei-Jin thinkers, often overlooked, have an important role to play.

Some scholars take *tian*, rather than *taiji*, to be the main candidate for transcendence in the early Chinese tradition. The late Confucian scholar Liu Shu-hsien argued for a particular type of transcendence in the Confucian tradition, connected to the concept of *tian*, although of a weaker kind than the contrastive transcendence considered here, by Huang, and others. Liu wrote:

> Heaven [*tian*] is transcendent in the sense that it is an all-encompassing creative power which works incessantly in the universe. It is not a thing, but it is the origin of all things. And it cannot be detected by sense perceptions, because its 'operations have neither sound nor smell.' But Heaven is also immanent in the sense that it penetrates deep in every detail of the natural order, in general, and of the moral order of man in particular. But Heaven in no sense should be regarded as something completely beyond nature; on the contrary, it is that which constitutes the warp and woof of nature.[60]

Part of the problem here is that Liu, like numerous other scholars, made claims about an overarching "Confucian tradition" and claims that *tian* is the transcendent entity discussed by this tradition. This is a problematic claim for a number of reasons. First, the notion of a unified "Confucian tradition" is no more coherent than that of a "Judeo-Christian tradition" (a construction Liu also used).[61] The reason for this is that many different schools and worldviews across thousands of years are lumped into these traditions, which are often very different and even contradictory, such that when we focus only on what is shared by these diverse traditions falling under such broad umbrellas, we can only have the vaguest and most philosophically empty of content.

It is a common move since the days of Zhu Xi (and one Liu made as well) to assume the "Confucian tradition" as defined by the so-called "Four Books": *Analects, Mengzi,* and two chapters of the *Liji,* the *Daxue* and *Zhongyong.*[62] If this defines the Confucian tradition, however, then this means that there was no Confucian tradition prior to the neo-Confucianism of the Song-Ming period, and that texts such as *Xunzi, Chunqiu Fanlu,* or *Fayan* are not Confucian. This is surely incorrect. Many scholars still tend to accept Zhu Xi's canon as definitive of Confucianism.[63] However, even if we follow this line and limit "Confucianism" to "Zhu Xi Confucianism," there is still a problem. The Four Books, while Zhu Xi interpreted them so as to impose coherence, are *not* coherent. These are very different texts written by different authors in different times,[64] and if we approach them without the preconceived idea that they must agree with each other (because they are the Confucian canon, after all!), we will find many disagreements and discrepancies between the texts. This is one of the fundamental problems with canon construction. Our tendency to read any canonical texts as offering a single coherent message leads us to ignore or reject obvious disagreements within the canon. Humans are creative and good at constructing interpretations to fit together things that disagree or contradict one another. This is apparent when we look at the way interpreters often read composite texts, such as the Confucian *Analects* or the Christian Bible. The *Analects,* we know today, was compiled from a collection of various Kongzi sayings, of multiple students, later figures, and followers. We should not expect, and indeed we do not find, consistency throughout the entire text. There are passages of the *Analects* that seem to directly contradict other passages on their face. Nonetheless, scholars will often attempt to explain away these contradictions through reinterpretation, nonliteral reading, and other techniques. Why do we do this?

We do it because we encounter the *Analects* as a single text, with the idea that it must therefore have a single and coherent message. If we encountered the various passages in the *Analects* in uncompiled form, through various recountings and fragments and oral traditions, would we treat the passages in the same way? Reading it as a single text, as canon, primes us to read it as coherent and unified.[65]

Liu focused particularly on the *Zhongyong* in his consideration of *tian* and transcendence, claiming "the ideas developed in this document are most typical of the Confucian reflection on the problem of transcendence and immanence."[66] Liu did not provide evidence for this, and we are inclined to disagree. While the *Zhongyong* certainly played an important role in the Confucian self-definition post-Zhu-Xi (and not a hegemonic one even then), issues concerning transcendence and immanence are found throughout Confucian literature, with the most robust consideration of the issues found in the texts of the early Han, in which metaphysics and cosmogonic thought became major areas of focus. Of texts we might call "Confucian," *Zhongyong* is perhaps one of the least concerned with metaphysics and cosmogony, and far more with moral self-cultivation. Perhaps it is the most metaphysics adjacent of the neo-Confucian "Four Books" (with the exception of a few passages of the *Mengzi*), but these are possibly the least metaphysically concerned texts of the wider tradition (with their centering by adherents at least partly the reason by the regular, but what seem to us baffling claims that early Chinese philosophers, and Confucians in particular, were not interested in metaphysics).[67]

A neglected area of early Chinese thought that has immense relevance for the transcendence debate is Eastern Han and Wei-Jin discussions of spontaneity and creation. Not only do these discussions shed light on conceptions of creation and generation adopted by early Chinese thinkers, but in their contrast and disagreement with earlier views, they demonstrate the existence of certain kinds of creative or agency-based transcendence that scholars such as Huang, Liu, and others deny.

We find the earliest discussion of the idea of "spontaneous generation" or "existence of-itself" (*zi sheng* 自生) in the *Lunheng* of the Eastern Han period thinker Wang Chong (27–100 CE). There, Wang develops an account of the generation of things such that they do not depend on agentive or deliberative creation (of the kind Huang claims is required for "creation" and thus objective transcendence). We can see in his most focused discussion of the topic, in the *Ziran* 自然 ("Spontaneity") chapter, Wang argues against the view that *tian* is responsible for the creation of things in the cosmos in an agentive sense—that is, that *tian* deliberately creates.[68] Wang claims that his argument for the spontaneous development of things in the cosmos is in opposition to those who accept the view that *tian* is a creative agent. Such people must have existed for Wang to be arguing against them—otherwise his position is incoherent. In the opening of the *Ziran* chapter, Wang writes:

或說以為天生五穀以食人，生絲麻以衣人。此謂天為人作農夫、桑女之徒也，不合自然，故其義疑，未可從也。

Some say that *tian* intentionally creates the five grains for humans to eat, and intentionally creates silk and hemp for humans to wear. To say this is to make *tian* a farmer for humans, or the mulberry girl attending to them. This is not consistent with [the principle of] spontaneity, thus we can cast doubt on this idea, and cannot go along with it.[69]

The agentive view of *tian* in itself, of course, does not demonstrate that *tian* is a transcendent entity, anymore that human agency demonstrates the transcendence of human agents. However, given other features of *tian*, and its role (in some texts) as the fundamental ground of creation, this conception of *tian* does seem to fit Huang's agency (or, as he puts it, "personality") requirement for creation. And indeed, Wang Chong himself distinguishes between agentive or deliberative creation, which he uses the term *wei* 為 to express, and non-agentive, nondeliberative creation (or generation), which he renders *zi sheng* 自生, connected to the broader concept of spontaneous action or action in-itself (*ziran* 自然).[70]

Against what he takes as this common view of *tian*'s agency, Wang argues that *tian* does not possess the necessary organs to have desires (according to a widespread and influential view found in medical texts such as the *Huangdi Neijing*, affective mental states, emotions, and desires are tied to the organs and their goal-directed activity[71]), and thus cannot create intentionally. *Tian* can still be said to be the source of things in some causal sense, but not in terms of deliberate (*wei*) creation. Wang makes a distinction here between agentive and non-agentive action in terms of intention, deliberation, and choice. This kind of non-agentive activity, according to Wang, is *wu wei*—a term deliberately playing on the earlier sense of *wu wei* found in texts such as the *Daodejing*. Wang writes:

天動不欲以生物，而物自生，此則自然也。施氣不欲為物，而物自為，此則無為也。

Tian moves, without desiring it, and things (*wu*) are generated (*sheng*)—and things are generated of themselves (*zi sheng*). These things are [thus] spontaneous (*ziran*). *Qi* is emitted without desire and things are created (*wei*)—and things are created of themselves (*zi wei*). Things are thus non-deliberately created (*wu wei*).[72]

On Wang's view, the generation of things from *tian* looks very much like a naturalistic causal process, absent agency, intention, or transcendence of any robust kind. *Tian* operates mechanistically, and this operation results in the formation of things (*wu* 物) from *tian*. Nothing Wang says here, of course, gives us any insight into the nature of *tian* itself and whether it can be considered substantially different from the things it generates. As with discussions of *tian* in other texts, it is said to be responsible for the generation of things, but according to Wang, this responsibility is agentless and nondeliberative.

According to Liu Shu-hsien, the concept of *tian* in Confucianism is of both a creative and pervasive entity, one that generates the world but does not stand apart from it, and is not seen as a "person."[73] While Wang Chong's conception of *tian* seems to fit with this picture, the conception of *tian* he argued against, which was shared by Confucians as well as others, does not. Liu "naturalized" *tian* in a way that cuts against much of the broader early Chinese tradition, in which there were numerous views of *tian*, spanning from the explicitly agentive, found in texts such as the *Mozi* and some Confucian texts, to the plainly naturalistic, found in texts such as Wang Chong's *Lunheng*.

Paul Goldin argues, just as Wang's discussion in the *Ziran* chapter shows, that at least some early Chinese thinkers did accept the concept of a creator existing outside of the natural order.[74] Early Han texts such as *Huainanzi* and unearthed texts such as *Taiyi Sheng Shui* demonstrate the existence of creation myths in early China as well as the concept of *creation* ex nihilo (which Goldin also rightly points out is far from obvious in ancient Greek texts) and discussion of the construction of the world from a preexisting order or a state in which there were no things (*wu* 物).[75]

In all, it is unclear that a focus on creation, while transcendence is often connected to the topic, will show us whether transcendence can be found in early China and where it is to be found. As we argued in previous chapters, there are numerous types of transcendence, and only contrastive transcendence will be up for issue in the creation debate. And there still may be contrastive transcendence in a tradition independently of the views on creation found in the tradition. Insofar as there are transcendent entities of a different substance or otherwise different nature than the rest of the (immanent) world, we have contrastive transcendence—whether or not the transcendent and immanent entities are related in terms of creation. It is conceivable that there could be some (contrastively) transcendent entity or entities not responsible for the creation of the world but that nonetheless exist. A view on which there is a creator substantively different from its creation certainly is one on which there is contrastive transcendence— but this is not the only way to have contrastive transcendence. If we can demonstrate that a tradition possesses such a view of a substantially distinct creator, we can show that it has contrastive transcendence. But since such a position is not necessary for contrastive transcendence, showing that a tradition does not have the concept of a substantially distinct creator *does not* show that it has no concept of contrastive transcendence. And even more than this, as we show above, the early Chinese tradition *does* have a concept of a substantively different creator. Not every early Chinese thinker accepts such a view, but this should not surprise us. The early Chinese philosophical tradition, like every other, contains multitudes. We should be wary of any claim that "Chinese thought" (or even "Daoist" or "Confucian" thought, for that matter) as a whole possesses some necessary feature. For any such generalization, exceptions can always be found. Philosophers in early China were just as diverse and contentious as philosophers elsewhere. Early Chinese philosophers were no more intellectually trapped by cultural and historical circumstances than were the philosophers of ancient Greece, early modern Europe, or contemporary academia. Yet we hardly ever read the views of the latter as culturally determined in the ways we still far too often read the views of the former.

The Fruits of Transcendence—A Conclusion

When we recognize that we can find numerous conceptions of transcendence and other non-naturalist concepts in early Chinese thought, this opens up a host of interpretive possibilities. Our understanding of early Chinese intellectual culture is broadened by recognizing the ways in which transcendence appears, in multiple forms, as well as understanding which types of transcendence are most prevalent in the early Chinese tradition. We propose that a far more useful way of approaching the question(s) of transcendence in early China is to ask *which kinds* of transcendence we find in early Chinese thought, which forms of transcendence are most adopted and discussed, and why this is the case. Why do we find relatively little contrastive transcendence, for example? How might this signal a disparity between early China and Western modernity? Why is there a tendency to understand the creative power of transcendent entities in terms of spontaneity and generation rather than agency? Once we move past the question of whether there *are* non-naturalist ideas in early China, we can move to the far more interesting questions of what these concepts were like in early China, what roles they played in both particular systems and broader swaths of the intellectual tradition, and in what ways early Chinese understandings of these concepts compare with those of other traditions.

We have offered here a preliminary sketch of such a project, demonstrating a number of ways we find transcendence emerging in early Chinese philosophical discourse. While we have sketched here some of the uses and reasons for introducing transcendence in various parts of the tradition, there is much more work to be done. There are a host of neglected concepts in early Chinese thought that have received insufficient attention due to persistent views that they "don't exist" or are otherwise unimportant in early Chinese thought. Whole areas of human inquiry are sometimes denied of early Chinese thought, including even basic areas such as metaphysics.[76] Concepts such as truth, substance, and philosophical positions such as "mind–body dualism," theism, creation—all of these have places in early Chinese thought.[77]

Interestingly, we rarely hear the kinds of omissive claims about Western thought that we often hear about early China. While one still encounters numerous claims about *dominant* strains of thought in the West, such as the Aristotelian conception of substance, which became influential in Medieval thought, or a general conception of mind–body dualism that can be found strongly in the work of Plato or Descartes, we don't find claims that such phenomena as process metaphysics, which rejects the centrality of substance, *didn't* exist in the West or that mind–body monism didn't exist in the West. There is a general recognition that numerous positions on these topics can be found in Western thought, and that even though certain positions may have been more widely influential, other options existed and were discussed. Nicholas Rescher argues that while "the mainstream philosophical tradition of the European West has been characterized by the dominance of a substance ontology,"[78] the roots of an alternative process ontology can be found in the same tradition, in the work of thinkers such as Heraclitus.[79]

What seems here extended to the Western tradition more readily than it is extended to Chinese thought is that there was in fact disagreement about fundamental philosophical outlooks and positions, that there was a variety of ways of understanding the world. The omissive views of Chinese thought mentioned above have their root in older scholarly understandings of Chinese thought as monolithic and determined by cultural elements in a way Greek or Western thought was/is not. To us, this appears to be simply a more subtle version of the old stereotype of Asian uniformity and collectivism.

There is also another driving force that lies behind these omissive accounts of Chinese thought. In many respects, the modern philosophical academy has an almost dogmatic presupposition that naturalism and atheism are the only respectable positions that "reasonable" people should or can hold. This seems, in many respects, part of the deeper story of the growth of the academic study of philosophy in the modern West, which often saw itself as the counterpoint to the Christian churches and their dogmas and doctrines. This heritage has had a profound impact on modern philosophy, not least in the instinct to associate thought that resembles Christianity as unphilosophical—or at least untrustworthy—and antiquated.

Of course, in itself, this idea or view of Christianity as outside the ambit of philosophical science is not key to our book. What is key is that this conception of Christian or more generally "religious" ideas as nonphilosophical or unreasonable prepares those who study Chinese thought to dismiss as invaluable or nonphilosophical anything they find therein which resembles the antiquated religious past of the West. In many ways, the naturalist reading of China has emerged from those who wish to emphasize the contrast between Chinese thought and classical Western thought on the one hand, and those who wish to show how Chinese thought can be trusted as part of the general atheistic and naturalist framework of the modern West.

Quite simply, this strikes us as a form of "cognitive imperialism," that assumes Chinese thought must sound like modern Western philosophy if it is to have any value. Consequently, those who interpret Chinese thought miss out on a vital question: How might early Chinese thinkers *critique* the naturalistic framework of the modern West? Might not the *Daodejing*, for example, heavily question the materialistic reductionism and devotion to empiricism marking modern Western philosophy? Might the authors of the *Chunqiu Fanlu* be horrified at how notions of worship and mystery of the ultimate have slipped from the modern West? All this seems to us quite possible, even probable, and seem questions worth considering when attempting to understand and describe the thought of early China.

Notes

Introduction

1 Roth, "Against Cognitive Imperialism," 1–26.
2 Granet, *La pensée chinoise*.
3 Peerenboom, *Law and Morality in Ancient China*, 59.
4 Even if Hansen is making the weaker claim that features of Chinese language *suggest* certain philosophical orientations, this is rendered problematic by our considerations below as well.
5 Hansen, *Daoist Theory*, 3. Heiner Roetz writes of Hansen's view that it is "linked to a well-known view of Chinese ethics as being holistic and heteronomous and lacking the ideas of freedom, individualism, and personal dignity." (Roetz, "Validity in Chou Thought," 70.
6 Hall and Ames, *Anticipating China*, 24.
7 Hall and Ames, *Thinking through Confucius*, 17.
8 Ibid.
9 The mystical and transcendence-heavy Neoplatonism of Plotinus existed within the exact same cultural and linguistic milieu of the naturalistic Epicureanism of Lucretius, for example.
10 It is far from clear what "naturalism" amounts to. We discuss this issue further in Chapter 1.
11 Fraser, "The Mohist Conception of Reality", 70.
12 Ibid.
13 Fraser, *Philosophy of the Mozi*.
14 Liu, "Chinese *Qi*-Naturalism and Liberal Naturalism," 59.
15 Hansen, *Daoist Theory*, 10.
16 Yearley, *Mencius and Aquinas*; and Stalnaker, *Overcoming Our Evil*.
17 Hall and Ames, *Thinking through Confucius*, 13; Hall and Ames, *Thinking from the Han*, 190.
18 Currently, we are planning a second volume on the concept of substance in early Chinese thought.

1 "Naturalism" in Western Philosophy and its Use in Scholarship on Chinese Thought

1 See Goetz and Taliaferro, *Naturalism*, 6. As Goetz and Taliaferro aptly put it, "We are in an intellectual climate in which there is a near consensus that naturalism is the philosophically correct dominant framework for nearly all areas of philosophical inquiry, but also no consensus over precisely what is meant by 'naturalism' and 'nature.'"

2 *Oratorio de Sinarum philosophia practica*. See Perkins, "Leibniz on the Existence of Philosophy in China," 61; see also von Collani, "China in the German 'Geistesgeschichte' in the Seventeenth and Eighteenth Centuries," 159–61.

3 Herbert, *Confucius*.

4 Thing such as "dark matter," for example, have never been experimentally detected, but are posited to make sense of our existing theories and observations.

5 Wang Shik Jang, discussing the view of David Hall and Roger Ames that we do not find transcendence in early Chinese texts, writes, "One of the significant reasons why they argue [that there is no transcendence in China] is that they want to construe Chinese religions as clear-cut contrasts to Western religions. In other words, Chinese religions can, they assume, function as a real alternative to dominant cultures and religions in the West." Jang, "Problem of Transcendence in Chinese Religions," 103–4. See also Hall and Ames, *Thinking from the Han*, 228.

6 See the Introduction on "contrastive" and "similarity" approaches to Chinese thought.

7 We maintain, as do an increasing (but still small) number of scholars (see McEvilley, *The Shape of Ancient Thought*; Kuzminski, *Pyrrhonism*), that both Islamic and Indian philosophy should be understood as belonging roughly to the same overarching tradition as European philosophy, a broader tradition we might refer to as the "Indo-European philosophical tradition." Linguists, archaeologists, and other scholars have long known that the languages and cultures of the various peoples of India, Persia, and Europe are ancestrally linked. Their languages all emerged from a common ancestor, Proto-Indo-European, which links the languages of these regions into a single language family. Likewise, culturally these regions are linked as well, with cultural elements drawn from the Proto-Indo-European people (previously known as *Aryans*), who likely originated in the central Eurasian Steppe and moved in a number of waves into Europe, the Middle East, and the Indian subcontinent. Though non-naturalist philosophical systems are not the only ones to be found in premodern Indo-European philosophy (the ancient Epicureans, Carvaka, and many others can be found), the massive influence of the Abrahamic and Vedic religions throughout much of the Indo-European tradition ensured that non-naturalist systems were dominant for much of the history of this tradition even through the modern period and until relatively recently in the West.

8 Bilgrami, "The Wider Significance of Naturalism."

9 Ibid., 23.

10 Berkeley, *A Treatise Concerning the Principles of Human Knowledge*, section 4.

11 Brightman, "The Definition of Idealism."

12 See Spinney, "Human Cycles," 488, and other papers mentioned in Konnikova, "Humanities Aren't a Science. Stop Treating Them Like One."

13 Indebted to conversations with Susan Schneider and James Beebe for this point.

14 Szabadvary, *History of Analyical Chemistry*, 45.

15 Which we do not, but this is an argument for another place.

16 Also called *de divisione naturae*, after the 1681 Thomas Gale edition of the work.

17 *De divisione naturae* I.1.

18 Hyman, Walsh, and Williams, eds., *Philosophy in the Middle Ages*, 3rd ed., 6.

19 Hilary, *Naturalism, Realism, and Normativity*, 9.

20 Boyd, Casper, and Trout, *Philosophy of Science*, 778.

21 Putnam, "The Content and Appeal of 'Naturalism.'"

22 Liu, "Chinese Qi Naturalism and Liberal Naturalism."

23 The rejection of transcendence is often a key component of such claims of naturalism. Lee writes, "By 'naturalism,' I mean an ancient Chinese philosophical orientation that seeks the source of normativity in the natural realm. In ancient China, the notion of 'transcendence'—the notion of absolute deity or the conception of Platonic 'Forms'— never occupied a central position in philosophical discourse." Lee, *Xunzi and Early Chinese Naturalism*, 2–3. As we argue below, this conception of transcendence (as well as others offered by scholars) is far too narrow.

24 "Modern ethical naturalism has the challenge of showing how normativity, broadly speaking, is a feature of the natural world—a description, roughly, acceptable in the language of modern natural science." Fraser, "*Dao* as a Naturalistic Focus," 267.

25 Liu, "Qi Naturalism."

26 McDowell called this "bald naturalism."

27 See Stoljar, *Physicalism*, chapter 10.

28 Burge, *Origins of Objectivity*, 296–7.

29 Including Mario De Caro and David Macarthur (see above), Hilary Putnam, John McDowell, Huw Price.

30 It is very unusual in our day to be wholly committed to non-naturalism, rejecting the naturalistic. The opposite, on the other hand, is very common. Generally non-naturalists of certain kinds will accept naturalism about very many aspects of the world, but will include non-natural entities, methods, and so on along with these in their systems.

31 The term "mainstream" is unfortunate, suggesting that topics outside of Chinese philosophy and other "non-Western" traditions are those with most traction and import. Sadly, this is largely the case. We do not use "mainstream" with any value implications—that is, the fact that contemporary philosophers in the West (and many other areas of the world) are working in areas in which they do not engage the ideas of "non-Western" philosophy (including Chinese philosophy) does not entail that these areas are more philosophically valuable than non-Western philosophy, even though the practices (and sometimes explicit claims) of mainstream philosophers often suggest that they believe this value claim. We thus use the term "mainstream" as a purely descriptive one, following general usage.

32 Ames and Hall, *Thinking through Confucius*, 11–29.

33 Ibid., 13; Hall and Ames, *Thinking from the Han*, 190.

34 Hall and Ames, *Thinking from the Han*, 189.

35 Fraser, in *The Philosophy of the Mozi*, xii, calls his project a "philosophical rehabilitation" of the *Mozi*. He writes that his aim is "to show that [Mohism] is both more plausible than it is typically taken to be and deeply instructive as to the shape a convincing normative theory might take." Part of this plausibility from a modern perspective relies on understanding the Mohist conception of *tian* as naturalistic.

36 Hall and Ames, *Thinking from the Han*, 220.

37 This is the position G. E. Moore famously (or infamously) argued against in his *Principia Ethica*, drawing on what he called the "naturalistic fallacy."

38 Gardner, *The Four Books*. Tu Weiming suggests that Carl Jung's characterization of the Chinese view as psychophysical in nature may have contributed to this. Tu, "An 'Anthropomorphic' Perspective on Creativity," 144.

39 Tiwald and Van Norden, *Readings in Later Chinese Philosophy*, 27. Ames and Hall reference an additional translation of *qi* as "hylozoistic vapors," *Focusing the Familiar*, 72.

40 There are a number of different kinds of "reduction" on offer, of course. What all of these hold in common though is that they accept that physics is fundamental and that any real entity or phenomena must ultimately be somehow reduced to it, whether in an explanatory or some other sense.

41 Chang, "Understanding *Di* and *Tian*," 108, 14–16. "*Tian* originally only referred to an anthropomorphic religious being, almost like a great 'man in the sky' as the character seemed to depict. It became a definite deity that chose the recipient of the mandate."

42 Xu, *Daojiao Shi* 道教史; Michael, *In the Shadows of the Dao*, 26.

43 Feng (Bodde trans.), …; Michael, *In the Shadows of the Dao*, 26.

44 See Kohn, *Early Chinese Mysticism*, chapter 1.

45 Kirkland, "Explaining Daoism," xi.

46 Alexus McLeod, in *The Philosophical Thought of Wang Chong*, argues against these readings of Wang as a scientific naturalist that were popular in the late nineteenth and early twentieth centuries.

47 Hu, "Scientific Spirit and Method in Chinese Philosophy," 31.

48 Paul Goldin, personal communication.

2 Rethinking Transcendence and Nature

1   Tanner, *God and Creation in Christian Theology*.

2   Ibid., 41.

3   Ibid., 40.

4   Ibid., 41.

5   Ibid.

6   Ibid.

7   Ibid., 45.

8   Ibid., 42.

9   Ibid., 46.

10 Hall and Ames, *Thinking through the Han*, 190.

11 The charge of ancient Greek thought as utterly dualistic is a standard trope of modern philosophy. Ironically, the modern understanding of dualism has much more to do with Rene Descartes than Greco-Roman or Christian thinkers, to which the term is often applied with impunity. While not entirely false—one can fairly say dualism was present in early Greek thought—the claim should be heavily qualified.

12 Li and Perkins, "Introduction" to *Chinese Metaphysics and Its Problems*, 1–15, here 3–4.

13 Ibid., 4.

14 Ibid., 4–5.

15 Ibid., 5.

16 Notably, some strains of liberal Protestant theology, such as that informed by commitments to Process philosophy, seem to accept the *categories* of transcendence and nature as they exist in the contrastive model of modernity, but also reject the truth of them. The difference is these strains of theology would also dispense with or heavily qualify divine transcendence, rather than question the conception of transcendence at work. For an example of such theology familiar to scholars of Chinese thought (though in this case, one not committed to a Process framework), see Neville, *God the Creator*.

17 Placher, *Domestication of Transcendence*, 1.
18 Ibid., 2.
19 Placher explicitly draws upon Tanner's terms.
20 Historically, apophaticism was associated with Neoplatonic thought, and recently has featured heavily in both nontheistic and theistic postmodern continental philosophy. However, by and large the Christian theological context is the main context associated with apophaticism in the history of Western thought. For an analysis of the beginnings of Christian apophaticism and its Greek heritage, see McGinn, *The Foundations of Mysticism*, as well as Hagg, *Clement of Alexandria and the Beginnings of Christian Apophaticism*. For a study of apophatic themes in modern literature and philosophy, see Knight, *Omissions Are Not Accidents*.
21 Ultimately, for Christian theologians these are two complementary procedures. See, e.g., the excellent study by Rocca, *Speaking the Incomprehensible God*.
22 See *Summa Theologiae* 1a q. 3.
23 Placher, *Domestication of Transcendence*, 6.
24 Ibid.
25 Ibid., 6–7.
26 Ibid., 111.
27 Ibid., 112.
28 Ibid.
29 Ibid. In a very different vein, Terrence W. Tilley has heavily critiqued the modern framework about evils which sought to explain them, often appealing implicitly to the kind of reductionism Placher mentions (though Tilley does not use these terms in his analysis). See Tilley, *The Evils of Theodicy*.
30 Placher, *Domestication of Transcendence*, 112.
31 This is taken from Augustine of Hippo, *Confessions* III, 6, 11.
32 This critique is primarily identified with the proponents of "radical orthodoxy," including John Milbank, Catherin Pickstock, and Graham Ward. For the paradigmatic presentation of this account, see Milbank, *Theology and Social Theory*, 2nd ed. For a response to this critique that defends Scotus, see Horan, *Postmodernity and Univocity*.
33 For a similar account of the two thinkers, see Griffin, *Leibniz, God and Necessity*.
34 Placher, *Domestication of Transcendence*, 87.
35 Dupré, "Transcendence and Immanence," 1–10, here 2.
36 Ibid., 2.
37 Ibid., 5.
38 Ibid.
39 Ibid., 3.
40 Ibid.
41 Ibid. Though he does not mention it explicitly, Dupre here is evoking theological debates in the wake of Heidegger's critique of "onto-theology." A great example of this literature is Jean-Luc Marion's *God without Being*, which attempts to articulate God's Being that is not articulated in terms of the experience of created being, but is beyond this ontic category.
42 Dupré, *Enlightenment and the Intellectual Foundations of Modern Culture*, 243.
43 Ibid.
44 Ibid., 243–56.
45 Ibid., 257.
46 We take this image of a "closed" system from the landmark work of Maurice Blondel, *L'action* (1893)—see Blanchette, *Action*. Blondel's language of Christian

metaphysics that is "open" to transcendence in contrast to modernity that is "closed" to transcendence became influential in especially Catholic critiques of modern philosophy.

47 Dupré, *Enlightenment*, 257–60.

48 Dupré, "Transcendence and Immanence," 9

49 See Genesis 1–2. The insight that Genesis 1–2 constitute different creation narratives stemming from two different editors (if not more) goes back at least to the research of Julius Wellhausen in the late nineteenth century. For a modern introduction and discussion of these claims about the layers of biblical authorship, see Friedman, *Who Wrote the Bible?*

50 Irenaeus, *Against the Heresies* in *The Ante-Nicene Fathers*, vol. 1. For an excellent study of this work and key themes, see Behr, *Irenaeus of Lyons*.

51 See Chapter 4.

52 The best treatment of this theme in Aquinas is Wippel, *Metaphysical Thought of Thomas Aquinas*.

53 See Wippel, *Metaphysical Thought of Thomas Aquinas*, 110–23. This is often connected in Thomistic scholarship to Aquinas's position that God is the act of being, i.e., God does not participate in a principle of being without which He would diminish, but His act is the act of being itself. For discussion, see Theron, "The Divine Attributes in Aquinas," 37–50.

54 For an overview and discussion of this aspect of Aquinas, see Levering, *Proofs of God*, 57–69.

55 *ST* Ia q. 2 art. 3 corp.

56 *ST* Ia q. 2 art. 3 corp. "*Quarta via sumitur ex gradibus qui in rebus invenientur.*"

57 *ST* Ia q. 2 art. 3 corp. "*Invenientur enim in reus aliquid magis et minus bonum et verum et nobile et sic de aliis huiusmodi.*"

58 *ST* Ia q. 2 art. 3

59 *De ente et essentia*, 13. "*Substantiarum vero quaedam sunt simplices et quaedam compositae, et in utrisque est essential, sed in simplicibus veriori et nobiliori modo, secundum quod etiam esse nobilius habent.*"

60 *ST* Ia q. 1 art. 5 corp.

61 See, e.g., De Nys, "God, Creatures, and Relations," 595–614.

62 *ST* Ia 1. 45 pr. "*utrum creatio sit aliquod ens in rerum natura.*"

63 *ST* Ia q. 45 pr.

64 For discussion of the Neoplatonic influence on Aquinas, see Hankey, *God in Himself*.

65 Tanner, *God and Creation in Christian Theology*, 42–5.

66 ST Ia q. 45 art. 3 obj. 1

67 *ST* Ia q. 45 art. 3 s.c. "*maius est fieri aliquid secundum totam subsantiam, quam secundum formam substantialem vel accidentalem.*"

68 *ST* Ia q. 45 art. 3. Resp.

69 This is also reminiscent of the emergence of the world from *dao* in Huang-Lao texts. The idea of 天人合一 is often taken as a statement of naturalism, but it seems to me to be closer to something like a statement of *imago Dei*.

70 *ST* Ia q. 45 art. 3 ad obj. 1. "*Sed relatio in Deo ad creaturam non est realis, sed secundeum rationem tantum.*"

71 *ST* Ia q. 45 art. 3. ad obj. 1. "*Relatio vero creaturae ad Deum est relation realis.*"

72 *ST* Ia q. 13 art. 1.

3 Naturalism and Non-Naturalism in the Han Dynasty

1 As Hans van Ess writes, "The evidence given by Sima Qian and Ban Gu is not sufficient to allow us to say anything about a philosophical or even a religious meaning of the term 'Huang-Lao.'" Van Ess, "The Meaning of Huang-Lao in *Shiji* and *Hanshu*."

2 Peerenboom, "*Heguanzi* and Huang-Lao Thought," 169.

3 Thus the strong concern with rulership in the Huang-Lao texts.

4 Chen and Sung, "The Doctrines and Transformation of the Huang-Lao Tradition," 254. Here, Chen and Sung specifically discuss the *Jingfa*, one of the *Huangdi Sijing* texts unearthed in the 1973 Mawangdui excavation.

5 Discussions of *dao* in early texts such as the *Daodejing* insist on its ultimate uncharacterizability—as in the claim in *Daodejing* 1: "the *dao* that can be a *dao* is not the constant *dao*" (道可道非常道).

6 In the *Mozi* we are enjoined to follow particular aspects of *tian*, such as *tian*'s will (*tian zhi* 天志) or *tian*'s intent (*tian yi* 天意)

7 The construction *shun dao* occurs once in the *Heguanzi* as well, the dating of which is controversial, and which contains a number of ideas shared with so-called Huang-Lao texts, which makes it possible that this is either an early Han text or one from the late Warring States linked with the naturalistic shift we discuss here.

8 *Heshangong* commentary, 21, 25.

9 *Chunqiu Fanlu* 77.1.

10 *Zhuangzi* 2.6.

11 *Zhuangzi* 4.2.

12 The discussion of the *dao* of the sage in *Zhuangzi* 6.4 suggests this.

13 The text here echoes *Daodejing* 25.

14 As with other Han constructions, the only Warring States texts we find referring to *dao li* are the *Xunzi*, *Hanfeizi*, and the highly suspect *Tianxia* chapter of *Zhuangzi*. The evidence from terminology and philosophical content incline us to think that *Tianxia* was written in the early Han, adding us to the company of those, according to David Nivison, "who think that the last chapter ([*Tianxia*], reviewing the Warring States philosophical scene) was written in the early Han and should be classed with other chapters that some scholars call 'syncretist.'" Nivison, "The Classical Philosophical Writings," in Loewe and Shaughnessy, *The Cambridge History of Ancient China*, 784.

15 Michael Nylan, "Yin-yang, Five Phases, and *qi*."

16 Often even within the same text, such as in the case of the numerous and not always consistent correlative systems outlined in the *Chunqiu Fanlu*. See Queen and Major, *Luxuriant Gems of the Spring and Autumn*, 448–9.

17 Brindley, *Music, Cosmology, and the Politics of Harmony in Early China*, 3–4.

18 Queen and Major, *Luxuriant Gems of the Spring and Autumn*, 27.

19 Ibid.; Loewe, *Dong Zhongshu, a "Confucian" Heritage and the Chunqiu Fanlu*, 16–17.

20 Queen and Major, *Luxuriant Gems*, 448:

> There is no indication, in either works confidently attributed to Dong or contemporaneous sources that give reliable information about him, that he ever incorporated Five-Phase concepts into his cosmological theories. In contrast, there is strong evidence that he drew heavily on yin-yang theory to formulate his general cosmological views and on the concept of *ganying* resonance to develop his interpretations of portents and anomalies.

21 Queen and Major, *Luxuriant Gems of the Spring and Autumn*, 449.
22 *Chunqiu Fanlu* 41.1.
23 *Huainanzi* 3.21.
24 *Chunqiu Fanlu* 40.1.
25 Unschuld, *Huang Di Nei Jing Su Wen*, ix.
26 *Huangdi Neijing Suwen* 3.6.
27 *Huainanzi* 7 Queen and Major, *Luxuriant Gems of the Spring and Autumn*.
28 *Lunheng*, chapter 6; McLeod, *Philosophical Thought of Wang Chong*.
29 *Zhuangzi* 15.2. A number of other texts offer similar formulations, such as the Heshanggong commentary on *Laozi* and Han texts such as *Yantielun* and *Hanshu*.
30 Brindley, *Individualism in Early China*.
31 The language here is reminiscent of the Mohist doctrine of *jian ai* 兼愛 (impartial care).
32 *Chunqiu Fanlu* 46.1.
33 *Chunqiu Fanlu* 58.1. Lau's edition of the text has this as chapter 59. See Queen and Major, *Luxuriant Gems of the Spring and Autumn*, 467.
34 *Chunqiu Fanlu* 43.2, Queen and Major, *Luxuriant Gems of the Spring and Autumn*.
35 *Chunqiu Fanlu* 58.1.
36 McLeod, *Philosophical Thought of Wang Chong*, chapter 5.
37 Despite the terms *yin* and *yang* being mentioned in only a single chapter of the *Daodejing* (42), where they seem to be understood as engendered by the "myriad things" (*wanwu*), the principles discussed in other chapters of the "mysterious" (*xuan*), "invisible" (*bu jian*), and the "valley" (*gu*) are commonly understood as referring to *yin* and their opposites to *yang*. *Yin* and *yang* thus associated with *dao* are discussed throughout the *Heshanggong* commentary.
38 *Baihutong*, *Wuxing* 3.
39 The *Taiyi Sheng Shui* is considered by a number of scholars to be a "companion text" to the *Laozi*. See Allen and Williams, *The Guodian Laozi*, 168–9; Brindley, *Music, Cosmology, and the Politics of Harmony in Early China*, 121.
40 Qiu Xigui disputes this connection, reading 恆 *heng* as 極 *ji*, making it equivalent to the 太極 *taiji* of the *Xici* commentary to the *Yijing*. Qiu, 《是"恆先" 還是 "極先"？》; Sixin, "A Study of the Concepts 'Heng' and 'Hengxian' in the *Hengxian* on Chu Bamboo Slips Housed at the Shanghai Museum," 212–13. Li Ling identifies *hengxian* with *dao*. Li, 楚簡《恆先》首章釋義 (Clarifications on the First Chapter of the Chu Bamboo Slips "Hengxian"), in 中國哲學史 (*History of Chinese Philosophy*) 3.
41 A number of scholars read *zi sheng* 自生 as "self-generating," including Brindley, Goldin, and Klein ("A Philosophical Translation of the *Heng Xian*"); Feng Cao (*Daoism in Early China: Huang Lao Thought in Light of Excavated Texts*), chapter 5; Wu Gengyou ("An Analysis of Philosophical Thought in Shanghai Museum Bamboo Manuscript Hengxian"); and Guo Qiyong ("Hengxian—The Lost Treatise on Forms and Names in Daoist-Legalist Thought"). There is another possible reading here, however, that can make this claim consistent with that earlier in the *Hengxian* that suggests that *qi* forms from earlier states—*zi* here can be read in the sense of "spontaneity", *ziran* 自然.
42 Perkins, "*Laozi* and the Cosmogonic Turn in Classical Chinese Philosophy."
43 Genyou, "Analysis of Philosophical Thought in Shanghai Museum Chu Bamboo Manuscript Hengxian," 68–9.
44 Goldin, "*Heng Xian* and the Problem of Studying Looted Artifacts."

45 *Han shu* 27/1317 [from Q,M]. Also see Queen and Major, *Luxuriant Gems of the Spring and Autumn*, 451.

46 *Baihutong* 9.1.

47 Graham, *Yin-Yang*, 16–24.

48 Ibid., 25, 41–2.

49 Queen and Major, *Luxuriant Gems of the Spring and Autumn*, 16–17. As Queen and Major argue, the text itself should be understood as a collected works text of *Gongyang* partisans, including Dong Zhongshu. Queen and Major attribute to Dong himself only a relatively small portion of the *Chunqiu Fanlu*. See also Loewe, *Dong Zhongshu, a "Confucian" Heritage and the Chunqiu Fanlu.*

50 *Huainanzi* 3.12, M,Q trans.

51 *Huangdi Neijing Suwen* 1.4, Unschuld trans., modified.

52 *Huainanzi* 2.6, Harold Roth trans., modified.

53 Michael Puett discusses these issues in the *Huainanzi* in his "Sages, Creation, and the End of History in the *Huainanzi*," in Queen and Puett, eds. *Huainanzi and Textual Production in Early China.*

54 The doctrine of original sin is accepted in many, but not all, Christian traditions. The notion of the fall and original sin, while deriving from Abrahamic sources, are unique to Christianity, as these doctrines are not found in Judaism and Islam, which generally understand the Genesis story differently.

55 *Huainanzi* 21.4. The "it" (*qi*) here is referring to *tian*, mentioned in the previous sentence. This is why we translate it as "disorder the regularities of nature" rather than "disorder its regularities," which is more literally correct.

56 *Huainanzi* 3.23.

57 Zhang, *Outlines of Chinese Philosophy* 中國哲學大綱, 66. Liu, "Chinese Qi-Naturalism and Liberal Naturalism," 64.

58 Liu, "In Defense of Qi Naturalism," 41–2.

59 The fact that the construction appears in the *Liezi* provides additional evidence that this text (at least certain sections of it as well as its organization) was constructed later than the traditional date given it, as most scholars now believe. If the *Liezi* was actually constructed in the early Warring States, that would make this use of the construction by far the earliest occurrence in known texts, with no others seen for hundreds of years.

60 Schwartz, "Transcendence in Ancient China," 66.

61 Needham, *Science and Civilization in China*, 582.

62 Ex. *Zhuangzi* 4.1. One passage (*Zhuangzi* 24.13) also speaks of following "the world" (順天下 *shun tian xia*).

63 *Xunzi* 5.5, 19.15–32. Also see *Analects* 11.20.

64 Lee, *Spirit, Qi, and the Multitude*, 275–6.

4 Transcendence of *Tian*?

1 Youlan 冯友兰, *Zhongguo Zhexue Shi* 中国哲学史, vol. 1, 35.

2 For examples of discussions of *tian* as a theistic concept (or not), see the following: Dubs, "Theism and Naturalism in Ancient Chinese Philosophy," 163–72; Eno, *Confucian Creation of Heaven*, 19–29; Loewe, *Faith, Myth, and Reason in Han China*, 17–24; Chung-ying, "Classical Chinese Views of Reality and Divinity," 113–33;

Louden, "'What Does Heaven Say?'" 73–93; Schwartz, *The World of Thought in Ancient China*, 50–5.

3 For a particularly helpful version of this discussion, see Pines, *Foundations of Confucian Thought*, 55–88.

4 Hall and Ames, *Thinking through Confucius*, 203.

5 Ibid., 206. In this context, Hall and Ames define transcendence as "fundamentally independent" (*Thinking through Confucius*, 205).

6 In addition to the well-known works of Tu and Mou, the embrace of religious perspectives of Confucianism including reference to transcendence is present in many essays from Weiming and Tucker, eds., *Confucian Spirituality*, vols. 1 and 2.

7 See Charbonnier, *Christians in China*, 246–70.

8 See Queen and Major, *Luxuriant Gems of the Spring and Autumn*. Queen and Major's is the first full translation of the *CQFL* in English. In subsequent references to the *CQFL*, we will cite dually from Queen and Major and the original text, taking the text divisions according to those used by the Chinese Text Project. Unless otherwise attributed, the translations are our own.

9 See, e.g., the opinion of the eminent Han historian Michael Loewe in *Dong Zhongzhu*.

10 For discussion of this scholarship, see Arbuckle, "Five Divine Lords or One (Human) Emperor?" 277–8; and Loewe, *Dong Zhongshu*, 6–17. Arbuckle provides more discussion of Chinese and Japanese scholarship on this question.

11 The first modern scholars to argue against the entire attribution of the *CQFL* to Dong Zhongshu were Keimatsu Mitsuo, "*Shanju Hanro* gogyo shohen gisaka ko" in *Kanazawa Daigaku ho bun gakubu ronshu (tetsugaku bungaku)*, 25–46, and Dai Junren, "Dong Zhongshu bu shuo wuxing kao," in *Guoli zhongyang tushuguan guankan*, 9–19. For English scholarship on these issues, see Queen, *From Chronicle to Canon*, 13–114; Queen and Major, "Introduction" to *Luxuriant Gems*, 1–35; Arbuckle, "A Note on the Authenticity of the Chunqiu Fanlu (Characters, 226–34; and Loewe, *Dong Zhongshu*, 6–17.

12 See Wang, "Dong Zhongshu's Transformation," 209–31. While agreeing with other scholars that the CQFL's *yin-yang* theory is unique to other similar cosmologies, Wang contends Dong's "renovations" of the system had a profound influence that allowed for gender inequality and subjugation in Chinese society. However, we would caution that the influence of Dong Zhongshu at least (and to some degree the CQFL) has come under scrutiny in recent decades of Han-era scholarship; see note 9 above.

13 For overview, see Queen and Major, *Luxuriant Gems*, 371–91.

14 *CQFL*, 43.1; Queen and Major, *Luxuriant Gems*, 394.

15 *CQFL*, 43.1; "是故天道十月而成."

16 *CQFL*, 44/43.2; Queen and Major, *Luxuriant Gems*, 395–6.

17 *CQFL*, 45; Queen and Major, *Luxuriant Gems*, 405.

18 *CQFL*, 45; Queen and Major, *Luxuriant Gems*, 406; "聖人視天而行."

19 *CQFL*, 44, Queen and major, *Luxuriant Gems*, 403.

20 The classic example from Hebrew Bible scholarship is how Genesis can be read in the context of responding to the Babylonian *Enuma Elish*. See, e.g., Matthews and Benjamin, eds. *Old Testament Parallels*, 11–20.

21 *CQFL*, 41; Queen and Major, *Luxuriant Gems*, 365.

22 *CQFL*, 41; Queen and Major, *Luxuriant Gems*, 365; "人之人本於天，天亦人之曾祖父也."

23 Hall and Ames, *Focusing the Familiar*, 80.

24 See Aristotle, *De caelo*, e.g., Book I.3.

25 *CQFL*, 43; Queen and Major, 402; see also Queen and Major, 411—"Heaven employs yang but does not employ yin"; Queen and Major, 417—"Heaven moves *yin-yang* to the left and right."

26 Even if these passages are interpreted metaphorically, the choice of these particular metaphors suggests something *like* agency, which is precisely our point.

27 See, e.g., *CQFL*, 416, which describes *tian's* intention as the pattern of mutuality existing between *yin* and *yang*.

28 *CQFL*, 46; Queen and Major, *Luxuriant Gems*, 409.

29 *CQFL*, 51; Queen and Major, *Luxuriant Gems*, 421.

30 *CQFL*, 44; Queen and Major, *Luxuriant Gems*, 402. Compare to *Daodejing*, 5.

31 *CQFL*, 44; Queen and Major, *Luxuriant Gems*, 402; "好仁而近."

32 *CQFL*, 44; Queen and Major, *Luxuriant Gems*, 400;
"凡舉歸之以奉人。察天之意，無窮極之仁也."

33 While the *CQFL* applies this in a cosmological context, one can hardly fail to recognize the similarities with the Mohist doctrine of *tian's* will and intention.

34 Arbuckle, "Inevitable Treason," 597.

35 See Arbuckle, "Inevitable Treason."

36 See Queen, *From Chronicles to Canon*, 85–93.

37 *CQFL*, 44.

38 De Bary et al. *Sources of the Chinese Tradition*, 160.

39 *CQFL*, 18; "故為人主者，法天之行."

40 The idea of humanity as the image of God is originally located in the Hebrew Bible, taken from Genesis 1:27. Historical-critical scholars of the Bible in the twentieth century tended to argue that the Hebrew meaning of the image of God is distinctively more holistic—i.e., embracing the bodily aspects of human being—than later Christian interpretations. See, e.g., von Ran, *Genesis*.

41 For theological discussion of this theme, see Levering, *Engaging the Doctrine of Creation*, 145–92; and Behr, "The Promise of the Image," 15–38.

42 *CQFL*, 44; Queen and Major, *Luxuriant Gems*, 399. Translation is via Queen/Major. We are not convinced *tian zhi shi* should be translated this way, because it implies the king simply acts with Heaven in mind. Saying the king is "only *tian zhi shi*" seems to associate the king rather with product or result of *tian's* activity. This makes more sense of how the *CQFL* sees the king as "extending Heaven's seasons," which is written as 施其時而成之. If the king is *tian's shi* then the *shi* he enacts toward the seasons seems to imply the king is the instrument through which *tian* acts, and not the king's act on its own.

43 *CQFL*, 44; Queen and Major, *Luxuriant Gems*, 399. Translation adapted from Queen and Major.

44 See *CQFL*, 24.

45 *CQFL*, 44; Queen and Major, *Luxuriant Gems*, 400.

46 *CQFL*, 44; Queen and major, *Luxuriant Gems*, 403.

47 *CQFL*, 44; Queen and Major, *Luxuriant Gems*, 404.

48 *CQFL*, 44; Queen and Major, *Luxuriant Gems*, 414.

49 *CQFL*, 24; Queen and Major, *Luxuriant Gems*, 258.

50 *CQFL*, 49; Queen and Major, *Luxuriant Gems*, 415.

51 See Brown, "Son of Heaven," 247–66.

52 *CQFL*, 25.

53 See Loewe, *Divination, Mythology, and Monarchy in Han China*; and Loewe, *Faith, Myth and Reason in Han China*, 80–103.

54 See, e.g., *CQFL*, 2.6.
55 It is worth asking whether the CQFL then ultimately sees *tian* in terms of the political vision of classical Confucianism as described by Loubna El Amine in *Classical Confucian Political Thought*, 177. El Amine argues that for classical Confucians, "Heaven provides the legitimacy for the political vision … without operating as an independent source of value," a view she contrasts to Mohism (see 177–9). Alternatively, perhaps El Amine has overlooked how *tian* functions as an "independent source of value" in earlier texts such as the *Mengzi* (see, e.g., 1A:7).
56 Ching, *Chinese Religions*, 5.
57 *CQFL*, 66; Queen and Major, *Luxuriant Gems*, 516.
58 *CQFL*, 66; Queen and Major, *Luxuriant Gems*, 516; "天者百神之君也."
59 Puett, *To Become a God*, esp. 31–117.
60 *CQFL*, 69; Queen and Major, *Luxuriant Gems*, 524.
61 *CQFL*, 68; Queen and Major, *Luxuriant Gems*, 521.
62 See Pankenier, *Astrology and Cosmology in Early China*, 83–148.

5 Does 天 *Tian* Will?

1 *Ming* takes a number of different senses across early Chinese texts. Its most well-known sense in connection with *tian* is something like that of "mandate," which connotes an aspect of destiny, fate, or allotment, along with entailing this fate as based on the agency of *tian*. See Slingeland, "Conception of *Ming* in Early Confucian Thought." *Ming* is not always connected to agency, however—in Eastern Han texts, such as *Lunheng*, *ming* is understood independently of a command or any agent-state, and is best translated as something like "allotment." *Ming* is also not often understood in these texts as ironclad or necessitating in the way fate is often understood in Western texts, as near deterministic.
2 The traditional Chinese story of Pangu 盤古 as original creature creating heaven and earth shows us an example of such a case.
3 *Summa Theologiae* Q.57, A.3. "God sees all things in His eternity, which, being simple, is present to all time, and embraces all time."
4 Vallat, "Al-Farabi's Arguments for the Eternity of the World and the Contingency of Natural Phenomena," 266–7.
5 According to Aquinas, God wills only himself, because any other object of God's will would make God dependent on something else, desirous and in need of something God does not already possess (*Summa Theologiae* Part 1 Q 19 article 2). This latter issue does not arise in early Chinese discussions of *tian*.
6 Frankfurt, "Freedom of the Will and the Concept of a Person," 15.
7 Ginet, "Freedom, Responsibility, and Agency," 86.
8 *Zhuangzi* 4.2.
9 Hansen, "Metaphysical and Moral Transcendence in Chinese Thought," in Mou, *Two Roads to Wisdom?*, 217.
10 Fraser, "The Mohist Conception of Reality," in Li and Perkins, eds., *Chinese Metaphysics and Its Problems*, 69.
11 Ibid., 20.
12 Ibid.
13 Ibid., 71.
14 Fraser, "Mohism."
15 *Summa Contra Gentiles* I.3.2., Anton Pegis trans.

16 *Mozi* 4.3.
17 *Mozi* 26.2.
18 *Mozi* 26.3.
19 Also discussed in *Mozi* 26.4.
20 This might be understood in terms of human punishments, natural disasters, or other incidents that negatively affect humans.
21 *Mozi* 27.4.
22 *Mozi* 26.6.
23 *Mozi* 27.3.
24 *Mozi* 27.6.
25 "Yet, in bestowing his goodness, he did not leave himself without witness, for he gave you rains from heaven and fruitful seasons, and filled you with nourishment and gladness from your hearts." Acts 14:17, New American Bible translation.
26 "So let man consider his food, that We pour down water in abundance; then We split the earth in fissures, and cause grains to grow therein, and vines and herbs, and olives and date palms, and gardens densely planted, and fruit and pastures, as sustenance for you and your flocks." *Quran* 80:24–32, Lumbard translation.
27 *Lunheng* 54.1-2; McLeod, *Philosophical Thought of Wang Chong*, 190–1.
28 Fraser, *Philosophy of the Mozi*, 106.
29 *Phaedo* 75a11-b8. Though see also David Sedley, "Form-Particular Resemblance in Plato's *Phaedo*."
30 *Summa theologiae*, I.19.10.
31 He writes in "The Mohist Conception of Reality" that early Chinese thinkers in general were naturalist in outlook.
32 *Philosophy of the Mozi*, 110.
33 *Mozi* 4.3. *Mozi* 26.2 discusses what tian desires (*yu*) and hates (*wu*).
34 *Huangdi Neijing Su wen* 24.
35 See Unschuld, *Huang Di Nei Jing Su Wen*, 228.
36 *Zhuangzi* 6.1 (其心志，其容寂…).
37 While a number of scholars have argued against the existence of a mind/body distinction in early China, these arguments require overlooking or radically reinterpreting what clearly seem like common distinctions between physical and mental phenomena. A number of recent studies push back on the "holistic" view of mind and body in early China, including Slingerland's *Mind and Body in Early China* and McLeod's forthcoming *The Dao of Madness*.
38 As Gregoire Espesset elegantly put it, "Repeated disasters (drought, rains, floods, hailstorms, earthquakes, epidemics, and famine) were seen as reflecting the loss of cosmic balance provoked by human misbehavior." "Later Han Religious Mass Movements and the Early Daoist Church," in Lagerwey and Kalinowski, *Early Chinese Religion, Part One*.
39 天欲雨 … *Hanshu, You xia zhuan* 23.
40 *Zhuangzi* 5.3 (天刑之，安何解？"If *tian* punishes him, how can he be let loose?").
41 37.1.

6 Transcendence in Relation: Humanity and *Tian* in Early Chinese Thought

1 For a general discussion of the theme of nature–human unity in East Asian thought, see Ivanhoe, *Oneness*, esp. 13–34.

2 See Hagen, *The Philosophy of Xunzi*; and Lee, *Xunzi and Early Chinese Naturalism*.

3 *Xunzi, Tianlun*, 2.

4 Xunzi defends learning at length across the text, but see especially the *Quanxue* chapter. In the *Fei Xiang* chapter, Xunzi attacks the pseudo-science of physiognomy. In the *Fei Shi Er Zi* chapter, he attacks many positions of his contemporaries.

5 See Machle, *Nature and Heaven in the* Xunzi, Machle, "Xunzi as a Religious Philosopher," 21–42; Kline and Tiwald, "Introduction" to *Ritual and Religion in the* Xunzi, 1–20.

6 For a recent book-length study of this theme in Chinese thought, see Brunozzi, *Himmel-Erde-Mench*.

7 *Xunzi, Tianlun*, 2.

8 Hagen, *The Philosophy of Xunzi*, 4.

9 Ibid.

10 Wang Xianqian 王先谦, compiler, *Xunzi Jijie* 荀子集解, ed. Chen Xiaohuan 沈嘯寰 and Wang Xingxian 王星贤 (Beijing 北京: Zhonghua Shuju 中华书局, 2014), 302. Wang Xianqian's edition included notations (*zhu* 注) made by Yang Jing in the Tang Dynasty.

11 *Guanzi, Zhou He*, 8. The *Guanzi* 管子 contains perhaps the oldest reference to the triad in the formulaic way that Xunzi puts it. This text features the full formula that "thus the sage forms a triad with *tian* and earth" (故曰聖人参于天地). The aspect of the formula that speaks to "forming a triad with *tian* and earth" (e.g., 参之天地) can be found in other texts where human agency is implied, but it is not in the formula we find with Xunzi. See, e.g., *Chu Ci, Jiu Zhang, Ju Song*, 1; *Guanzi, Xing Shi*, 1; *Mozi, Fei Gong Xia*, 1; *Zhuangzi, Shi Bing*, 1; *Shenzi, Wei De*, 1. Note these texts are not central to the *Ru* tradition. It is likely the triad conception entered *Ru* literature through Xunzi, due to his time at the Jixia academy.

12 *Liji, Kongzi Xian Ju*, 5.

13 *Xunzi, Tianlun*, 1.

14 Ibid.

15 Lin, "The Image and Status of Shamans in Ancient China," 397–458. Lin's helpful background essay shows how shamanistic practices and traditions were very real competitors for political influence in early China.

16 Machle, "Xunzi as a Religious Philosopher."

17 Goldin, *Rituals of the Way*, 51.

18 Ibid., 52–4.

19 Lee, *Xunzi and Early Chinese Naturalism*, 23.

20 Cheng, *Histoire de la pensée chinoise*, 215. "*Xunzi, pour sa part, dissocie clairement le domaine cosmologiuque du Ciel et le domaine éthico-politique de l'homme.*"

21 *Xunzi, Tianlun*, 1. "故明天人之分，則可謂至人矣."

22 *Xunzi, Tianlun*, 2. "不為而成，不求而得."

23 *Xunzi, Tianlun*, 2. "與天爭職."

24 *Xunzi, Tianlun*, 2.

25 Ibid.

26 Ibid.

27 *Xunzi Jijie*, 302. "既天道难测，故圣人但修人事，不务役虑于知天也."

28 Hagen, *The Philosophy of Xunzi*, 57.

29 Ibid., 15–16.

30 *Xunzi, Tianlun*, 4.

31 Ibid.

32 See, e.g., *Bhagavad Gita*, chapters 9–10.
33 See, e.g., Williams, *The Ground of Union*.
34 Rahner, *The Trinity*, esp. 21–4.
35 *Xunzi, Tianlun*, 10. "故君子敬其在己者，而不慕其在天者."
36 *Xunzi, Tianlun*, 10.
37 Dubs, "Theism and Naturalism in Ancient Chinese Philosophy," 163–72.
38 "Ritualization as Domestication: Ritual Theory from Classical China." Ritual Dynamics and the Science of Ritual, Volume I: Grammars and Morphologies of Ritual Practices in Asia. Edited by Axel Michaels, Anand Mishra, Lucia Dolce, Gil Raz, and Katja Triplett (Wiesbaden: Harrassowitz Verlag, 2010), 365–76.
39 *Liji, Liyun*, 14.
40 *Xunzi, Wangzhi*, 18.
41 Wang E 王锷, "*Liji*"*Chengshu Kao* 《礼记》成书考 (Beijing: Zhonghua Shuju, 2007).
42 Wang, *"Liji" Chengshu Kao*, 239–46.
43 Ibid., 244–6.
44 *Liji, Liyun*, 21.

7 天理 *Tian li*—The Patterns of *Tian* and *Dao*

1 While there is wide philosophical disagreement about just how to understand what laws of nature are (see John Carroll, "Laws of Nature," *SEP*), most philosophers agree that laws of nature are somehow descriptions of reality, describing how objects do and will interact.
2 Ziporyn, *Ironies of Oneness and Difference*, 87.
3 Ibid., 22.
4 *Shuowen Jiezi*, 147, 理.
5 Roth, "The Classical Daoist Concept of *Li* and Early Chinese Cosmology."
6 For example, *Mengzi*, 6A7, *Xunzi*, 1.16, 2.12, 3.9.
7 *Liji*, 6.63.
8 Scholars who translate *li* as "pattern" include Harold Roth, Kwong-loi Shun, A. C. Graham, Hyo-Dong Lee, Stephen Angle, and Justin Tiwald.
9 Not to be confused with the common connection between ritual (*li* 禮) and *yi*.
10 *Mengzi*, 6A7.
11 Ziporyn, *Beyond Oneness and Difference*, 21. Angle and Tiwald, *Neo-Confucianism*, 29.
12 Tang Junyi, 中國哲學原論, ch. 1. Ziporyn, "Form, Principle, Pattern, or Coherence?," 403.
13 Contrasted with a number of other senses of *li* Tang describes.
14 Ziporyn, "Form, Principle, Pattern, or Coherence?," 405.
15 We also find the equivalent construction 天之理 *tian zhi li* in these texts.
16 *Zhuangzi*, 3.2, 14.3; *Chunqiu Fanlu*, 25.1, 27.2, 41.1, ch. 77; *Huainanzi*, 1.5.
17 The traditional distinction is attributed to Guo Xiang (d. 312 CE) who compiled the text. This distinction of chapters has also more recently been argued for by Liu Xiaogan (*Classifying the Zhuangzi Chapters*).
18 *Zhuangzi*, 3.2.
19 See Mollgaard, *An Introduction to Daoist Thought*, 52.
20 *Zhuangzi* 1.3 associates the "spirit person" with the "perfected person" and the "sage": 至人無己，神人無功，聖人無名.

21 Selover, *Tianli renyu*. This opposition can also be found in *Liji* 19.7-8.

22 Li, *Tao Encounters the West*, 61.

23 Chong, *Zhuangzi's Critique of the Confucians*, 59.

24 This is of course not all there is to be said for the distinction between *tian* and
    humanity. While they are used as contrastive terms, in early Han cosmology the
    "naturalistic shift" draws a closer connection between *tian* and humanity, as seen in
    texts such as *Huainanzi* (e.g., the discussion of the resemblance between the two in
    3.21) and *Chunqiu Fanlu* (49.1, 55.1). The view develops on which the two ultimately
    share the same nature. This is only possible, of course, along a background in which
    the two are originally contrastive concepts, similar to other well-known contrastives
    in early Chinese texts, such as *jun-chen* 君臣, *da-xiao* 大小, *hao-wu* 好惡, or even
    shi-fei 是非.

25 Chong, *Zhuangzi's Critique of the Confucians*, 59.

26 Esther Klein also challenges the received view of the Inner Chapters in "Were there
    'Inner Chapters' in the Warring States?"

27 *Zhuangzi*, 14.3.

28 The importance of the concept of *ziran* is sometimes attributed to Guo Xiang rather
    than to the authors of the *Zhuangzi*. Fu Weixun argues that Guo developed the
    philosophical conception of *ziran*, which does not occur often in the *Zhuangzi* itself
    ("Creative Hermeneutics," 128). The number of times of the term's occurrence does
    not necessarily demonstrate whether the concept is a philosophically important one.
    Tian li likewise only appears three times in the entire *Zhuangzi*, but it is of clear and
    necessary philosophical import.

29 See Coutinho, *Zhuangzi and Early Chinese Philosophy*, 32–3.

30 See McLeod, *The Philosophical Thought of Wang Chong*, 186–99. *Ziran* is a feature
    of *tian* itself in the *Zhuangzi* (莊子哲學討論集 *Zhuangzi zhexue taolun ji*, 164),
    associating *ziran* with *tian ran* (*tian*-like [action]).

31 Harold Roth argues that the *Zhuangzi* was compiled in Liu An's court in "Who
    Compiled the *Chuang Tzu*?"

32 *Huainanzi*, ch. 6.4.

33 Blanc, *Huai-nan Tzu*, 8–9.

34 About which we are doubtful, despite the clear importance of *ganying* in the
    Huainanzi. This is because in general we resist the idea that there is a single central
    concept unifying the *Huainanzi*—even its synthetic methodology makes use of a
    number of different styles of unifying disparate things, with organizing things within
    the *ben-mo* (root-branches) structure being a prominent one.

35 It may be the case that the *xiao zhi–da zhi* (lesser knowledge–greater knowledge)
    distinction drawn in the *Zhuangzi* is meant to apply here as well—so that *tian li* are
    not known in the lesser sense but are in the greater sense. There is no explicit case
    made for this, however, and we leave discussion of it here as a possibility consistent
    with the text.

36 *Zhuangzi*, 15.2.

37 Roth, "The Classical Daoist Conception of Li and Early Chinese Cosmology," 167.
    Heshanggong 65 reads: 順者，　天理也 ("what they follow is the *tian li*").

38 McLeod, "Disordering Regularities and the Human Completion of the Cosmos in the
    Huainanzi."

39 *Liji*, 19.7.

40 Wang Yangming's view of *li* is exactly along these lines as well.

41 *Zhuangzi*, 2.7. We translate *ai* 愛 here as "emotional commitment" in order to show the point of the passage in attachment to things, rather than the particular sense of "love" or "care" often associated with *ai*.

42 Wayne Alt makes a similar point, arguing that while Zhuangzi "recommended that we not make moral distinctions, ... he recognized that we need some distinctions to survive, and that others are essential for a creative and happy life." Alt, "Zhuangzi, Mysticism, and the Rejection of Distinctions," 2.

43 Guo Xiang's commentary on the passage suggests this. See Ziporyn, *Zhuangzi*, 149.

44 Chris Fraser argues that the *Zhuangzi* makes an even more radical claim, that "no single, ultimate value or principle unifies all moral norms. ... There will be no general, systematic theory of right and wrong by which we can resolve all moral questions." Fraser, "*Zhuangzi* and the Heterogeneity of Value".

45 While we cannot assume that all of these texts shared views about what *li* is, the view of the dependence of "things" on *li* seems to be common across a variety of texts, suggesting that it is part of a shared broad conception (or "thin account") of *li* across texts.

46 This is far from the only time this question arises in the Chinese tradition. There has been a great deal of debate over the issue of the ontological priority of 理 *li* or 氣 *qi* in the work of neo-Confucian philosophers such as Zhu Xi. For the neo-Confucians, *qi* plays a similar role to *wu* (things) in early texts, as beginning in the early Han (and based on earlier suggestions), *qi* becomes largely understood as the basic substance of things, a kind of "psychophysical stuff" constituting the things of the world.

47 *Chunqiu Fanlu*, 26.1.

48 非秦之伐周，漢之伐秦，非徒不知天理，又不明人禮。

49 *Chunqiu Fanlu*, 41.1.

50 This is connected to the concept of *ganying*, which Major, Queen et al. translate as "sympathetic resonance," although the exact term is not used in that text.

51 *Huainanzi*, 3.21.

52 Openings or orifices, places where the body's internal contents are uncovered by flesh—the eyes, ears, nostrils, mouth, anus, and genital opening. (It's unclear whether there are ten for females, as there is both urethra and vaginal opening.)

53 Early Chinese calendrics, as in other areas, maintained a 360-day variable calendar, adjusted to take account of the roughly 5.25 additional days that the Gregorian calendar solves with the "leap year."

54 Possibly a reference to each of the major jointed structures in the arms and legs—two each of the upper arm, lower arm, and hand, and two each of the upper leg, lower leg, and foot.

55 This is part of the reason Ames and Rosemont translate *de* as "excellence" in their translation of the *Analects*—although Ames has also understood it specifically morally, rendering it "excelling morally" in *Confucian Role Ethics*, 207.

56 *Zhuangzi*, 16.2.

57 Hansen reads *every* use of *dao* in this way, as something like "course." Ziporyn also translates it as "course." Ames translates it as "way-making," focusing on what he takes to be the processual nature of *dao* (see Ames and Hall, *Dao De Jing*). There have been numerous debates between scholars on the topic of *dao*. We maintain, however, that there is no one sense of *dao* expressed in all uses of the term in early Chinese texts, or even within single texts such as the *Zhuangzi*. We find numerous senses throughout this text and the wider tradition. We find little need for taking one of the senses to be the primary, grounding, or "true" sense of the term—they are simply different senses.

58 Hall and Ames, *Dao De Jing.*
59 Ziporyn, *Zhuangzi.* Hansen, *A Daoist Theory of Chinese Thought.*
60 Roth, "Who Compiled the Chuang-tzu?"; "The Laozi in the Context of Early Daoist Mystical Praxis."
61 This is not to deny that a Daoist tradition formed at some point in early Chinese history, but rather that pre-Han texts should not be seen as representative of this tradition, which formed as such post-Sima Tan, rather than before he formulated the *jia* category. There certainly are family resemblances between the texts Sima Tan deemed part of the "*dao jia*," but this is better explained by appealing to particular popular strains of thought during the Warring States, rather than to any "school" affiliation or interests.
62 *Early Chinese Mysticism*, 29, 66. *Daoist Mystical Philosophy.*
63 *Cultivating Perfection*, 64–7.
64 *Genuine Pretending*, 165: "A religious reading ... as representing 'the mysterious union with Dao' somewhere 'far beyond the world' is certainly justified if one is inclined to approach the *Zhuangzi* with intentions of a spiritual ascent to some higher realm."
65 Mainly for the reasons discussed in Chapter 1.
66 *Genuine Pretending*, 11–12.
67 According to Thomas Michael, the twentieth-century scholar Xu Dishan was the first to maintain a distinction between *daojiao* and *daojia* as two distinct phenomena, in his 1934 *Daojiao shi* 道教史 ("History of *Daojiao*") (*In the Shadows of the Dao*, 26). This distinction was borrowed by Feng Youlan, whose work aimed to make Chinese philosophy "modern" and palatable to Western scholars. Cleaving off seemingly "religious" aspects of the Daoist tradition served this purpose well, as the mid-twentieth century was the height of the analytic movement in philosophy, for which commitment to scientific naturalism and empirical science rose to the level of dogma.
68 *In the Shadows of Dao*, 26.
69 Scare quotes here due to the fact that Roth questions, as do we, the usefulness of school categorizations for Warring States texts. Roth, "Laozi in the Context of Daoist Mystical Praxis."
70 *Original Tao*, 152. We devote much of the discussion in chapters below to apophaticism in early Chinese texts.
71 Roth, "The Laozi in the Context of Daoist Mystical Praxis," 77; *Guanzi*, 36.5.
72 *Guanzi*, 36.8. Earlier in the chapter, another claim of the emptiness of *tian's dao* is found, similar to the passage quoted above, but adding that the emptiness of *dao* makes it "without shape" (*wu xing* 無形).
73 *Zhuangzi*, 4.2. See also the discussion of this passage in Chapter 5.
74 This statement is echoed in *Daodejing*, chapter 37.
75 See McLeod, "In the World of Persons."
76 Itself closely related with the "Zhuangist" tradition of the *Zhuangzi*—see Roth, "Who Compiled the Chuang-tzu?"; Klein, "Were there 'Inner Chapters' in the Warring States?"
77 As do a number of other chapters in the *Huainanzi*, including chapter 3 (*Tianwen*). See McLeod, "Human Construction of the Cosmos ..." (forthcoming).
78 Puett, *To Become a God*, 3.
79 Particularly important in this regard are Brook Ziporyn's two volumes *Ironies of Oneness and Difference* and *Beyond Oneness and Difference.*
80 Wing-tsit Chan, *A Source Book in Chinese Philosophy*, 634; Perkins, "Metaphysics in Chinese Philosophy," *Stanford Encyclopedia of Philosophy.*

8 Changing without Change: *Dao* and Causation in Early Daoism

1 Alexander, *Lao-tsze, the Great Thinker, with a Translation of His Thoughts on Nature and Manifestations of God.*

2 Ibid., 55.

3 *Hanfeizi*, 5.1. "道者萬物之始，是非之紀也。"

4 Hyo-dong Lee has attempted to provide a panentheistic conception of *dao* following neo-Confucian sources. See Lee, "The Heart-Mind of the Way and the Heart-Mind are Non-Dual, 37–58.

5 For example, the approaches of Baruch Spinoza and the Process philosophy movement.

6 See Dodds, OP, *The Unchanging God of Love*, 1–4. Particularly in his footnotes, Dodds notes the remarkable and universal agreement of the Christian tradition before the modern period regarding the immutability of God, which is in contrast to the widespread assumption now of God's mutability.

7 This is a common critique against the immutability and/or impassibility of God. For a helpful study and example of such a critique, see Fiddes, *The Creative Suffering of God.*

8 See, e.g., Hartshorne, *The Divine Relativity.*

9 Properly speaking, divine immutability is not a question Aquinas discusses in the *ST*. Rather, it falls under the ambit of the *quaestio* on divine simplicity and related issues. Aquinas directly addresses immutability in the *Summa Contra Gentiles* Book I cap. 16, under the terms of proving why "there is no passive potency in God" (*quod in Deo non est potential passiva*). He also addresses divine immutability in the broader context of *De Potentia* qq. 7–8. For background on Aquinas's study of God in the *ST*, see especially the following: Garrigou-Lagrange, O.P., *The One God*; Gilson, *The Philosophy of St. Thomas Aquinas*, 98–127; Torrell, *La "Somme de théologie" de saint Thomas d'Aquin*; Te Velde, *Aquinas on God: The "Divine Science" of the Summa Theologiae*, esp. 123–46.

10 For discussion of this framework as it specifically applies to Aquinas, see Rota, "Causation," 104–14.

11 See Thomas, *Summa Contra Gentiles*, I.16.

12 Such change or motion is often discussed in the context of the distinction between matter and form in literature on Aquinas. See Wippel, *The Metaphysical Thought of Thomas Aquinas*, 296–312; and Brower, "Matter, Form, and Individuation," 85–103.

13 The Christian tradition does speak of generation within the Trinity, but this is a unique species of generation that is analogous to creaturely generation (within species) and is sharply distinguished from the act of creation. For this reason, Trinitarian generation is usually described as "filiation" (the generation of the Son), and "spiration" (generation of the Holy Spirit). For background and further discussion of Trinitarian ways of speaking of generation, see Emery, OP, *The Trinity*, esp. 83–110, and Friedman, *Medieval Trinitarian Thought from Aquinas to Ockham*, 5–49.

14 Aquinas does not mean that God cannot be an object of acts such as contemplation or prayer. Rather, he means God cannot receive the action of another as a grammatical object receives the action of verbs in a sentence.

15 *Summa Contra Gentiles*, I.16.5.

16 See Dodds, *The Unchanging God of Love*, 153–60. As Dodds notes, Aquinas does not deny all motion in God (since God loves the world and is Trinity in Aquinas's theology), but denies any motion that is *change* in God.

17 Specifically, following A. C. Graham, scholars generally hold that the *Liezi* is from the fourth century CE. However, Ronnie Littlejohn has recently complicated this account by observing that the *Liezi* may contain passages that are part of the *Zhuangzi* that have been thought lost for a long time. In this sense, the *Liezi* perhaps reflects earlier Daoist thought, even if the later date is accurate. For Graham's position on the dating of the *Liezi*, see Graham, "The Date and Composition of the *Lieh-tzu*," 216–82. See also Littlejohn, "The *Liezi's* Use of the Lost *Zhuangzi*," 31–49.

18 See Chan, *Two Visions of the Way*. Chan hypothesizes that the commentary dates from the Late Han, and it eventually came to be ascribed to the mythical figure of *Heshanggong* as the Huang-Lao tradition developed (see pp. 89–118 for specifics of this account). For our purposes, the main value is that the commentary likely represents early interpretations of the *Laozi*, though we should note some scholars hold it is of a much later date.

19 Van Norden, "Method in the Madness of the *Laozi*," 187–210, here 194–5.

20 See discussion by Moeller, *The Philosophy of the* Daodejing, 9–10 and related discussion on 21–32.

21 *DDJ*, 25.

22 Guying, *Lao Tzu: Text, Notes, and Comments*, trans. Rhett Y. W. Young and Roger T. Ames, 143; see also p. 145 for a similar position. In the most recent Chinese edition of Chen's work, *Laozi Zhu Yi Ping Jie*, 152, he retains the comment regarding the absolute and eternal nature of the *dao* (道的绝对性和永存性), but the latter half of his comment has been edited out. However, the spirit of the comment remains present in Chen's comment that the *dao* does not share in the "cycles, changes, or dissolution" of the phenomenal world (道…但它本身不会随着运转变动而消失, p. 157).

23 *Heshanggong Laozi*, 25."無匹雙." (Hereafter, *Heshanggong*.)

24 Wang Bi, *Daode Zhenjing Zhu*, 25. 無物之匹故曰獨立.

25 *Heshanggong*, 25.

26 Wang Bi, *Daode Zhenjing Zhu*, 25.

27 See Allan, "The Great One, Water, and the *Laozi*," 237–85.

28 *DDJ*, 57.

29 Xiaogan, "Laozi's Philosophy," 71–100, here 88. Liu contends that the *Laozi* takes "desireless activity" not to mean the cessation of all desires, but only "the ordinary desires of common rulers and people" (88). However, Edward G. Slingerland has employed H. Creel's distinction between "contemplative" and "purposive" Daoism to great effect in showing that the meaning of "without desire" in the *Laozi* is deeply contested in the Daoist tradition, with some arguing it should mean being without desire at all. For discussion, see Slingerland, *Effortless Action: Wu-wei as Conceptual Metaphor and Spiritual Ideal in Early China*, 107–17.

30 See inter alia, *DDJ*, 37.

31 *Huainanzi*, 1.13. Text division here cited according to divisions in Major, et al., ed. and trans., *The Huainanzi*.

32 See Roth, "*Huainanzi*," 341–65, here 348. Roth argues that the opening chapter of the *Huainanzi* takes the perspective that "everything within Heaven and Earth is both natural and supernatural, secular and sacred," such that "these patterns, sequences, propensities, and natures are themselves holy or divine" (348). This description would seem to lean toward describing the *Huainanzi* as defending "immanent transcendence" wherein nature is considered in "transcendental" ways.

33 *DDJ*, 40.

34 *Heshanggong*, 40 "本者 道之所以動"

35 Originally a Neoplatonic concept, this schema of *exitus–reditus* has had profound impact on the Christian theological tradition.

36 *Heshanggong*, 40.

37 Chen Guying, *Laozi Zhu Yi Ping Jie*, 211.

38 Allan and Williams, *The Guodian* Laozi, 158. At this conference, scholars noted that the Guodian *Laozi* does not attribute *xing* to *dao*, but it does say *dao* has a *zhuang* or form.

39 See Möller, *In der Mitte des Kreises*, 38–48. Möller identifies the imagery of the wheel (*der Rad*) with the empty (and therefore formless) center as the image that "opens a path the the Daoist world of images and providesa orientation or framework by which to bring together the individual motives and themes which differ among various Daoist texts" (*das Bild des Rades…Es eröffnet einen Zugang zur daoitischen Bilderwelt und stellt eine Orientierungshilfe oder einen Rahmen bereit, um die einzelnen Motive und Themen der verschiedenen daoistischen Texte aufeinander zu beziehen*), here p. 38.

40 *Heshanggong*, 40.

41 Scholars have heavily debated the precise relationship between *you* and *wu* with regard to *dao*. See chapter 9, note 22.

42 *DDJ*, 25 does use *wu* to describe *dao*, but this is subject to two qualifications. First, it is clear from context that if *dao* is a *wu*, it is so in ways radically different than other *wu*. For this reason, this seems to be less a claim about *dao* and more a linguistic attempt to articulate the positive existence of *dao*. Second, the Guodian *Laozi* does not use the word *wu* in this passage, but *zhuang* (see note above). We think this would suggest an attempt to clarify an earlier reading. At the very least, it seems positively clear that *dao* is not a *wu* in the sense of undergoing processes of death and decay.

43 Perenboom, *Law and Morality in Ancient China*, 33–6. More recently, James Behuniak, Jr. has argued that the Mawangdui variants of the *Laozi*—while predating the Wang Bi received text—includes a Huang-Lao alteration of *DDJ* 22. See Behuniak, Jr., " 'Embracing the One' in the *Daodejing*," 364–81, here 365.

44 See, e.g., Mary Bockover, "Daoism, Ethics, and Faith," 139–53.

45 *Huainanzi*, 2.13.

46 For a helpful discussion of the theme of death in the *Liezi*, see Jones, "When Butterflies Change into Birds," 241–53.

47 *Liezi*, 1.6. Text cited according to Ctext divisions.

48 See Jones, "When Butterflies Change into Birds," 249.

49 *Liezi*, 1.5.

50 *Liezi*, 4.9.

51 Ibid.

52 Ibid.

53 *Xici Shang*, 5. Cited according to Ctext divisions.

54 *DDJ*, 42.

55 Wang, *Yinyang*, 50.

56 *DDJ*, 42.

57 *Heshanggong*, 42.

58 Ibid.

59 See Wang, *Yinyang*, 52–3.

60 For a still excellent general study of the cosmology of the *Huainanzi*, see Le Blanc, *Huai-nan-tzu*, 191–206.

61 *Huainanzi*, 2.1.

62 Ibid.

63 Ibid.
64 *Huainanzi*, 2.1–2.2.
65 See Major, *Heaven and Earth in Early Han Thought*, 25. Major sees the cosmology of *Huainanzi* chapter 3 (the *Tianwen* chapter) as an "amplification" of the end of chapter 2.
66 *Huainanzi*, Major et al., *The Huainanzi*, 115.
67 See Le Blanc, *Huai-nan-tzu*, 191–4.
68 See Michael, "The That-Beyond-Which of the Pristine Dao," 101–26, here 108–10. Michael suggests that the *Liezi* strategically avoids explicitly mentioning the *dao* in its cosmology due to the namelessness of the "pristine" *dao*. This indirectly supports our reading here.
69 *Liezi*, 1.2.
70 Ibid.
71 *Liezi*, 1.3.
72 Ibid.

9 Transcendence and Generation: Pseudo-Dionysius and the Daodejing

1 Such a definition of transcendence is part of, though not the entirety, of Hall and Ames's definition of transcendence in *Thinking through the Han*, 190.
2 Often, the apophatic aspects of the *DDJ* fall under the question of the religious nature of the text. The strongest reading—and we believe convincing—account of the *DDJ* as promoting a genuinely religious path of inner self-cultivation that contextualizes the apophatic elements of the text comes from the many writings of Harold D. Roth on the subject. Among other of Roth's works we cite below, a helpful general study about inner cultivation in the Daoist spiritual tradition is Roth, "The Inner Cultivation Tradition of Early Daoism," 123–48.
3 See Schwitzgebel, "Zhuangzi's Attitude Toward Language and His Skepticism," 68–96; and Berkson, "Language: The Guest of Reality," 97–126. Both Schwitzgebel and Berkson argue that Zhuangzi's view of language is not nearly as radically skeptical as he makes it sound, and rather as a "therapeutic" aim for his critique of language.
4 See Lau, Introduction to *Tao Te Ching*, 15–16; Graham, *Disputers of the Tao*, 219–21; Schwartz, *The World of Thought in Ancient China*, 192–201; and Nuyen, "Naming the Unnameable," 487–97.
5 The texts here refer to those said to be authored by Dionysius the Areopagite. In Acts 17:34, this figure is named as one who heard the preaching of the Apostle Paul and converted. The texts now studied as the Dionysian corpus were authored by a later anonymous figure, likely around the sixth century AD, and thus modern scholars refer to the author as "Pseudo-Dionysius," which we employ here.
6 Scholars of Dionysius are now in universal agreement that Pseudo-Dionysius is more impacted by Proclean Neoplatonism than Plotinian. For discussions of this opinion and evidence for it, see Saffrey, "New Objective Links between the Pseudo-Dionysius and Proclus," 54–63.
7 In this sense, the *MT* is a complementary piece to the *DN*. For an overview and study of the *MT* itself, see Rorem, *The Dionysian Mystical Theology*.

8   Lubheid, trans. *Pseudo-Dionysius*, 135. We have drawn upon Lubheid's translation
     in consultation with the text of the Dionysian corpus in the *Patrologia Graeca* vol.
     III, comp. J. P Migne, accessed August 15, 2019 from https://archive.org/details/
     Patrologia_Graeca_vol_003. The latter contains all the texts of the Dionysian corpus.
     A modern critical edition of the text is available via Suchla, ed. *Corpus Dionysiacum*,
     2 vols.

9   Lubheid, *Pseudo-Dionysius*, 138.

10   See Perl, *Theophany*, 13–16; and Craig Rhodes, "Pseudo-Dionysius' Concept of God,"
     306–18.

11   Lubheid, *Pseudo-Dionysius*, 136.

12   See Rorem, *Pseudo-Dionysius*. As Rorem puts it, "It is not sufficient to elevate one's
     mind from one level of conceptuality to another, since all that the mind can conceive
     still ultimately falls short of the transcendence of God" (p. 9). We agree with Rorem's
     account of Pseudo-Dionysius, but stress that "falling short" is not the same as
     "erroneous."

13   See Darley, "Hyperousios," 865–88. Darley examines how the basic idea of *hyperousios*
     in the Dionysian corpus was treated in three fundamentally different directions
     by Jean-Luc Marion ("without"), Jacques Derrida ("super"), and Thomas Aquinas
     ("unlimited"). Perhaps more importantly, Darley's article shows the extent to
     which the interpretations of *hyperousios* found in Marion and Derrida, at least,
     are contextualized by broader preoccupations of twentieth-century continental
     philosophy that color how the term is understood.

14   See, e.g., *Patrologia Graeca*, 284C.

15   Rorem, *The Dionysian Mystical Theology*, 9.

16   *Patrologia Graeca*, 588A; see also Lubheid, *Pseudo-Dionysius*, 50.

17   Lubheid, *Pseudo-Dionysius*, 50.

18   For commentary, see Rorem, *Pseudo-Dionysius*, 134–5.

19   See, e.g., Pope Paul VI, "Dogmatic Constitution on Sacred Scripture—*Dei Verbum*,"
     (1965) accessed August 15, 2019 from http://www.vatican.va/archive/hist_councils/
     ii_vatican_council/documents/vat-ii_const_19651118_dei-verbum_en.html. See esp.
     section 11.

20   Lubheid, *Pseudo-Dionysius*, 49.

21   Ibid.

22   Ibid., 53.

23   Ibid., 54. *Patrologia Graeca*, 593C-D.

24   See *Patrologia Graeca*, 593D.

25   Ibid., 288.

26   See Rorem, *Pseudo-Dionysius*, 136–7.

27   See Knepper, *Negating Negation*. Our argument is similar to Knepper's in that we
     do not think Dionysius is attempting an "apophatic abandonment" which Knepper
     defines as "the ultimate and complete negation of all things of an absolutely and
     unqualifiedly ineffable God" (p. xi). However, we also do not go as far as Knepper,
     who holds that the positive names Dionysius applies to God are "the divine causes
     of the intelligible properties in which beings participate" (p. xii). Clearly there is a
     generative link between God as *hyperousia* and the world of being, but it does not
     seem right to think of the names Pseudo-Dionysius applies to God as causes in their
     own right (as though each property was isolated from the divine essence) but speak to
     the general principle of God as generative cause, which we stress in our interpretation.

28   Lubheid, *Pseudo-Dionysius*, 66.

29 Louth, *Denys the Areopagite*, 81–8.
30 Ibid., 85.
31 Ibid.
32 Ibid., 87.
33 Lubheid, *Pseudo-Dionysius*, 66.
34 Ibid., 72.
35 Ibid., 73.
36 Ibid.
37 Ibid., 74.
38 Ibid., 75.
39 See Lubheid, *Pseudo-Dionysius*, 73. The Pseudo-Dionysian conception of God as "formless" considers form as an aspect of creaturely being. It should not be confused with the arguments in favor of God having a form such as one finds in Aquinas (wherein God is said to be His own form in an Aristotelian sense) or in the twentieth-century theologian Hans Urs von Balthasar (wherein God's *Gestalt* is conceived as the luminous and numinous *gloria Dei*). For these accounts of God as having form, see Aquinas, *ST* Ia q. 3 art. 2, and Balthasar, *The Glory of the Lord*, 419–511.
40 Generally speaking, most Daoist scholars note that for Daoist texts, the *dao* as "nothing" is not nihilistic, but a kind of testimony to the generative creativity of *dao*. For helpful discussion of this, see Chai, "Meontological Generativity," 303–18.
41 We do not mean to imply Hall and Ames's argument of the aesthetic vs. logical worldview.
42 It is notable that some modern scholars have attempted a kind of *rapprochement* between the Daoist theme of nothing and themes in Continental philosophy, especially those inspired by Martin Heidegger. See, e.g., Tongdong, "An Ontological Interpretation of *You* (Something) (有) and *Wu* (Nothing) (无) in the *Laozi*," 339–51; Guenter, "Heidegger and Laozi," 39–59; Wenning, "Kant and Daoism on Nothingness," 556–68.
43 See Csikszentmihalyi, "Mysticism and Apophatic Discourse in the *Laozi*," 33–58. Csikszentmihalyi associates the apophaticism in the *DDJ* with the passages using direct contradictions (see 43–51). We are here using apophatic in the more general sense of "negation," within which contradiction is an important strategy in texts such as the *DDJ*, but not the only or even necessarily primary form.
44 See *DDJ*, 25. Liu Xiaogan helpfully discusses how this passage's description of the *dao* as "great" (*da* 大) illustrates the "difficulty" (*mianqiang* 勉強) of attempting to understand *dao*, which "obscures" (*mohu* 模糊) knowledge or familiarity (*renshi* 認識). See Liu Xiaogan, *Laozi Gu Jin* 老子古今, Volume 1 (Beijing: Zhongguo Shehui Kexue Chubanshe, 2006), 295–7.
45 See Liu, *Laozi Gu Jin*, 295. In explaining why *dao* is difficult to understand, Liu writes, "This is because *dao* is the foundational 'greatness' of the cosmos and the myriad creatures, and so it exceeds our bodies, and even what all human beings have the power to know."
46 *DDJ*, 42.
47 *Heshanggong*, 42. "道使所生"
48 For a helpful discussion of various interpretations of this passage from the commentarial tradition, see Liu, *Laozi Gu Jin*, 438–40.
49 See Liu, *Laozi Gu Jin*, 440–2.
50 *DDJ*, 1.
51 Ibid.

52 As Chen Guying observes, the commentarial tradition has often read *DDJ*, 1 and 40 in
    unison. See Chen, *Laozi Zhu Yi Ji Pingjie*, 52–3.
53 *DDJ*, 40.
54 *Heshanggong*, 40.
55 *Huainanzi*, 2.1.
56 *Huainanzi*, 2.2.
57 *Huainanzi*, 2.6.
58 See, e.g., *DDJ*, 14, 21, and 25.
59 A. C. Graham famously suggests dispensing with the label "Daoist" and using
    "Laoist" and "Zhuangist" in its place. These labels are based on the assumption that
    the *Zhuangzi* and *Daodejing* represent at time very divergent views; more recently,
    scholars have argued for a greater unity among the early traditions. We lean toward
    a unitive view of early Daoism, but use "Laoist" and "Zhuangist" here as ways of
    indicating differences within a tradition or perspective, rather than divergences.
60 See Perkins, "The *Mozi* and the *Daodejing*," 18–32. Perkins argues these two texts
    should be read as "emerging from a context of shared concerns and commitments"
    (19), one of which is the nature of the ultimate. Perkins argues that the *DDJ* is
    pushing against the Mohist anthropomorphic conception of *tian* and asserting
    a more "naturalistic" *dao* freed from anthropomorphism and the consequent
    anthropocentrism of the Mohists (see 21–6).
61 See Chung-ying, "Dimensions of the *Dao* and Onto-Ethics in Light of the *DDJ*,"
    143–82, here 148. Noting the interdependence of something like transcendence
    and immanence in the *DDJ*, Chung argues, the best way to conceive the *dao* is to
    consider it as both transcendent and immanent, as both originating and supporting,
    as both self-fulfilling and others-fulfilling, and to see its transcendence as linked to its
    immanence and vice-versa … It is before the world and yet continues to produce the
    world as if it is dependent and or [sic] as something to be depended on. This is the
    origin of the world, which also depends on the world for creative self-definition, self-
    manifestation, and self-sustenance.
62 Hall, "Process and Anarchy," 271–85, here 280.
63 See Bockover, "Daoism, Ethics, and Faith."
64 Roth, "Daoist Apophatic Mediation," 84–128, here 89.

10 *You* and *Wu*: Cataphasis and Apophasis

1 The beginning of *Huainanzi*, 2 contains a reading of a passage from *Zhuangzi*, 2,
   reading the passage as outlining a cosmogony in which all things emerge from an
   original non-being. This understanding is almost certainly very different than that
   intended by the original author of the *Zhuangzi* passage, as becomes clear from its
   context in *Zhuangzi*, 2.
2 *De divisione naturae (Periphyseon)*, I.11.
3 In this, Eriugena resembles the Neoplatonists as well as other philosophers we see
   who hold a similar position, such as Pseudo-Dionysius and Origen in the Christian
   tradition; Solomon ibn Gabirol in the Jewish tradition; and Ibn Sina, Ibn Arabi,
   and Suhrawardi and the philosophers of the Illuminationist school in the Islamic
   tradition, among others.
4 *De divisione naturae*, I.14.

5 Ibid.
6 Ibid.
7 Ibid.
8 *Abhidharmakosa*, I; Mark Siderits, *Buddhism as Philosophy*, 56–7.
9 *Zhuangzi*, 2.10.
10 *Zhuangzi*, 2.4.
11 *Zhuangzi*, 6.1.
12 *Zhuangzi*, 2.6.
13 *Zhuangzi*, 2.14, 4.2.
14 *Zhuangzi*, 2.14.
15 The greater/lesser knowledge distinction is discussed in *Zhuangzi*, 1.1, 2.2, and 26.6. See also Donald Sturgeon, "*Zhuangzi*, Perspectives, and Greater Knowledge."
16 Chai, "The Apophatic Trace of Derrida and Zhuangzi"; Komjathy, *The Daoist Tradition*; Franke, *Apophatic Paths from Europe to China*, "Classical Chinese Thought and the Sense of Transcendence"; Juillien, *Detour and Access*.
17 Franke, *Apophatic Paths from Europe to China*, 69–70.
18 For example, discussions of *dao* in *Zhuangzi*, 4: early on it claims "*dao* does not like to be scattered" (夫道不欲雜), while later it claims that *dao* "collects in emptiness" (唯道集虛). Later, in *Zhuangzi*, 6.3, we find "*dao* has essence and integrity, but is without doing and without form" (夫道，有情有信，無為無形).
19 *Daodejing*, 1.
20 *Phaedo*, 74–6, *Republic*, 514 (analogy of the cave).
21 *Parmenides*, 130–1.
22 *Enneads*, V.1.
23 Hall, "Culture of Metaphysics," 275; Yonghua Ge, whose position we agree with here, points out that "if immanence were the only character of the *Dao*, it would be unnecessary to distinguish between the nameable *dao* and the unnameable *Dao*." Ge, "Transcendence, Immanence, and Creation," 91.
24 Ge, "Transcendence, Immanence, and Creation," 91. In Brown and Franke, *Transcendence, Immanence, and Intercultural Philosophy*.
25 Ge, "Transcendence, Immanence, and Creation," 91.
26 We do not intend to make the stronger claim that such a distinction concerning the *dao* is a generally accepted Daoist idea or that it can be found in *all* Daoist texts. For one, there is the difficult issue of parsing texts and discerning authorship—an issue we do not want to wade into here. It is enough for us to show that there are at least some texts and thinkers within the early Daoist tradition that seem to have something like Eriugena's conception of *dao* and the two modes of access of *dao*.
27 Song, *A Study of Comparative Philosophy of Religion on "Creatio Ex Nihilo" and "Sheng Sheng,"* Ph.D. dissertation, Boston University, 227.
28 The idea of "holism" is often used for this purpose. A clear statement of this is made by Jana Rosker, who writes:

> The immanent notions which essentially define Chinese philosophy are the necessary results of the holistic worldview. If there is no division between two worlds (material/spiritual or subjective/objective), it is difficult to determine which of the two might be more important or even absolute. And this is precisely why most of the main traditional Chinese philosophical discourses do not include the notion of transcendence, in the sense of transcending from one into another (usually "higher") sphere. (*Traditional Chinese Philosophy and the Paradigm of Structure*, 11)

29 *Daodejing*, 4, *Daodejing*, 25.
30 Song, *Comparative Philosophy of Religion*, 230.
31 *Daodejing*, 2.
32 Ibid., 23.
33 Ibid., 38.
34 Barbour, *Religion in an Age of Science* (Gifford Lectures 1989–91, vol. 1), 144.
35 Augustine of Hippo, *City of God*, 11.2.
36 *Enneads*, VI 9.6:

> Neither can [the One] have will to anything; it is a Beyond-Good, not even
> to itself a good but to such beings only as may be of quality to have part with
> it. Nor has it Intellection; that would comport diversity; nor Movement, it is
> prior to Movement as to Intellection. ... This Principle is not, therefore, to be
> identified with the good of which it is the source; it is good in the unique mode
> of being The Good above all that is good. (MacKenna, trans.)

37 *Enneads*, V 1.7.
38 道生一，一生二，二生三，三生萬物。 *Dao* generates the one, the one generates
    two, two generates three, and three generates myriad things.
39 *Enneads*, V.1.
40 *Enneads*, VI.9: "The One is only itself and really itself, while every other thing is
    itself and something else" (in Zimmerman, "Does Plotinus Present a Metaphysics of
    Creation?" *Review of Metaphysics*, 67).
41 *Enneads*, VI.8. (Zimmerman, trans.).
42 *Enneads*, V.1 (MacKenna, trans.).
43 *Enneads*, V.4: "The activity generated from the perfection in [the One] and its
    coexistent activity acquires substantial existence ... and arrives at being and
    substance—the Intellect and the whole intelligible nature" (Zimmerman, trans.).
44 As Plotinus writes (*Enneads* III.7), nothing can be predicated thus of the One—"not
    even majesty can be predicated of it" (MacKenna, trans.).
45 Ames, "Getting Past Transcendence," 24.
46 *Mozi*, ch. 31.
47 *Huainanzi*, 2.1.
48 Franke, "All or Nothing?," 8.
49 Neville, *Behind the Masks of God*; and "From Nothing to Being." See also Ge, "*Creatio
    Ex Nihilo* and Ancient Chinese Philosophy."
50 Song, *Comparative Philosophy of Religion*.
51 Huang, *Confronting Confucian Understandings of the Christian Doctrine of Creation*;
    Song, *Comparative Philosophy of Religion*, 24.
52 Mote, "The Cosmological Gulf between China and the West," 7.
53 Isaeva, *From Early Vedanta to Kashmir Shaivism*, 42; Dasgupta, *History of Indian
    Philosophy, Vol. 1*, 469–70. Also see Shah-Kazemi, *Paths to Transcendence*, 10–11, for a
    discussion of the connection between this idea and transcendence.
54 *Enneads*, V.2.1:

> The One is all things and no one of them; the source of things is not all things;
> all things are its possession—running back, so to speak, to it- or, more correctly,
> not yet so, they will be. ... It is precisely because that is nothing within the One
> that all things are from it: in order that Being may be brought about, the source
> must be no Being but Being's generator, in what is to be thought of as the primal
> act of generation.

55 Indeed, this is a difficulty that theistic philosophers, accepting a divine that is both transcendent and an agent, have spent thousands of years trying to resolve.

56 In his commentary to the *Taijitu shuo*, Zhu Xi explains *taiji* as associated with *li* 理 (pattern, principle).

57 Zhou Dunyi, *Taijitu shuo*.

58 The beginning of *Hengxian*, for example, attributes to *hengxian* (which Brindley, Goldin, and Klein translate to "the primordial state of constancy") a lack—"*hengxian* is without things" (*hengxian wu you* 恆先無有). See Brindley, Goldin, and Klein, "A Philosophical Translation of the *Heng Xian*," 146.

59 *Zhuangzi*, 6.3.

60 Liu, "The Confucian Approach to the Problem of Transcendence and Immanence," 49.

61 We find a multitude of different views in a tradition as diverse, widespread, and long-lasting as the Confucian tradition. These features of a Confucian tradition make it nearly impossible to locate universally shared features throughout the wider tradition. Insofar as we can locate such features, they will necessarily be vague, overly broad, and generally unhelpful. Such traditions are better understood in terms of ancestral connection and family resemblance than in terms of essential features.

62 Daniel Gardner describes the constitution of the "Four Books" as Confucian canon in the Song in the introduction to his *The Four Books: The Basic Teachings of the Later Confucian Tradition*. He writes: "By the end of the Song period, these four texts had come to constitute a collection, the Four Books, and had displaced the Five Classics as the authoritative, central texts within the canon." *The Four Books*, xxi.

63 According to Rifeng Tang, Mou Zongsan was committed to the idea that understanding these texts was necessary for understanding early (pre-Qin) Confucianism. Tang, "Mou Zongsan on Intellectual Intuition," 331.

64 Wenyu Xie points out, for example, that at least parts of the *Zhongyong* could not have been written before the Qin, as the text itself refers to the unification of written characters. Xie, "The Concept of *Cheng* and Confucian Religiosity."

65 Michael Hunter discusses the "canonization" of the *Analects* in *Confucius Beyond the Analects*, 165–6. He writes: "… the notion of the *Lunyu* as a legitimately archaic text … postdates the rise of the *Lunyu* by several decades […]. … the traditional view of the *Lunyu* is best read as an invented backstory for a text whose status by the late Western Han had become unassailable." See also Makeham, *Transmitters and Creators*; Gardner, *Zhu Xi's Reading of the Analects*.

66 Liu, "The Confucian Approach to the Problem of Transcendence and Immanence," 45.

67 Tucker, "Japanese Confucian Philosophy," SEP: "Early Confucians had not typically discussed metaphysics, apparently thinking that common sense assumptions about the reality of this world were not in question." Robert Neville writes: "Confucianism does not have a densely elaborated history of metaphysical discussions, as the Western and South Asian traditions have. Confucius himself sometimes turned aside metaphysical questions." He then points to Zhou Dunyi's *Taijitu shuo* as an example of a possible metaphysics in China. This overlooks the enormous amount and concentration on metaphysics in late Warring States and especially early Han thought, going far beyond Zhou Dunyi's paragraph-long description of his *taijitu* ("diagram of the supreme ultimate"). Some scholars, perhaps most prominently A. C. Graham (in *Yin Yang and the Nature of Correlative Thinking*), have argued (incorrectly in our estimation) that early Chinese correlative cosmology should not be understood as metaphysics, but if one is taking Zhou Dunyi's cosmogonic thought as representing metaphysics, we find something far more robust in early Han texts (from which Zhou

clearly drew heavily). Compared to the voluminous and elaborate cosmogonic and metaphysical explanations of early Han texts, Zhou Dunyi's *Taijitu shuo* is but a mere footnote or aside, almost impossible to make sense of on its own.

68   *Lunheng*, 53.
69   *Lunheng*, 53.1.
70   The latter concept which seems almost indistinct from that of *wu wei* 無為, which Wang understands as something like "non-deliberate action."
71   *Huangdi Neijing Suwen*, 3.3 discusses the connection between anger and the physical state. Wang Bing's commentary discusses the role of anger on organs in greater detail: "in case of anger the kidney receives harm; in severe cases the flow of *qi* is interrupted. In case of great anger the *qi* flows contrary to its normal direction and the yang *qi* cannot descend" (Unschuld and Tessenow, trans., 68).
72   *Lunheng*, 53.3.
73   Liu, "The Confucian Approach to the Problem of Transcendence and Immanence," 45.
74   Goldin, "The Myth That China Has No Creation Myth."
75   Goldin, "Myth," 6–9.
76   This claim, while not as prevalent as it once was, still has adherents. Joseph Needham wrote: "It is frequently said that before the Neo-Confucians China had no metaphysics in the strict sense …." *Science and Civilization in China, Vol 2*, 467.
77   For some recent work arguing these points, see Slingerland, *Mind and Body in Early China*; Goldin, "The Myth That China Has No Creation Myth"; McLeod, *Theories of Truth in Chinese Philosophy*.
78   Rescher, *Process Metaphysics*, 51.
79   Ibid., 9.

Bibliography

Primary Sources

All primary source materials from Chinese texts have been cited from the Chinese Text Project, unless otherwise listed below.Sturgeon, Donald. *Chinese Text Project: A Dynamic Digital Library of Premodern Chinese*. https://ctext.org, accessed October 10, 2019.

Secondary Sources

Alexander, G. G. *Lao-tsze, the Great Thinker, with a Translation of His Thoughts on Nature and Manifestations of God*. London: Trubner, 1895.

Allan, Sarah. "The Great One, Water, and the *Laozi*: New Light from Guodian." *T'oung Pao* LXXXIX (2003): 237–85.

Allan, Sarah, and Crispin Williams. *The Guodian* Laozi: *Proceedings of the International Conference, Dartmouth College, May 1998*. Berkeley, CA: Society for the Study of Early China, 2000.

Alt, Wayne. "Zhuangzi, Mysticism, and the Rejection of Distinctions." *Sino-Platonic Papers*, no. 100. Philadelphia: Department of Asian and Middle Eastern Studies University of Pennsylvania, 2000.

Ames, Roger T. *Confucian Role Ethics: A Vocabulary*. Hong Kong: Chinese University of Hong Kong Press, 2010.

Ames, Roger T. "Getting Past Transcendence: Determinacy, Indeterminacy, and Emergence in Chinese Natural Cosmology." In *Transcendence, Immanence, and Intercultural Philosophy*, edited by Nahum Brown and William Franke, 3–34. London: Palgrave Macmillan, 2016.

Ames, Roger T., and David L. Hall, *Dao De Jing: A Philosophical Translation*. New York: Ballantine Books, 2010.

Ames, Roger T., and David L. Hall, trans. *Focusing the Familiar: A Translation and Philosophical Interpretation of the Zhongyong*. Honolulu: University of Hawaii Press, 2001.

Angle, Stephen, and Justin Tiwald. *Neo-Confucianism: A Philosophical Introduction*. Walden, MA: Wiley, 2017.

Aristotle, *On the Heavens* [*De caelo*]. Translated by W. K. C. Guthrie. Loeb Classical Library. Cambridge, MA: Harvard University Press, 1939.

Aquinas, Thomas. *Summa Theologica [Summa theologiae]*. Translated by the Fathers of the English Dominican Province. New York: Benzinger, 1948.

Aquinas, Thomas. *De ente et essentia*. Torino: Marietti, 1957.

Aquinas, Thomas. *Summa contra gentiles*. Translated by Anton C. Pegis, FRSC. Notre Dame, IN: University of Notre Dame Press, 1955–7.

Arbuckle, Gary. "Five Divine Lords or One (Human) Emperor? A Problematic Passage in the Material on Dong Zhongshu." *Journal of the American Oriental Society* 113 no. 2 (April–June 1993): 277–80.

Arbuckle, Gary. "Inevitable Treason: Dong Zhongshu's Theory of Historical Cycles and Early Attempts to Invalidate the Han Mandate." *Journal of the American Oriental Society* 115 no. 4 (October–December 1995): 585–97.

Arbuckle, Gary. "A Note on the Authenticity of the Chunqiu Fanlu (characters): The Date of Chunqiu Fanlu Chapter 73 'Shan Chuan Song (characters)' ('Praise-ode to Mountains and Rivers')." *T'oung Pao* second series 75 nos 4–5 (1989): 226–34.

Augustine of Hippo, *Confessions*. Translated by Henry Chadwick. New York: Oxford University Press, 1991.

Augustine of Hippo, *City of God*. Translated by G. R. Evans. New York: Penguin, 2003.

Bai Tongdong. "An Ontological Interpretation of *You* (Something) (有) and *Wu* (Nothing) (无) in the *Laozi*." *JCP* 35 no. 2 (2008): 339–51.

Barbour, Ian G. *Religion in an Age of Science*. San Francisco, CA: Harper & Row, 1990.

Behr, John. *Irenaeus of Lyons: Identifying Christianity*. New York: Oxford University Press, 2013.

Behr, John. "The Promise of the Image." In *Imago Dei: Human Dignity in Ecumenical Perspective*, edited by Thomas Howard, 15–38. Washington, DC: Catholic University of America Press, 2013.

Behuniak, James Jr. "'Embracing the One' in the *Daodejing*." *PEW* 59 no. 3 (July 2009): 364–81.

Berkeley, George. *A Treatise Concerning the Principles of Human Knowledge*. Edited by Thomas J. McCormack. Mineola, NY: Dover, 2003.

Berkson, Mark. "Language: The Guest of Reality—Zhuangzi and Derrida on Language, Reality, and Skillfulness." In *Essays on Skepticism, Relativism, and Ethics in the Zhuangzi*, edited by Paul Kjellberg and Philip J. Ivanhoe, 97–126 (Albany, NY: SUNY Press, 1996).

Bilgrami, Akeel. "The Wider Significance of Naturalism: A Genealogical Essay." In *Naturalism and Normativity*, edited by Mario de Caro and David Macarthur, 23–54. New York: Columbia University Press, 2010.

Blondel, Maurice. *Action: Essay on a Critique of Life and a Science of Practice*. Translated by Olivia Blanchette. Notre Dame, IN: University of Notre Dame Press, 1984.

Bockover, Mary. "Daoism, Ethics, and Faith: The Invisible 'Goodness' of Life." *Journal of Daoist Studies* 4 (2011): 139–53.

Boyd, Richard, Philip Casper, and J. D. Trout, eds. *The Philosophy of Science*. Cambridge, MA: MIT Press, 1991.

Brightman, E. S. "The Definition of Idealism." *Journal of Philosophy* 30 no. 16 (1933): 429–35.

Brindley, Erica Fox. *Individualism in Early China: Human Agency and the Self in Thought and Politics*. Honolulu: University of Hawaii Press, 2010.

Brindley, Erica Fox. *Music, Cosmology, and the Politics of Harmony in Early China*. Albany: State University of New York Press, 2012.

Brindley, Erica Fox, Paul R. Goldin, and Esther Klein, trans. "A Philosophical Translation of the *Heng xian*." *Dao* 12 no. 2 (2013): 145–51.

Brower, Jeffrey E. "Matter, Form, and Individuation." In *The Oxford Handbook of Aquinas*, edited by Brian Davies and Eleonore Stump, 85–103. New York: Oxford University Press, 2012.

Brown, Joshua R. "'Son of Heaven': Developing the Theological Aspects of Mengzi's Philosophy of the Ruler." In *The Bloomsbury Research Handbook of Early Chinese Ethics and Political Philosophy*, edited by Alexus McLeod, 247–66. London: Bloomsbury Press, 2019.

Brown, Nahum, and William Franke, eds. *Transcendence, Immanence, and Intercultural Philosophy*. London: Palgrave Macmillan, 2016.

Burge, Tyler. *Origins of Objectivity*. Oxford: Oxford University Press, 2010.

Cao, Feng. *Daoism in Early China: Huang Lao Thought in Light of Excavated Texts*. New York: Palgrave Macmillan, 2017.

Carroll, John W., "Laws of Nature." In *The Stanford Encyclopedia of Philosophy*, edited by Edward N. Zalta (Fall 2016 Edition), https://plato.stanford.edu/archives/fall2016/entries/laws-of-nature/.

Chai, David. "The Apophatic Trace of Derrida and Zhuangzi." In *Contemporary Debates in Negative Theology and Philosophy*, edited by Nahum Brown and J. Aaron Simmons, 239–61. Cham: Palgrave Macmillan, 2017.

Chai, David. "Meontological Generativity: A Daoist Reading of the Thing." *PEW* 64 no. 2 (April 2014): 303–18.

Chan, Alan K. L. *Two Visions of the Way: A Study of the Wang Pi and the Ho-Shang Kung Commentaries on the Lao-Tzu*. Albany, NY: SUNY Press, 1991.

Chang, Ruth. "Understanding *Di* and *Tian*: Deity and Heaven from Shang to Tang Dynasties." *Sino-Platonic Papers* no. 108. Philadelphia: Dept of Asian and Middle Eastern Studies University of Pennsylvania, 2000.

Charbonnier, Jean-Pierre MEP. *Christians in China: A.D. 600 to 2000*. Translated by M. N. L. Couve de Murville. San Francisco, CA: Ignatius Press, 2007.

Chen Guying 陳鼓應. *Lao Tzu: Text, Notes, and Comments*. Translated by Rhett Y. W. Young and Roger T. Ames. San Francisco, CA: Chinese Materials Center, 1977.

Chen Guying 陳鼓應. *Laozi zhuyi ji pingjie* 老子注译及评介. Beijing: Zhonghua Shuju, 2015.

Chen, L. K., and Winnie Sung, "The Doctrines and Transformation of the Huang-Lao Tradition." In *Dao Companion to Daoist Philosophy*, edited by LiuXiaogan 劉笑敢, 241–64. New York: Springer, 2015

Cheng, Anne. *Histoire de la pensée chinoise*. Paris: Éditions du Seuil, 1997.

Cheng Chung-ying. "Classical Chinese Views of Reality and Divinity." In *Confucian Spirituality*, vol. 1., edited by Tu Weiming and Mary Evelyn Tucker, 113–33. New York: Crossroad, 2003.

Cheng Chung-ying. "Dimensions of the *Dao* and Onto-Ethics in Light of the *DDJ*." *JCP* 31 no. 2 (June 2004): 143–82.

Ching, Julia. *Chinese Religions*. Maryknoll, NY: Orbis Books, 1993.

Chong, Kim-Chong. *Zhuangzi's Critique of the Confucians: Blinded by the Human*. Albany: State University of New York Press, 2016.

Coutinho, Steve. *Zhuangzi and Early Chinese Philosophy: Vagueness, Transformation, and Paradox*. Farnham: Ashgate, 2004.

Csikszentmihalyi, Mark. "Mysticism and Apophatic Discourse in the Laozi." In *Religious and Philosophical Aspects of the* Laozi, edited by Mark Csikszentmihalyi and Philip J. Ivanhoe, 33–58. Albany: State University of New York Press, 1999.

Csikszentmihalyi, Mark, and Philip J. Ivanhoe, eds. *Religious and Philosophical Aspects of the* Laozi. Albany: State University of New York Press, 1999.

Dai Junren, "Dong Zhongshu bu shuo wuxing kao." *Guoli zhongyang tushuguan guankan* 2, no. 2 (1968/10): 9–19.

Dainian, Zhang 張岱年. *Zhongguo zhexue dagang* 中國哲學大綱 [*The Outlines of Chinese Philosophy*]. Beijing: Zhonghua shuju, 2017.

Darley, Alan Philip. "Hyperousios: God '*Without* Being,' '*Super*-Being,' or '*Unlimited* Being'?" *Heythrop Journal* LVIII (2017): 865–88.

Dasgupta, Surendranath. *History of Indian Philosophy. Volume 1*. Cambridge: Cambridge University Press, 1961.

Davies, Brian, and Eleonore Stump, eds. *The Oxford Handbook of Aquinas*. New York: Oxford University Press, 2012.

De Bary, William T., et al. *Sources of the Chinese Tradition. Volume 1*. New York: Columbia University Press, 1969.

De Nys, Martin J. "God, Creatures, and Relations: Revisiting Classical Theism." *Journal of Religion* 81 no. 4 (2001): 595–614.

Dishan, Xu 許地山, *Daojiao Shi* 道教史. Changchun: Jilin, 2016.

Ding Sixin. "A Study of the Concepts '*Heng*' and '*Hengxian*' in the *Hengxian* on Chu Bamboo Slips Housed at the Shanghai Museum." *Frontiers of Philosophy in China* 11 no. 2 (June 2016): 206–21.

Dodds, Michael J. OP. *The Unchanging God of Love: Thomas Aquinas and Contemporary Theology on Divine Immutability*. Washington, DC: Catholic University of America Press, 2008.

Dubs, Homer H. "Theism and Naturalism in Ancient Chinese Philosophy." *PEW* 9 no. 3–4 (October 1959–January 1960): 163–72.

Dunyi, Zhou 周敦頤, *Taijitu shuo xiangjie* 太極圖詳解. Compiled by Zhang Boxing 張伯行. Beijing: Xuefan chubanshe, 1990.

Dupré, Louis. *The Enlightenment and the Intellectual Foundations of Modern Culture*. New Haven, CT: Yale University Press, 2004.

Dupré, Louis. "Transcendence and Immanence as Theological Categories." *Catholic Theological Society of America: Proceedings of the 31st Annual Convention, June 9–12, 1976*. New York: Catholic Theological Society of America, 1976, 1–10.

El Amine, Loubna. *Classical Confucian Political Thought*. Princeton, NJ: Princeton University Press, 2015.

Emery, Gilles OP. *The Trinity: An Introduction to the Catholic Doctrine on the Triune God*. Translated by Matthew Levering. Washington, DC: Catholic University of America Press, 2011.

Eno, Robert. *The Confucian Creation of Heaven: Philosophy and the Defense of Ritual Mastery*. Albany: State University of New York Press, 1990.

Espesset, Gregoire. "Later Han Religious Mass Movements and the Early Daoist Church." In *Early Chinese Religion: Part One: Shang through Han (1250 BC-220 AD)*, edited by John Lagerwey and Mark Kalinowski, 1061–1102. Leiden: Brill, 2009.

Eriugena, John Scottus. *Periphyseon: On the Division of Nature*. Translated by Myra I. Uhlfelder. Indianapolis, IN: Bobbs-Merrill, 1976.

Fiddes, Paul S. *The Creative Suffering of God*. New York: Oxford University Press, 1988.

Fingarette, Herbert. *Confucius: The Secular as Sacred*. New York: Harper & Row, 1972.

Flood, Gavin, and Charles Martin, trans. *The Bhagavad Gita: A New Translation*. New York: W. W. Norton, 2012.

Franke, William. "All or Nothing? Nature in the Chinese Tradition and the Apophatic Occident." *Comparative Philosophy* 5 no. 2 (2014): 4–24.

Franke, William. *Apophatic Paths from Europe to China: Regions without Borders*. Albany: State University of New York Press, 2018.

Franke, William. "Classical Chinese Thought and the Sense of Transcendence." In *Transcendence, Immanence, and Intercultural Philosophy*, edited by Nahum Brown and William Franke, 35–66. London: Palgrave Macmillan, 2016.

Frankfurt, Harry G. "Freedom of the Will and the Concept of a Person." In *What is a Person?*, edited by Michael F. Goodman, 127–44. Clifton, NJ: Humana Press, 1988.

Fraser, Chris. "*Dào* as a Naturalistic Focus." In *Ethics in Early China: An Anthology*, edited by Chris Fraser, Dan Robins, and Timothy O'Leary, 267–96. Hong Kong: Hong Kong University Press, 2011.

Fraser, Chris. "The Mohist Conception of Reality." In *Chinese Metaphysics and Its Problems*, edited by Chengyang Li and Franklin Perkins, 69–84. Cambridge: Cambridge University Press, 2015.

Fraser, Chris. *The Philosophy of the Mòzǐ: The First Consequentialists*. New York: Columbia University Press, 2016.

Fraser, Chris. "Mohism." In *The Stanford Encyclopedia of Philosophy*, edited by Edward N. Zalta (Winter 2015 Edition), https://plato.stanford.edu/archives/win2015/entries/mohism/.

Fraser, Chris. "*Zhuangzi* and the Heterogeneity of Value." In *New Visions of the* Zhuangzi, edited by Livia Kohn, 40–58. St. Petersburg, FL: Three Pines Press, 2015.

Friedman, Richard Elliott. *Who Wrote the Bible?* San Francisco, CA: HarperOne, 1987.

Friedman, Russell L. *Medieval Trinitarian Thought from Aquinas to Ockham*. New York: Cambridge University Press, 2010.

Fu Charles Wei-Hsun. "Creative Hermeneutics: Taoist Metaphysics and Heidegger." 3 (1976): 115–43.

Gardner, Daniel K., trans. *The Four Books: The Basic Teachings of the Later Confucian Tradition*. Indianapolis, IN: Hackett, 2007.

Garrigou-Lagrange, Reginald OP. *The One God: A Commentary on the First Part of St. Thomas Aquinas' Summa*. Translated by Dom. Bede Rose, OSB. St. Louis, MO: B. Herder Bok, 1943.

Genyou, Wu. "An Analysis of Philosophical Thought in Shanghai Museum Bamboo Manuscript Hengxian." In *Chu Region Bamboo and Silk Manuscripts Research, Part Two*, edited by Ding Sixin. Wuhan: Hubei, 2005.

Gilson, Etienne. *The Philosophy of St. Thomas Aquinas*. Edited by G. A. Elrington. Translated by Edward Bullough. New York: Dorset Press, 1987.

Ginet, Carl. "Freedom, Responsibility, and Agency." *Journal of Ethics* 1 (1997): 85–98.

Goetz, Stewart, and Charles Taliaferro, *Naturalism*. Grand Rapids, MI: Wm B. Eerdmans, 2008.

Goldin, Paul. "*Heng Xian* and the Problem of Studying Looted Artifacts." *Dao* 12 no. 2 (2013): 153–60.

Goldin, Paul. "The Myth That China Has No Creation Myth." *Monumenta Serica* LVI (2008): 1–22.

Goldin, Paul. *Rituals of the Way: The Philosophy of Xunzi*. Chicago, IL: Open Court, 1999.

Graham, Angus C. "The Date and Composition of the *Lieh-tzu*." In *Studies in Chinese Philosophy and Philosophical Literature*, 216–82. Albany: State University of New York Press, 1990.

Graham, Angus C. *Disputers of the Tao: Philosophical Argument in Ancient China*. Chicago, IL: Open Court, 1989.

Graham, Angus C. *Yin-Yang and the Nature of Correlative Thinking*. Singapore: Institute of East Asian Philosophies, 1986.

Granet, Marcel. *La pensée chinoise*. Paris: Éditions Albin Michel, 2012.

Griffin, Michael V. *Leibniz, God and Necessity*. Cambridge: Cambridge University Press, 2012.

Guenter, Wohlfart. "Heidegger and Laozi: *Wu* (Nothing): On Chapter 11 of the *Daodejing*." Translated by Marty Heitz. *JCP* 30 no. 1 (2003): 39–59.

Guo, Qiyong. 郭齊勇 "Hengxian—The Lost Treatise on Forms and Names in Daoist-Legalist Thought." 《恆先》——道法家形名思想的佚篇 In *Jianghan Forum Collection of Papers* no. 8 (2004): 5–9.

Hagen, Kurtis. *The Philosophy of Xunzi: A Reconstruction*. La Salle, IL: Open Court, 2007.

Hagg, Henny Fiska. *Clement of Alexandria and the Beginnings of Christian Apophaticism*. New York: Oxford University Press, 2006.

Hall, David L. "The Culture of Metaphysics: On Saving Neville's Project (from Neville)." *American Journal of Theology and Philosophy* 18 no. 3 (1997): 195–214.

Hall, David L. "Process and Anarchy: A Taoist Vision of Creativity." *PEW* 28 no. 3 (July 1978): 271–85.

Hall, David L., and Roger T. Ames. *Thinking through Confucius*. Albany: State University of New York Press, 1987.

Hall, David L., and Roger T. Ames. *Thinking from the Han: Self, Truth, and Transcendence in Chinese and Western Culture*. New York: State University of New York Press, 1998.

Hankey, Wayne J. *God in Himself: Aquinas' Doctrine of God as Expounded in the* Summa Theologiae. New York: Oxford University Press, 1987.

Hansen, Chad. *A Daoist Theory of Chinese Thought: A Philosophical Interpretation*. New York: Oxford University Press, 1992.

Hansen, Chad. "Metaphysical and Moral Transcendence in Chinese Thought." In *Two Roads to Wisdom? Chinese and Analytical Philosophical Traditions*, edited by Bo Mou, 197–228. Chicago, IL: Open Court, 2001.

Hartshorne, Charles. *The Divine Relativity: A Social Conception of God*. New Haven, CT: Yale University Press, 1948.

Horan, Daniel P. OFM. *Postmodernity and Univocity: A Critical Account of Radical Orthodoxy and John Duns Scotus*. Minneapolis, MN: Fortress Press, 2014.

Huang, Paulos. *Confronting Confucian Understandings of the Christian Doctrine of Creation: A Systematic Theological Analysis of the Basic Problems in the Confucian-Christian Dialogue*. Leiden: Brill, 2009.

Hunter, Michael. *Confucius beyond the Analects*. Leiden: Brill, 2017.

Hyman, Arthur, James Walsh, and Thomas Williams, eds. *Philosophy in the Middle Age: The Christian, Islamic, and Jewish Traditions*, 3rd ed. Indianapolis, IN: Hackett, 2010.

Irenaeus of Lyons. *Against the Heresies* in *The Ante-Nicene Fathers*, vol. 1. Translated by Alexander Roberts and James Donaldson. Edinburgh: T&T Clark, 1867; reprinted. Peabody, MA: Hendrickson, 1996.

Isaeva, Natalia V. *From Early Vedanta to Kashmir Shaivism: Gaudapada, Bhartrhari, and Abhinavagupta*. Albany: State University of New York Press, 1995.

Ivanhoe, Philip J. *Oneness: East Asian Conceptions of Virtue, Happiness, and How We Are All Connected*. New York: Oxford University Press, 2017.

Jang, Wang Shik. "The Problem of Transcendence in Chinese Religions: From a Whiteheadian Perspective." In *Whitehead and China: Relevance and Relationship*, edited by Xie, Wang, and Derfer, 101–12. Frankfurt: Ontos Verlag, 2005.

Jones, David. "When Butterflies Change into Birds': Life and Death in the *Liezi*." In *Riding the Wind with Liezi: New Perspectives on the Daoist Classic*, edited by Ronnie Littlejohn and Jeffrey Dippmann, 241–53. Albany: State University of New York Press, 2011.

Juillien, François. *Detour and Access: Strategies of Meaning in China and Greece*. Translated by Sophie Hawks. New York: Zone Books, 2000.

Keimatsu Mitsuo. "*Shunju Hanro* gogyo shohen gisaka ko." *Kanazawa Daigaku ho bun gakubu ronshu (tetsugaku bungaku)* 6 (1959): 25–46.

Kirkland, Russell. "Explaining Daoism: Realities, Cultural Constructs, and Emerging Perspectives." In *Daoism Handbook*, edited by Livia Kohn, xi–xviii. Leiden: Brill, 2000.

Kjellberg, Paul, and Philip J. Ivanhoe, eds. *Essays on Skepticism, Relativism, and Ethics in the* Zhuangzi. Albany, NY: SUNY Press, 1996.

Klein, Esther. "Were There 'Inner Chapters' in the Warring States? A New Examination of Evidence about the Zhuangzi." *T'oung Pao* 96 no. 4–5 (2010): 299–369.

Knepper, Timothy D. *Negating Negation: Against the Apophatic Abandonment of the Dionysian Corpus*. Cambridge: James Clarke, 2014.

Knight, Christopher J. *Omissions Are Not Accidents: Modern Apophaticism from Henry James to Jacques Derrida*. Toronto: University of Toronto Press, 2010.

Kohn, Livia. *Early Chinese Mysticism: Philosophy and Soteriology in the Taoist Tradition*. Princeton, NJ: Princeton University Press, 1992.

Kohn, Livia. *Taoist Mystical Philosophy: The Scripture of Western Ascension*. Albany, NY: SUNY Press, 1991.

Komjathy, Louis. *The Daoist Tradition: An Introduction*. London: Bloomsbury, 2013.

Konnikova, M. "Humanities Aren't a Science. Stop Treating Them Like One." In *Scientific American*, August 10, 2012. http://blogs.scientificamerican.com/ literally-psyched/2012/08/10/humanities-arent-a-science-stop-treating-them- like-one/, accessed May 7, 2019.

Kuzminski, Adrian. *Pyrrhonism: How the Ancient Greeks Reinvented Buddhism*. Lanham, MD: Lexington Books, 2008.

Lagerway, John, and Marc Kalinowski, eds. *Early Chinese Religion. Part One: Shang through Han (1250 BC–220 AD)*. Leiden: Brill, 2009.

Lau, D. C., trans. *Tao Te Ching*. New York: Penguin, 1963.

Le Blanc, Charles. *Huai-nan-tzu: Philosophical Synthesis in Early Chinese Thought: The Idea of Resonance (Kan-ying 感應) with a Translation and Analysis of Chapter Six*. Hong Kong: Hong Kong University Press, 1985.

Lee, Hyo-Dong. *Spirit, Qi, and the Multitude: A Contemporary Theology for the Democracy of Creation*. New York: Fordham University Press, 2014.

Lee, Hyo-Dong. "The Heart-Mind of the Way and the Heart-Mind Are Non-Dual: A Reflection on Neo-Confucian Panentheism." In *Panentheism across the World's Traditions*, edited by Lorilai Biernacki and Philip Clayton, 37–58. New York: Oxford University Press, 2014.

Lee, Hyo-Dong. *Xunzi and Early Chinese Naturalism*. Albany: State University of New York Press, 2005.

Levering, Matthew. *Engaging the Doctrine of Creation: Cosmos, Creatures, and the Wise and Good Creator*. Grand Rapids, MI: Baker Academic, 2017.

Levering, Matthew. *Proofs of God: Classical Arguments from Tertullian to Barth*. Grand Rapids, MI: Baker Academic, 2016.

Li, Chengyang. *The Tao Encounters the West: Explorations in Comparative Philosophy*. Albany: State University of New York Press, 1999.

Li, Chengyang, and Franklin Perkins, eds. *Chinese Metaphysics and Its Problems*. Cambridge: Cambridge University Press, 2015.

Li, Xueqin 李学勤, 楚簡《恆先》首章釋義 (Clarifications on the First Chapter of the Chu Bamboo Slips "*Hengxian*"), in 中國哲學史 (*History of Chinese Philosophy*), 2002.

Lin Fu-Shih. "The Image and Status of Shamans in Ancient China." In *Early Chinese Religion: Part One: Shang through Han (1250 BC–220 AD)*, edited by John Lagerwey and Mark Kalinowski. Leiden: Brill, 2009.

Littlejohn, Ronnie. "The *Liezi's* Use of the Lost *Zhuangzi*." In *Riding the Wind with Liezi: New Perspectives on the Daoist Classic*, edited by Ronnie Littlejohn and Jeffrey Dippmann, 31–49. Albany: State University of New York Press, 2011.

Littlejohn, Ronnie, and Jeffrey Dippmann, eds. *Riding the Wind with Liezi: New Perspectives on the Daoist Classic*. Albany: State University of New York Press, 2011.

Liu, Shu-Hsien. "The Confucian Approach to the Problem of Transcendence and Immanence." *PEW* 22 no. 1 (1972): 45–52.

Liu, Jeeloo. "Chinese *Qi*-Naturalism and Liberal Naturalism." *Philosophy, Theology and the Sciences* 1 no. 1 (2014): 59–86.

Liu, Xiaogan 劉笑敢, ed. *Dao Companion to Daoist Philosophy*. New York: Springer, 2015.

Liu, Xiaogan. *Classifying the Zhuangzi Chapters*. Ann Arbor: Center for Chinese Studies University of Michigan, 2003.

Liu, Xiaogan. "Laozi's Philosophy: Textual and Conceptual Analyses." In *Dao Companion to Daoist Philosophy*, 71–100. New York: Springer, 2015

Liu, Xiaogan. *Laozi Gu Jin* 老子古今. *Volume 1*. Beijing: Zhongguo Shehui Kexue Chubanshe, 2006.

Loewe, Michael. *Divination, Mythology, and Monarchy in Han China*. New York: Cambridge University Press, 2008.

Loewe, Michael. *Dong Zhongshu, a "Confucian" Heritage and the Chunqiu Fanlu*. Leiden: Brill, 2011.

Loewe, Michael. *Faith, Myth, and Reason in Han China*. Indianapolis: Hackett, 2005.

Louden, Robert B. "'What Does Heaven Say?': Christian Wolff and Western Interpretations of Confucian Ethics." In *Confucius and the* Analects: *New Essays*, edited by Bryan W. Van Norden, 73–93. New York: Oxford University Press, 2002.

Louth, Andrew. *Denys the Areopagite*. London: Continuum Books, 2001.

Lubheid, Colm, trans. *Psuedo-Dionysius: The Complete Works*. Mahweh, NJ: Paulist Press, 1988.

Machle, Edward. "Xunzi as a Religious Philosopher." In *Ritual, Religion, and the Xunzi*, edited by T. C. Kline III and Justin Tiwald, 21–42. Albany: State University of New York Press, 2014.

Major, John S. et al., trans. *The Huainanzi: A Guide to the Theory and Practice of Government in Early Han China*. New York: Columbia University Press, 2010.

Major, John S. *Heaven and Earth in Early Han Thought: Chapters Three, Four, and Five of the* Huainanzi. Albany: State University of New York Press, 1993.

Makeham, John. *Transmitters and Creators: Chinese Commentators and Commentaries on the* Analects. Cambridge, MA: Harvard University Asia Center, 2003.

Marion, Jean-Luc. *God without Being*. Chicago, IL: University of Chicago press, 1991.

Matthews, Victor H., and Don C. Benjamin, eds. *Old Testament Parallels: Laws and Stories from the Ancient Near East*, 3rd ed. Mahweh, NJ: Paulist Press, 2007.

McEvilley, Thomas. *The Shape of Ancient Thought: Comparative Studies in Greek and Indian Philosophies*. New York: Allworth Press, 2002.

McGinn, Bernard. *The Foundations of Mysticism: Origins to the Fifth Century*. New York: Crossroad, 1995.

McLeod, Alexus. *The Philosophical Thought of Wang Chong*. New York: Palgrave Macmillan, 2018.

McLeod, Alexus. *The Dao of Madness: Mental Illness and Self-Cultivation in Early Chinese Thought*. New York: Oxford University Press (forthcoming).

McLeod, Alexus. "Disordering Regularities and the Human Completion of the Cosmos in the *Huainanzi.*" *Dao: A Journal of Comparative Philosophy*

McLeod, Alexus. "In the World of Persons: The Personhood Debate in the *Analects* and *Zhuangzi.*" *Dao* 11 (2012): 437–57.

McLeod, Alexus. *Theories of Truth in Chinese Philosophy: A Comparative Approach*. Lanham, MD: Rowman and Littlefield International, 2016.

Michael, Thomas. *In the Shadows of the Dao: Laozi, the Sage, and the* Daodejing. Albany: State University of New York Press, 2015.

Michael, Thomas "The That-Beyond-Which of the Pristine Dao: Cosmogony in the *Liezi.*" In *Riding the Wind with Liezi: New Perspectives on the Daoist Classic*, edited by Ronnie Littlejohn and Jeffrey Dippmann, 101–26. Albany: State University of New York Press, 2011.

Milbank, John. *Theology and Social Theory*, 2nd ed. Cambridge, MA: Blackwell, 2006.

Moeller, Hans Georg. *The Philosophy of the* Daodejing. New York: Columbia University Press, 2006.

Moeller, Hans-Georg. *In der Mitte des Kreises: Daoistisches Denken*. Berlin: Verlag der Weltreligionen im Insel Verlag, 2010.

Moeller, Hans-Georg, and Paul J. D'Ambrosio. *Genuine Pretending: On the Philosophy of the Zhuangzi*. New York: Columbia University Press, 2017.

Møllgaard, Eske. *An Introduction to Daoist Thought: Action, language, and Ethics in Zhuangzi*. London: Routledge, 2007.

Moore, G. E. *Principia Ethica*. New York: Cambridge University Press, 1993.

Mote, Frederick W. "The Cosmological Gulf between China and the West." In *Transition and Permanence: Chinese History and Culture: A Festschrift in Honor of Dr. Hsiao Kung-ch'üan*, edited by David C. Buxbaum and Frederick W. Mote, 3–22. Hong Kong: Cathay Press, 1972.

Needham, Joseph. *Science and Civilization in China. Vol. II: The History of Scientific Thought*. Cambridge: Cambridge University Press, 1956.

Neville, Robert Cummings. *Behind the Masks of God: An Essay toward Comparative Theology*. Albany: State University of New York Press, 1991.

Neville, Robert Cummings. *God the Creator: On the Transcendence and Presence of God*. Chicago, IL: University of Chicago Press, 1968.

Neville, Robert Cummings. "From Nothing to Being: The Notion of Creation in Chinese and Western Thought." *Philosophy East and West* 30 no. 1 (January 1980): 21–34.

Nivison, David S. "The Classical Philosophical Writings." In *The Cambridge History of Ancient China: From the Origins of Civilization to 221 B.C*, edited by Michael Loewe and Edward L. Shaughnessy, 745–812. New York: Cambridge University Press, 1999.

Nuyen, A. T. "Naming the Unnameable: The Being of the *Tao.*" *JCP* 22 no. 4 (December 1995): 487–97.

Nylan, Michael. "Yin-yang, Five Phases, and *qi.*" In *China's Early Empires: A Re-Appraisal*, edited by Michael Nylan and Michael Loewe, 398–414. Cambridge: Cambridge University Press, 2010.

Pankenier, David W. *Astrology and Cosmology in Early China: Conforming Earth to Heaven*. Cambridge: Cambridge University Press, 2013.

Peerenboom, Randall. "*Heguanzi* and Huang-Lao Thought." *Early China* 16 (1991): 169–86.

Perenboom, Randall. *Law and Morality in Ancient China: The Silk Manuscripts of Huang-Lao*. Albany: State University of New York Press, 1993.

Perkins, Franklin. "The *Laozi* and the Cosmogonic Turn in Classical Chinese Philosophy." *Frontiers of Philosophy in China* 11 no. 2 (2016): 185–205.

Perkins, Franklin. "Leibniz on the Existence of Philosophy in China." In *China in the German Enlightenment*, edited by Bettina Brandt and Daniel Leonhard Purdy, 60–79. Toronto: University of Toronto Press, 2016.

Perkins, Franklin. "Metaphysics in Chinese Philosophy." In *The Stanford Encyclopedia of Philosophy*, edited by Edward N. Zalta, Summer 2019 Edition, https://plato.stanford.edu/archives/sum2019/entries/chinese-metaphysics/.

Perkins. Franklin. "The *Mozi* and the *Daodejing*." *JCP* 41 nos. 1–2 (March–June 2014): 18–32.

Perl, David. *Theophany: The Neoplatonic Philosophy of Dionysius the Areopagite*. Albany: State University of New York Press, 2007.

Pines, Yuri. *Foundations of Confucian Thought: Intellectual Life in the Chunqiu Period, 722–453 B.C.E.* Honolulu: University of Hawaii Press, 2002.

Placher, William C. *The Domestication of Transcendence: How Modern Thinking about God Went Wrong*. Louisville, KY: Westminster John Knox Press, 1996.

Plato. "Phaedo." In *Five Dialogues*, translated by G. M. A. Grube. Indianapolis, IN: Hackett, 1981.

Plato. *Republic*. Translated by Robin Waterfield. Oxford: Oxford University Press, 1998.

Plotinus. *The Enneads*. Translated by Stephen Mackenna. London: Penguin, 1991.

Pope Paul VI, "Dogmatic Constitution on Sacred Scripture—*Dei Verbum*," 1965. Accessed August 15, 2019, from http://www.vatican.va/archive/hist_councils/ii_vatican_council/documents/vat-ii_const_19651118_dei-verbum_en.html.

Puett, Michael J. *To Become a God: Cosmology, Sacrifice, and Self-Divinization in Early China*. Cambridge, MA: Harvard University Asia Center for the Harvard-Yenching Institute, 2002.

Puett, Michael J. "Sages, Creation, and the End of History in the *Huainanzi*." In *The Huainanzi and Textual Production in Early China*, edited by Sarah A. Queen and Michael Puett, 269–90. Leiden: Brill, 2014.

Puett, Michael J. "Ritualization as Domestication: Ritual Theory from Classical China." In *Ritual Dynamics and the Science of Ritual, Volume I: Grammars and Morphologies of Ritual Practices in Asia*, edited by Axel Michaels, Anand Mishra, Lucia Dolce, Gil Raz, and Katja Triplett, 365–76. Wiesbaden: Harrassowitz Verlag, 2010.

Putnam, Hilary. *Naturalism, Realism, and Normativity*. Cambridge, MA: Harvard University Press, 2016.

Putnam, Hilary. "The Content and Appeal of 'Naturalism.'" In *Naturalism in Question*, edited by Mario De Caro and David Macarthur, 59–70. Cambridge, MA: Harvard University Press, 2004.

Qiu Xigui 裘锡圭. *Shi "heng xian" haishi ji xian*? 《是"恆先" 還是 "極先"？ 》中国简帛学国际论坛, Taipei: National Taiwan University, 2008.

Queen, Sarah A. *From Chronicle to Canon: The Hermeneutics of the* Spring and Autumn, *According to Tung Chung-shu*. Cambridge: Cambridge University Press, 1996.

Queen, Sarah A., and John S. Major, eds and trans. *Luxuriant Gems of the Spring and Autumn*. New York: Columbia University Press, 2015.

Rahner, Karl. *The Trinity*. Translated by J. F. Donceel. London: Continuum, 2001.

Rescher, Nicholas. *Process Metaphysics: An Introduction to Process Philosophy*. Albany: State University of New York Press, 1996.

Rhodes, Michael Craig. "Pseudo-Dionysius' Concept of God." *International Journal of Philosophy and Theology* 75 no. 4 (2014): 306–18.

Rocca, Gregory P. *Speaking the Incomprehensible God: Thomas Aquinas on the Interplay of Positive and Negative Theology*. Washington, DC: Catholic University of America Press, 2004.

Roetz, Heiner. "Validity in Chou Thought: On Chad Hansen and the Pragmatic Turn in Sinology." In *Epistemological Issues in Classical Chinese Philosophy*, edited by Hans Lenk and Gregor Paul, 69–113. Albany: State University of New York Press, 1993.

Rorem, Paul. *The Dionysian Mystical Theology*. Minneapolis, MN: Fortress Press, 2015.

Rorem, Paul. *Pseudo-Dionysius: A Commentary on the Texts and an Introduction to Their Influence*. New York: Oxford University Press, 1993.

Rosker, Jana S. *Traditional Chinese Philosophy and the Paradigm of Structure (Li 理)*. Newcastle upon Tyne: Cambridge Scholars, 2012.

Rota, Michael. "Causation." In *The Oxford Handbook of Aquinas*, edited by Brian Davies and Eleonore Stump, 104–14. New York: Oxford University Press, 2012.

Roth, Harold D. "Against Cognitive Imperialism: A Call for Non-Ethnocentric Approach to Cognitive Science and Religious Studies." *Religion East and West* no. 8 (October 2008): 1–26.

Roth, Harold D. "The Classical Daoist Concept of *Li* 理 (Pattern) and Early Chinese Cosmology." *Early China* 35–6 (2012–13): 157–83.

Roth, Harold D. "Daoist Apophatic Mediation: Selections from the Classical Daoist Textual Corpus." In *Contemplative Literature: A Comparative Sourcebook on Meditation and Contemplative Prayer*, edited by Louis Komjathy, 84–128. Albany: State University of New York Press, 2015.

Roth, Harold D. "*Huainanzi*: The Pinnacle of Classical Daoist Syncretism." In *Dao Companion to Daoist Philosophy*, edited by Liu Xiaogan 劉笑敢, 341–65. New York: Springer, 2015.

Roth, Harold D. "The *Laozi* in the Context of Daoist Mystical Praxis." In *Religious and Philosophical Aspects of the* Laozi, edited by Mark Csikszentmihalyi and Philip J. Ivanhoe, 59–96. Albany: State University of New York Press, 1999..

Roth, Harold D. *Original Tao: Inward Training (Nei-yeh) and the Foundations of Taoist Mysticism*. New York: Columbia University Press, 1999.

Roth, Harold D. "Who Compiled the *Chuang Tzu*?" In *Chinese Texts and Philosophical Contexts: Essays Dedicated to A. C. Graham*, edited by Henry Rosemont, 79–128. La Salle, IL: Open Court, 1991.

Saffrey, Henri-Dominique. "New Objective Links between the Pseudo-Dionysius and Proclus." In *Neoplatonism and Christian Thought*, edited by Dominic J. O'Meara, 54–63. Norfolk, VA: International Society for Neoplatonic Studies, 1982.

Schwartz, Benjamin I. "Transcendence in Ancient China." *Daedalus* 104 (1975): 57–68.

Schwartz, Benjamin I. *The World of Thought in Ancient China*. Cambridge, MA: Belknap Harvard, 1985.

Schwitzgebel, Eric. "Zhuangzi's Attitude toward Language and His Skepticism." In *Essays on Skepticism, Relativism, and Ethics in the* Zhuangzi, edited Paul Kjellberg and Philip J. Ivanhoe, 68–96. Albany: State University of New York Press, 1996.

Sedley, David. "Form-Particular Resemblance in Plato's *Phaedo*." *Proceedings of the Aristotelian Society* 106 (2006): 309–25.

Selover, Thomas. "*Tianli renyu*." In *The Encyclopedia of Confucianism*, edited by Xinzhong Yao. 2-volume set. New York: Routledge, 2013.

Shah-Kazemi, Reza. *Paths to Transcendence: According to Shankara, Ibn Arabi, and Meister Eckhart*. Bloomington, IN: World Wisdom, 2006.

Shih, Hu. "The Scientific Spirit and Method in Chinese Philosophy." *Philosophy East and West* 9 no. 1/2 (1959): 29–31.

Siderits, Mark. *Buddhism as Philosophy: An Introduction*. New York: Routledge, 2016.

Slingerland, Edward G. "The Conception of *Ming* in Early Confucian Thought." *PEW* 46 no. 4 (1996): 567–81.

Slingerland, Edward G. *Mind and Body in Early China: Beyond Orientalism and the Myth of Holism*. New York: Oxford University Press, 2018.

Slingerland, Edward G. *Effortless Action: Wu-wei as Conceptual Metaphor and Spiritual Ideal in Early China*. New York: Oxford University Press, 2003.

Song Bin. *A Study of Comparative Philosophy of Religion on "Creatio Ex Nihilo" and "Sheng Sheng"*, PhD dissertation, Boston University.

Spinney, Laura. "Human Cycles: History as Science." *Nature* 488 no. 7409 (2012): 24–6.

Stalnaker, Aaron. *Overcoming Our Evil: Human Nature and Spiritual Exercises in Xunzi and Augustine*. Washington, DC: Georgetown University Press, 2006.

Stoljar, Daniel. *Physicalism*. New York: Routledge, 2010.

Sturgeon, Donald. "*Zhuangzi*, Perspectives, and Greater Knowledge." *PEW* 65 no. 3 (2015): 892–917.

Suchla, Beate Regina, ed. *Corpus Dionysiacum*. 2 Vols. Berlin: Walter de Gruyter, 1990–91.

Szabadváry, Ferenc. *History of Analytical Chemistry*. Translated by Gyula Svehla. Oxford: Pergamon Press, 1966.

Tang, Junyi 唐君毅. *Zhongguo zhexue yuanlun* 中國哲學原論. Taipei: Xuesheng shuju, 1986.

Tang, Rifeng. "Mou Zongsan on Intellectual Intuition." In *Contemporary Chinese Philosophy*, edited by Chung-ying Cheng and Nicholas Bunnin, 327–46. Malden, MA: Blackwell.

Tanner, Kathryn. *God and Creation in Christian Theology: Tyranny or Empowerment?* Minneapolis, MN: Fortress Press, 2005.

Te Velde, Rudi. *Aquinas on God: The "Divine Science" of the Summa theologiae*. New York: Ashgate, 2006.

Theron, Stephen. "The Divine Attributes in Aquinas." *Thomist* 51 no. 1 (January 1987): 37–50.

Tiwald, Justin, and Bryan W. Van Norden, eds. *Readings in Later Chinese Philosophy: Han Dynasty to the 20th Century*. Indianapolis, IN: Hackett, 2014.

Torrell, Jean-Paul OP. *La "Somme de théologie" de saint Thomas d'Aquin*. Paris: Éditions du Cerf, 1998.

Tu, Wei-ming. "An 'Anthropocosmic' Perspective on Creativity." *Procedia Social and Behavioral Sciences* 2 (2010): 7305–11.

Tucker, John. "Japanese Confucian Philosophy." In *The Stanford Encyclopedia of Philosophy*, edited by Edward N. Zalta, Spring 2018 Edition, https://plato.stanford.edu/archives/spr2018/entries/japanese-confucian/.

Unschuld, Paul U. *Huang Di Nei Jing Su Wen: Nature, Knowledge, and Imagery in an Ancient Chinese Medical Text*. Berkeley: University of California Press, 2003.

Vallat, Philippe. "Al-Fārābī's Arguments for the Eternity of the World and the Contingency of Natural Phenomena." *Interpreting the Bible and Aristotle: The Alexandrian commentary tradition between Rome and Baghdad*, edited by Josef Lössl and John W. Watt, 259–86. Aldershot: Ashgate, 2011.

van Ess, Hans. "The Meaning of Huang-Lao in *Shiji* and *Hanshu*." *Études chinoises* 12 no. 2 (1993): 161–77.

Van Norden, Bryan W. "Method in the Madness of the *Laozi*." In *Religious and Philosophical Aspects of the* Laozi, edited Mark Csikszentmihalyi and Philip J. Ivanhoe, 187–210. Albany, NY: SUNY Press, 1999.

von Balthasar, Hans Urs. *The Glory of the Lord: Volume I: Seeing the Form*. Translated by Erasmo Leiva-Merikakis. Edited by Joseph Fessio S. J. and John Riches. San Francisco, CA: Ignatius Press and Crossroad, 2009.

von Collani, Claudia. "China in the German 'Geistesgeschichte' in the Seventeenth and Eighteenth Centuries." In *China and Christianity: Burdened Past, Hopeful Future*, edited by Stephen Uhalley, Jr. and Xiaoxin Wu, 149–61. London: M. E. Sharpe East Gate, 1999.

von Rad, Gerhard. *Genesis: A Commentary*. Translated by John H. Marks. Philadelphia, PA: Westminster Press, 1972.

Wang, E 王锷. "*Liji*"*Chengshu Kao* 《礼记》成书考. Beijing: Zhonghua Shuju, 2007.

Wang, Robin R. "Dong Zhongshu's Transformation of *Yin-yang* Theory and Contesting of Gender Identity." *PEW* 55 no. 2 (April 2005): 209–31.

Wang, Robin R. *Yinyang: The Way of Heaven and Earth in Chinese Thought and Culture*. New York: Cambridge University Press, 2012.

Wenning, Mario. "Kant and Daoism on Nothingness." *JCP* 38 no. 4 (December 2011): 556–68.

Williams, A. N. *The Ground of Union: Deification in Aquinas and Palamas*. New York: Oxford University Press, 1999.

Wippel, John F. *The Metaphysical Thought of Thomas Aquinas: From Finite Being to Uncreated Being*. Washington, DC: Catholic University of America Press, 2000.

Wolff, Christian. *Oratorio de Sinarum philosophia practica*. Frankfurt: Andreae and Hort, 1726.

Xianqian, Wang 王先谦, compiler. *Xunzi Jijie*荀子集解. Edited by Chen Xiaohuan沈嘯寰and Wang Xingxian 王星贤. Beijing: Zhonghua Shuju, 2014.

Xie, Wenyu. "The Concept of *Cheng* and Confucian Religiosity." *Journal of East-West Thought* 1 no. 2 (2012): 91–106.

Yearley, Lee H. *Mencius and Aquinas: Theories of Virtue and Conceptions of Courage*. Albany, NY: SUNY Press, 1990.

Yonghua, Ge. "Transcendence, Immanence, and Creation: A Comparative Study of Christian and Daoist Thoughts with Special Reference to Robert Neville." In In *Transcendence, Immanence, and Intercultural Philosophy*, edited by Nahum Brown and William Franke, 79–102. London: Palgrave Macmillan, 2016.

Yonghua, Ge. "*Creatio Ex Nihilo* and Ancient Chinese Philosophy: A Revisiting of Robert Neville's Thesis." *PEW* 68 no. 2 (April 2018): 352–70.

Youlan, Feng 冯友兰. *Zhongguo zhexue shi* 中国哲学史, vol. 1. Chongqing: Chongqing Chubanshe, 2009.

Yu-lan, Feng. *A History of Chinese Philosophy. Volume 1: The Period of the Philosophers (from the Beginnings to Circa 100 B.C.)*, 2nd ed. Translated by Derk Bodde. Princeton, NJ: Princeton University Press, 1952.

Ziporyn, Brook. "Form, Principle, Pattern, or Coherence? *Li* in Chinese Philosophy." *Philosophy Compass* 3 no. 3 (2008): 401–22.

Ziporyn, Brook. *Ironies of Oneness and Difference: Coherence in Early Chinese Thought; Prolegomena to the Study of* Li 理. Albany: State University of New York Press, 2012.

Ziporyn, Brook, trans. *Zhuangzi: The Essential Writings, with Selections from Traditional Commentaries*. Indianapolis, IN: Hackett, 2009.

Index

Printed in Dunstable, United Kingdom